Business Opportunities in Vietnam

THIS SIGNIFICANT NEW book will be relevant to a wide variety of readers; not only will it help businessmen understand the forces which are shaping Vietnam's rapidly changing investment climate, but it will guide policymakers in the ASEAN region (and beyond) in their efforts to assist in its re-integration into the world economy, will be useful to aid organisations which are attempting to formulate viable programmes to fill strategic gaps in its development process, and will help researchers in development economics and related fields understand the intricate dynamics of its struggle to move from a command to a market-driven economy....The quality of the overall research product is impressive; it appears far more rigorous than normally found in a book intended to guide potential investors. There is something in this volume for everyone with an interest in Vietnam, and I recommend it highly.

Mr Mai Kim Dinh
Coordinator of Vietnam Programme
Hanns Seidel Foundation

Titles in the Nanyang Business Report Series

Business Opportunities in Penang, Malaysia

Business Opportunities in Sichuan Province, China

Business Opportunities in India

Business Opportunities in the Philippines

Business Opportunities in Myanmar

Business Opportunities in the Yangtze River Delta, China

Business Opportunities in Vietnam

For further enquiries, information or feedback on the series, please write to the Editor at e-mail: prenhall@singnet.com.sg or Simon & Schuster (Asia) Pte Ltd, 317 Alexandra Road, #04-01 IKEA Building, Singapore 159965.

NANYANG BUSINESS REPORT SERIES

Business Opportunities in Vietnam

Edited by

Tan Teck Meng (Dean)
Low Aik Meng (Vice Dean and Director of MBA Programme)
John J. Williams (Chief Coordinator, Business Study Mission)
A. Lee Gilbert (Coordinator, Business Study Mission)
Luu Trankiem (Coordinator, Business Study Mission)

Nanyang Technological University
Singapore

Prentice Hall
Singapore New York London Toronto Sydney Tokyo

First published 1997 by
Prentice Hall
Simon & Schuster (Asia) Pte Ltd
317 Alexandra Road
#04-01 IKEA Building
Singapore 159965

Printed in Singapore

5 4 3 2 1   01 00 99 98 97

ISBN 0-13-754342-5
ISBN 0-13-754334-4 (pbk)

Library of Congress Cataloging-in-Publication Data

Business opportunities in Vietnam / edited by Tan Teck Meng ... [et al.].
p. cm. -- (Nanyang business report series)
Includes bibliographical references.
ISBN 0-13-754334-4 (pbk.)
1. Vietnam--Economic conditions. 2. Vietnam--Economic policy.
3. Investments, Foreign--Vietnam. 4. Business enterprises-
-Government policy--Vietnam. I. Tan, Teck Meng. II. Series.
HC444.B868 1997
332.6'73'09597--dc21   97-3479
CIP

Prentice Hall International (UK) Limited, *London*
Prentice Hall of Australia Pty. Limited, *Sydney*
Prentice Hall Canada Inc., *Toronto*
Prentice Hall Hispanoamericana, *S.A., Mexico*
Prentice Hall of India Private Limited, *New Delhi*
Prentice Hall of Japan, Inc., *Tokyo*
Editora Prentice Hall do Brasil, Ltda., *Rio de Janeiro*
Prentice Hall, Inc., *Upper Saddle River, New Jersey*

CONTENTS

BUSINESS ATTITUDES AND BEHAVIOURAL ISSUES

SINGAPORE'S INVESTMENT INITIATIVES

ABOUT THE EDITORS

TAN TECK MENG is Professor and Dean at the Nanyang Business School. Since joining academia in the early 1970s, Professor Tan has combined his university responsibilities with extensive consultancy work, largely in the field of accountancy. He holds senior positions on a number of institutional boards and committees in Singapore including the Accounting and Auditing Services Working Group of the Economic Committee, the Public Accountants Board, the Board of Directors of Singapore Reinsurance Corporation Limited, the Institute of Certified Public Accountants of Singapore (ICPAS) Annual Report Award Competition Committee and the Income Tax Board of Review. Professor Tan is founding Director of the Entrepreneurship Development Centre (ENDEC) and in 1992 was elected to the Board of Governors of the MIT Sloan School of Management Society for Senior Executives. He is a council member of the ICPAS.

LOW AIK MENG is Associate Professor and Director of the MBA programme at the Nanyang Business School. He worked for five years as an accountant and an internal auditor before joining academia in 1975. He was Vice Dean of the Faculty of Accountancy and Business Administration at the National University of Singapore until he joined the Nanyang Technological University in 1987. He is currently Vice Dean at the Nanyang Business School and has been the Director of its very successful MBA Programme since its inception in 1991. Under his leadership, the MBA Programme has been building a network of contacts with businesses and government bodies in Singapore and overseas. He spearheads the thrice-yearly Business Study Missions which are an integral part of the MBA Programme. Associate Professor Low continues to be active in the accountancy profession and serves on several committees in the Institute of Certified Public Accountants of Singapore.

JOHN J. WILLIAMS is Associate Professor at the Nanyang Business School and Chief Coordinator of the MBA Business Study Mission programme. He has taught and carried out research projects in several countries including Canada, the U.S., Kenya and Singapore. Throughout the latter part of the 1980s, Dr. Williams served as Vice-Chairman and Chairman of the Final Accreditation Exam Board for the Society of Management Accountants of Canada, which admitted him as a Fellow in the Society in 1992. Although active in consulting for government agencies in the U.S. and Canada during this period, he has published extensively in leading academic and professional journals and he continues to pursue the study of emerging regional economies in the Asean region.

A. LEE GILBERT in his first overseas assignment for SRI International introduced strategic technology planning to the Ministry of Health of the Kingdom of Saudi Arabia. As Deputy Director of the Institute of Systems Science, he led executive education, and initiated a longitudinal study of the transfer and use of information technology in Singapore. As Future Information Systems faculty Fellow at Harvard Business School, he authored teaching cases portraying technology transfer in Asia. More recently, as Regional Adviser for Technology Transfer and Development for the United Nations Secretariat, Dr. Gilbert advised governments throughout the region, and helped organise the first International Investment Forum in Vietnam, which attracted more than 300 overseas investors. Now Director of the new MBA programme in International Business for the Nanyang Business School in Singapore, his research and publication addresses strategic planning and technology policy.

LUU TRANKIEM was Chairman of the Marketing and International Business Department at California State University, a past Regional President of the Academy of International Business and a Fellow of the Ford Foundation. He was Associate Governor of the National Bank of Vietnam, President of Vietnam Chamber of Commerce in America, CEO of Delta Savings Bank, Executive Director of the Los Angeles World Trade Center and President of Strategic Development International Corporation. He has authored four books in Marketing/International

Business and over forty journal articles, monographs and professional papers.

PREFACE

The Nanyang Business School, the largest school in Singapore's Nanyang Technological University, requires every candidate for its Master of Business Administration degree to complete a Business Study Mission (BSM). The main purpose of these organised visits to other countries is to ensure that our MBA participants acquire skills in understanding overseas investment opportunities and evaluating the business climate in which such investments must operate. The Business Study Mission also supports the national economic strategy which, in recent years, has focused on the development of an "external wing" to balance a strong, but relatively small, internal economy.

This volume contains business reports originating from the Business Study Mission to the Socialist Republic of Vietnam in March of 1996. Over an 11 day period, more than 70 participants from the Nanyang Business School MBA programme explored the climate for business enterprises in Hanoi, Da Nang, Hue, and Ho Chi Minh City. Typically, these participants have five years or more of business experience as middle managers in medium-to-large Singapore-based enterprises. During the six months prior to the BSM, participants were engaged in specific lectures and workshops, carried out desk research and interviewed managers who have extensive experience in Vietnam. Following the BSM, the participants transformed their learning experience in Vietnam into the chapters presented here, under the able guidance of their mission supervisors who have expertise in selected functional areas.

Many knowledgeable analysts see Vietnam as a potential "Tiger", following the much earlier economic courses set by South Korea and Taiwan. With its 75 million disciplined people, many of whom are relatively well-educated and eager to move forward, the nation seems poised to take a fast track toward economic development. Growth rates averaging 10% over the decade since *doi moi* policies opened the economy confirm this potential. In the words of Nguyen Duc Hung, Ambassador of the Socialist Republic of Vietnam, expressed at a speech given in Singapore in September 1996, "Vietnam has a rich traditional culture with unique national characteristics formed and accumulated over thousands of years. My people wish to befriend all countries in the world community. When men approach one another with a sincere and open heart, they will naturally and eventually become friends in need and in deed".

However, the country and its overseas partners must join together to overcome many serious obstacles including ancient port and transport infrastructures, inadequate mechanisms governing commercial relationships and a lack of skilled managers. This volume, therefore, carefully investigates the institutional context for foreign investment, examines several key sectors of the economy, and analyses the experiences of pioneering joint ventures. The objective is to develop and communicate an in-depth understanding of investment opportunities, and the ingredients and behaviours necessary to succeed at doing business in Vietnam in this first phase of its re-integration into the world economy through membership in ASEAN.

The Chairman of the Vietnam National Administration for Tourism, Mr. Do Quang Trung, officially opened the business study mission on 4 March 1996 at the Hanoi Hotel after opening addresses by Dr. Cham Tao Soon, President of Nanyang Technological University, and Professor Tan Teck Meng, Dean of the Nanyang Business School. The Minister of Tourism delivered the keynote address for a two-day conference focused on the theme "Vietnam and Singapore in the Asean Age" attended by our participants, and guests from the educational and business communities. Other prominent speakers included Professor Nguyen Mai, former Vice Chairman of the State Committee for Co-operation and Investment (SCCI); Professor Ho Sy Thoang, CEO and President of Petrovietnam; Ms. Pham Chi Lan, Secretary-General of the Vietnamese Chamber of Commerce and Industry; Mr. Nguyen Minh Tu of the Central Institute of Economic Management; and Professor Le Van Vien, Director of the Department for Foreign Relations of the Hanoi People's Committee.

On the following day, participants joined parallel discussions on three main topics: Financial Services and Banking Systems, Technology Transfer and Education, and Tourism and Hospitality Services. After an informal discussion with Singapore Ambassador to Vietnam, Mr. Toh Hock Ghim, participants undertook site visits to acquire first-hand impressions of how business is actually conducted on the ground and then they liaised with members of the Singapore business community in Vietnam.

Vice Minister of Finance, Dr. Nguyen Sinh Hung, chaired the parallel session on financial services and banking systems which featured detailed briefings from Ms. Nguyen Thi Cuc of the General Department of Taxation, Mr. Bradley Babson of the World Bank, and Mr. Bui Van Mai of the Vietnam Auditing Company. The investor's perspective was provided by Mrs. Iris Fang, CEO of Standard Chartered Bank (Vietnam), and a group of expert panelists from leading international banks and professional service firms active in Vietnam.

In the parallel session on technology transfer and education projects, Professor Pham Minh Hac of the Ministry of Education and Training provided an overview of the structure of the educational establishment while Mr. Do Van Loc of the Ministry of Science, Technology, and the Environment shared his insights on the new role of information technology. Professor Pham Minh Ha of Hanoi Technological University and project director Suzanne Hosley of the Vietnam Management Initiative at the National Economics University contributed greatly to our understanding of manpower development issues in technology transfer, as did Mr. John Theaker of the Swedish International Development Agency.

At the parallel session on tourism and hospitality service projects, Mr. Bui Xuan Nhat, Vice Chairman of the Vietnam National Administration for Tourism (VNAT), presented the Master Plan for Tourism. Mr. Vu The Binh demonstrated prototypes of multimedia tools developed by VNAT to promote tourism and this was followed by Mr. Nguyen Van Thiem of VNAT who explained the national plan to develop manpower in the tourism industry. Mr. Mai Kim Dinh of the Hanns Siedel Foundation provided the perspective of a leading overseas non-governmental organisation engaged in training activities. Panelists from several hospitality and property development projects provided the perspective of joint venture partners engaged in these activities.

The focus of the agenda in Central Vietnam was to gain an understanding of the development issues for tourism-related activities in this beautiful area. After arriving in Da Nang, the participants inspected the ancient trading port of Hoi An on foot before touring the coastal road along the Hai Van Pass route to Hue. The seminar in Hue was co-hosted at the Century Riverside Inn by the People's Committee, tourism officials, and Hue University. The speakers included Mr. Pham Van Duong of the Binh Tri Thien Province People's Committee; Mr. Nguyen Thanh Dan of the Office of Tourism; Dr. Nguyen The Huu, President of Hue University; and Ms. Nguyen Thi Kinh, the Vice President of Hue University. Following the seminar on the master plan for development of the region, participants visited the well-restored ruins of the ancient imperial capital of the *Nguyen* kings, designated a world heritage site by the United Nations, toured the tomb of Emperor Tu Duc and then returned to the hotel to prepare for a moonlight cruise on the Perfume River.

Arriving in Ho Chi Minh city the next day, mission participants met with local and overseas business people over dinner, and undertook follow-up visits necessary to complete their field research for the BSM Chapters. The dinner speakers included Singapore Consul, Mr. Goh Seow Kwang; Dominique Rohner of the Swiss-AIT Management Development Programme; Mr. Lonh Bao Nguyen of SRG-Nielson; and Mr. Binh Nguyen of Federal Express Indochina. Their frank assessments of the dynamic economy in the south helped balance our perspective of the overall business climate.

In ordering the contents of this book, several features are noteworthy. First, the chapters have been packaged into sections which roughly proceed from macro issues to functional areas of law, tax, trade regulations and accounting, to specific economic sectors and special issues. Second, each major section is concluded by a synopsis which integrates the preceding chapters and sharpens the major future challenges and opportunities. Third, each main chapter is intended to stand on its own merit and, thus, marginal replication of important background information is unavoidable in several chapters.

The knowledge amassed by the MBA participants through the experience of this mission to Vietnam is enormous. It is our hope that sharing the contents of this book will be insightful for understanding the environment and specific contexts which presently exist in Vietnam concerning a variety of business opportunities. To be sure, the book's appeal is global as well as regional: to firms or entrepreneurs eager to provide capital, human resource training or technology; to institutional agencies, public or private, contemplating trade or infrastructure development; to organisations servicing expatriate subsidiary operations in Vietnam; to executives and managers of professional services; and to educational institutions for pedagogical and research purposes.

Editors:
TAN Teck Meng
LOW Aik Meng
John J. WILLIAMS
A. Lee GILBERT
LUU Trankiem

ACKNOWLEDGEMENTS

Many individuals and organisations assisted tremendously to make the Business Study Mission to Vietnam a success. In Hanoi, we were particularly fortunate to have the sponsorship of the newly formed Vietnam National Tourism Administration (VNAT) and the Central Institute of Economic Management (CIEM). Thanks are extended particularly to the management team at VNAT led by Administrative Head, Mr. Nghiem Van Ky; Personnel and Training Director, Mr. Nguyen Van Thiem; plus Tourism Information Center Director, Mr. Vu The Binh. Collectively, these individuals carefully arranged all logistics for the mission and provided access to the tourism authorities visited in each province. We also thank Dr. Le Dang Doanh, Director of the prominent think tank which advises the central government on economic issues. He was instrumental in developing an adequate understanding of the current business climate and investment opportunities and, in conjunction with Mr. Nguyen Minh Tu from CIEM, offered a special parallel seminar session for government economists at which Emeritus Professor Lim Chong Yah, Chairman of Singapore's National Wage Council, shared some lessons from Singapore's development experience.

To the educational establishment led by Professor Pham Minh Hac, First Vice Minister of the Ministry of Education and Training, we extend our gratitude for providing full access to the critical issues in manpower development as well as for facilitating fruitful discussions with the Ministry and direct contact with several universities responsible for various aspects of business education. These contacts led to signed memoranda of understanding with the National Economics University, Hanoi Technological University, the Foreign Trade University and Hue University with the intent to co-operate in curriculum development, faculty development and exchange, and training activities.

We are grateful to the many speakers, member panelists and business people who gave untiringly of their time and knowledge throughout the mission: In Hue, thanks to all the individuals who provided cultural and historical insights about Vietnam. Their hospitality was overwhelming and they added that special cultural dimension to our economic knowledge which is fundamental to understanding how business functions in Vietnam's society. A very special thanks also to the student interns whose English language skills and cultural knowledge contributed to a better understanding of Vietnam by our MBA participants.

Thanks go to the many pre-trip seminar speakers in Singapore who helped us prepare for the BSM to Vietnam. Without question, we are proud of the MBA participants who prepared well for the mission and conducted themselves professionally on a difficult information-gathering, and exhausting, trip. A special acknowledgement is extended to the diligent supervising efforts of Dr. Choo Teck Min, Dr. Roger Marshall, Dr. Jon Kendall, Dr. Luu Trankiem, Dr. Ian McGovern and Mr. Peter Low.

Finally, our sincere thanks to MBA director, Associate Professor Low Aik Meng, for marshalling together all of the talent and resources necessary to make the BSM a success. Thanks also to the MBA office, to Grace Cheng and Adelene Ang for attending to incredible administrative details; without their efforts the trip would not have worked. Thanks to Linda Chua for meticulous proofing; to our publisher, Prentice Hall, for their guidance; and to Shirley Ong and especially Alison Soo for her painstaking efforts in bringing this book to completion.

INTRODUCTION

Chapter 1

Vietnam in the ASEAN Era

BY
TAN Teck Meng
LOW Aik Meng
John J. WILLIAMS
GILBERT A. Lee
LUU Trankiem

INTRODUCTION

SINCE OPENING ITS doors in the mid-1980s, the Vietnamese economy has grown at more than 8% annually. The driving forces underpinning this developmental success are 75 million relatively literate, healthy and hard-working people complemented by a rich endowment of natural resources, substantial injections of foreign direct investment and technology transfer. With its admission as a full member of the Association of Southeast Asian Nations (ASEAN) on 18 July 1995, Vietnam closed its era of isolation. ASEAN member nations have already committed substantial resources, currently more than US$3 billion, to the development of its economy. Singapore-based firms are active in Vietnam and they represent its third-largest overseas source of investment capital. The potential for sustained economic growth is indeed solid. However, the idiosyncratic nature of a centrally-planned economy moving toward a market-oriented system is an enigma to potential investors. Thus, there is a need to understand the mechanisms which underpin the present transition of Vietnam's economy.

VIETNAM IN TRANSITION: AN OVERVIEW

Beginning in the early 1980s, Vietnam initiated a series of steps designed to move the Vietnamese economy from a centrally-planned system to a more mixed, market-oriented system. Early reforms were hesitant, but events forced the government to adopt a more radical approach to stimulate economic growth and to help restore Vietnam's position in the international community. The 1986 shift to the *doi moi* economic renovation policy was prompted by a series of economic and political crises. The international embargo which followed the invasion of Cambodia effectively isolated Vietnam from most Western nations while a series of internal economic policy failures fuelled hyper-inflation and falling production.

Soon after these events, the collapse of the Soviet empire disrupted trade among Vietnam and pro-communist block nations, and aid from these sources dried up. The government responded to this challenge by providing generous incentives for investors and enacting a broad range of economic reforms which effectively replaced central planning with the market system over a five-year period. Trading became the primary activity for the early investors.

Under the direction of reformist Prime Minister Vo Van Kiet, the government was able to control inflation, stabilise its currency and evolve a new basic legal infrastructure to accommodate foreign investment. Renovation of its agricultural sector was a key development goal. Here, radical revision of land rights laws, combined with the shift to market mechanisms, led to sharply increased yields by the late 1980s. The rapid exploitation of its rich oil and gas resources provided much-needed foreign exchange. Aid from Western nations increased when the U.S. lifted its embargo in 1994. The government invested much of this new capital in reconstructing a war-damaged physical infrastructure and upgrading its neglected roads, ports and telecommunications facilities. These moves gradually attracted foreign investors with a long-term outlook, mainly in the energy, manufacturing, services and hospitality sectors.

However, the reform government experienced difficulty in implementing many of its newly formulated laws. Many Vietnamese administrative mechanisms, originally intended to support a centrally-planned economy, were inadequate following the shift to a market economy. This gave rise to an era of administrative reforms which has continued to the present time. New accounting and tax systems are being patterned largely on international practices. The 1995 restructuring of the central government greatly reduced the number of agencies which oversee the activities of foreign investors. This was an important step toward integrating foreign investment policy with domestic implementation measures. A new *Civil Code* promises to rationalise the legal infrastructure and the 1996 Commercial Code will pave the way for the harmonisation of the legal system with its trading partners.

During this period of economic evolution, the political structure in Vietnam has remained remarkably stable. The Vietnam Communist Party exerts influence over the military, police and government machinery through a 19-member Politburo led by Secretary General Do Muoi. By shifting the role of the Party away from operational issues, the 1992 Constitutional reforms paved the way for the introduction of administrative reforms. Legislative power now falls to the National Assembly which not only formulates laws but, also, shapes economic and foreign policy, and oversees all of the state agencies.

VIETNAM'S KEY ECONOMIC FEATURES

Vietnam is currently the second most populous country in the fast-growing ASEAN region with 80% of its 75 million people living in the countryside. The population is quite youthful; approximately 50% of its people are under the age of 30. Its labour force is relatively well-educated and skilled and salary expectations of US$100 per month are well below the ASEAN average. The literacy rate in Vietnam is approximately 86%, good by ASEAN standards.

Achieving Sustained Improvements in Economic Performance

Annual GDP growth over the ten-year period from 1985 has averaged 8.2%, improving in 1995 to 9.3%. Annual total industrial output growth averaged 13% over the same period. The government's announced goal is to raise per capita GDP from US$200 to US$500 by the year 2000, which would generate a sizeable middle class.

The most notable achievements of the economic renovation policy are the control of hyper-inflation, and overcoming the economic crisis and depression during the difficult 1986 to 1991 period. The high inflation rate of 750% in 1986 was arrested and reduced to 68% in 1991. Over the past five years, inflation has hovered around 9.5%

per annum.

A High Degree of Political Stability

Vietnamese leaders are pragmatic and forward-looking in their efforts to introduce the benefits of a market economy. Unlike some of its neighbours, Vietnam has experienced no threat of a coup or military take-over. The Vietnamese people are disciplined and well aware that this transformation to a market economy will not be easy. They have been warned by their leaders that the desired reforms can be accomplished only if both domestic and external resources are used effectively and some short-term hardships are endured.

Self-sufficiency in Food Production

Moving from a position of near-famine in 1986, Vietnam undertook a number of steps to privatise the agricultural sector. By 1988, it had achieved strong production surpluses for many agricultural products. Most notably, Vietnam has emerged as the world's third largest rice producer with ample surpluses available for export.

A Quality Labour Pool

Vietnam has a highly skilled and literate work force. Many of their professionals have attended some of the best universities in Czechoslovakia, Hungary, East Germany and Russia and have gained valuable work experience. As a result, Vietnamese that are hired for many of the new investment projects need only minimal retraining. Executives of joint ventures projects claim that Vietnamese workers learn fast and adapt easily to modern practices. However, its socialist tradition has produced awkward relationships between labour and management.

An Attractive Investment Climate

Vietnam's foreign-investment laws are among the most liberal in Asia. All imported equipment, machinery, semi-processed products, component parts and raw materials for the manufacture and assembly of products destined for foreign markets are exempt from duties and taxes. In addition to tax holidays, preferential treatment brings tax rates to as low as 10%. There are also provisions for loss carryovers and reimbursement of taxes paid on profits and reinvested dividends.

Vietnam's largely untapped natural resources are without parallel in the region. In addition to oil and gas reserves, reportedly among the world's largest, there are large proven deposits of minerals and ores in the northern and central regions of the country. With a coastline of nearly 2,000 miles, Vietnam has a seafood industry that provides an important source of protein for its population and also generates foreign exchange earnings. There are more than 740,000 acres of water suitable for the inland cultivation of fish and shrimp.

Vietnam has comparative advantages in agriculture, light industry, energy and tourism due to the relatively low cost of labour. These are the areas where the government wishes to attract the majority of investment.

The current focus of Vietnam's financial policy is the promotion of domestic savings and investment as current levels are perceived to be constraining further development. Increasing government expenditures on infrastructure development is being met by increasing revenues and external financing while the cost of servicing the debt is declining. Vietnam is establishing a debt market in 1997 and is planning to set up a securities market by the end of 1998.

Incentives are provided for companies investing in high priority areas such as labour-intensive or export-based operations, infrastructure development, exploitation of natural resources, as well as companies practising import substitution and those earning foreign exchange. The tax base has been broadened and applied to all sectors of the national economy with the goal of removing subsidies to state enterprises. Corporate taxes are structured to provide incentives for foreign investment in Vietnam, particularly in areas such as infrastructure construction where the economy needs development.

Import and export trade has increased since 1993 while the current account deficit and the trade balance have increased as well. More of the same is expected for the next two years. External debt is expected to reach US$21.4 billion in 1995. A large portion of Vietnam's debt is being recycled, particularly with Japan and European countries. The debt-service ratio is expected to be manageable at 12% of exports in 1994 and 1995.

FOREIGN DIRECT INVESTMENT PATTERNS

Since the birth of the *Foreign Investment Law* in 1988, Vietnam has attracted over US$18 billion as of the end of August 1996 (see Table 1–1). Foreign investors are most active in oil and gas exploration and in the tourism industry. These two sectors also have the largest projects. Tourism activities are particularly visible in large cities where many large hotels are under construction. In garments, footwear, and seafood processing industries, investors from Taiwan, Hong Kong, Singapore, Korea and Japan have developed several large- and medium-scale export-oriented projects using low cost local labour.

TABLE 1–1
Foreign Investment since 1988

Years	1988–90	1991	1992	1993	1994	1995	1996*
No. of Projects	281	155	193	265	343	370	61
Capital invested	1,615	1,278	1,967	2,688	3,588	6,215	1,120

* January to August 1996.
Source: MPI – up to 23 August 1996.

These countries were the earliest investors and they account for over one-half of total foreign investments to date (see Table 1–2). About two-thirds of their proposed investments are for projects located in the south, despite the government's encouragement and promotion of investment in all parts of the country (see Table 1–3). Foreign investors prefer to have their projects in the south where the infrastructure is better than in the north and management skills are more readily available.

The majority of foreign investment projects to date are joint ventures, mostly with state-owned enterprises (SOE) or state agencies, which often contribute their capital in the form of land use (see Table 1–4). The *Foreign Investment Law* allows for 100% foreign-owned projects but relatively few of the approved projects are of this type. Part of the reason is because foreign investors prefer to have local counterparts in their projects to benefit from their familiarity with Vietnam's system which, until recently, was still closed. It is also difficult for foreign investors to obtain rights to use land unless they engage in a joint venture.

TABLE 1–2
Leading Foreign Investors in Vietnam (US$ Million)

Countries	No. of Projects	Capital Invested	Percentage of Total
Taiwan	256	4,008	18.3%
Japan	154	2,413	11.0%
Singapore	140	2,374	10.8%
Hongkong	186	2,305	10.5%
South Korea	163	2,166	9.9%
United States	61	1,285	5.9%
Malaysia	48	925	4.2%
Thailand	63	666	3.0%
France	75	655	3.0%
Australia	48	621	2.8%
United Kingdom	19	485	2.2%
Indonesia	14	240	1.1%
Philippines	14	218	1.0%
Other		3,528	
Total		21,889	
ASEAN		**4,423**	**20.2%**

Source: MPI as of 23 August 1996.

TABLE 1–3
Top Localities Receiving Foreign Investment (US$ Million)

Provinces/Cities	No. of Projects	Capital Invested	Percentage
South	1,050	12,177	64.00
North	529	6,854	36.01
Ho Chi Minh City	538	5,719	30.05
Hanoi	272	3,506	18.42
Dong-Nai	166	2,428	12.76
Song Be	70	447	2.35
Haiphong	56	978	5.14
VungTau	63	873	4.59
Tay Ninh	10	157	.82

Source: MPI – up to 23 August 1996.

One problem with the joint venture form in Vietnam is that major decisions must be approved by all parties to the venture regardless of their relative shares in the firm. Foreign investors who choose the joint venture route thus lose control of their venture. If they try to go it alone, on the other hand, they run into the difficulty of renting land for their projects. A revision of the *Foreign Investment Law* in 1992 now allows private local companies to enter into joint venture agreements with foreign investors.

TABLE 1–4
Forms of Foreign Investment

Forms of Foreign Investment	Number	Capital Invested	Percentage
Joint Venture	1,048	13,164	67.61
100% Foreign Capital	371	321	23.94
Others (Business Co-operation)	131	252	8.45

Source: MPI – up to 23 August 1996.

LONG-TERM IMPACT OF VIETNAM'S ENTRANCE INTO ASEAN

The entry of Vietnam into ASEAN should have positive implications for all members. One consequence of its entry is the enhancement of the ASEAN market to 400 million people. The other ASEAN countries already enjoy significant trade and investment with Vietnam and this trend should accelerate with Vietnam's full membership. Although Vietnam's GDP is a tiny portion of the total ASEAN GDP, its annual growth of more than 8% means that its contribution to the region's economy should grow rapidly.

The impact of ASEAN membership is a source of mutual benefit to Vietnam and its neighbours in several respects. For example, Vietnam gains greater access to foreign investment capital and regional markets while other members, such as Singapore, gain access to its growing markets and cheap labour. Seen from this perspective, entry into ASEAN is only a first step towards Vietnam's re-integration within the region. In addition, Vietnam must harmonise certain key laws and administrative procedures (such as customs and immigration) so that they are compatible with the laws and procedures in place throughout the region.

It is likely that Vietnam will be invited to join the Asia-Pacific

Economic Co-operation (APEC) group in late 1997. However, it is possible for Vietnam to participate in relevant APEC working groups prior to admission. This step would help Vietnamese enterprises adapt to the rapidly opening regional economy. Even though Vietnam is temporarily exempt from the ASEAN Free Trade Area (AFTA), it must accelerate its internal reforms to prepare for the competitive challenge posed by AFTA. In an open regional economy, the country's enterprises would be at a dual disadvantage: first, their managers are relatively young and inexperienced; and secondly, they now operate in a restrictive and protective environment.

Beyond the region, ASEAN membership for Vietnam is a first step toward the interaction required for re-integration into the world economy. Through this membership, Vietnam will have full access to ongoing forums between ASEAN and its dialogue partners (including the U.S. and Japan), as well as with ASEAN's consultative partners (including China). As these relationships grow, and Vietnam is increasingly perceived by the world community as a peaceful and responsible member, doors should open to enable a full normalisation of economic and political relationships. This would enhance the value of those pioneering investments able to withstand the challenges of the current era.

ASEAN is steadily moving toward a regional organisation. From the time of its inception, ASEAN has had the goal of eventually representing all countries in Southeast Asia. ASEAN grew from five to six members with the addition of Brunei in 1984 and now from six to seven with Vietnam's formal inclusion. From here, ASEAN looks forward to including other countries such as Laos which is already an observer, and Cambodia which has made steps toward observer status. Myanmar is following close behind. With the entry of these countries ASEAN would become a ten-country regional organisation. The advantages for Vietnam, therefore, from its ASEAN membership are manifold.

Another issue that Vietnam faces is lack of membership in the World Trade Organisation (WTO) where it is currently an observer. This is an important priority for Vietnam and another major step in its re-integration into the world community. Membership, of course, will depend on the pace of economic reform in Vietnam and the country's willingness to work towards the standards required by the WTO.

With this cursory overview of Vietnam's changing character and its earnest endeavours to join the global investment community, there is evidence of unparalleled opportunity for business and trade within Vietnam. However, a more detailed understanding of its transitional changes, new reforms, infrastructure development and industry-sector opportunities is prerequisite for doing business in Vietnam. The contents of this volume are specifically directed towards enriching this understanding.

ORGANISATION OF CHAPTER CONTENTS

The remainder of this book comprises six major sections plus a concluding chapter. Each section has been arranged to deal with a significant economic focus impacting potential business and investment opportunities in Vietnam. However, notwithstanding this effort to consolidate the economic focus of each section, there is considerable diversity in the information content within each section. Thus, a synoptic chapter concludes each section with the express purpose of synthesising the major themes of each chapter and, further, of highlighting the implications of these themes for doing business in Vietnam.

The section on Macro Policy and Reform starts with Chou *et al.* exploring different aspects of Vietnam's foreign investment policies and strategies for growth in Chapter 2. In Chapter 3, Chan *et al.* examine the government's macro economic reform measures through the lens of monetary policy while Ang *et al.*, in Chapter 4, pursue the efforts of major reforms in the banking system during the *doi moi* era. Chapter 5 shifts outward and Tan *et al.* embrace the broader Mekong basin region where Vietnam is a dynamic component followed by McGovern's synopsis and commentary on the breadth of macro economic reforms in Chapter 6.

The next section, Infrastructure for Development, commences with Pham *et al.* tracing the impact of regulations, financing and market development specifically on trading activities. In Chapters 8 and 9, Chionh *et al.* and Au Yong *et al.* detail the legal environment for foreign investment, and tax incentives and accounting issues, respectively. In Chapter 10, Choo provides an overview of these mechanisms and examines the implications of some impending modifications to them.

The section on Technology Transfer begins with Lee *et al.*'s analysis of the telecommunication industry in Chapter 11 followed by Lee *et al.*'s assessment, in Chapter 12, of the potential and impediments underlying the development of Vietnam's Internet industry. Chapter 13 is empirical in nature, but unique. Here Ang *et al.* explore characteristics related to the human factor which is probably the most important element in technology transfer. Chapter 14 concludes this section with Kendall summarising the technology transfer issues and illuminating new business opportunities.

The next section, Services Sectors, draws on three of the most vital service industries to Vietnam's sustained economic expansion. After Tan *et al.* review the challenges and opportunities in the banking sector in Chapter 15, Chan *et al.* and Ong *et al.* cover the education and hospitality sectors in Chapter 16 and 17, respectively. In Chapter 18, Marshall consolidates the issues in these sectors and suggests extended business and investment opportunities.

Turning to the section on Business Attitudes and Behavioural Issues, Chapters 19, 20 and 21 are empirically based and attempt to capture and explain prevailing beliefs and values currently held by a cross-section of managers operating in Vietnam. First, in Chapter 19, Tan *et al.* examine different ethical standards in individuals from various cultural settings in Vietnam. This is followed, in Chapter 20, by Lam *et al.*'s exploration of non-economic risk assessment activities. After Loo and Sum pursue a cross-cultural comparison of hospitality managers' performance expectations in Chapter 21, Low concludes the section with a synopsis and commentary in Chapter 22.

The final major section, Singapore's Investment Initiatives, deals with specific types of linkages between Vietnam and Singapore. The special features and advantages of the Vietnam-Singapore Industrial Park are featured by Agustono *et al.* in Chapter 23. In Chapter 24, Low *et al.* use a survey questionnaire to present current problems in the construction and building development sector while in Chapter 25, Quah *et al.* present a cross-cultural comparison of management practices between Singaporean and Vietnamese enterprises. Luu sums up the issues on regional interaction in Chapter 26.

In Chapter 27, Lall concludes the book with some potential suggestions on what the future holds for businesses and investors interested in Vietnam. Finally, there are considerable references throughout the book to various regions and cities located in Vietnam. To facilitate an understanding of relative locations, a territorial map of Vietnam is presented in Figure 1–1.

FIGURE 1–1
Map of Vietnam

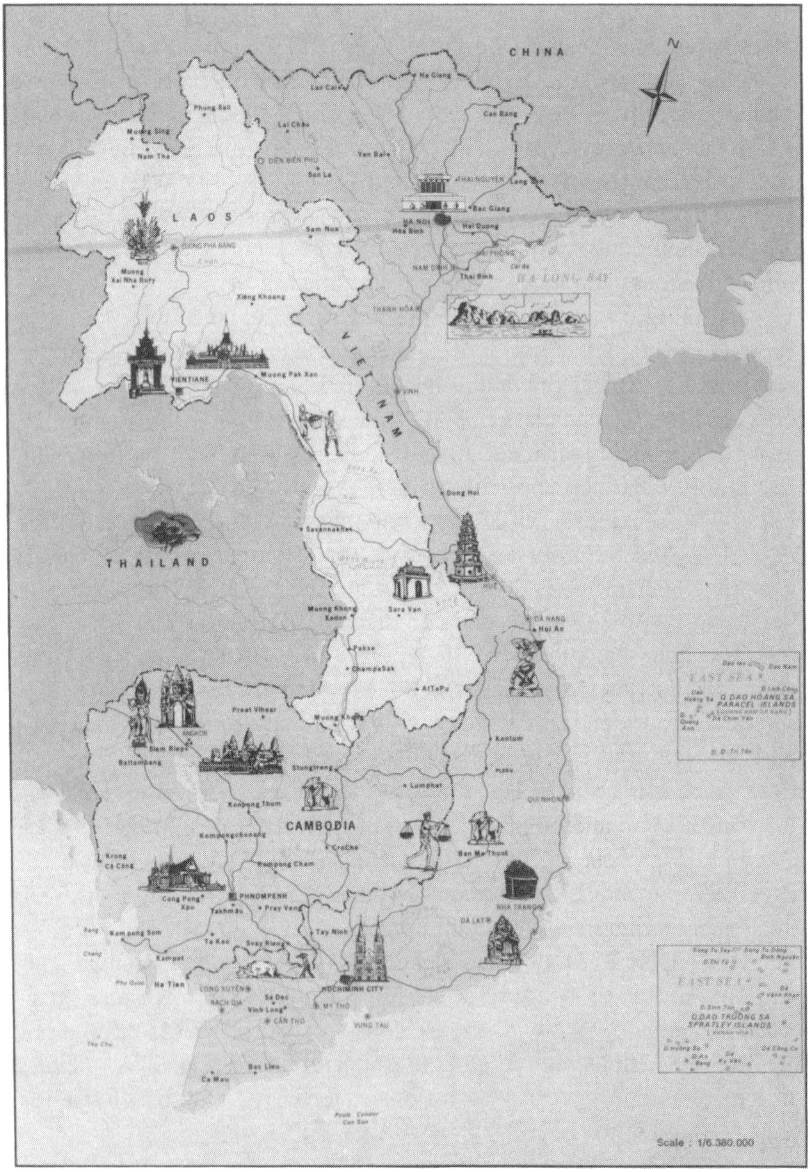

Source: Vietnam National Administration of Tourism, Hanoi, Vietnam, 1995.

REFERENCE

Vietnam Business Journal, 1996 issues, URL: http://www.viam.com/

MACRO POLICY AND REFORM

Chapter 2

Foreign Investment in Vietnam: Promotion Policies and Strategies*

BY
CHOU Cher Hoong
Jennifer GAN
Henry LIM
TAN Meng Heng

INTRODUCTION

IN NOVEMBER 1995, the *Conference on Tax and Investment in the Emerging Economies in the Asia-Pacific Region* was held in Singapore. As one of the speakers, the Vietnamese Vice-Minister for Finance, Dr. Nguyen Sinh Hung, highlighted the Vietnamese government's aim to speed up economic development to close the gap that exists with other capitalist economies in the region (for example, Malaysia, Thailand and Indonesia). To achieve its aim, the government: "... intends to pay attention to a maximum and efficient mobilisation of external sources of capital, modern technology and management expertise".

The Vietnamese government estimates that to generate an annual gross domestic product (GDP) growth rate of 9 to 10% for the period 1996 to 2000, Vietnam will need to mobilise as much as US$20 billion from external capital sources (Nguyen Sinh Hung, 1995b). This chapter critically examines the appropriateness and adequacy of Vietnam's foreign investment policies *vis-à-vis* this objective and the schemes or incentives introduced to attract foreign direct investment (FDI).

---

* The authors are grateful for the guidance and assistance provided by Dr. Ian McGovern.

FOREIGN INVESTMENT POLICIES

The government appears to view FDI as the main engine of growth for the Vietnamese economy. It officially welcomes all forms of FDI provided that the activities of investors do not conflict with Vietnamese traditions and values. In particular, FDI is to take a central role in establishing an export-oriented economy; in generating employment and alleviating poverty; and in improving the technical skills of its people. In formulating FDI policies to match these roles, the government identified the following sectors (Coopers and Lybrand, 1994):

(i) activities bringing in foreign currency, such as tourism and oil exploitation;
(ii) export-oriented manufacturing industries;
(iii) labour-intensive industries using Vietnamese raw materials and natural resources;
(iv) infrastructure development; and
(v) hi-tech industries using skilled labour.

The government is encouraging investments in the northern and central regions of the country instead of concentrating its efforts only on Ho Chi Minh City in the south. To achieve these objectives, the government adopted a two-pronged approach. At the macro level, it is building an economic and legal framework conducive to doing business. This includes an amendment to the constitution in 1992 to "ensure no nationalisation of the assets of investors" (State Committee for Co-operation and Investment (SCCI), 1995) and promulgation of the *Law on Foreign Investment* (LFI) which provides the legal foundation for establishing foreign enterprises in Vietnam. To make it easier for potential investors to obtain a license to operate a business enterprise in Vietnam, the government promises to streamline administrative procedures. For example, in January 1996 the State Planning Committee and the SCCI merged into the new Ministry of Planning and Investment (MPI) which intends to provide a "one-stop" processing service for investors seeking investment license approval.

At the micro level, specific initiatives were taken to attract the kind of foreign investment desired by the government. Thus, projects with more than 500 employees, that use advanced technology, or export at least 80% of total production, are to be given a preferential profit tax rate of 20%[1] for a period of between five to ten years commencing from the year following the issuance of the investment licence. In addition, investments in infrastructure construction, exploitation of natural resources other than oil and gas, and investments in less favourable areas (mountainous areas and areas with unfavourable natural, social or economic conditions), are to have a profit tax rate of only 15%.

To attract foreign investment into export-oriented manufacturing industries as well as to spread the foreign investment projects throughout the whole country, the government established export processing zones (EPZs) in different parts of the country. EPZs offer a free trade environment, access to infrastructure and even better incentives than offered elsewhere. So far, six zones have licenses in Vietnam: Tan Thuan and Linh Trung (both on the outskirts of Ho Chi Minh City in the south), Haiphong (in the north), Da Nang (in the centre), Can Tho (in the Mekong Delta), and Noi Bai (outside Hanoi in the north) (Fforde and Goldstone, 1995).

Recently, the government introduced a scheme to lease out land at a relatively lower cost to companies willing to set up industrial parks. This allows the government to transfer the burden of infrastructure development within these parks to the companies that set them up.[2] The government also commissioned two separate companies to carry out feasibility studies for setting up two high-technology parks.[3] In addition to tax incentives, the government also encourages investments in infrastructure projects and operates a scheme where investors can build and operate the infrastructure[4] (such as roads or bridges) for a number of years before transferring the infrastructure development to the government (Nguyen Minh Tu, 1996).

---

1 The standard profit tax rate for foreign investment is 25%.

2 This is unlike the case of EPZs where infrastructure development is the responsibility of the government.

3 These parks are analogous to the industrial parks except that they are meant to bring together companies involved in high-technology industries.

4 This is known as build-operate-transfer (BOT).

CURRENT INVESTMENT PROMOTION POLICIES AND STRATEGIES

Activities to Generate Foreign Currency

In the mid-1980s the Vietnamese government began liberalising the economy. This eventually increased the demand for foreign currencies as locals increased their consumption of imports, and this had an adverse impact on the current account balance. Table 2–1 indicates that from 1991 to 1994 Vietnam's current account balance was in deficit, although much of this was actually due to capital imports rather than expenditures on imported consumer goods. To improve its external balance of payments situation, the government is seeking investments both in industries that will earn the needed foreign currencies for capital imports and in import-substitution industries.

TABLE 2–1
Current Account Balances from 1991 to 1994

	1991	1992	1993	1994
Current Account Balance ($ billion)	–188	–36	–758	–960

Source: Mai Kim Dinh, 1996.

The government particularly is encouraging investments in tourism and energy resources (mainly oil and gas). For tourism, Vietnam can rely on its many historical sights to attract visitors. Central Vietnam also has a superb coastline with beautiful scenery and secluded bays which hold great potential for development as holiday resorts. In addition, the cooler mountainous parts of Vietnam also have a possibility for tourist development. Focusing on the tourism sector is also a way of enabling the central region to catch up with the northern and southern regions in terms of economic development. The oil sector has been targeted because of its potential as a major foreign currency earner. The added attraction is that because of the location of energy reserves, development of this industry can benefit the poorer central region of Vietnam.

Export-oriented Policies

Apart from tourism and energy, the government is encouraging a wide range of both import-substitution and export-oriented industries. There are a number of export-oriented policies that the government has implemented. Apart from the use of tax incentives, the government has set up various export processing zones (EPZs). The usefulness of EPZs is especially apparent in developing countries like Vietnam where there are still very strong trade barriers, including high import tariffs[5] and export taxes. EPZs should allow for a liberalised trade policy only in selected areas while maintaining a protectionist stance in the rest of the country for developing domestic industries to mature.

However, the direct benefits from EPZs (to the implementing country) may not be as substantial as they seem. For example, the average number of workers employed in a large EPZ is about 30,000, a small number considering Vietnam's need to absorb high unemployment. Foreign exchange earnings from exports of production within EPZs have also been as low as 10% of the export value. Studies also show that out of about 90 EPZs operating in the world, only 25% are considered to be successful and, even in these, success is often limited to specific areas of the economy (Fforde and Goldstone, 1995).

Labour-intensive Industries

Considering that Vietnam is in the early stages of economic development, one of the main concerns is to make sure that its population is gainfully employed. This helps fuel economic growth and also moves people away from the poverty line and attendant social ills. Vietnam's unemployment rate is estimated to be between 25 and 30%. In fact, this is probably a gross underestimate because predominately agricultural countries have a lot of disguised unemployment in their agricultural sector. FDI in labour intensive industries can help to provide jobs, both in industry and in agri-business (processing of agricultural produce) and, thus, it can alleviate many problems in the rural areas. Moreover, Vietnam is a country that is richly endowed with natural resources including coal, oil and gas, iron ore and bauxite (see Table 2–2).

---

[5] Having high import tariffs is biased against exports as tariffs on final goods make import-substitution industries more profitable while import tariffs on intermediate goods (or inputs) increase the production costs of exports (*East Asian Executive Reports*, February 1994).

TABLE 2–2
Natural Resources in Vietnam

Natural Resource	Regions with Significant Deposits	Current Estimated Capacity
Coal	North-eastern province of Quang Ninh, Thai Nguyen Basin in the nearby province of Bac Thai, Red River Delta	20 to 30 billion tonnes
Oil and gas	South Con Son Basin, Mekong Basin	20 million tonnes
Gas	South Con Son Basin, Bach Ho	2 trillion cubic feet
Iron ore	Thach Khe, Lam Dong, Lang Son	500 million tonnes
Bauxite	Thach Khe, Lam Dong, Lang Son	4 billion tonnes

Source: Fforde and Goldstone, 1995.

High-technology Industries

With today's rapid changes and developments in technology, the Vietnamese believe that they can leap-frog over the traditional phases of economic growth. According to Nguyen Sinh Hung (1995a), being a backward agricultural country that started a few decades later than many countries in the region and in the world, it is the aim of the Vietnamese government to shorten the gap in development compared with other countries in the region and in the world. It is from this perspective that Vietnam is trying to promote high-technology industries.

An important factor that the government is relying on in pursuing this policy is the high literacy rate of the population. Vietnam's literacy rate of 83.8% is higher than that of many other developing Asian countries (Fforde and Goldstone, 1995). This outcome reflects a good education system, though the system is currently undergoing considerable adaptation to meet the needs of a modern market economy. Current foreign investors testify to the good educational training and learning abilities of the Vietnamese workers and this is an important factor in the government's drive to support high-technology industries.

However, although the government's intention may be to "leap-frog" the development process and move into high technology industries, an overriding consideration is the creation of more jobs. These are likely to be found in labour-intensive industries. The government, therefore, is very selective in its promotion of high-technology industries since these tend to be highly capital intensive and they are not able to generate the number or types of job required.

Infrastructure Development

Since it is a developing country, there are many infrastructural problems that need to be addressed in Vietnam. Infrastructure development is always one of the biggest problems facing such economies and it is a catch-22 situation: the government needs foreign funds to build the infrastructure to support economic development but foreign investors often do not invest if there is inadequate infrastructure.

To overcome this problem, the government recently introduced build-operate-transfer (BOT) schemes. Under such schemes, investors build and operate the needed infrastructure (such as a road, railway or a bridge) for a stated period of time before handing it over to the government. The scheme is attractive as it does not require the government to invest any funds in the infrastructure development.

However, while the government may designate certain projects for BOT operations, a major drawback is that these projects are carried out by profit-motivated private investors who expect a reasonable balance between risk and return. Also, private investors may decide to stop the project at any time to cut losses if anticipated profits seem unattainable. A further concern is that private investors may not maintain the infrastructure particularly well as the time for the transfer approaches. There is no doubt, however, that BOT is a viable option for many projects and one that the Vietnamese government is eager to exploit.

Regional Economic Development

The country's three most developed cities are Ho Chi Minh City in the south, and Hanoi and Haiphong in the north. Comparatively, the least developed parts of the country are in the central region.

At first, the government attempted to develop the more rural central region by stipulating specific geographical areas where foreign investors could invest. However, this approach did not succeed in attracting foreign investment and there are a number of highly publicised failures (e.g., withdrawal of the French oil company "Total"). The policy has not provided a good foundation for long term co-operation.

The government recently changed its strategy and now employs a softer approach towards persuading private investors to move their investments into those regions. This involves moving state-owned enterprises (SOEs) into those regions first, as an example to others, to show them that there is money to be made, and to provide an industrial base. For instance, Petrovietnam (a SOE) will establish an oil refinery in central Vietnam. It welcomes joint ventures with foreign investors.

The government has adopted a policy of using the natural endowment in each region to attract the desired FDI. This approach is in contrast to Thailand which divided the country into three investment promotion zones and offered varying degrees of incentives for each region, with remote areas being granted more incentives (see Table 2–3).

Agricultural Sector Development

Examination of official investment guidelines, and the *Law on Foreign Investment,* indicates that Vietnam has made little concerted effort to seek FDI in its agricultural sector. This is surprising considering Vietnam's huge agricultural sector which employs about 65% of the country's total workforce and accounts for one-half of the gross national product (*CIA World Fact Book*, 1995). The Vietnamese have chosen instead to rely more on domestic funds and aid to develop this sector of the economy. Perhaps the reason for choosing this strategy is to avoid being overly reliant on foreign influence in such an important sector of the economy.

However, raising domestic funds is inhibited by the infancy of the domestic banking sector. A large amount of domestic funds circulate outside the formal banking system and this limits access. Furthermore, since all land belongs to the state and individuals only have land-use rights, there is a lack of pledgeable securities that can be used to secure loans from banks. Therefore, unless Vietnam is prepared to attract foreign investment into this sector, the agricultural sector may not be able to develop to its full potential.[6] As noted above, FDI could

---

[6] It appears that the government may be having a change of heart about this strategy. During a recent seminar for foreign business executives, top government officials made a sales pitch to foreign investors with the aim of attracting more than $1 billion in foreign investment by the year 2000 to build up the

provide jobs in agri-business in the rural areas and thus alleviate some of the problems of the rural poor. So far, however, the government has not moved very far in this direction.

Comparison of Vietnamese FDI Promotion Policies with Selected Countries

The investment policies and strategies adopted by the Vietnamese government are quite similar to those pursued by the governments of Malaysia, Thailand and Poland[7] (see Table 2–3). All four countries seeks FDI in export-oriented and labour-intensive industries. To a certain extent, Thailand and Malaysia encouraged import-substitution industries in the early years of development. Ensuring the simultaneous economic development of the various regions of the country was also actively pursued by both countries.

However, while Vietnam does not offer special incentives (apart from giving general tax incentives) for investments in difficult areas, the Thai government takes a different approach. Thailand is divided into three zones, with the less developed zones receiving greater investment incentives. The success of this strategy todate has been mixed, and the Thai Board of Investment still has difficulty in attracting FDI outside of Bangkok and the eastern seaboard (Economic and Social Committee for Asia and the Pacific (ESCAP); 1995b, 1995c).

In contrast to Vietnam, both Thailand and Malaysia actively pursue FDI in their agricultural sectors. For example, Malaysia's 1986 *Promotion of Investment Act* listed agricultural production, integrated agriculture, and the processing of agricultural produce among the list of products and activities where foreign investment is encouraged (Economic and Social Committee for Asia and the Pacific (ESCAP), 1995a). Similarly, in Thailand a large number of individual product groups in the agriculture, livestock and fishing sectors were listed in the activities eligible for investment promotion (Peat Marwick Suthee, 1994). Malaysia has also adopted a more general strategy in its export promotion drive.

---

farm, fish and forestry industries (see "Vietnam Seeks US$1 billion in Form Investment", clari-world.asia.south-east, 10 May 1995).

7 Malaysia and Thailand were chosen for comparison because they are second generation newly industrialised economies which are at least a few steps ahead of Vietnam in economic development. They also have a large agricultural sector like Vietnam. Poland was chosen because, like Vietnam, it dismantled a command economy in favour of a market economy.

TABLE 2–3
FDI Promotion Policies of Malaysia, Thailand and Poland

Malaysia	Thailand	Poland
Investment policies are geared towards reducing Malaysia's dependence on primary resources and reducing the economic imbalance in ownership and control of various sectors of the economy. While FDI is actively sought for all of the industries, preference are given to export-oriented, capital intensive industries which utilise locally available resources. Industrial projects that depend on domestic markets as well as those involving extraction of non-renewable domestic resources require substantial Malaysian equity. FDI is also encouraged in the agricultural sector.	In the 1960s and 1970s, the Thai Government concentrated on encouraging import substitution industries. During the 1980s, a strong emphasis was placed on promoting exports to strengthen the country's foreign exchange position. Efforts were geared towards encouraging foreign companies to use Thailand as a production base for exports. Most export activities were labour intensive. The 1990s is shifting to industrial deepening and broadening. The Thai government is encouraging more localisation. Considerable effort is geared towards the creation of industrial linkages. Another important theme is industrial decentralisation.	The Polish government adopted a liberal policy with regards to FDI where, except for a few strategic areas in the Polish economy, foreign investment does not need any governmental approval. In many ways, foreign investors are given the same rights and treatment as domestic investors including land ownership rights. However, where accrued foreign investment exceeds ECU 2 million in high-technology sectors, in regions of high unemployment, or in industries whose exports exceed 20% of total sales, investors are entitled to income tax exemptions.

Sources: Tan and Lim (1992); Peat Marwick Suthee (1994); Coopers and Lybrand (1992 and 1994); Hong Kong Trade Development Council (1994); Department of Promotion and Information of Poland (1996); and Confederation of British Industry (CBI) (1994).

Poland has adopted a very liberal policy towards FDI, especially in the area of land ownership rights where foreign investors are given the same rights and treatment as domestic investors. This is significantly different from the strategy adopted by Vietnam which, because of its political history, allows neither its own citizens nor foreign investors to own any land. This has created a barrier to investments in the country (see Table 2–4).

TABLE 2–4
Foreign Direct Investment Capital by Economic Sectors: 1988 to 1995

Sectors	Capital Committed (US$ million)	Percentage
Industrial	8,927	45.97
Hotel, tourism	6,472	33.33
Oil and gas	1,125	5.79
Transport, telecommunications	1,067	5.49
Projects in EPZs, industrial zones	537	2.77
Agriculture, fishery, forestry	370	1.91
Services, bank, finance	352	1.81
Others	570	2.94

Source: Nguyen Mai, 1996.

ADEQUACY OF INCENTIVES OFFERED

Given the appropriateness of the investment promotion policy as well as the strategies adopted to achieve that policy, the remaining question concerns the effectiveness of the incentives. A review of Table 2–4 below might lead to the conclusion that the various incentives offered were effective in helping the economy to attract most of the desired types of foreign investment. Almost one-half of the total foreign capital commitments lie in the industrial sector. The tourism sector (including hotels) accounts for about one-third of capital commitments. An examination of the projects that were in operation as at 31 December 1994 (see Table 2–5) lead to similar conclusions. Of the total realised foreign investment, 39% was in the industrial sector followed by tourism (20%) and oil and gas (12%).[8]

[8] It should be noted that due to differences in classification it is not possible to compare the amount of capital commitments against realised commitments.

TABLE 2–5
Projects in Operation by Economic Sector at 31 December 1994

Sectors	Projects	Total Capital (US$ million)	Percentage
Industrial	547	4,306	39
Tourism (including hotels)	113	2,235	20
Oil and Gas	26	1,302	12
Services	134	1,254	10
Transport and communications	28	951	9
Export processing zones	28	388	4
Agriculture, forestry and food industry	74	369	3
Banking and Finance	15	177	2
Industrial zones	2	167	1
Others	22	85	0

Source: SCCI, 1995.

However, interviews with foreign investors in Vietnam revealed a number of current problems which continue to hinder investments. These include the following areas:

(i) *Tax System:* Although the tax incentives given to foreign investors appear to be very generous, they may not be that attractive. This is because the main concession given is in the area of profit tax. A Hanoi-based tax consultant claimed that he had yet to see foreign companies registering sufficient profits to benefit from these incentives.

On the other hand, investors are greatly affected by the turnover tax imposed by the government.[9] This may be one main reason why foreign investors are less than enthusiastic about the EPZs and industrial zones encouraged by the government. It is well aware of the problem and promises actions to streamline and revise the tax structure. One of the improvements being considered is the replacement of the turnover tax with a value-added tax

[9] This tax applies to both locals and foreign businesses.

(VAT).[10] The ultimate success of the VAT is uncertain since one of the impediments to its implementation is Vietnam's lack of a proper accounting system.

Even if the government is able to streamline its tax regime, effort is required to ensure that the tax laws are correctly implemented by the various local authorities. Anecdotal evidence from investors indicates that misinterpretation of the tax laws by local authorities has led to great inconvenience. For example, under the tax laws, Vietnamese nationals who earn more than VND 6,300,000 per month (about US$600) are subject to an additional rate of 30% on the amount exceeding VND 6,300,000. One local authority misinterpreted the law and applied it to companies with total monthly wage bills exceeding VND 6,300,000 instead of to individuals. This oversight involved many rounds of talks and clarifications with the central authorities before the case was finally straightened out.

(ii) ***Repatriation of Profits and Assets:*** Another issue relates to the repatriation of profits and assets. The government guarantees that foreign organisations and private persons investing in Vietnam have the right to repatriate profits derived from business operations in Vietnam. However, before a foreign investor can do so, the company's paid-up capital must be increased. In other words, if the company is registered with an authorised capital of US$10 million, then the foreign investor would have to make sure that the paid-up capital is also US$10 million before there can be any repatriation of profits out of Vietnam.

(iii) ***Land Lease:*** Foreign investors are given special privileges in the form of reduced rent for land leased from the state. For example, if a foreign investor is operating in a particularly difficult area or in a number of special fields that need incentives to induce invested capital, then a maximum reduction of 50% of the rent is allowed. Again, this sounds attractive. However, the problem faced by investors is the short lease given which makes it difficult for investors to recoup sufficiently the investment made. One example in point is the proposed Vietnam-Singapore Industrial Park (VSIP). The Singaporean consortium wanted to lease the pro-

---

[10] The VAT differs from the turnover tax in the sense that the former only taxes the firm on the value added to the products sold. Turnover tax, on the other hand, applies to the absolute value of sales.

posed site for the VSIP for a period of 90 years but the Vietnamese government is considering only a 50 year lease.

(iv) ***Lack of Incentives to Promote Tourism:*** For promoting tourism, the government has not offered many incentives apart from concessions in building hotels and infrastructure such as seaports and airports. The fact that Vietnam is able to attract a relatively large amount of foreign investment into this sector, despite the lack of specific incentives, is testimony to the tourist potential of the country (Nguyen Van The, 1996).

Indeed, central Vietnam holds great potential for the tourism trade with its many historical sights. It also holds potential for the promotion of tour packages that include some neighbouring countries such as Laos and Cambodia along specific themes (such as war relics, ancient cultures and so forth). The government is well aware of the tourism potential, especially in the central region, and it has already drawn up a Tourism Master Plan. However, based on conversations with both central and local authorities, it would appear that little effort has been made in marketing this opportunity to potential investors.

(v) ***Uncertain and Difficult Investment Climate:*** Apart from investment promotion policies, foreign investors also assess the attractiveness of the overall investment climate in the country before making a decision. In this respect, current investors are finding problems with the frequent changes made to the various investment regulations which are often made without any forewarning or proper dissemination of information to the concerned parties. For example, decrees may be issued without any explanation or warning which ban particular products from import. Alternatively, the government may announce that a particular business activity will no longer be approved for joint ventures. Another example is the frequent changes made to the various tax rates which makes it extremely difficult for investors to carry out any meaningful assessment of potential investments.

Another major problem is red tape. *Asiaweek* (16 June 1995) reported that the "lingering problems of red tape, unclear or incomplete laws, petty corruption, and poor infrastructure are testing the patience of investors." In his visit to Hanoi in 1995, Singapore Senior Minister, Mr. Lee Kuan Yew, was reported to have remarked that "without slashing red tape and graft, Vietnam could lose investment to its neighbours" (*Asiaweek*, 16 June 1995).

THE SUCCESS OF VIETNAM'S FDI POLICY

The objectives that the government set out for FDI are largely being achieved and the adopted policies are consistent with the roles expected of FDI. The policy of encouraging FDI in export-oriented manufacturing industries should result in the establishment of an export-oriented economy. Targeting FDI in labour-intensive industries as well as infrastructure developments should also help to generate employment and alleviate poverty. Moreover, focusing FDI in high technology industries should help improve the technical skills of the people. Overall, the government appears to be able to attract the type of investments that it is seeking and the incentives, regulations and policies governing business operations as a whole, are consistent with its plans on FDI.

Vietnam as a Foreign Investment Location

Most of the empirical research on the motivation behind foreign investment (as opposed to the alternative of international trade) tends to suggest four main groups of reasons why firms seek to invest abroad: marketing factors, barriers to trade, cost factors and investment climate (see Table 2–6) (Czinkota *et al.*, 1994).

Vietnam's large population provides a potentially lucrative market for investors while entry into Vietnam can also serve as a springboard for tapping the potential markets of neighbours in the Mekong Basin. The cost of doing business is also generally lower *vis-à-vis* other relatively more developed countries around the region.

While the investment climate, as noted above, may be somewhat difficult and uncertain, the general attitude of the government towards foreign investment is encouraging. It is genuinely interested in attracting foreign investors into the country. It is also aware of many of the problems that foreign investors are facing with the changes to existing investment policies, rules and steps that are being taken. Political stability can also be expected in the foreseeable future.

TABLE 2–6
Determinants of Foreign Direct Investment

Marketing Factors
1 Size of market
2 Market growth
3 Desire to maintain share of market
4 Desire to advance exports of parent company
5 Need to maintain close customer contact
6 Dissatisfaction with existing market arrangements
7 Export base
8 Desire to follow customers
9 Desire to follow competition

Barriers to Trade
1 Government-erected barriers to trade
2 Preference of local customers for local products

Cost Factors
1 Desire to be near source of supply
2 Availability of labour
3 Availability of raw materials
4 Availability of capital/technology
5 Lower labour costs
6 Lower transport costs
7 Lower overhead production costs
8 Financial (and other) inducements by government
9 More favourable cost levels

Investment Climate
1 General attitude towards foreign investment
2 Political stability
3 Limitation on ownership
4 Currency exchange regulations
5 Stability of foreign exchange
6 Tax structure
7 Familiarity with country

General
1 Expected higher profit
2 Other

Source: Organisation for Economic Co-operation and Development, *International Investment and Multinational Enterprises* (Paris: OECD, 1983) p. 41, as quoted in Czinkota *et al.*, 1994.

Overall, Vietnam scores high as a suitable investment location in terms of current cost factors and investment climate. In addition, as the market develops there will be an increasing need for companies that currently rely on trade with Vietnam to take into account marketing factors and the likelihood of increasing barriers to trade. As a result, FDI is likely to increase significantly in Vietnam during the next decade.

FUTURE DEVELOPMENTS

Foreign investors will tend to become more selective in the future as the economy matures. For example, greater emphasis will probably be placed on high-technology industries instead of labour-intensive ones. In this respect, it is interesting to note that during the recent World Trade Organisation conference in Singapore (1996), the idea of an ASEAN investment area was mooted. According to Mr. Tunky Ariwibowo, Indonesian Industry and Trade Minister, the purpose of this area would be to help investors exploit the unique comparative advantage of individual member countries so that they could distribute their investment projects in different ASEAN countries. However, such a concept may be at odds with Vietnam's intention to attract FDI in high-technology industries.

Also mentioned was the idea that uniform incentives should be adopted for attracting FDI. This would tend to favour more developed countries, such as Malaysia and Thailand, since Vietnam would not be able to offer more attractive incentives *vis-à-vis* its ASEAN partners. Therefore, it will be interesting to see how Vietnam balances its own FDI needs against those of the greater ASEAN family that it has fought so hard to be a part of. Vietnam also needs to monitor the development of its immediate neighbours Cambodia, Laos and especially Myanmar. These economies are expected to develop rapidly in the coming years and, thus, compete with Vietnam in attracting FDI.

CONCLUSION

Vietnam considers FDI as the engine of growth for its transitional economy. It has mapped out extensive roles for FDI in an effort to transform the old economy into a more market-oriented system. To achieve this aim, a relatively attractive investment promotion package has been put in place.

Among other things, the government is revamping the legal and tax structures and has introduced many incentives to make the investment climate conducive for foreign investors. On balance, it seems that the government is achieving success in attracting the type of foreign investment that it wants. Moreover, Vietnam also appears to possess locational factors that generally encourage multinational corporations to invest in the country. However, further actions are still required to ensure Vietnam's continued attractiveness. These include:

(i) Further streamlining and simplifying the tax and legal systems to make these systems pro-business (such as through the establishment of contract law and other business laws);
(ii) Re-examining various tax incentives in view of the problems highlighted above;
(iii) Reconsidering strategies adopted for the development of the tourism and agricultural sectors; and
(iv) Reviewing the policies on land ownership (Pham Chi Lan, 1996).

If these actions are undertaken, then Vietnam is likely to be successful in attracting new FDI despite competition from elsewhere in the region. Although there are rumblings of discontent from some investors, Vietnam's current investment policies appear to be a step in the right direction. Overall, there is a need to further fine-tune policies at this stage rather than to adopt a radically different approach.

REFERENCES

"Bumps on the Road – Investors in Vietnam Ask if Returns Match Risk", *Asiaweek*, 16 June 1995.

CIA World Fact Book, "World Factbook Data on Vietnam", available at website:www.odci.gov/cia/publications/95fact/vm.html (1995).

Confederation of British Industry, *Doing Business in Poland*, Kogan Page, London, 1994.

Coopers and Lybrand, *Malaysia: A Guide for Businessmen and Investors*, Coopers and Lybrand, Singapore, 1992.

Coopers and Lybrand, *Vietnam: A Guide for Businessmen and Investors*, Coopers and Lybrand, Singapore, 1994.

Czinkota M.R., I.A. Ronkainen and M.H. Moffett, *International Business*, Harcourt Brace College Publishers, New York, 1994.

Department of Promotion and Information of Poland, "Political and Economic Promotion" available at website: 158.66.233.27/mszdpi/imszl.hmtl (10 April 1996).

Economic and Social Committee for Asia and the Pacific, *Foreign Investment Guidelines: Malaysia*, United Nations, Bangkok, 1995a.

Economic and Social Committee for Asia and the Pacific, *Foreign Investment Guidelines: Thailand*, United Nations, Bangkok, 1995b.

Economic and Social Committee for Asia and the Pacific, *Foreign Investment Incentive Schemes: Vietnam*, United Nations, Bangkok, 1995c.

Editorial, *East Asian Executive Reports*, February 1994.

Fforde A. and A. Goldstone, *Vietnam to 2005: Advancing on All Fronts*, Economist Intelligence Unit, London, 1995.

Hong Kong Trade Development Council, *Poland: Export and Investment Opportunities*, Research Department, Hong Kong, 1994.

Mai Kim Dinh, Director, Hanns Seidel Foundation, Seminar on "Vietnam", Hanoi, Vietnam, 5 March 1996.

Nguyen Mai, Vice Chairman, State Evaluation Commission, Ministry of Planning and Investment, Seminar on "Opening the Investment Climate for ASEAN", Hanoi, Vietnam, 5 March 1996.

Nguyen Minh Tu, Deputy Director, Central Institute for Economic Management, Seminar on "Economic Reform and Investment", Hanoi, Vietnam, 5 March 1996.

Nguyen Sinh Hung, Vice Minister for Finance, *Vietnam Desires a Tighter Co-operation with Countries in the Region for the Purpose of Mutual Development and Prosperity*, Paper presented at the Conference on Tax and Investment in the Emerging Asia-Pacific Economies, Singapore, 24–25 November 1995a.

Nguyen Sinh Hung, Vice Minister for Finance, *Investment Policies and Incentives to Attract Foreign Investment in Vietnam*, Paper presented at the Conference on Tax and Investment in the Emerging Asia-Pacific Economies, Singapore, 24–25 November 1995b.

Nguyen Van The, Deputy Chairman, People's Committee, Seminar on "Master Development Plan for Hue", Hue, Vietnam, 8 March 1996.

Peat Marwick Suthee, *Investment in Thailand*, Chuan Printing Press, Singapore, 1994.

Pham Chi Lan, General Secretary, Vietnam Chamber of Commerce and Industry, Presentation on "Industry-Government Relations in Vietnam", Hanoi, Vietnam, 8 March 1996.

State Committee for Co-operation and Investment, *Guide-Book for Foreign Investors in Vietnam*, Investment Transaction Center, Hanoi, Vietnam, 1995.

Tan C. L. and T. S. Lim, *Malaysia – Business and Investment Opportunities*, Cassia Communications, Singapore, 1992.

"Vietnam Seeks US$1 billion in Farm Investment" available at newsgroup: clari.world.asia.south-east (10 May 1995).

Chapter 3

Compatibility of Vietnam's Monetary Policy with Reforms*

BY
CHAN Hiang Tiak
LOH Choon Cheong
TAKAHASHI Teruyuki

INTRODUCTION

THIS CHAPTER TAKES a macro perspective of the Vietnam economy and examines the implementation of monetary policy in the country. Since the current discussion touches upon issues related to Vietnam's two currencies, some background material on monetary policy prior to 1991 is provided along with a framework for evaluating the effectiveness of new monetary reforms. These reforms are directed at gaining control of inflation and stabilising interest rates, which both have serious implications for investment and business in Vietnam. Finally, the chapter considers reforms in the banking system which are inexorably

* A number of individuals contributed their time and valuable information. Special thanks are extended to Mr. Anthony Chan, Fortune Hotel, Hanoi Vietnam; Mr. Chuyen D. Uong, Deputy General Manager, Citibank, Hanoi Vietnam; Ms Iris Fang, Chief Executive, Standard Chartered Bank, Hanoi Vietnam; Dr. Nguyen Minh Tu, Director, Central Institute For Economic Management (CIEM), Hanoi Vietnam; Mr. Nguyen Van Cung, Director, Vietnam Bank for Agriculture, Thua Thien Hue Province Branch Vietnam; Dr. Tar, Ministry of Finance, Vietnam; Dr. Ton Si Kinh, Vice Director, Institute of Economic Research, Ho Chi Minh City Vietnam; and Mr. Phan Uu Hoang, Tutor, Foreign Trade College, Hanoi Vietnam. The authors are grateful to Dr. Jon Kendall for his guidance and assistance.

linked to exchange rate controls and investor attitudes.

FRAMEWORK FOR ANALYSIS

There are three widely used definitions of money. M1, the narrow definition, consists of currency held by the public plus demand deposits (accounts from which funds may be withdrawn on demand) at commercial banks. This is the most liquid form of money. M2, a broader definition, consists of M1 plus other chequing, notice and personal term deposits at commercial banks. These term deposits are held by households and firms and may not be withdrawn on demand without penalty. M3, the broadest definition of money, includes large denomination time deposits in addition to M2 (Champ and Freeman, 1994; Auerbach, 1989).

The basic objective of monetary policy is to achieve various economic targets through changing the demand and supply of money in an economy. Governments generally use monetary policy to control inflation, stimulate growth and instil market confidence in the economy. In the paragraphs below, the factors that affect the demand and supply of money are examined.

The Demand for Money

Individuals hold money for various reasons. Keynes (1936) suggested that there are three motives for holding money. The first is a transaction motive. Individuals hold money for the convenience of being able to make regular payments for goods and services. The second is a precautionary motive. Individuals hold money in excess of what is needed for regular transactions in case of unexpected purchases. Third is a speculative motive. Individuals sometimes hold money because they are uncertain about the monetary value of other assets. The first two motives relate to the primary function of money as a medium of exchange, and the speculative motive relates to the function of money as a store of value.

In considering how much money to hold, an individual is likely to consider the need to hold money and the cost of holding money. For example, as the level of income increases, an individual is likely to hold more money because consumption is likely to rise with income. Also, if the banking system in a country is inefficient, then the individual would need to hold more money to meet contingent needs. On the other hand, the cost of holding money is the interest rate that the individual foregoes by not putting money in the bank. If the cost is high, the individual would want to hold less money (Baumol, 1952; Tobin, 1956).

Therefore, a government can control the demand for money by changing the cost of holding money. For example, if the interest rate is increased, people would deposit more with the bank and the demand for money is reduced. Conversely, the demand for money can be increased with lower interest rates.

The Supply of Money

The supply of money in an economy is affected by how government finances its expenditures. Governments, though sovereign in many countries, are also subject to budget constraints. They need to find sources of income to finance expenditures.

Governments can raise money through various means. The main source of income is usually taxes. But if a government spends above and beyond what it expects to collect through taxes, then additional income must be raised either by printing more paper money, also known as fiat money, or by borrowing from the public. In the latter case, the government would issue treasury bonds.

Suppose the government chooses to print more fiat money to pay for its expenditures. If there is no corresponding increase in real output, then the increase in the amount of fiat money would result in higher prices. This in turn lowers the value of the fiat money that the public holds. Thus, the printing of fiat money is equivalent to a tax on holding the local currency (seigniorage tax) by the public. However, if the government often resorts to printing fiat money to raise funds for expenditures, then people learn to anticipate this action and minimise their demand for money. They resort to storing and accumulating their wealth in some other less inflation-sensitive assets so as to avoid being taxed. Consequently, seigniorage tax is lower in future periods.

In practice, most governments issue bonds to finance their budget deficits. These bonds can either be bought by the public (which includes individuals and commercial banks) or the central bank. The first case is a borrowing from the public. In order to make it attractive for the public to hold government bonds, it is likely for the government to offer higher returns on the bonds. This has the effect of raising interest rates. The money raised from the public sale of bonds can then be channelled back to the market when the government pays for its expenditures. There is thus no increase in the monetary base.

However, there is the danger of the government "crowding-out" private investment as individuals who bought government bonds may have switched from holding other forms of capital which yielded a lower rate of return than the rate offered by government bonds. On the other hand, if the government raises funds by selling bonds to the central bank, otherwise known as monetising the debt, then the government is given a cheque to be drawn on the central bank. This has the effect of increasing the monetary base. Coupled with the money multiplier effect, the increase in money supply at equilibrium will be greater than the increase in the monetary base (Champ and Freeman, 1994).

Another way that the government can influence the supply of money is through setting reserve requirements by the central bank. Commercial banks are required to keep a certain percentage of their deposits in the form of cash or deposits with the central bank. An increase in the reserve requirement means a reduction in the amount of funds available for loan by the banks. This has the effect of reducing the money supply. Conversely, a decrease in the reserve requirement has the opposite effect.

Condition for Effective Monetary Policies

For the government to effectively employ monetary policies to stimulate economic growth, it must have control over the currency that is in circulation in the economy. This means that the currency in circulation must be the fiat money of the country. In order to ensure this in an open economy, the government needs to restrict the use over time of any foreign currencies (Champ and Freeman, 1994, p. 77).

Using effective monetary policies, the government can vary the demand and supply of money to control the economy. By contracting the supply of money and increasing its demand, the government can reduce prices, increase saving and encourage investments.

MONETARY POLICIES IN VIETNAM

Using the framework established above, the following sections provide a history of the monetary policies in Vietnam and discuss the government's effort to gain control of the monetary market. They also examine various monetary policies employed by the Vietnamese government and discuss their effect and implications, if any, on foreign businesses in Vietnam.

The Background of Monetary Policy in Vietnam

Vietnam was reunified in 1975. Since then, the nation has experimented with several modes of economic policy. The process can be divided into three distinct stages which are described sequentially.

(i) ***After the War (1976 to 1979):*** Soon after the war, the Vietnamese leadership tried to establish an integrated system of central planning for the whole country. It converted many of the large and medium-sized firms in the south into state-owned enterprises (SOEs) and the smaller ones into co-operatives (Spoor, 1995).

However, there was still a differential between the wealth of the people in the north and in the south. Therefore, in May 1978, the government introduced a new currency to replace the old one. This drastic change totally eroded and diminished the savings of many people and enterprises in the south (Quinlan, 1995, pp. 42–3). The policy achieved its objective of eliminating personal wealth.

(ii) ***Early Attempts at Reform (1980 to 1986):*** Overall, the result of the government's centrally-planned economy was that economic growth was stifled and production declined. By the end of the 1970s, the government had recognised that changes were necessary.

The Sixth Plenum of the Central Committee sanctioned steps to reform the economy. This initiated a period during which policy makers experimented with policies in a trial-and-error process in an attempt to encourage economic liberalisation. Selected private enterprises were allowed to operate with more autonomy but with less financial subsidy from the government. A quota and contract system was introduced to the agricultural sector. The result was an improvement in production (Quinlan, 1995, p. 44; Hirasawa, 1994, p. 56).

However, this improvement was not sustainable. By 1985, the stimulative effect of the reform had worn off. Food shortages and the rapid increase in money supply due to the government's printing of money to meet expenditures caused a major inflation (Quinlan, 1995, p. 46). On 14 September 1985, the government recalled all of the old Dong (Vietnamese currency) and replaced it with a new Dong which was denominated at ten times the value of the old Dong. This action caused panic in the market and people dumped Dong in favour of commodities and staples (Brahm, 1995, p. 75). Inflation in subsequent years spiralled upwards (Quinlan, 1995). The economic situation which ensued prompted the government to consider more radical measures to reform the economy.

(iii) ***Doi Moi (December 1986 to Present):*** *Doi Moi* was introduced in December 1986 at the Sixth National Congress. It involved a series of economic changes whereby the leadership established stronger policies to promote economic renewal. The strategic thrust of *doi moi* was to liberalise and deregulate the economy (Quinlan, 1995, p. 48). Policies introduced during *Doi Moi* are presented in Table 3–1.

TABLE 3–1
***Doi Moi* Policies**

Year	Policy
Early 1987	Remove restrictions on private sector's involvement in trade.
July 1987	Raise prices of non-essential consumer goods and adjust them in line with market realities.
July 1987	Restructure the banking system, separating commercial banking from the central bank's functions.
October 1987	Raise prices of essential consumer goods to free market levels.
November 1987	Grant state enterprises greater autonomy.
December 1987	Encourage foreign investment through the *Foreign Investment Law*.
March 1988	Dismantle the state enterprise planning apparatus.
March 1988	Grant legal status and rights to the private sector and family oriented economic entities.
April 1988	Recognise the role of individual and family units in the rural economy.
April 1988	Abolish price controls and grant farmers the right to sell their products on the market.
July 1988	Adjust prices of government agricultural subsidies to eliminate the gap between official and free market prices.
October 1988	Introduce new foreign exchange regulations.

Source: Compiled from Brahm, 1995.

In 1989, the government increased the interest rate to a level higher than the inflation rate. This policy effectively put a stop to the high inflation rate and restored the confidence in the Dong. In 1991, the state bank stabilised the exchange rate by reducing the supply of Dong and increasing the demand for it at the same time. Also in 1991, the government stopped printing money to finance its budget deficit. All of these policies taken together helped Vietnam to significantly restore its economy. The effects of these monetary policies are examined in further detail in later sections of this chapter.

Gaining Control of the Monetary Market

In Vietnam, there are two prominent currencies in circulation: the Vietnamese Dong and the U.S. dollar. There are several reasons for this situation. Since 1975, the Vietnamese people have had more confidence in the dollar than the Dong. This is partly because of the severe devaluation of the Dong between 1985 and 1991. The U.S. dollar was plentiful due to remittances from overseas Vietnamese. Moreover, it was a stable currency. It, thus, became the preferred currency. A second reason for the greater confidence in the dollar is that up to 1993, the highest denomination of the Dong was only 5,000 (US$0.50). This caused a major practical problem in the use of Dong because large stacks of money were required for transactions.

Because the dollar is outside the control of the Vietnamese authority,[1] greater confidence in the dollar made it more difficult to implement monetary policies. The official estimate of the amount of dollars in circulation is US$600 million while the unofficial estimate is US$2 billion (Balfour, 1996; Vatikiotis, 1994).

In 1994, the government started to reduce the dominance of dollars in the economy. A senior government official said "the intention is not to hurt the people but to restore order" (*The Straits Times*, 10 August 1994).

To achieve the objective, the Vietnamese government stipulated that companies in Vietnam must invoice their customers in Dong for domestic transactions starting from 1 October 1994 (*The Straits Times*, 10 August 1994). The government's aim was to "gradually narrow the scope of utilisation of the U.S. dollar inside the country, first of all in credit operations and in payments within the country,

---

1 Based on interviews with various individuals in Hanoi, including Dr. Tar, Ministry of Finance, March 1996.

between businesses and the banks" (*Business Times*, 13 June 1994).

However, most shops in Vietnam are quite willing to accept U.S. dollars as a means of payment. Interviewees in Vietnam confirmed that the government has not strictly enforced the rule. The reality is that the government cannot ban the use of dollars because of the shortage of Dong in the marketplace. There simply is not enough Dong to support all the transactions that are taking place. Also, the government cannot just print more money because it needs to maintain tight control over the amount of currency in the market to curb inflation (Vatikiotis, 1994, p. 50).

Making the local banking system more efficient might help. One banker[2] mentioned that the inter-bank clearing system would be implemented next year (1997); this would improve the circulation of Dong, thus increasing the money multiplier factor. For foreign businesses venturing into Vietnam, it is reassuring that the government appears not to have any intention of further controlling the conversion of Dong to dollars.[3]

Financing of State Budget Deficits

Vietnam's state budget is burdened by several factors. One is the subsidy to state-owned enterprises (SOEs). These were introduced during the days of the centrally-planned economy. SOEs produce according to quotas set by the central government and do not have to concern themselves with operational efficiency or productivity. As a result, the government has to subsidise the shortfall between the price their products are sold for in the market and their actual cost of production (Vu, 1995, pp. 17–30). A second factor is price subsidy. Prior to 1989, the Vietnamese government purchased goods at world market prices and sold these in the domestic market at much reduced prices, thus subsidising local consumption to the tune of hundreds of billions of Dong each year. A third factor is the inefficient tax collection system. The system for tax assessment and collection in Vietnam is not very well developed. This has aggravated the budget deficit problem since there is a big gap between what the government should be collecting and what has actually been collected (Vo, 1995, pp. 71–83).

Prior to 1991, the Vietnamese government financed its budget

---

[2] Ms. Iris Fang, Chief Executive, Standard Chartered Bank, Hanoi, Vietnam.

[3] Dr. Tar, Ministry of Finance, Vietnam, March 1996.

deficits by printing more fiat money. This contributed to high inflation because the supply of money increased without real economic growth. The effect of this can be observed in Table 3–2 where the increase in Hanoi's consumer price index (CPI) closely followed the increase in the supply of money.

TABLE 3–2
Growth in M1 and CPI (Inflation): 1986 to 1992
(Annual Changes in Percentages)

	1986	**1987**	**1988**	**1989**	**1990**	**1991**	**1992**
M1	512	273	400	130	34	72	20
Hanoi CPI	487	317	311	35	67	67	17

Source: State Bank of Vietnam and various IMF reports.

However since 1991, the government has stopped printing money to finance its deficits.[4] Instead, the government has turned its fund raising efforts to issuing government bonds for sale to the public. About 300 billion Dong of bonds were issued by the end of 1995.[5]

Based on interviews with bankers and officials in Vietnam, it seems unlikely that the Vietnamese government would resort to printing money again to finance its deficit in the near future. There are several reasons that support this assessment. First, the government is committed to keeping the inflation rate below 10% this year (1996).[6] Any increase in the money supply would jeopardise this objective; secondly, the price liberalisation policy (discussed below) which reduced the government subsidy of prices and SOEs has already helped to reduce the budget deficit.

Increase in Interest Rates

One of the major problems that plagued the Vietnamese economy was high inflationary pressures. From 1986 to 1988, inflation ranged from 300 to 500% per year. During this period, inflation rates were much higher than the interest rates offered on deposits by the banks. This

---

4 Dr. Tar, Ministry of Finance, Vietnam, March 1996.

5 Dr. Nguyen Minh Tu, Director, Central Institute For Economic Management (CIEM), Hanoi, March 1996.

6 Dr. Tar, Ministry of Finance, Vietnam, March 1996.

meant that real interest rates were negative. Consequently, people as well as organisations started to hedge against inflation by hoarding goods. There was no confidence in the Vietnamese Dong as people kept their holdings of the local currency to a minimum (De Vylder, 1995).

In April 1989, the Vietnamese government took a very bold step in the fight against inflation. The state bank, under the direction of the Vietnamese government, raised the interest rate on savings and deposits to a level higher than the inflation rate. The bank interest rate on savings was raised to 9% per month and the three-month fixed deposit rate was increased to 12% per month while inflation was averaging 3.3% per month.

By setting the interest rate on savings and deposits at a level well above the inflation rate, the Vietnamese government created a positive real interest rate. Since the interest rate on deposits was higher than that of inflation, the accumulation of goods became relatively expensive. In the past, some state enterprises used to accumulate goods sufficient for a year's requirements and ordinary households hoarded basic consumer goods. All these practices came to a halt with the increase of the interest rate above the inflation rate. Enterprises started to unload their hoarded goods onto the market to avoid bankruptcy. Where there was previously a shortage of goods in the market, a surplus of food and consumer goods was created. This had the indirect impact of reducing prices and lowering inflation (Vo, 1995, p. 73).

Higher interest rates on savings and deposits also encouraged the public to put their money in the banks. The higher rate of personal savings, as indicated by an increase in deposits, enables the Vietnamese government to mobilise domestic funds for economic development projects instead of having to print more money or borrow from the international market at higher interest costs.[7]

Another impact brought about by the rise in interest rates was the effect it had on SOEs. Due to the high interest rates, many SOEs were not able to service their debts to the banks, despite the fact that their loans were already subsidised by the banks which charged them a rate lower than that paid to depositors. Besides having to liquidate their inventory in order to avoid bankruptcy, the SOEs were also forced to re-organise their operations in order to be more profitable. Workers

---

[7] Dr. Tar, Ministry of Finance, Vietnam, March 1996.

were shed and production reduced or streamlined to improve efficiency (Vo, 1995).

However, the positive real interest rate did not last. The real interest rate became negative again in 1990 and 1991 (see Table 3–3). As a result, people reverted to holding gold and U.S. dollars in their attempt to hedge against inflation, thus pushing up the prices of assets.

TABLE 3–3
Rate of Fixed Interest on Bank Time Deposits of SOEs and the Rate of Inflation in Percentage per Month

Month	Interest Rate	Inflation Rate
1989		
November	2.6	2.6
December	2.6	3.0
1990		
January	2.6	2.9
February	2.4	3.8
March	1.8	1.9
April	1.8	2.5
May	1.8	2.6
June	1.8	2.1
July	1.8	3.6
August	1.8	5.7
September	1.8	4.3
October	1.8	6.1
November	1.8	7.9
December	1.8	8.8

Source: Vo, 1995.

The government has since reverted to a policy of higher interest rates. In 1995, the annual interest rate was 21% while the inflation rate was 12.7%.[8] The situation has again boosted confidence in Dong and the amount of Dong being converted to U.S. dollars and gold has declined.

However, for how long the interest rate can remain this high is yet to be seen. An adverse effect of the high interest rate is that the cost of capital to private investors is also high. This discourages capital investment and the growth of businesses. Consequently, it also

8 Dr. Tar, Ministry of Finance, Vietnam, March 1996.

reduces the tax income of the government. At some point in time, the government must reduce the interest rate in order to expand the economy.

Price Liberalisation

Under the old centrally-planned economy, prices of most products were fixed by the central authorities. This increased the burden of the government because it had to purchase goods in the international market at a high price and then sell the goods in the local market at a lower price (Vo, 1990).

All of this changed in the second quarter of 1989 when the government set about liberalising the prices of most goods. By the end of the year, the state only retained control over the prices of essential products like transportation, communication, electricity, petroleum and cooking oil. Some other important basic products, such as rice, had their prices regulated by indirect means,[9] but by and large, prices of most products were allowed to adjust to the free market rate.

However, the situation may not be as clear-cut as it appears. For example, a government official[10] asserted that since 1992, only the price of electricity has been regulated while prices of staples such as rice have been free from intervention by the government. This, however, was contradicted by a lecturer[11] from the Foreign Trade College who pointed out that the Ministry of Finance had intervened when the price of cement doubled in March 1995. It was his impression that the price of sugar is also monitored. Further, in Ho Chi Minh City, a senior official[12] said that the government controls the price of three items namely, electricity, water for urban areas and rentals of state-owned houses and land.

Given the above conflicting views on the scope of the Vietnamese government's price control policy, it seems reasonable for foreign investors involved in projects relating to products which are "not sensitive" in nature to exercise more caution in case the government decides to intervene with their prices.

---

9 For example, subsidising the cost of transporting rice from the south (where it is in abundance) to the north.

10 Dr. Tar, Ministry of Finance, Vietnam, March 1996.

11 Mr. Phan Uu Hoang, Lecturer, Foreign Trade College, Hanoi, Vietnam, March 1996.

12 Dr. Ton Si Kinh, Vice Director, Institute of Economic Research, Ho Chi Minh City, Vietnam, March 1996.

REFORM OF THE BANKING SYSTEM

In 1988, Vietnam's banking system was restructured to separate the central banking functions from commercial banking. This has allowed commercial banks to concentrate on making loans to businesses for economic expansion (Baker and McKenzie, 1995). With the high economic growth that Vietnam is experiencing, commercial banking (which comprises trade and development banks, foreign banks, joint venture banks, shareholding banks, credit organisations and financial companies) is expanding rapidly. Nonetheless, the commercial banking sector is still dominated by the state-owned banks whose loan portfolio consists mainly of loans to state enterprises (Brahm, 1995).

To control the supply of money through the banking system, the Vietnamese government has stipulated reserve requirements which average about 15% of the total deposits (The Economist Intelligence Unit, 1994). However, the effectiveness of this system is hindered because the state-owned banks do not necessary comply with the policy.[13] Also, an informal credit market exists in the economy and "billions of Dong do not go through the formal banking system at all".[14]

This informal market exists for three reasons. First, unlike in the formal commercial banking sector where there are very stringent rules for granting credit to only apparently economically viable projects, it is much easier to obtain a loan in the informal credit market.[15] Secondly, state enterprises and the central government account for the major share of available bank credit, thus limiting the access to loans by individual entrepreneurs and small-scale private companies. Therefore they have to turn to the informal credit market. Thirdly, people in Vietnam are generally reluctant to use the formal banking system. This is because there is a fear that the government may find out about their wealth. Also, since the current tax assessment and collection system is not well developed, tax evasion is easy and people do not want to provide an avenue for the government to monitor their

---

[13] Dr. Nguyen Minh Tu, Director, CIEM, Hanoi, March 1996.

[14] Ms. Iris Fang, Chief Executive, Standard Chartered Bank, Vietnam, March 1996.

[15] Ms. Iris Fang, Chief Executive, Standard Chartered Bank, Vietnam, March 1996.

income.[16]

There are other problems facing the banks in Vietnam. Banks (especially state-owned commercial banks) are still required to provide subsidised credit to unprofitable state companies. The fact that the assets of state companies belong to the state means that banks do not have any meaningful collateral. In the event that state companies go bankrupt, it is difficult for banks to recover their loans since any money that state companies have belongs to the government. A lack of clear rules about creditors' rights greatly increases the risk to banks, not least when lending to state units, which are frequent defaulters (Brahm, 1995, p. 53). Moreover, there is a lack of experienced bankers in the stated-owned banks. However, the situation is likely to improve because foreign banks and institutions are currently training Vietnamese bankers. A government official expressed optimism that these people would eventually find their way into the government banks and reform them.

It appears that the Vietnamese government is determined to continue the reform of the banking system. There is evidence to suggest that there will be more liberalisation in this sector in the near future.

Exchange Rate Control

Foreign exchange control in Vietnam is administered by the state bank (*Global Investor*, 1994a, p. 48). In the years immediately after the war, the Dong was valued slightly below one U.S. dollar. However, as the economic situation in Vietnam deteriorated, this official rate became unrealistic. On 14 September 1985, the government issued a new Dong that was denominated at ten times the value of the old Dong. As mentioned earlier, the effect of the sudden change caused panic in the market and people rushed to dump Dong in favour of purchasing commodities and staples. This sparked a spiralling inflation which lasted four years (Brahm, 1995, p. xvi).

The government took a series of moves to readjust the value of Dong but were not able to stop its fall. The Dong was devalued many times to close the gap between the official and black market rate. By late 1991, it was valued at 12,000 to one U.S. dollar (Brahm, 1995, p. 75). The market confidence in Dong was low.

In late 1991, the state bank carried out a bold step to stabilise the

---

[16] Interviews with various parties, including Dr. Nguyen Minh Tu, Director of CIEM, Hanoi; and Mr. Anthony Chan, Fortune Hotel, Hanoi, Vietnam.

Dong. Just before an important new year holiday, when the demand for money was high, it stopped the supply of Dong to the market, creating a shortage in supply. At the same time, it sold its gold reserves in the market which increased the demand for money. Within a matter of weeks, the Dong rate was stabilised at 10,500 to one U.S. dollar (Brahm, 1995, p. 76).

In March 1996, the official Dong exchange rate available at the banks was very close to the 11,000 Dongs per U.S. dollar rate that was quoted in the unofficial market. This indicates that there was no artificial fixing of the exchange rate by the state bank. Officials of the government that were interviewed[17] emphasised that the government is determined to maintain the exchange rate at the present level. This is in line with a statement by deputy Governor, Nuygen Ngoc Oanh, of the state bank in June 1994 that the bank did not "want to devalue the Dong, although a small change may be possible. It must be consistent with controlling and stabilising the inflation rate" (*Global Investor*, 1994b). Other bankers[18] that were interviewed also expressed high confidence in the stability of the Dong and cited inflationary control as the main reason.

CONCLUSION

In summary, a foreign investor considering investment in Vietnam can expect several trends. First, the inflation rate for 1996 is likely to be below 10% and should remain stable for the near future. Secondly, the interest rate should remain above the inflation rate for at least the short run. Thirdly, the supply of money should be stable because the government can sell bonds to finance its expenditures instead of printing more money. Consequently, the exchange rate of Dong should stabilise at the current level. It is quite unlikely that the Dong will devalue. Finally, the banking system will improve and, therefore, the government will have better control over its monetary market. Thus, more money will pass through the banking system as confidence increases. This development represents further opportunities for for-

---

[17] Dr. Tar, Ministry of Finance and Dr. Nguyen Minh Tu, Director, Central Institute For Economic Management, Vietnam.

[18] Ms. Iris Fang, Chief Executive, Standard Chartered Bank, Hanoi, Vietnam, and Mr. Chuyen D. Uong, Deputy General Manager, Citibank, Hanoi, Vietnam.

eign banks.

However, there are several pending risks. First, the government regulations could change with unpredictable results, although the overall direction is unlikely to change. Furthermore, the Vietnamese government will continue with its policy of making Dong the dominant currency in the economy. But the strategy it might use to increase the use of Dong and reduce the circulation of the U.S. dollar remains to be seen. However, it is very likely that the use of the U.S. dollar will be further tightened. Secondly, the government may revert to price controls for some important commodities. Finally, if the interest rate is reduced significantly at some stage, then this may again lead to inflation as in 1990 and 1991.

REFERENCES

Auerbach Robert D., *Money, Banking and Financial Markets*, Third Edition, Macmillan Publishing Company, New York, 1989.

Baker and McKenzie, *Fundamental Considerations – Business Forms for Foreign Investors in the Socialist Republic of Vietnam*, Hanoi, March 1995.

Balfour Frederik, "Why Are We In Vietnam?", *Institutional Investor*, Vol. 30, January 1996, pp. 115–6.

Baumol William, "The Transactions Demand for Cash: An Inventory Theoretic Approach," *Quarterly Journal of Economics*, November 1952, pp. 545–56.

Brahm Laurence J., *Vietnam Banking and Finance*, Butterworths Asia, Singapore, 1995.

Champ Bruce and Scott Freeman, *Modelling Monetary Economies*, John Wiley & Sons, New York, 1994.

De Vylder Stefan, "State and Market in Vietnam – Some Issues for an Economy in Transition", in *Vietnam in a Changing World*, edited by Irene Norlund, Carolyn L. Gates and Vu Cao Dam, Curzon Press, Richmond, Surrey, 1995.

Editorial, *Business Times*, 13 June 1994.

Editorial, *The Straits Times*, 10 August 1994.

Euromonitor, *The World Economic Factbook*, 1994.

Hirasawa Katsuki, *Overseas Business Now – Vietnam*, Sogo Horei Shuppan Kabushiki Kaisha, Tokyo, Japan, 1994.

Keynes J. M., *The General Theory of Employment, Interest and*

Money, Macmillan, New York, 1936, Chapter 13.

Nguyen Sinh Hung, *Investment Policies and Incentives to Attract Foreign Investment in Vietnam,* Paper presented at the Conference on Recent Developments on Emerging Asia-Pacific Economics, Singapore, 24–25 November 1995.

Price Waterhouse, *Vietnam A Guide For The Foreign Investor,* Hong Kong, July 1994.

Quinlan Joseph P., *Vietnam Business Opportunities and Risks,* Pacific View Press, Berkeley, California, 1995.

Spoor Max, "State Finance in the Socialist Republic of Vietnam", in *Post-war Vietnam: Dilemmas in Socialist Development*, edited by David G. Maar and Christine P. White. *SEAP* Finance, Singapore, published for the Asian Studies Association of Australia by Heinemann Education Books, 1995.

Standard Chartered Bank, "Vietnamese Dong", *Global Investor*, November 1994a, pp. 48–50.

"State Bank of Vietnam", *Global Investor*, November 1994b, p. 47.

The Economist Intelligence Unit, "Indochina: Vietnam, Laos, Cambodia", *EIU Country Profile,* Hong Kong, 1994.

Tobin James, "The Interest-Elasticity of Transactions Demand for Cash," *Review of Economics and Statistics*, August 1956.

Vatikiotis Michael, "The Buck Stops Here", *Far Eastern Economic Review,* 25 August 1994, pp. 49–50.

Vo Dai Luoc, "Monetary Stabilisation – The Vietnamese Experience", in *Vietnam in a Changing World,* edited by Irene Norlund, Carolyn L. Gates and Vu Cao Dam, Curzon Press, Richmond, Surrey, 1995.

Vo Nhan Tri, *Vietnam's Economic Policy Since 1975*, Institute of Southeast Asian Studies, Singapore, 1990.

Vu Tuan Anh, "Economic Policy Reforms", in *Vietnam in a Changing World,* edited by Irene Norlund, Carolyn L. Gates and Vu Cao Dam, Curzon Press, Richmond, Surrey, 1995.

Chapter 4

Reforms in Vietnam's Financial and Banking System*

BY
Ben ANG
Siew Hock
LEE Boon Leng
TAN
Teng Keong
TAN Tong Aik

INTRODUCTION

VIETNAM HAS EXPERIENCED significant economic progress since *doi moi* (economic renovation) in 1986. These achievements have been reflected in the strong average GDP growth rate of 8.2% over the last five years. Inflation has dropped from 487% in 1986 to 12.4% in 1995 and per capita income has grown steadily to around US$200 in 1995. Vietnam's planners have estimated that the country needs US$42 billion in the next five years to double the per capita income to US$400. Of the total amount, US$13 billion to

* We are grateful to the following individuals for interviews which have contributed to the information contained in this chapter: Dr. Nguyen Minh Tu, Director, Central Institute For Economic Management (CIEM); Nguyen Van Cung, Director, Vietnam Bank of Agriculture, Thua Thien Hue Province Branch; Luu H. Le, Senior Vice President, Bank of America, Vietnam Country Manager and Indochina Representative Office; Ms. Iris Fang, Chief Executive Officer, Standard Chartered Bank Vietnam; Mr. Lee Kau Fu, KPMG Peat Marwick, Vietnam; Dr. Ton Si Kinh, Vice Director, Institute of Economic Research, Ho Chi Minh City; Dr. Han Manh Tien, Director, Consulting and Research Company for Technology Transfer and Investment; Mr. Richard Irwin, Price Waterhouse Vietnam; Ms. Ha Ngoc Van, Deputy Chief Representative, Barclays Bank PLC; and Mr. Chan Kok Choy, GM VID Public Bank. We are also grateful to Dr Jon Kendall for his guidance and assistance.

US$14 billion will come from foreign direct investment, US$7 billion to US$8 billion from overseas development aid sources, and an ambitious US$21 billion from domestic sources (Folkmanis, 1996a). Given the substantial size of the amount to be raised domestically, the financial system in Vietnam has to be further developed to keep pace with the developments in other sectors of the economy such as manufacturing and construction. This will ensure that the financial system can support, and not stifle, the growth in other sectors without being over dependent on foreign sources of funds. A developed banking system will also ensure that an entrepreneurial spirit is not choked because of any imbalance in the mobilisation of capital towards a few selected sectors of the economy.

In line with *doi moi*, the financial system has experienced some reforms. This chapter considers some major reforms that have taken place in the financial system in Vietnam. These include changes in the way that banks are funding their operations; the gradual deregulation of interest rates; and the attraction of funds from the private sector.

Despite reforms which have made the financial system more efficient, there are still some outstanding issues that the Vietnamese government has to focus on in order to realise further improvements in the efficiency of the financial system. These issues include lending to state-owned enterprises and bad debts; the complicated system of collateral; and establishing a stock market in Vietnam.

BACKGROUND

Following the founding of the Socialist Republic of Vietnam, all monetary policies and credit operations in Vietnam were controlled by the Ministry of Finance (Ngyuen and Pham, 1994, p. 8). Similarly, the responsibility to ensure financing for the resistance against the French also rested with the Ministry. The instruments available for effecting such control were much more limited in comparison to the present. Revenue sources were also limited and when the financing requirement for the resistance increased, the Ministry was forced to issue more money to meet its expenditure requirement. This in turn had disastrous impacts on production and social life, and brought about serious inflation in 1950 and 1951.

After the Second Party Congress in February 1951, the government set a target for fiscal management to centralise budget operation control. This was aimed at increasing revenues and reducing expenditures to ensure financing for the resistance, to enhance production development, and to balance the state budget. The tax system was restructured in order to increase production while the main source of revenue was agricultural taxes.

On 6 May 1951, the National Bank of Vietnam (NBV), which was subsequently renamed the State Bank of Vietnam (SBV) in 1960, was set up for purposes of issuing bank notes, increasing revenues, managing national reserves and controlling inflation. The bank was fully independent and autonomous. It performed both central bank and commercial bank functions. During the war against the French, the bank played a pivotal role by lending heavily to essential trading services and production units in order to continue exporting agricultural and farm products and, in return, import industrial and other necessary goods to fight the war.

As in the case of the NBV, the SBV was also instrumental during the Vietnam-American War by ensuring constant economic re-orientation and avoiding the destruction of the economy by the Americans. The SBV actively helped important production units evacuate and relocate, and to continue producing and building up inventories. Its role was to ensure adequate financing for vital industries to produce and import critical products. The SBV was responsible for receiving aid donated by foreign allies. It also had to set up a special payments system to serve the battlefield in the south.

Following unification of the country in 1975 and the nationalisation of the banking sector, the SBV became the sole provider of almost all domestic financial services. There were two other specialised banks reporting to the SBV, namely the Bank for Foreign Trade of Vietnam (Vietcombank) and the Bank of Investment and Development Bank (BIDV). The Vietcombank was in charge of trade finance and foreign exchange functions while the BIDV took care of long term financing for public works.

Being the only banks serving the needs of the whole country, both the NBV and the SBV played important roles in the country's war victories. By 1988, however, the Vietnamese government recognised the limitation of a unified banking system in supporting the government's policy to develop the economy and attract foreign investors. The monobank structure was inefficient in handling the many diverse banking functions as well as having to operate as a central bank. Recognising the need for an efficient banking system to mobilise capital for economic development, the government enacted a set of sweeping reforms that created a two-tier banking sector during the period 1988 to 1990. The reorganisation of the banking system which established the SBV as the central bank and monetary authority of the country was officially recognised in the form of the *Decree Law on the State Bank of Vietnam* adopted by the State Council on 23 May 1990 (Brahm, 1995, p. xiv).

Under this new system, the SBV was entrusted with central banking responsibilities such as regulating the money supply, supervising credit and the banking functions of the newly autonomous commercial banks, as well as other macro management functions. The commercial banking operations which the SBV used to perform were handed over to the newly spun-off commercial banks, including the Industrial and Commercial Bank of Vietnam (ICBV) and the Agricultural Bank of Vietnam (ABV). As a result of further reforms enacted in 1991 and 1992, a new banking structure emerged with the inclusion of shareholding joint stock banks, foreign banks and representative offices, joint venture banks, housing banks, and urban and rural credit co-operatives.

THE CURRENT BANKING SYSTEM

With the creation of the two-tier structure, local banks, foreign banks and financial institutions have been allowed to operate in Vietnam. The current banking system has a variety of structures which are shown in Table 4–1. The functions of the various types of banks are described in the following sections.

TABLE 4–1
Current Banking System

Type	Number
State-owned commercial banks	4
Foreign banks	19
Joint venture banks	4
Representative offices	67
Joint stock banks	45
Credit co-operatives	69

Source: *Vietnam Economic News,* January 1996.

State Bank of Vietnam

The SBV performs the role of the central bank of Vietnam. Its responsibilities include:

(i) ***Formulating Monetary and Financial Policy:*** The SBV formulates policies for financial reform and economic development, and is responsible for monetary reform and intervention. It also enforces the laws and regulations under its authority. In formulating monetary policies, the SBV aims to stabilise prices in the economy. It can achieve this through controlling interest rates or varying the money supply. As a result of a tight monetary policy, inflation was brought down from triple digits in 1989 to 14.4% in 1994. The SBV also manages foreign exchange controls in Vietnam. It is involved in setting regulations for transactions, lending, borrowing and other operations based on foreign currencies.

(ii) ***Issuing Vietnamese Currency:*** The SBV, with permission from the Prime Minister, is also responsible for issuing, organising, circulating and setting the value of the Vietnamese Dong. It also has the right to determine various features, such as denominations, size and design of bank notes and coins.

(iii) ***Acting as a Central Bank for Other Banks:*** The SBV supervises the operations of the various banks and financial institutions and imposes safety measures such as liquidity ratios, minimum reserve ratios and other required ratios to ensure that they have adequate liquidity. The SBV also allows banks and financial institutions to maintain deposit accounts with it. In the event of urgent needs for cash, the SBV is a lender of last resort to the banks and financial institutions.

(iv) ***Acting as a Banker for Government:*** The SBV is instrumental in advising the government on monetary affairs and financial reforms. It helps in managing the state budget and acts as a bank to the state treasury. Together with the Ministry of Finance, the SBV acts as an agent for the state treasury in issuing short- and long-term government securities that can be used to raise funds to cover any deficit in the budget. The SBV also represents the government in dealing with international credit and banking institutions.

(v) ***Regulatory and Licensing Authority:*** The SBV has the authority to issue regulations, notices and guidelines to regulate the activities of commercial banks and financial institutions in Vietnam. Approval of the SBV is also required before a new bank or financial institution can be established.

State-owned Commercial Banks

Under the current banking system in Vietnam, there are four state-owned banks. These are the Bank for Foreign Trade (Vietcombank), the Vietnam Investment and Development Bank (VIDBank), Industrial and Commercial Bank of Vietnam (ICBV) and the Agricultural Bank of Vietnam (ABV). As a group, the state-owned commercial banks accounted for about 87% of commercial bank operations in Vietnam in 1994. Each of these state-owned commercial banks is responsible for servicing a distinct segment of the country's financial needs.

(i) ***Bank for Foreign Trade:*** Vietcombank operates primarily as a trade financing bank for the entire country. Its primary responsibility is to handle foreign trade transactions and, hence, it has expertise in foreign currency trading and financial relationships with over 700 banks in 85 countries. Vietcombank recently became the first bank in Vietnam to issue a pay-later credit card.
(ii) ***Industrial and Commercial Bank of Vietnam:*** ICBV provides mainly commercial banking services. Its principal customers are transport, telecommunication and industrial companies.
(iii) ***Vietnam Investment and Development Bank:*** VIDBank functions as a development bank which funds various infrastructure and investment projects. As such, about 80% of its funds come directly from the state budget. Only about 20% of its loans are made to the private sector.
(iv) ***Agricultural Bank of Vietnam:*** ABV offers a broad range of credit services and other financial assistance to rural farmers and rural regional enterprises. It also undertakes financial support for rural development projects.

Although the reforms in 1990 were intended to create a separation of the functions between the management of SBV and the state-owned banks, the former still directly influences the management of the state-owned banks. This is because the general director of each state-owned bank must be nominated by the governor of the SBV and approved by the Prime Minister. In fact, the governor manages and supervises the activities of each state-owned bank down to the level of the deputy director (Brahm, 1995, p. 29). It is envisaged that the SBV will probably release this influence over the state-owned banks if they are corporatised.

Joint Stock Banks

Joint stock banks are commercial financial institutions that are established between different state-owned enterprises, state-owned enterprises and private enterprises, or entirely among private interests. Numerous privately owned joint stock banks have been authorised to operate and they are regulated by the *Decree Law on Credit Institutions*. While the scope of their services is limited to collecting short- and long-term deposits, and granting short- to long-term credit, these banks provide additional credit facilities to accommodate the rapidly expanding volume of business. Among the banks in this category are Dainam Bank, Nam Phuong Bank, Cholon Bank, Saigon Credit and Housing Bank.

Foreign Banks and Representative Offices

Participation by foreign banks in Vietnam has increased recently through the establishment of branches, representative offices or joint venture banks. However, their operations have been constrained by, among other factors, restrictive government foreign exchange regulations such as the inconvertibility of the Dong.

The operations of foreign banks are further complicated by the ambiguous regulations on collateral for domestic lending. Accepting physical assets in Vietnam as pledged collateral against loans is currently a problem for banks, because although buildings can be privately owned and mortgaged, the underlying land is owned by the state and allocated to firms or individuals for specific purposes and time periods. Thus, banks are prevented from establishing clear title to the collateral. In addition, the lack of rigorous financial disclosure rules in Vietnam makes it impossible for banks to adequately value the assets and financial position of local borrowers.

Despite the problems that foreign banks face, most of them are taking a long-term view and appear to be willing to accept short term losses to maintain a foothold in what promises to become a lucrative market. In fact, some foreign banks, such as Malaysia's Public Bank (*Malaysia Business Times*, May 1996) and France's Credit Lyonnais (Reuters, 18 May 1996), are not only undaunted by the present difficulties but intend to expand their operations to areas like Haiphong and Danang.

Vietnam needs approximately US$40 billion to US$45 billion in investments to maintain a GDP growth of 9 to 10% over the next few years. It plans to attract over US$25 billion in foreign investment over the next 10 to 15 years and another US$4.5 billion will be mobilised through the domestic banking system. Foreign banks stand to gain a great deal of business providing short-term trade financing and medium-term loan syndication. Vietnam authorities appear amenable to improvements in banking standards and practices and are generally committed to upgrading the banking sector to international standards. Some bankers believe that the SBV will make the Dong freely convertible and that a stock exchange will be opened soon.

REFORMS IN THE FINANCIAL SYSTEM

There have been some major reforms recently in the financial system aimed at improving overall efficiency. In this section, changes in the sources of funds in the financial system, the liberalisation of interest rates and the government's efforts to attract funds from the private sector are considered.

Sources of Funds in the Financial System

Banks in Vietnam traditionally have relied heavily on the SBV for their funds. However, as inflation surged as high as 487% in 1986 and 67% in 1990, the SBV had no choice but to restrict the supply of money. This action severely affected the availability of funds to the banks and forced them to tap the private sector for funds. In this regard, the local banks have been very successful despite the increasing competition from foreign banks which, however, are only allowed to offer current account facilities and not savings accounts.

At present, local banks account for 80 to 90% of all domestic deposits and loans (Vu, 1995). To help banks attract more savings, the SBV made fundamental changes in September 1994 when it announced the deregulation of interest rates and allowed local banks to determine their own rates. Some banks responded by offering rates that are higher than the recommended rate, which is still controlled by the SBV. However, the number of personal savings accounts has increased only marginally, by about 0.2%, since then.

The establishment of an inter-bank market for the Dong in 1993 and one for foreign currencies in 1994 has also helped banks to raise funds. In fact, foreign banks have become increasingly active in both markets. Foreign banks' share of credit extended to the inter-bank markets in 1995 grew by 27.8% relative to 1994 and accounted for over 32% of their total outstanding credit. This reflects their interest in the development of credit institutions in Vietnam. Another reason for this growth is the fact that the legal framework and financial position of enterprises in Vietnam do not meet the safety requirements of foreign banks. In other words, foreign banks are generally not very comfortable with the financial position or the accuracy of the financial statements of most Vietnamese companies and, as such, they are less willing to grant loans.

On the other hand, since the SBV presently acts as guarantor for loans made to state-owned commercial banks, foreign banks are more willing to lend to them in the inter-bank markets. With the participation of the foreign banks, the inter-bank market will continue to grow in effectiveness for the trading of forward, swap and options transactions. The present guarantees by the SBV, resulting from risky collateral, will eventually be replaced by treasury bills and bonds once these become widely held and traded.

Besides tapping the savings of the private sector and the inter-bank market, Vietnam will increasingly seek overseas financing from foreign banks for direct loans and refinancing facilities. Until recently, the main impediment to Vietnam's ability to raise substantial amounts of new loans from overseas lenders was its substantial foreign debt, officially estimated to be about US$8 billion, or 54% of GDP, and approximately two thirds of which is in arrears. However, on 17 May 96, Vietnam signed an agreement with the "London Club" group of creditors to restructure a debt of US$800 million owed to foreign commercial creditors which were mainly Japanese banks who had lent to Vietnam in the late 1970s (Chalmers, 1996). The agreement, which includes a 50% forgiveness option on the principal amount owed (estimated to be US$400 million), is essential to improving Vietnam's credibility in the international financial markets which was damaged when it stopped servicing its commercial debt. It is also an essential step for the integration of Vietnam into the international financial community and will pave the way for Vietnam to issue international bonds and borrow again from commercial banks.

However, it can be argued that Vietnam should not be too aggressive in raising funds through international bonds at this time because it would have to offer excessively high interest rates to compensate for the country's high risk. Furthermore, the World Bank has indicated its preference for Vietnam to settle the 9.8 billion Roubles debt with Russia before it issues bonds. This is in dispute because of the rapid depreciation of the Rouble from US$1/0.51 Roubles, when the money was lent, to the recent rate of US$1/4750 Roubles. Nevertheless, Vietnam's deal with its creditors is a sign that the government views the international financial market as a very important source of funds and, therefore, it is taking the necessary steps to improve Vietnam's credit profile.

Development loans have been another source of funds aimed at meeting Vietnam's financing needs. Loans have been granted by organisations, such as the Asian Development Bank (ADB) and World Bank in the past, and this will continue in the near future as Vietnam is still in the infant stage of economic growth. Recently, the ADB agreed to grant Vietnam loans worth more than US$1.5 billion over the next four years. In 1996, the ADB will lend US$310 million for development of public works (Miller, 1996). The World Bank, which has committed US$1.1 billion in loans to Vietnam since 1993, is currently considering providing another US$1.5 billion in loans over the next three years (Folkmanis, 1996a).

Over the last few years, the financial system has reduced its dependence on the SBV for funding. One new source of funds which banks will devote increasing amounts of effort towards is the savings of the private sector. With growing confidence in the financial system, it is expected that more savings will accumulate in the banks. The inter-bank, as well as foreign financial markets, will also grow in importance not only as a source of funds but also as a source of knowledge for local banks.

Deregulation of Interest Rates

Another reform deals with the control of interest rates by the SBV. This has been one of the main tools for exercising monetary control. In the past, the structure and level of interest rates on both savings and loans were set by the SBV. Traditionally, these rates have been very high, even after the abolition of the 15% turnover tax on banks' net interest income in December 1995. Concern over the high rates has been acknowledged by Deputy Prime Minister, Phan Van Khai, who recently called for lower interest rates on loans despite the banks' complaints about narrowing margins (*Vietnam News*, May 1996).

Due to the need to fight hyper-inflation in the late 1980s and early 1990s, the government set interest rates higher than the inflation rate. Furthermore, as in the case of many emerging economies, there was a multitude of interest rates which were differentiated according to economic sectors as part of the government's measures to control credit allocation (World Bank, 1995). This resulted in banks setting different interest rates without regard to the specific risks in each sector.

This situation closely resembled that in South Korea in the early 1980s when the government controlled interest rates and intervened in credit allocation to prevent massive corporate bankruptcies. Since the early 1990s, the South Korean banking system has been shaken by bankruptcies of companies that were beneficiaries of these policy loans and, subsequently, they took excessive risks on the assumption that the government would always be there to bail them out. Another consequence was the under-development of the South Korean banking system relative to the manufacturing sector's phenomenal growth because the government's intervention had prevented banks from functioning autonomously and, therefore, acquiring good credit skills and risk management.

Apparently realising these unfavourable consequences, the SBV has been gradually liberalising interest rates. At present, the SBV recommends a minimum savings rate and a maximum lending rate which are about 1.6 and 2.2% per month, respectively. In addition, the SBV has also abandoned setting sector-specific interest rates and instead, has differentiated them according to whether the loans are fixed or for working capital requirements. However, this differentiation has resulted in an inverted rate structure where the recommended interest rate on loans for fixed capital is lower than for working capital. This does not reflect the maturity or credit risk premium and, thus, it discourages term loans by banks.

For the short term, the SBV should probably continue to recommend interest rates as it is doing at present. Full liberalisation of interest rates does not appear likely in the immediate future because the financial position of banks is still not sound. They have small profit margins and large amounts of non-performing assets. Full liberalisation may result in banks targeting risky borrowers and this may further harm profitability and soundness. At the macro economic level, the country is not robust enough for a complete liberalisation of interest rates. Vietnam has barely achieved success in restraining inflationary pressure using interest rate controls. As such, a full liberalisation of interest rates coupled with the lack of monetary policy instruments may result in inflation swinging out of control.

Attracting Funds from the Private Sector

In addition to the formal financial system in Vietnam, a huge informal market exists for lending and borrowing by individuals and small businesses. The informal market takes on many forms including direct loans between individuals, such as family members, friends and money lenders, or participation in a mutual credit association called *hui* which is similar to the *tontine* in Singapore in the 1970s. In such an arrangement, members of a rotating credit/savings system contribute some money, less the interest proposed for the month, to a pool. The member who offers the highest interest rate will be entitled to the whole amount as a loan which will be repaid in instalments. The process repeats itself in the second month and so on.

The informal market is characterised by interest rates that are about three times higher (6 to 10% per month) than that offered by banks and the loans are normally short-term in nature. As compared to formal interest rates which have an inverted structure, the informal rates exhibit a positive relationship with the longer term loans at higher rates. Lending and borrowing procedures are simple and convenient. Because most borrowers rarely can provide any collateral, the lenders are exposed to great risks and, hence, the existence of a higher interest premium.

Despite the higher risks, lenders have been willing to lend since most Vietnamese do not trust banks. The distrust can be traced to the historical legacy of the SBV as a mono-bank not geared towards serving the individual and the collapse of several credit co-operatives since 1989. This situation is common in countries where the financial system is rather undeveloped, such as in Russia, and even South Korea where a kerb market was still very active in the early 1990s.

In Vietnam, the informal market has been able to co-exist with formal lenders such as the Agribank or Vietcombank due to the historical inefficiencies of the formal lenders in the remote rural areas. Formal lenders were not able to satisfy the financing requirements of rural households and businesses. This outcome arose because of the government's policy of channelling more funds to high priority sectors at the expense of others, and "crowding-out" by the state-owned enterprises which were traditionally the preferred customers of the formal lenders. The formal lenders also have not been willing to extend loans with a maturity long enough so that income can be generated to make repayments, because of the inverted interest rate structure and the lack of long-term funds. The formal lenders' requirement for collateral, which most borrowers in the rural sector could ill afford, further perpetuate an informal market which accounts for about 70% of the rural sector's loans.

The informal market was very active during the period 1989 to 1992 when the banking system could not cope with the sudden and huge capital requirements that followed in the wake of the introduction of *doi moi*. Since this market was unregulated and comprised informal arrangements, lenders lost a lot of money in 1992 and 1993 when borrowers could not pay up or simply disappeared with the money. The number of rural credit co-operatives which also acted as informal financial institutions declined sharply from about 7,500 in 1990 to only about 69 in 1994 (World Bank, 1995).

In the last few years, the government's efforts to reduce these informal market activities have been rather successful. Initial reforms in the financial system, including re-orienting the banking industry toward market principles, limiting the SBV to a traditional central bank role, and developing a domestic industry by allowing more privately owned banks, have raised the efficiency of the domestic banking industry and marginally boosted the confidence of the public. The Agribank's growing emphasis on small private farmers and rural businesses, improved operational efficiency. Rationalised branch networks have also contributed to the reduction in informal market activities. However, despite the common belief that the informal market is shrinking, its present size is estimated to be about US$5 billion. As such, this market will still serve as a significant adjunct to the formal banking system.

The significance of a shrinking informal market is that some funds circulating in this market will eventually find their way into the formal financial system. This will boost to a great extent the amount of funds available in the financial system. The increased funds can then be mobilised to meet the development needs of the country and thus reduce reliance on foreign funds. Barring any significant increase in inflation, this will also help to lower future interest rates in Vietnam.

Although the Vietnamese government is committed to improving the financial system, it needs to take steps in particular to increase the efficiency of financial intermediation even further in the rural sector in order to attract more funds to flow from the informal market to the formal financial system. One way of achieving this is to introduce more competition into the rural sector as the Agribank now dominates the sector. Not only might other banks be allowed to serve the rural sector but the government also could allow these banks access to the inter-bank markets and the refinancing facility of the SBV. The Agribank also needs to strengthen its operational efficiency and ability to reach out within the rural sector. As for procedures, the Agribank needs to re-evaluate its requirement on collateral and perhaps focus on a borrower's ability to pay out of operating revenues. Over time as the average Vietnamese becomes more confident in the formal financial system, previously immobilised funds held in the form of U.S. dollars and gold will make their way into the banks.

OUTSTANDING INEFFICIENCIES

Although Vietnam has achieved significant success in improving the overall efficiency of the financial system through enlarging the sources of funds, liberalisation of interest rates, and attracting funds from the informal market, there are still some outstanding inefficiencies in the system. These inefficiencies include the trend of favouring loans to state-owned enterprises, the lack of significant progress in streamlining the complicated laws on collateral, and establishing a stock market as an alternative for raising funds.

Lending to State-owned Enterprises and Bad Loans

The dominance of state banks, with an estimated 60% market share in the lending and deposit markets, and their historically close relationships with state-owned enterprises, has ensured easier access to credit for the latter group both in the past and at present. The existence of an underdeveloped mortgage financing market, where laws on collateral are complicated, also favours foreign banks in lending to companies that are connected to the government because they are normally guaranteed against default. This trend, if unchecked, will continue to smother the amount of financing available to private enterprises and will result in their returning to the informal market for funds.

The trend of favouring loans to state-owned enterprises has also raised some serious concerns about the financial strength of the domestic banking system. State banks do not recognise the concept of non-performing loans. Moreover, the tax laws are similarly structured and they do not allow for provisions against bad loans. Hence, there are basically no incentives for banks to clean up their books. As a result, most banks have undisclosed amounts of bad debts that could trigger a major crisis. The amount of bad loans is estimated to be approximately US$300 million and they are mainly loans to state-owned enterprises before 1988. It is crucial that provisioning for these loans begins immediately in order to avoid the tangle of debt such as is found in China between the state financial system and the state-owned enterprises. Making such provisions would greatly increase public confidence. To raise the level of confidence in the financial system further, the government might consider implementing some type of deposit insurance.

Collateral

The various pieces of legislation governing collateral are rather ill defined and lack cohesion at present. For instance, the types of collateral for loan are defined in the *Ordinance on Civil Contracts* (1990) and not in the *Ordinance of Economic Contracts* which is applicable to registered businesses. The latter ordinance merely provides that performance associated with this type of contract may be secured by mortgage property or guarantees in accordance with the applicable law. However, it does not define the type of property nor the applicable law regarding guarantees.

In general, the various ordinances and SBV resolutions provide that the following items may be used as collateral:

(i) mortgages on real estate such as housing, production and storage facilities, and equipment;
(ii) pledges of refined gold and other precious metals, and other personal property including savings passbooks;
(iii) cash collateral; and
(iv) guarantees supplied by third parties and duly secured by a mortgage or a pledge.

The 1989 SBV resolution also provides the following conditions:

(i) the loan amount should not exceed 80% of the value of the asset pledged;
(ii) the value of the asset, subject to the security interest, should be agreed mutually between the parties and recorded in a statement certified by the notary public or the People's Committee in the absence of the former;
(iii) once an asset is pledged it cannot be used as collateral for another loan simultaneously; and
(iv) pledged assets, except for real estate assets, must be held by the lender until the loan is satisfied.

Notwithstanding these provisions, all banks have their own internal guidelines with regard to the types of collateral which are acceptable for loans. This is because the regulations governing collateral are not well developed in Vietnam. As a result, most banks in Vietnam primarily lend money to state-owned enterprises and not to the private sector since the former generally have lower credit risk and are better able to provide adequate collateral.

One of the main problems with regard to collateral arises from mortgages on real estate which are used to secure loans from banks. This issue is tied to the existence of various pieces of legislation governing ownership/rights on land use. Under the *Law of Land 1993*, all land is the property of the people. This same piece of legislation also confirms the private right to use such land. However, it does not address the ownership/rights use with respect to housing which is covered in the *Ordinance on Residential Housing*. Hence, the land law and the ordinance affirm the right of the owner of the housing, and the land user, to mortgage their respective rights. However, it is not clearly stated how the right can be transferred from one party to another. It also does not address the manner in which the mortgages are created, enforced and liquidated in the event of default. These issues are mainly addressed in the *Ordinance on Civil Contracts* which applies exclusively to civil contracts. Thus, it is legally unclear as to how a mortgage in an economic contract is to operate.

Another problem is that the legal mechanism to resolve issues relating to a loan contract is ambiguous and rather time consuming. This is because there are several ordinances which provide the procedures for handling different contracts and situations. Because these ordinances were implemented on an *ad hoc* basis as stop gap measures to address certain loopholes, they were not rationalised very well, thus causing ambiguity. For prompt enforcement and liquidation of collateral at present, most default cases are settled out of court through a resolution committee which consists of representatives from the People's Committee, the Department of Police, the Department of Finance, SBV, State Prosecutor, courts, economic arbitration groups, and the lending banks' shareholders, depositors and management committee. Nevertheless, the enforcement of the judgment is difficult. The last resort, then, is to obtain a judicial judgment from the People's Court of Vietnam.

The current state of regulations governing collateral is not likely to improve significantly in the near future as there are many issues that the government has to address. However, the first issue that the government needs to address is providing a cohesive and transparent system of legislation for prompt enforcement and liquidation of collateral in default situations. Once this framework is in place, the government can then consider allowing multiple collateral on the same asset as in other countries, so as to mobilise more funds into the banking system. A well regulated system of collateral is very important because foreign banks will understand it and have confidence in the enforceability of the collateral in a loan agreement. This development would encourage more active lending by foreign banks to Vietnamese companies.

Stock Market as a Financing Alternative

At present, Vietnam has a small primary market for the issue of treasury bills and bonds, bonds issued by state-owned enterprises and state commercial banks, and shares issued by shareholding companies and state run enterprises that have been equitised (the Vietnamese term for privatisation). The market is still in its infancy with the value of all shares and bonds at about US$600 million (Nguyen, 1995) and the participants are mainly from Hanoi and Ho Chi Minh City. The main instruments in this market – treasury bills and bonds – have been issued since 1991, but it was only in June 1995 that an auction system was introduced. The auctions are not held regularly. There were only six auctions and all of the issues were oversubscribed as of mid-1996. Banks tend to favour such instruments in view of the high yields and relatively lower risks.

The recent auction of six-month bills raised US$4.5 million at a yield of 12.3% per annum (Hargrove, 1996a), while nine-month bills also raised US$4.5 million at a yield of 10.6%. Issues of bonds by the state-owned enterprises and banks are not very significant at present and, therefore, the primary market mainly comprises government treasury issues. The secondary market for trading these instruments is virtually non-existent at the moment due to a lack of depth. Recently, the Governor of SBV announced that auctions of treasury bills will be held every two weeks (Hargrove, 1996b). This is another step towards starting a healthy secondary market, which is a prerequisite to having more companies raising capital in the market.

The Vietnamese government originally planned to have a stock exchange in either Hanoi or Ho Chi Minh by the end of 1995. However, the plan did not materialise for several reasons. First, to have a stock exchange, Vietnam must have enough companies that are well managed and issue shares that can be traded on the exchange. Presently, there are about 100 companies that have issued shares but most of them are small companies with a small number of shareholders. Thus, to build a critical mass of shareholding companies, the government embarked on a three-year programme to equitise state enterprises. So far, five state enterprises have been equitised and another ten out of a total of about 5,000 to 6,000 state enterprises have been designated to be equitised by the end of 1997 (Folkmanis, 1996b). In the past, registration was voluntary. A decree issued on 7 May 1996 also granted incentives, such as a 50% tax break on profits for two years, to encourage state-operated companies to sell shares.

However, the equitisation programme has not yielded the desired results. The absence of an emerging Vietnamese middle class hampers the plan since foreigners are not allowed to participate in the programme. The lack of management skills also means that equitised companies will not experience any immediate improvement in efficiency and this will not make equitised companies any more desirable than other non-equitised enterprises. State companies are also used to operating with a high degree of financial secrecy which makes it difficult to value companies and thus attract investors (Folkmanis, 1996c). Finally, without a stock market, the equitisation programme will have difficulty in achieving its objective because there will be insufficient liquidity to attract potential investors, thus putting the planners in a catch-22 situation.

Secondly, inadequate accounting standards have impaired investors' ability to value companies accurately. Nevertheless, there has been some progress in shifting Vietnamese accounting standards to international standards. The Ministry of Finance is working on a circular to state enterprises that sets out the financial information required by international accounting standards, for potential investors to be able to assess their operations.

The third factor that has hindered Vietnam's stock exchange plans is the absence of stock market expertise in Vietnam. In fact, the concept of stocks is still something strange to most Vietnamese. This will continue to be a problem in the near future. However, Vietnam has recently signed two separate US$1 million co-operation agreements with the U.K. and South Korea to provide training for the operation of a stock market. Vietnam should have no problem in obtaining help from other countries in this respect.

Due to the existing myriad problems, the formation of a stock exchange is still a long way off. In the near future, it will be rather difficult for Vietnam to raise capital through the stock market to fund investment needs. Also, the government's attempts at mobilising capital from workers and the private sector through the equitisation programme is likely to have limited success. Nevertheless, the Vietnamese government should attempt to speed up the formation of a stock market as an avenue for raising funds in order to meet part of its massive funding requirement. In designing a stock market, the government should consider the need for limited foreign participation even in the early stages. Although there are genuine fears about foreign participation, there are also benefits such as the additional funds and liquidity afforded, and the transfer of technical, professional and regulatory expertise. Foreign participation will also help to overcome domestic individual investors' scepticism and mistrust of the formal financial institutions. The experiences of South Korea and Taiwan show that, given sufficient attractions, capital controls can remain stringent without deterring foreign investors (Chapman, 1996).

CONCLUSION

Vietnam has made significant progress in reforming its banking and financial systems. The financial system is attracting funds through new sources, such as the private sector and the inter-bank market, and there is a high possibility in the near future that the international financial market will be involved as well. These new sources will eventually increase the size of funds available in Vietnam and benefit investors. Together with the deregulation of interest rates, there is a possibility for lower interest rates and, thus, lower operating costs. A reduction in the size of the informal market activities will translate into even more funds for the formal financial system and it will also benefit investors.

To support economic development plans, the financial system must undergo further reforms to make it more efficient in mobilising capital. The government has to ensure an efficient allocation of funds and streamline its laws on collateral. These measures will eventually raise the level of confidence in the financial system. The government also has to step up efforts in developing a stock market in order to mobilise even more capital for development.

The government is determined that reforms will not fail because the development of the financial system is central to further economic growth. Given the increasing number of foreign banks and representative offices in Vietnam, there is some indication of a growing confidence in the economic potential of Vietnam and the stability of the financial system.

REFERENCES

Brahm J. Lawrence, *Vietnam Banking and Finance*, Butterworths, Asia, Singapore, 1995.

Chalmers John, *Vietnam Clinches Deal With Foreign Creditors*, Reuters, 18 May 1996.

Chapman Mathew, "Vietnam Transition Under Threat", *Peregrin Securities*, 14 March 1996.

Credit Lyonnais to Boost Vietnam Loans, Reuters, 13 May 1996.

Folkmanis Jason, "World Bank Chief to Recommend US$1.5 Billion in New Loans for Vietnam", *Bloomberg*, 9 May 1996a.

Folkmanis Jason, "Vietnam to Require Sale of Shares in State-Run Companies", *Bloomberg*, 22 May 1996b.

Folkmanis Jason, "Vietnam Unveils Incentives for State-Run Firms to Sell Shares", *Bloomberg*, 14 May 1996c.

Hargrove Kenny, "Vietnam Says Treasury Bills to be Every 2 weeks", *Bloomberg*, 12 April 1996b.

Hargrove Kenny, "Vietnam Sells 6-month Treasury Bills Raising US$4.5m", *Bloomberg*, 15 March 1996a.

Miller J. Lee, "Asian Development Banks to Lend Vietnam US$1.5 Billion Over 4 Years", *Bloomberg*, 2 May 1996.

Nguyen Cong Nghiep, "Vietnam, Towards a Securities Market", Seminar on Securities Market, Nanyang Technological University, July 1995.

Ngyuen Duc Thao and Pham Dinh Thong, *Vietnam Banking System and Its Payment Modalities*, Statistical Publishing House, Hanoi, 1994.

"Public Bank Opens 4th Branch in Vietnam", *Malaysia Business Times*, 21 May 1996.

"Vietnam's Deputy PM Urges Cuts in Interest Rates", *Vietnam News*, 10 May 1996.

Vietnam Economic News, Vol. V, 4 January 1996, p. 31.

Vu Arthur, "A Fistful of Bucks – Mobilising Retail Banking", *Vietnam Today*, Vol. 4, Issue 5, 1995.

World Bank, "Financial Sector Review, An Agenda for Financial Development", World Bank, Washington, DC, 1 March 1995.

Chapter 5

Regional Economic Co-operation: The Mekong Basin*

BY
TAN Siak Lim
Michael CHUA Lee Huat
HO Yik Joon
NG Chee Kin

INTRODUCTION

THIS CHAPTER EXAMINES an area of Southeast Asia that is currently attracting a great deal of attention. The area is known as the Greater Mekong Subregion (GMS) or Mekong Basin. It comprises the economies of Cambodia, Laos, Myanmar, Thailand, Yunnan (China) and Vietnam. The current interest began with an initiative by the Asian Development Bank (ADB) in the early 1990s to encourage co-operation between the countries of the GMS. The chapter highlights current proposals for the Subregion and examines its potential as an integrated economic subregion of Southeast Asia.

More specifically, and given the focus of this book, the role of Vietnam within the Mekong Basin is assessed. The first two sections provide background information on the Mekong river economies, and some of the ADB and other initiatives which are likely to influence current and future development and economic co-operation among the countries in the GMS. The third section focuses on some of the key developments within Vietnam itself. Finally, an attempt is made to assess Vietnam in the context of likely developments within the

* The authors are grateful to Dr. Ian McGovern for his guidance and comments.

Mekong Basin over the next decade or so. The underlying theme of the chapter is that Vietnam has a potentially significant role to play, given its size and location, but that events within the region outside its control, particularly the role played by Thailand, will determine the extent to which it does become a major player in the GMS.

THE MEKONG RIVER ECONOMIES[1]

The Mekong river rises in Tibet and flows from the high peaks of southwest China's Yunnan province to Myanmar, Thailand and Laos. It continues through Cambodia and, finally, empties into the southern Vietnamese delta south of Ho Chi Minh City. The six countries that comprise the Mekong Basin not only share common borders but their cultures and histories are also inextricably linked through centuries of conflict, trade and transmigration. And because of their size and geographical location, between China and India, these six countries have the potential to play a significant role in the future of Asia. In short, the major features of the GMS are:

(i) The Mekong river runs though or alongside all the six countries, playing a key role in agriculture, forestry, fishing, energy, and providing an important mode of transportation.
(ii) All but one (Thailand) of the six Mekong economies are in varying stages of transition from highly centralised, planned economies to more market-oriented, open economies.
(iii) The sweeping economic reforms across the Subregion, involving a change in national focus from inward-looking development to outward-oriented trade and investment, have opened up new horizons and opportunities for economic co-operation.
(iv) With the notable exception of Thailand, there is a need for considerable development of economic and commercial infrastructure to enable the Mekong Basin economies to compete effectively, even on a limited scale.
(v) Again with the notable exception of Thailand, there is a severe lack of capital for funding current and future economic development.
(vi) To a great extent, they share a common cultural heritage. Thailand, Laos and Yunnan also share the same language roots.

[1] Most of this section is taken from Korsmoe, 1995.

In addition to the above features, the population of the six GMS countries are shown in Figure 5–1 beginning clockwise with Laos (i.e., 4.2 million).

Figure 5–1
Subregional Populations (in millions), 1990

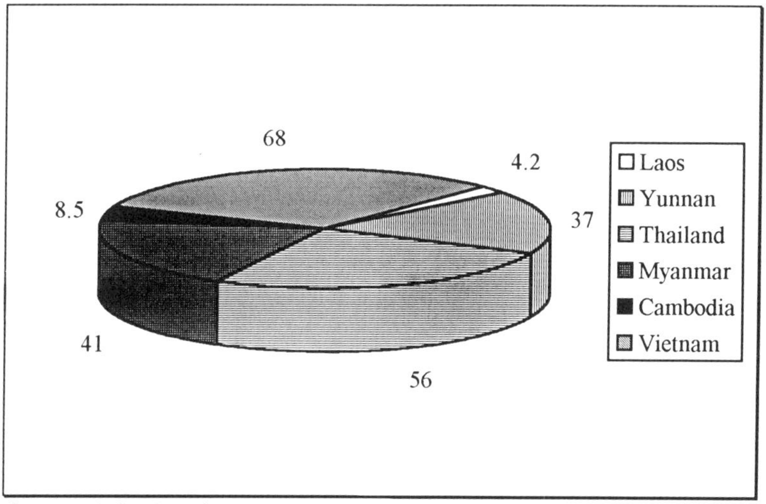

Source: Asian Development Bank.

GREATER MEKONG SUBREGION ECONOMIC CO-OPERATION[2]

The ADB initiative

Although there have been a number of previous attempts to foster some degree of co-operation in the Mekong Basin, the recent ADB initiative which began towards the end of 1991 appears to be the most promising. Not only does it come at the right time, with the cessation of most of the hostilities in the region, but it is also committed to funding many of the proposed projects and arranging private funding for much of the remaining funding requirements. The "Mekong Six" were previously looked upon as a non-cohesive subregion of East

2 This section is taken from *The Sunday Times*, 1995, and *ADB*, 1994, unless otherwise indicated.

Asia with little potential for co-operation, due to centuries of ethnic wars, colonial politics and superpower rivalries, which created fundamental distrust between them. The ADB, however, realised the potential in the region and decided to encourage the development of a regional infrastructure. This would help to integrate the GMS economies and, thus, assist them in integrating into the East Asian economic mainstream. The ADB is now taking a leading role as a facilitator in arranging co-operation among the countries involved.

If the experiences of Southeast Asia's neighbours are any guide (see World Bank, 1993), then we might expect a natural process of integration within the Subregion as countries begin to rise above subsistence levels and benefit from the growth in trade and inward direct foreign investment. This is likely to be accelerated by Vietnam's recent admission into ASEAN and the anticipated inclusion of Cambodia, Laos and Myanmar within the next two years.

However, there are significant obstacles to the development process. The most fundamental of these is the problem of inadequate domestic resources due to low *per capita* incomes. In Cambodia, Laos and Vietnam, for example, the lack of savings and financial resources greatly hampers the task of rebuilding the commercial and physical infrastructure, most of which was badly damaged during almost 40 years of conflict.

During the 1991 ADB conference on the GMS, infrastructure development was identified as the priority area for co-operation. Although economic co-operation in the GMS is intended to centre around trade and investment, the numerous projects that have been proposed or implemented so far are primarily concerned with the development of transportation networks and basic infrastructure. The purpose is to strengthen linkages among the participating countries as a catalyst for further co-operation in business and investment. In the area of energy co-operation, the six countries have agreed to shift from self-sufficiency to a more integrated approach to energy development. Co-operation is especially evident in the electric power and gas sub-sectors where energy demand in the Subregion is expected to grow very rapidly over the next 25 years.

Improved infrastructure was considered by all participants of the 1991 ADB conference to be the key prerequisite for economic growth with the most urgent need being in the field of transportation. Many of the proposals stemming from the conference pertain to the improvement of road, rail, air and water transportation systems. Some of these proposals call for the rehabilitation of existing facilities, some call for the extension of existing facilities, while others call for the construction of new facilities. Poor infrastructure is a major impediment to trade and co-operation in the GMS. The transportation infrastructure, despite substantial assistance from donor countries and multilateral organisations and investments by the countries themselves, requires further major commitments before minimum standards can be satisfied.

Many examples can be cited where inadequate transportation facilities frustrate subregional development and trade opportunities within the GMS. First, for landlocked Laos, access to the sea is along the country's undeveloped road network to seaports in other countries, and this requires the co-operation of Thailand, Vietnam and Cambodia. Not only must Laos improve its own road network but it must also rely on its neighbours to upgrade their own connecting roads between Laos and the ports. This puts Laos at a serious disadvantage for integrating itself into the regional (let alone the world) economy.

Secondly, the lack of rail links in northern Laos to the Thai railway system across the border from southern Laos, hinders the development of Laos' rich potash, iron ore, copper and other mineral resources. This is particularly frustrating given that the new bridge across the Mekong river between Thailand and Laos could provide direct access for Laos to the richer markets of Thailand and Southeast Asia.

Finally, Yunnan province is quite distant from coastal facilities with the closest major port being Haiphong harbour in northern Vietnam. There is currently no southward transportation link that provides Yunnan with access to the richer markets of Southeast Asia, nor the ASEAN countries with an overland route to southern China.

Given these problems, a number of projects have begun, aimed at improving communications within the Subregion (see Appendix 5–1 for a more comprehensive overview). These include:

(i) ***Subregional Road Projects:*** Some of these road projects are already underway while some are still proposals. The plan is for comprehensive road links between all the member countries of the GMS.

(ii) ***Subregional Railway Projects:*** Most of these are simply improvements to existing lines although a few new lines are planned.

(iii) ***Subregional Airport Projects:*** Most of the proposals here are for the upgrading of existing airports although a few new airports are being considered in some of the more remote areas.

(iv) ***Telecommunication Co-operation:*** Improvements in telecommunications is a major priority and a number of projects (mostly joint ventures) are already underway.

(v) ***Energy Co-operation:*** Once again, this is a major priority given the potential in this area. However, because these investments typically require large amounts of capital and raise sensitive environmental issues, they pose considerable challenges for co-operation. Most of the potential hydroelectric and petroleum developments require Subregional co-operation in order to proceed. Since this sector is so sensitive from a security standpoint, co-operative energy development is difficult to implement. Laos aims to be a major player in the hydroelectric field, but it is not the only potential source of hydroelectricity. Other projects are also under consideration in the region, some of which involve the use of the Mekong river itself.

(vi) ***Oil and Gas Projects:*** Although still at an early stage, there are a number of oil and gas projects already underway in the GMS and others are being proposed. As with hydroelectric power, this sector is a major priority given its potential as a foreign currency earner.

(vii) ***Irrigation:*** A Vietnamese Master Plan for the Mekong Delta submitted to the Vietnamese government by the State Planning Committee in co-operation with the World Bank and the United Nations Development Programme (UNDP), indicates that a relatively simple gate dam on the Tonle Sap (in Cambodia) could hold back flood waters in the great lake. The dam could then periodically release the water during the dry season for the Cambodian and Vietnamese farmers and fishermen's best use (Truong and Vu, 1995).

Although the most important areas for co-operation identified in the ADB master plan are trade, investment, transportation, communications, energy, water resources, and tourism, the understanding is that growth should not be achieved at the expense of the region's natural resources and natural beauty. Thus, there are also plans for co-operation in the areas of environmental protection and human resource development. Major strategic health projects also on the development agenda include HIV and AIDS prevention, and malaria control projects, both of which require joint action among the countries in the Subregion.

The Thai Initiative

Thailand, with its strategic geographical position, is now playing a crucial role in linking the countries in the Mekong Basin with the ASEAN countries and the outside world. Thailand's advantages include its location and the close historical, cultural and social ties that exist between Thailand and its neighbours. In the north and northeast, Thailand has been forging closer economic co-operation with the Mekong Basin countries to strengthen economic ties in six areas: energy, infrastructure (including transport networks and telecommunications), trade and investment, tourism, human resources, and the environment. Thailand accounts for about two-thirds of total subregional energy demand and is a supporter of well-planned energy management for the Subregion.

In the area of human resource development, the Thai government firmly believes that co-operation is an effective means of increasing the efficiency, well-being and income of the Subregion's population. The government is therefore establishing a centre (at Khon Kaen in north-eastern Thailand) for training in agriculture, health, finance, hotel management and developmental planning in the Subregion. The courses will be opened to participants from all Mekong Basin countries. Another important policy of the Thai government is to protect and preserve the environment in the Subregion, particularly addressing problems of deforestation, soil erosion and salinity, water pollution, hazardous wastes, degradation of urban environment and pollution.

ASEAN'S Mekong Basin Initiative[3]

At the Fifth ASEAN Summit held in Bangkok on 14–15 December 1995, the ASEAN leaders responded favourably to a proposal by Singapore that the group should co-operate in developing the Mekong Basin. ASEAN leaders discussed ways in which their countries could play an active role in Cambodia, Laos and Myanmar, and ways of getting the ASEAN private sector to be the locomotive for growth. It

---

[3] This section is based on *The Straits Times* 1995(a) and 1995(b) as well as ADB, 1994.

was suggested that the Mekong Basin provided a good opportunity for developing a "growth triangle" concept which has already been adopted elsewhere in Southeast Asia (see Thant *et al.*, 1994). It was also suggested that if ASEAN was confident about the opportunities and stability of the region, it could help the private sector to create an infrastructural fund specially dedicated to those countries.

In a similar initiative, the governments of Singapore and Thailand are assessing ways in which they can work together to develop the Subregion. There is a feeling by both sides that Singapore's expertise in infrastructure, coupled with Thailand's understanding of the region, could provide worthwhile opportunities for companies from both countries.

In summary, co-operation between the GSM countries emphasises infrastructure development, particularly in the areas of trade, investment, transportation, communications, energy, water resources and tourism. However, effective environmental management and human resource development are crucial in any bid to achieve sustainable economic growth. The Mekong Basin governments are aware of this and these two issues have not been neglected. With the basic infrastructure in place, the entire Mekong Basin has the potential to take off to form a mainland Southeast Asian economic subregion. If it does so, it is quite probable that Thailand will be a major player, given its cultural links with and geographic location at the heart of the Subregion.

VIETNAM

Introduction

The second part of this chapter deals with Vietnam, as the largest and most developed of the transitional economies in the GMS. Before evaluating Vietnam's current and potential role within the GMS, a brief overview of Vietnam might prove useful.[4]

Vietnam lies on the eastern coast of the Indochina Peninsula, with a total land area of 329,000 square kilometres. It is bordered by China to the north, Laos to the west and Cambodia to the southwest. The country comprised 44 provinces, cities and special zones. Its major

---

[4] This section relies heavily on Nguyen and Grub, 1992, and the *Economist*, 1995.

cities are Ho Chi Minh City in the south, Hanoi and the port of Haiphong in the north, and the industrial city and port of Da Nang in central Vietnam.

Vietnam's rapid economic growth in recent years has been primarily as a result of inward foreign direct investment. Vietnam has become one of the latest attractions for investors searching for new, large markets and low cost production sites. One of Vietnam's major resources is its people. It has a population of approximately 74 million (1994) and almost 40% of the population are less than 15 years old.

The nation's labour force continues to grow substantially at an annual rate of around 3.5%. Per capita income is at US$240 (1994) though there is considerable variability between both the north and south, and between the urban and rural areas. The workforce is fairly well-educated with a literacy rate of around 85%. Labour costs are significantly lower than those in most Southeast Asian countries, with some foreign joint ventures paying their Vietnamese employees the minimum wage of US$35 a month.

Like many other socialist countries, Vietnam was affected by the collapse of the Soviet Union in 1991. Financial assistance from the Soviet Union, totalling around US$1 billion per annum, collapsed and Vietnam had no alternative sources of overseas aid. In addition, foreign trade between the Soviet Union and Vietnam came to a virtual halt when Moscow demanded that Hanoi pay for its imports in hard currency at world prices. Consumer prices soared from 36 to 129% in 1989, and the Dong (Vietnamese currency) lost two-thirds of its value. Real GDP growth in 1990 and 1991 declined to around 5%.

As a result, Vietnam stepped up its economic reforms and opened trade links with non-communist countries. Its balance of payments then began to improve and the Dong stabilised. Foreign investment also increased significantly and in 1992 it totalled about US$2 billion. By 1993 the worst was over. The economy had expanded by 8.3% in 1992 and exports jumped nearly 30% producing a substantial trade surplus – the first in decades. In addition, the Vietnamese government managed to bring down the inflation rate to 7%. Over the last few years, the Dong has been relatively stable and has shown only a slight depreciation against the U.S. dollar (Economist Intelligence Unit, 1993; Economist Intelligence Unit, 1995; *Far Eastern Economic Review*, October 1995).

On the political front, Vietnam became the seventh member of ASEAN in July 1995. In addition, an economic co-operation agreement with the European Union (EU) was also signed in July 1995. The accord with the EU, which had been under discussion for over two years, covers a range of economic and trade related issues and gives Vietnam a number of valuable trading privileges. Vietnam intensified its diplomatic links with the world and has increased its trade with many countries, especially those in Asia. Japan resumed its aid to Vietnam in 1992. Former French President Mitterrand visited Hanoi in February 1993 and was the first Western head of state to be in Vietnam since 1975. Finally, in August 1995, Vietnam established formal diplomatic relations with the U.S., to complete a round of vital political initiatives.

Vietnam's most immediate goal now is to upgrade trade ties, specifically to gain Most Favoured Nation (MFN) status and other commercial privileges, which would greatly assist its bid to break into U.S. markets. The granting of Generalised System of Preferences (GSP) privileges which would give it valuable trading exemption privileges is even further down the road. To be eligible for GSP privileges, Vietnam must first be designated a Beneficiary Developing Country (BDC) which, in turn, requires that it be granted MFN status. However, many countries are already according Vietnam various trading privileges in anticipation of a freer trading and investment climate during the next few years.

Key Development Priorities

Poor infrastructure remains one of the biggest barriers to sustained growth and development in Vietnam. It needs huge amounts of foreign investment to improve these facilities. The transportation system is far from satisfactory as only 25% of the 105,000 kilometre of roads are paved. Highways around major cities and key ports are in poor condition and many bridges need repair. Only three ports (Haiphong, Da Nang and Ho Chi Minh City) are capable of handling container ships of significant size. However, even here the equipment and facilities need to be upgraded. Only about one-third of the goods are transported by rail, truck, air or ship. The remainder is moved by traditional means such as bicycles, bullock carts and small boats. As a consequence, distribution tends to be localised and distribution channels short. The telecommunications system is also inadequate. Power failure happens frequently. For example, in Ho Chi Minh City, power blackouts last an average of three hours a day (HKTDC, 1993).

The government recognises that infrastructure problems are the major constraint on Vietnam's growth and development. Therefore, in order to achieve the target of industry's contribution to GDP of between 26–27% by the year 2000, it aims to boost investment in energy, fuel, transport, communications, irrigation and other infrastructure projects. Current infrastructure problem areas and government policy targets are outlined below.

(i) ***The Energy Sector:*** In the energy sector, oil product consumption rose by 20% in 1993, more than double the annual GDP rate, and this trend has continued in 1994 and 1995. Almost all of Vietnam's oil products have to be imported. Although crude oil output is rising, demand is expected to outstrip supply for the next five to ten years. Vietnam's oil production, all of which is exported, is likely to rise from the 1994 level of around 140,000 bpd (barrels per day) to approximately 400,000 bpd by the end of the decade. In addition, gas is also quickly becoming a top priority with the aim being to replace expensive oil product imports to local power stations with local gas supplies. To fully fund energy sector projects, however, officials estimate that around US$600 million will have to be spent annually between 1995 and 2000 (Economist Intelligence Unit, 1995).

(ii) ***The Electricity Sector:*** In the electricity sector, Vietnam plans to raise power output from 14 billion KWH in 1994 to 25 billion KWH by the year 2000. This will involve the construction of 6 new power plants, 3 of which are needed in the very short-term given the ongoing power shortages which seriously affect industrial production in the south during the hot dry season. Of the three power plants required to meet immediate demand, two (a thermo-electric facility and a hydro-electric facility with a capacity of 600 and 400 megawatts, respectively) are to be built in the south while the third (a thermo-electric power facility with a capacity of 600 megawatts) will be located in the north. Over the medium-to-long term, the government aims to build three additional facilities. They include another major hydro-electric plant with a capacity of 2,500 megawatts and two thermo-electric facilities with a capacity of 1,000 megawatts each (Economist Intelligence Unit, 1995).

(iii) ***The Transport Sector:*** In the transport sector, the government is giving priority to roads linking Vietnam with neighbouring countries. The country's three international airports are also to be upgraded. Within Vietnam itself, the government is targeting the railway network, giving top priority to improving both the trans-Vietnam railway (it currently takes three days to travel from Ho Chi Minh City to Hanoi) and the rail link between the northern port of Haiphong and the Chinese border.

(iv) ***Irrigation Projects:*** Finally, major irrigation projects are being completed and targeted for the central region of the country. Dikes in the northern and central regions are currently under repair and new irrigation projects will be implemented in the Mekong and Red river deltas.

(v) ***Required Investment:*** According to the Vietnamese government, around US$40 to 50 billion in investment will be required to sustain double-digit growth from 1995 to the end of the decade, of which 35 to 40% will have to be devoted to infrastructure projects. The government hopes that around one-half of this total will come from foreign sources such as direct investment, aid and concessionary loans, with the reminder coming from the increased mobilisation of domestic savings. However, it is also likely that Vietnam will need to secure commercial loans to make up any shortfall (*Business Times,* 1995).

The ruling Communist Party of Vietnam has committed itself to becoming an industrialised socialist country by the year 2020. Although economic reforms have helped the country to progress over the last ten years, the year 2020 as a target to become an industrialised country is extremely ambitious. For example, Malaysia has also set the year 2020 as its target to be an industrialised nation and, yet, it is starting from a much higher level of economic development (Economist Intelligence Unit, 1993 and 1995).

Vietnam and the Mekong Economy

As mentioned previously, Vietnam is strategically located within the Greater Mekong Subregion. Its coastline stretches 3,400 kilometres and it borders China to the north, Laos to the west and Cambodia to the southwest.

To the north, links with China have been slow to develop but the recent moves to re-establish the rail link between Beijing and Hanoi are encouraging. Given Vietnam's common border with Yunnan

Province, improving communications with Yunnan are a logical first step, and this will eventually result in easier access for Yunnan to the South China Sea. The benefits to Vietnam are less easily identified at this stage given that the Vietnamese are unlikely to find an attractive market in Yunnan. However, in the longer term, the establishment of trade links is likely to be advantageous to both sides.

Vietnam's accessibility to the sea has made it a natural route to serve Laos, its landlocked neighbour. There are a number of proposed infrastructural developments, but one that may have particular significance for Indochinese co-operation is the proposed Chan May deep-water port and industrial zone in central Vietnam (see Appendix 5–2). Landlocked Laos could benefit significantly from the development of the Chan May seaport which is only about 30 kilometres away from the Laos border. The building of a system of seaports in central Vietnam at Chan May, Lien Chieu and Dung Quat, will be one of Vietnam's top priorities. The ports will link central Vietnam with Laos, Myanmar and other countries via the Trans-Asia Highway. These ports have the potential to serve a significant role in the development of the Mekong Subregion.

The opening up of the Bangkok-Phnom Penh-Ho Chi Minh-Vung Tau road will eventually provide southern Vietnam with access to new markets to the west and this could prove to be a significant development in the region. Co-operation with Cambodia has been rather low key in recent years and official trading links are almost non-existent. However, there has been a considerable amount of cross-border smuggling, a practice that is prevalent across all Mekong Basin borders (ADB, 1994). In addition to co-operating on the road project, negotiations are also taking place between Cambodia and Vietnam on co-operative use of the Mekong river. As mentioned above, proposals have been made for using the waters of Cambodia's Tonle Sap Lake for joint irrigation.

Taken together, all of these projects are contributing to a considerable change in the attitudes of the Mekong Basin economies toward one another. For the first time in decades, there is a feeling that the time is right for the countries of the Mekong Basin to join the mainstream economies of Southeast Asia. Given its size and the commitment of the government to a more open economic system, Vietnam is likely to be a major player in these developments.

Vietnam and ASEAN

Even before Vietnam became the seventh member of ASEAN in July 1995, there was considerable activity by ASEAN companies in Vietnam. In particular, Singaporean companies have invested heavily in Vietnam, though most of this has been in property development (*Vietnam Economic Times*, 1996). One Singaporean infrastructure project that is in progress is a joint venture involving the Neptune Orient Line (NOL), a Singaporean government-linked company. The company is planning to build and operate a container port at Tan Thuan, six kilometres southeast of Ho Chi Minh City. The US$50 million project will be developed jointly by Singaporean, Japanese, Taiwanese and Vietnamese partners. Another major investment by Singapore is the Vietnam-Singapore Industrial Park (VSIP) just outside Ho Chi Minh City, which is to be based on Singapore's successful industrial park model used in Singapore and Batam (Indonesia).

A number of Malaysian and Philippine companies have also been active in Vietnam but, so far, home-grown ASEAN companies (as opposed to MNCs based in ASEAN countries) have not played a leading role. Notably absent from Vietnam (given Thailand's desire to be a key player in the Subregion) are Thai companies. However, this may change since the Thais are making increasing overtures to the Vietnamese in the hope of improving both political and commercial ties.

The Future

With peace returning to the Subregion, many infrastructure-related projects are now either in the pipeline or underway to boost the economic development of the Subregion (thanks mainly to the ADB initiative). The most significant projects are those related to the development of seaports, airports, road, rail and telecommunications networks, all of which are vital to support business activities. If the plans are successful, this region will offer a highly attractive location in Asia for foreign investors looking for high growth.

It is worth noting that over the next decade, this may reinforce the gravitational shift of business attention northwards (a shift that has become increasingly apparent, for example, among foreign investors) and away from the traditional Southeast Asian economies, with Singapore playing its entrepôt role at the centre. For example, with the successful construction of the Chan May port in central Vietnam, together with the construction of the east-west road extending all the way from the port to Bangkok, the business community will have a number of options when deciding on how best to transport goods to and from northeast Asia. Currently, goods are often trans-shipped through Singapore on their way to Europe and northeast Asia but, five to ten years from now, there are likely to be a number of alternatives.

In summary, Vietnam is the largest transitional economy within the Mekong Subregion and since 1991 it has stepped up its economic reforms and opened trade links with non-communist countries. However, there is common agreement that the top priority must be infrastructural development. The Vietnamese government sees the co-operation with ASEAN and other Mekong economies as a key component in its efforts to build a market-oriented economy. As it progresses, its links to Mekong partners will assume greater importance, if for no other reason than its reliance on them for transportation and water use.

It now seems certain that Cambodia, Laos and Myanmar will be joining ASEAN within the next two years (leaving Yunnan as the only Mekong Basin area outside ASEAN). ASEAN membership may have the effect of cementing the ties between the Mekong economies and making co-operation easier. In addition to this is the desire by Thailand, Malaysia and Singapore to play an active role in the development of the Subregion, and the ADB's intention to play a facilitating role. Thus, the Mekong Basin initiative is gathering momentum for all of these reasons. The question most relevant to this chapter concerns the role that Vietnam is likely to play in these developments.

In the early stages (during the next few years), Vietnam's role is likely to be modest and limited to co-operation on cross-border infrastructure projects. However, over the next decade, if Vietnam develops in the way that many analysts believe that it will, then it is likely to play an increasingly important trading role. With the largest population in the Mekong Basin and its ideal geographical location on the South China Sea, Vietnam is an attractive location for foreign investment and a future alternative to Thailand for servicing the Mekong Basin economies. The main impediments to foreign investment at this stage are the lack of a sound legal business framework that foreign investors can rely on and appropriate human resource development policies. However, these are manageable problems that the Vietnamese are likely to resolve.

Since Vietnam can be viewed as a future alternative production and servicing location to Thailand, the role of the latter during the next decade is of more than passing interest. These two countries are the biggest economies in the Mekong Basin and, although at this stage Vietnam is no threat to Thailand, in the coming years Vietnam's cost advantage may make it much more competitive in some (probably low-technology) industries. Thailand is, of course, aware of this possibility. This is one of the reasons why Thai businesses are so eager to be actively involved in the Subregion. Given the opportunity, they would also like to be more active investors in Vietnam. The extent to which they are successful in doing this might determine the future shape of the Mekong Basin.

APPENDIX 5–1

COMMUNICATIONS PROJECTS PROPOSED OR UNDERWAY IN THE MEKONG BASIN

Given the infrastructural problems faced by the Mekong Basin economies, a number of projects have been started or are under consideration to improve communications within the Subregion. These include the following projects.

Subregional Road Projects

(i) ***Laos/Yunnan Province:*** There is a road link connecting with the Yunnan road system to improve communications between Yunnan and Thailand.
(ii) ***Thailand/Laos/Vietnam:*** Upgrading of the road from Nakhon Phanom in Northeast Thailand, through Laos, to Vinh (on Vietnam's coast) gives producers in Laos and Thailand better access to Vietnam and the South China Sea.
(iii) ***Laos/Thailand:*** A second bridge is planned across the Mekong river (to be paid for by Thailand) which will improve the link between the two countries. This will increase access for Laos to the South China Sea (see the Thai-Lao Friendship Bridge).
(iv) ***Cambodia/Laos:*** Rehabilitation of the most dilapidated sections of the primary network in Cambodia, including temporary structures and key provincial roads, will improve the link between Cambodia's interior and its coast, and between Cambodia and

Laos.

(v) ***Vietnam/Cambodia/Thailand:*** Rehabilitation of the Ho Chi Minh-Phnom Penh-Bangkok road will reduce travel time between the three cities giving Cambodia and Vietnam access to the richer Thai markets, and providing Thailand with a direct overland route to the South China Sea.

(vi) ***Myanmar/Yunnan Province:*** The proposed road improvement between Kunming (Yunnan) and Ruili (northern Myanmar), known both as the Dian Mian Road and the Stilwell Road, will improve Myanmar's link to the Chinese transportation network and improve Yunnan's access to markets in Myanmar and Thailand. Some 320 kilometres of the 900 kilometres road are now being upgraded.

(vii) ***Myanmar/Thailand:*** There is construction and upgrading of sections of the Asian Highway, including the planned A2 route crossing the Salween River at Ta Kaw and linking with Thailand via Kengtung and Hpayak. This improvement will eliminate a weak link in the road system that connects Southeast Asia with South and West Asia.

(viii) ***Thai-Lao Friendship Bridge:***[5] This bridge is 1,174 metres and it is the first major bridge over the Mekong river just upstream from Nong Khai, Thailand. It has been under construction since 1993 and was officially inaugurated on 8 April 1994. It is a symbol of improved relations between Thailand and Laos. For Australia, which financed the US$30 million bridge, it symbolises a larger diplomatic and commercial role.

Trade, tourism and investment between Thailand and Laos is expected to surge sharply with the opening of the bridge because it relieves a transportation bottleneck. According to Thai customs officials, about 2,000 trucks board the ferry at Nong Khai to cross the river into Laos each month. The bridge will provide an important door to the outside world for landlocked Laos where the only route to the sea is through ports on the Gulf of Thailand and in Vietnam. It is also a key link in a planned road network that will eventually stretch from Singapore to Beijing.

Subregional Railway Projects

(i) ***Vietnam/Yunnan Province:*** The reconstruction of the railway

---

5 Most of this section is taken from Fairclough, 1994.

bridge at the border, along with changing the gauge on Vietnam's side, will link the rail systems of Vietnam and the People's Republic of China.

(ii) ***Myanmar/Yunnan Province:*** Extension of the Kunming-Dali line to Lanping (ongoing), followed by an extension to Xizang (Tibet) and Wanding, a border town near Myanmar, will lead to the linkage of the two national railway systems. Another plan is to construct a spur line from Baoshan (Yunnan) to Myitkyina in Myanmar.

(iii) ***Yunnan Province/Myanmar/Laos:*** Extension of two railway lines (Xiangyun-Jinghong and Yuxi-Jinghong) from Yunnan to the Myanmar-Laos-Thailand "Golden Triangle" will link all four countries and facilitate the flow of goods and passengers.

(iv) ***Vietnam/Cambodia/Thailand:*** Rehabilitation of Cambodia's railway system will greatly improve the flow of goods and passengers between Bangkok, Phnom Penh, and eventually Ho Chi Minh City.

Subregional Airport Projects

(i) ***Laos:*** The upgrading of airports at Luang Prabang and Pakse will improve access to these cities for tourists and business people, and facilitate the development of a Subregional air network.

(ii) ***Yunnan Province:*** The upgrading of the airport at Kunming (in progress) and the procurement of 50-passenger water-landing planes will increase access to Yunnan for business travellers and tourists. There is a feasibility study underway for a new airport at Jinghong

(iii) ***Cambodia:*** The upgrading of airports at Phnom Penh and Siem Reap will improve access to tourist destinations as well as the capital. There is a feasibility study underway for a new airport at Sihanoukville.

(iv) ***Myanmar:*** A feasibility study is underway for a new airport at Hanthawaddy.

Telecommunications Projects

(i) ***Cambodia:*** There is a US$10 million satellite telecommunications project in Phnom Penh by OTC International of Australia.

(ii) ***Vietnam:*** OTC International of Australia has a ten-year contract to upgrade and manage Vietnam's international telephone service.

(iii) ***Vietnam:*** Marconi of Italy is installing a fibre optic cable between Hanoi and Ho Chi Minh city, serving all major centres along the route.
(iv) ***Myanmar:*** Siemens is assisting in improving the country's telecommunications systems.

Subregional Hydro-electric Projects

(i) ***Laos:*** Hydro-electric power projects are planned for Laos to serve the whole of the Mekong Basin, especially Thailand (Theun-Hinboun hydro-power project).
(ii) ***Myanmar/Thailand:*** The Salween river hydro project, including the diversion of water from the Salween river in Myanmar to the Chao Phraya river in Thailand is underway.
(iii) ***Vietnam/Cambodia:*** Development of the Pleikrong and Yali Falls sites on the Upper Se San river in Vietnam will provide energy for the central and southern portions of the country. A grid system could also serve portions of Cambodia.
(iv) ***Yunnan/Thailand/Myanmar:*** Plans for developing eight hydropower stations on the middle and lower sections of the Lancang (Mekong) river in Yunnan with an installed capacity of 14,810 megawatts are underway. The province already produces four million kilowatts which satisfies provincial demand but they are looking to export power. These stations will produce up to ten million kilowatts of power. Provincial authorities intend to sell their surplus power to other provinces in China and other countries.

Subregional Oil and Gas Projects

(i) ***Myanmar/Thailand:*** A gas pipeline linking reserves in the Gulf of Martaban (Myanmar) with markets in Thailand is under consideration.
(ii) ***Vietnam/Thailand:*** A gas and oil pipeline linking reserves in southern Vietnam with markets in Thailand is under review.
(iii) ***Myanmar/Cambodia/Thailand/Vietnam:*** A gas pipeline between Yandana (Myanmar), Bangkok, Phnom Penh, Ho Chi Minh City and Vung Tao (Vietnam) is under consideration.
(iv) The development funds required for these projects are huge; one phase of the Theun-Hinboun power project alone will cost about US$1 billion. The key challenge for the "Mekong Six", therefore,

is to find innovative ways to mobilise private capital and to channel this into priorities in the Subregion.

APPENDIX 5–2

CHAN MAY PORT AND INDUSTRIAL ZONE[6]

In February 1996, the central Vietnamese province of Thua Thien – Hue revealed a master plan for a deep-water port and an industrial zone at Chan May, Horizon Bay, 49 kilometres north of the ancient capital of Hue. If approval is given, the deep-water port, coupled with an industrial zone, will be the country's second largest complex after Dung Quat, the site of Vietnam's future oil refinery. The 7-kilometre wide bay has an average depth of 9 to 14 metres. It is free from reefs and can accommodate vessels of up to 50,000 TDW (tonnes dead weight) at low tide. The project envisages the construction of a 1.8 kilometre long wave-dike, making the port 10 kilometres long and enabling it to handle ships of up to 70,000 TDW. It is projected that the port's cargo handling capacity could reach 25 million tonnes per year. Presently, Vietnam has a current total capacity of 25 million tonnes/year. Planners believe that because of its favourable geographical, geologic and hydrological conditions, Chan May is set to become a versatile deep-water port, handling cargo, containers, tourists and deep-sea fishing vessels.

In addition, land adjoining Chan May Bay is close to Highway 1A (the main north-south highway) and it is suitable for an industrial zone. The Industrial Zone Master Plan includes a container port with a capacity of one million containers a year; several hi-tech industrial facilities (covering 200 hectares); electricity and electronics facilities (200 hectares); shipyard and engineering facilities (200 hectares); textiles and handicraft facilities (200 hectares); agriculture-forestry processing facilities (300 hectares); seafood processing facilities (200 hectares); construction materials facilities (450 hectares); cement plants (producing 5 million tonnes a year); a dump site for oil and gas; and residential areas for workers. The Chan May Industrial Zone would not be too far away from the 500 kilowatts power transmission line and it could be easily supplied from the 220 kilowatts national grid. Two natural lakes, 12 kilometres southwest of the industrial zone,

[6] Source: Thoal Linh, 1996.

would supply the newly developed region with 117,000 cubic metres of water per day.

According to the Master Plan, Chan May city would be situated in the east and west of the Industrial Zone and have a population of between 150,000 and 200,000. It plans to construct high-rise office buildings and hotels at the edge of the mountains. Much nearer to the sea, a commercial centre and several residential villas will be constructed. Because of its strategic tourist location, situated between world-famous tourist cities such as Hue, Hoi An, My Son, and Da Nang, and close to older resorts such as Canh Duong and Bach Ma in the National Park 1,450 metres above sea-level, Chan May could be developed into a large tourist site comprising 500 hectares for villas and bungalows and 500 hectares for swimming beaches.

REFERENCES

ADB, *Economic Co-operation in the Greater Mekong Subregion: Toward Implementation*, Asia Development Bank, Manila, 1994.

"Backing for Mekong Basin Project", *The Straits Times*, 15 December 1995b.

Economist Intelligence Unit, "Indochina: Vietnam, Laos, Cambodia. Country Report: Analysis of Economic and Potential Trade" *Economist*, 1993.

Economist Intelligence Unit, "Vietnam, Country Report, 3rd Quarter 95", *Economist*, 1995.

Fairclough G., "Spanning The Divide", *Far Eastern Economic Review*, 21 April 1994, p. 23.

"Gateway to Business in Indochina and ASEAN", *The Sunday Times*, 3 December 1995.

Hong Kong Trade Development Council (HKTDC), "Trade Development in Vietnam, Market Prospects and Investment Environment", HKTDC Research Department, June 1993.

Korsmoe S., "Riding The Mekong", *Vietnam Economic Times*, Issue No. 13, May 1995, pp. 14–5.

Nguyen X. O. and T. B. Grub, *Vietnam: The New Investment Frontier in Southeast Asia*, Times Academic Press, Singapore, 1992.

"Report on Vietnam", *Business Times*, 17 November 1995.

"Singapore is Vietnam's Top Investor for 1994", *The Straits Times*, 2 January 1995a.

"Special Report on Singapore", *Vietnam Economic Times*, Issue No. 28, August 1996.

Thant M., M. Tang and H. Kakazu, *Growth Triangles in Asia: A New Approach to Regional Economic Co-operation*, Oxford University Press, London, 1994.

Thoal Linh, "New Port, Industrial Zone Proposed", *Vietnam News*, 13 February 1996.

Truong V. K. and M. S. Vu, "Can Tho: Hub of the Delta Heartland", *Vietnam Economic Times*, May 1995, p. 16–21.

"Vietnam: Trade and Investment Special Report", *Far Eastern Economic Review*, 26 October 1995, pp. 47–57.

World Bank, *East Asian Miracle: Economic Growth and Public Policy*, Oxford University Press, London, 1993.

Chapter 6

A Synopsis of Macro Policy and Reform

BY
Ian McGOVERN

INTRODUCTION

THE FIRST SECTION of this book explored various macro economic aspects of the Vietnamese economy. Among the many issues that need to be addressed there are four which are particularly important at this stage of Vietnam's development, and they are the basis of the first four chapters of this book:

(i) inward foreign direct investment (FDI);
(ii) financial/monetary policy;
(iii) the financial system; and
(iv) Vietnam's growing regional role.

FOREIGN DIRECT INVESTMENT

Chapter 2 provides a detailed analysis of Vietnam's foreign investment promotion strategy. The Vietnamese government has earmarked a central role for FDI in its plans to modernise the economy and to transform it from a centrally-planned to a more market-oriented economy. The government recognises the importance of FDI and, yet, like many other transitional economies, it feels more than a degree of ambivalence towards foreign investors. Recent adverse press reports concerning the behaviour of foreign managers towards their Vietnamese workers (*Far Eastern Economic Review*, 1995, 1996), the corrupting influence of foreign advertising on Vietnamese culture (*The Straits Times*, 2 February 1996) and, more recently, the government's much publicised difficulties with foreign investors (*The Straits Times*, 1 January 1996) all highlight the often prickly relationship between the Vietnamese and their foreign counterparts.

To a great extent, this response is hardly surprising. The Vietnamese government is trying to cope with the transition to a market economy while at the same time trying to protect its economy, culture, and power base from what it sees as the worst excesses of the free market economy. Unfortunately, it has no blueprint to follow and is making up the rules as it goes along. The resulting uncertainty and unpredictability is a major concern for foreign investors. It is much more than a minor irritation. The recent changes in the licensing procedure for law firms, for example, penalises those firms which entered the market first, and makes a mockery of the much touted strategic concept of "first mover advantage" (*Saigon Times*, 16 December 1996). Clearly, in the view of investors (and more importantly, potential investors), the government still has some way to go before it sets its house in order.

In Chapter 2, the authors dealt specifically with the government's strategy for attracting foreign investors. The chapter began with an overview of the government's economic policy and FDI's intended central role within that policy. A review of the policy shows clearly that the government sees a role for FDI in almost every aspect of industrial and commercial development. The authors note that the government has developed a two-pronged approach to investment promotion. At the macro level, it is trying to build an economic and legal framework that is conducive to doing business. At the micro level, the government is offering specific incentives to attract the kind of investment it wants. In practice, the latter is being done on a case-by-case basis, though there are general guidelines on what incentives are available. The chapter goes on to explain the main incentives in some detail and the rationale behind them.

The authors comment that unlike its neighbour Thailand, for example, Vietnam does not use preferential zoning for its promotional privileges but relies instead on the natural endowments of each region. As a consequence, the kind of incentives that are offered to foreign investors in remote areas of central Vietnam are similar to the incentives given to investors in the main industrial areas around Ho Chi Minh City, Hanoi and Haiphong. Given Vietnam's well-publicised difficulty in getting foreign companies to invest in these less attractive areas, a change in policy may be overdue.

The chapter concluded on a relatively upbeat note. After making a number of observations on the tax and legal systems, and land ownership, the authors concluded that, in general, the policies are well founded and consistent with the government's development objectives. They point out that despite the many problems faced by investors, the need is probably for more fine-tuning of current investment promotions rather than instituting wholesale change.

VIETNAMESE MONETARY POLICY

The second critical issue is the state of the Vietnamese financial system. The whole financial sector has had to be restructured to accommodate the market economy and, although considerable improvements have been made, there is still cause for concern. There are two strands to this problem. The first is the Vietnamese government's monetary policies; the second is the structure of the financial and banking system itself. Chapter 3 addresses the issue of monetary policy.

There is general agreement (see Chapter 3) that by and large the Vietnamese monetary authorities have implemented sensible monetary policies in recent years. In Chapter 3, the authors first explain the basics of monetary policy and then go on to discuss the unique circumstances that Vietnamese authorities faced as a consequence of having implemented a centrally-planned economy for the whole country after reunification in 1975. As the authors point out, the first critical decision was the introduction of a new currency in 1978 which effectively wiped out much of the personal wealth held in the southern part of the country. The legacy of this is that, even today, the government has difficulty in getting the Vietnamese to use the banking system: many of them prefer instead to keep their wealth outside the formal sector in the form of gold or foreign currencies (usually American dollars). Subsequent reforms during the 1980s led to hyper-inflation and this was only brought under control in the early 1990s with the introduction of punitive interest rates which drastically reduced the demand for money.

To put it simply, the monetary authorities have been concerned with managing inflation, increasing their control of the money supply, maintaining the stability of the currency and liberalising the market price mechanism. There appears to have been three elements in this policy. The first of these was the punitive interest rate regime mentioned above, which brought inflation under control. Although the policy severely damaged many businesses (including state-owned enterprises) it was successful in ridding the economy of hyper-inflation. With inflation down to a more or less manageable figure, the second element of the policy has been to try and reduce Vietnam's reliance on the U.S. dollar, thereby strengthening the authorities' hold over the money supply. Government directives in 1994 stipulated that customers must be billed in Dong (the Vietnamese currency), though this has met with limited success due to the shortage of Dong. At the time of writing, there is still considerable reliance on payments in U.S. dollars and most sellers are willing (if not eager) to accept payment in dollars. The third element of monetary policy has been to try and improve the market mechanism by reducing price subsidies and price controls. Once again, this has severely affected many domestic firms, especially the state-owned enterprises which have enjoyed considerable protection under central planning.

Overall, the Vietnamese government's policy of tight money and price liberalisation have met with approval from most analysts. There are still worries, particularly on the extent to which inflation can be kept down, as the economy grows and bottlenecks occur. However, the economy looks in much better shape than it did just a few years ago and the government appears to be aware of the dangers. As the authors conclude, there are grounds for believing that monetary policy is more or less on track.

THE FINANCIAL SYSTEM

Underpinning the government's whole monetary policy is the reform of the financial and banking system. Governments may formulate monetary policy but it is the institutions that are instrumental in the implementation of such policies. It is through the banking and financial system, and through the activities of their central bank, that governments carry out their monetary policy.

Unfortunately for the Vietnamese, a legacy of their previously centrally-planned economy is a financial and banking system that is not particularly suited to the workings of a market economy. The government, therefore, is involved in a wholesale reform of the banking and financial system to make it better suited to the needs of the market economy and to be more responsive to the government's new monetary policies. Chapter 4 of this book focused on the reform of Vietnam's financial and banking system, examining the reforms that have taken place so far, and assessing the extent to which they are consistent with the government's plans for the development of the economy.

The chapter started with a summary of Vietnam's financial institutions, taking the 1950s as its starting point. Once again, as with Chapter 3, this historical perspective is important in that it puts into context the difficulties faced by the current authorities. Decisions taken decades ago by policy makers faced with supporting a war economy have resulted in a philosophy and legacy that is difficult to shake off. As the authors point out, it was not until the end of the 1980s that the State Bank of Vietnam (SBV) ceased to be the sole provider of almost all domestic banking services. Today, the SBVs role is very much that of a traditional central bank and a host of other institutions have taken responsibility for the various aspects of the financial and banking sector. It is here that the historical context becomes important. It must have been very difficult politically to change a system and a way of thinking that had been prevalent for almost 40 years. As investors and foreign governments complain about the slow pace of change in Vietnam, they might do well to reflect on the enormous psychological adjustment that had to take place just for Vietnam to get to where it is today.

The chapter highlights many of the problems to be found in the current system and comments on the slow pace of change. It also addresses the interesting issue of informal credit, a phenomenon that is prevalent across the whole of East Asia. In countries such as Thailand (where it is well established in the Thai-Chinese business community), informal credit results from a credit shortage; but in Vietnam, it is strongly influenced by the people's mistrust of the banking system. This "cultural" dimension of informal credit is important to take into account when assessing the authorities' ability to reduce the size of the informal sector.

Chapter 4 ended with a relatively upbeat assessment of the financial system. The government seems well aware of the importance of reform, and although a workable legislative framework still seems a long way down the road, there appears to be growing confidence within the business community that the government is on the right track.

REGIONAL DEVELOPMENT

The final chapter in this section was a little different from the previous three in that the focus was not on domestic issues but on Vietnam's regional involvement. Chapter 5 focused on Vietnam as part of the Mekong Basin, which comprises Cambodia, Laos, Myanmar, Thailand, Yunnan (China) and Vietnam. Vietnam's role in ASEAN is discussed briefly, and so is ASEAN's role in Vietnam, but this is done in the wider context of the Mekong Basin. The rationale behind this chapter is that no book on Vietnam would be complete without an understanding of the wider context in which Vietnam's development will take place. Plans for the economic development of the Mekong Basin are now well underway and are likely to have far-reaching effects on Vietnam's development.

The background to the chapter is the Asian Development Bank (ADB) initiative to create a community of countries in mainland South-east Asia, linked by the Mekong River (Asian Development Bank, 1994). The official name given by the ADB to this area is the Greater Mekong Subregion (GMS) but, increasingly, it is becoming known as the Mekong Basin. Within the Mekong Basin, the only industrially developed country is Thailand; the remainder (with one exception) are transitional economies, moving from centrally-planned to more market-oriented economic systems. The exception is Myanmar which, though a strong socialist country, does not really have a system of central planning.

The purpose of Chapter 5 was two-fold. First, it attempted to explain what is happening in the region and, thus, provides this book on Vietnam with a regional perspective. The infrastructural developments in the region are of such significance that if only one-half are realised over the next ten years, they will radically affect the business potential of the Mekong Basin. Some of these infrastructural developments are specific to particular countries (for example, the building of a new airport in northern Laos, or a new port in central Vietnam). However, most of them depend on cross-border co-operation (such as irrigation plans for the Tonle Sap lake in Cambodia to feed the Mekong Delta in Vietnam; or upgrading the road link between Ho Chi Minh City, Phnom Penh and Bangkok). The master plan is extremely ambitious and it will take at least a decade to become a reality. However, some projects will be completed within a year or so (for example, the international road mentioned above). The most recent press releases on the Mekong Basin are very upbeat and they quote ADB sources as saying that the planning stage is now over and the implementation stage has begun (*The Straits Times*, 29 August 1996).

Secondly, the chapter sought to assess the implications for Vietnam of what is happening in the region. To do this, the authors examined the role of ASEAN in the Mekong Basin in terms of what individual member countries are doing in the region and what ASEAN as a group proposes to do. Some countries (notably Singapore) are strong investors in Vietnam and they are firmly committed to developing their operations there in anticipation of the growth of the Mekong Basin. Other countries (notably Thailand) are less active in Vietnam but very active in the region as a whole. Companies from Malaysia, Singapore, Thailand and the Philippines are all very active in the region but some of them find it easier than others. Singapore, for example, has a strategy for the region and tends to use its Government-Linked Companies (GLCs) as the spearhead for Singaporean investment overseas (*The Straits Times*, 13 September 1996).

The government is very supportive of its own companies and encourages them to go regional and follow the GLCs. At the other extreme, Thai companies receive almost no help from their government and they are expected to rely on their entrepreneurial skills and contacts in the region.

As a group, ASEAN has plans to develop the Mekong Basin and a number of working groups have been set up (ASEAN, 1996). One of the most notable projects that will almost certainly go ahead is a rail link between Singapore, Kuala Lumpur, Bangkok, Phnom Penh, Ho Chi Minh City and Hanoi, before carrying on up to Beijing (*The Straits Times*, 31 May 1996). In addition, Singapore and Thailand have plans for some of their companies to link up and jointly exploit opportunities in the region. Overall, the level of ASEAN involvement is still quite low but the Mekong Basin as a concept is growing in importance to ASEAN. This is understandable given that the remaining Mekong Basin countries (with the exception of Yunnan) are likely to be members of ASEAN within two or three years.

SUMMARY AND COMMENTS

The four chapters in this section address some of the most critical issues facing the Vietnamese government in its attempt to make the transition from a centrally-planned to a more market-oriented economy. These issues are not unique to Vietnam but they are largely unique to that small group of "transitional" economies located in Asia. They are different, for example, from the transitional economies of the old Eastern Europe (Poland, Hungary, and so forth) in that the Asian transitionals are struggling to make the changes from a much lower level of economic development than that faced by the European transitionals. In addition, although both groups of transitional economies have a rich supranational neighbour, ASEAN has been less inclined than the European Union to provide funding for developing its poorer neighbours. In fact, the ADB has publicly appealed to ASEAN to be more generous toward the poorer countries in the region (*The Straits Times*, 31 August 1996). As a consequence, the Asian transitionals have had to rely more on the ADB and on foreign investment, and it is in this context that the development of Vietnam needs to be viewed. Without ADB funding and foreign investors, Vietnam simply could not cope with the transition to a market economy.

Given the crucial role of foreign investment, and the need to make the country more attractive to foreign investors, the government is faced with a number of difficult problems. First, there is the difficulty of handling the transition itself. The sheer complexity of dismantling one administrative system and replacing it with another is often not appreciated by outsiders and they wonder why Vietnam is so slow to change. But it takes more than administrative changes to make a new system. Legislative changes are the easy part but they must be accompanied by a new way of thinking within the country, and it is this change in the country's "mind-set" that takes time.

Secondly, the government has to balance the needs of the country and its people against the needs of foreign investors. These do not always coincide. FDI often means job losses as well as new jobs, and this leads to the creation of prosperous urban enclaves surrounded by the poorer rural areas. Foreign investors are there to make money whereas the government has to consider the wider interests of society. As a consequence, it is hardly surprising that the government moves slowly. It has no blueprint for success and is understandably nervous as it moves through the transition.

Thirdly, because of its recent history, Vietnam has inherited a legacy of mistrust within its commercial community. People do not trust the financial institutions and, in many cases, they do not trust those whose job is to enforce laws (where such laws exist) related to business dealings. Consequently, the Vietnamese people are still more likely to hoard their wealth out of sight of the government and the tax authorities, and out of the reach of the formal banking sector. Once again, it is difficult to see how this will change until the Vietnamese regain their trust. This time, it is the mindset of the Vietnamese people, and not their leaders, that needs to change.

Given all of these problems, and seen in this light, it is surprising to think how far Vietnam has come in such a short time. The Vietnamese government has made mistakes, they have upset foreign investors, and they have failed to regain the trust of their own business community. But at the same time, they have made a remarkable transition in the space of ten years. Even two years ago, few would have thought that Vietnam would become a member of ASEAN so soon, and that ASEAN companies would be queuing up to invest in the country.

Vietnam, today, is very different from the Vietnam of just a few years ago and the pace of change is quickening, albeit not as fast as some vested interests would like. Overall, the government is cautious, and afraid of making catastrophic and irreversible mistakes. But as the authors of all four chapters note, there is room for optimism that Vietnam is making progress. If the pace seems a little slow at times, and the government a little indecisive, the words of the late economist John Maynard Keynes may be reassuring: "It is better to be approximately right, than precisely wrong". By and large, the consensus seems to be that Vietnam is getting it approximately right.

REFERENCES

Basic Framework of ASEAN-Mekong Basin Development Co-operation, Press release, ASEAN, Kuala Lumpur, 17 June 1996.

"Culture Shock: Korean Employers Irk Vietnamese Workers", *Far Eastern Economic Review*, Hong Kong, 22 August 1996.

Economic Co-operation in the Mekong Subregion: Toward Implementation, Asian Development Bank, Manila, 1994.

"First Mercedes Rolls Out of EDB-Daimler Vietnam Plant", *The Straits Times*, Singapore, 13 September 1996.

"Love Thy Neighbour", *Far Eastern Economic Review*, Hong Kong, 10 August 1995.

"Mekong Forum Issues Appeal to Fund 100 Priority Projects", *The Straits Times*, Singapore, 31 August 1996.

"Planning Over – Mekong Area Nations Move into Implementing Projects", *The Straits Times*, Singapore, 29 August 1996.

"Special Report on Changes to Business Law", *Saigon Times*, Ho Chi Minh City, 16 December 1996.

"Three Firms Invited to Replace Total in Viet Refinery Deal", *The Straits Times*, Singapore, 1 January 1996.

"Trans-Asian Rail Route Gets Green Light", *The Straits Times*, Singapore, 31 May 1996.

"Viets Launch Offensive Against Social Evils", *The Straits Times*, Singapore, 2 February 1996.

INFRASTRUCTURE FOR DEVELOPMENT

Chapter 7

Trading with Vietnam: Regulations, Financing and Market Development*

BY
PHAM Uyen Nguyen
YEE Jenn Jong
Adeline SUM
CHAN Yew Fook

INTRODUCTION

VIETNAM'S FOREIGN TRADE grew from a mere US$0.7 billion in 1988 to US$11.2 billion in 1995. Exports grew at an average rate of 25% yearly from 1990 to 1995 (Vietnam Central Institute of Economic Management, 1996). The *doi moi* policy of economic renovation has opened up vast opportunities for trading with Vietnam. This chapter examines the environment for trading with Vietnam and focuses on issues relating to trade regulations, trade financing and market

* *The authors wish to thank the following persons for their valuable assistance: Mr. Junichi Itoh, Managing Director, and Ms. Pham Thi Thu Hang, executive staff, Nissho Iwai, Ho Chi Minh City office; Mr. Edward Kan, Chief Representative, Intraco Hanoi office; Mr. Lim Kian Boon, Chief Representative, Intraco Ho Chi Minh City office; Mr. Goh Seow Kwang, Regional Director, Singapore Trade Development Board, Ho Chi Minh City office; Mr. Leon Khor, Centre Director, Singapore Trade Development Board, Hanoi office; Mr. Do Trung Ta, Director, Vietnam Ministry of Finance; Mdm. Pham Chi Lan, Secretary General, Vietcochamber; and Mr. Le Trung Kien, General Director, Ha Thanh Group Co. Ltd., Hanoi. The authors are also grateful for the comments and encouragement from Dr. Roger Marshall on earlier drafts of this chapter.*

development. The purpose is to provide foreign traders with a good understanding of the Vietnam market and its trading environment. Case studies of local and foreign trading houses' operations in Vietnam are provided to illustrate key issues.

HIGHLIGHTS OF VIETNAM'S FOREIGN TRADE

Trade Performance

Growth and diversification of foreign trade have been among the most notable of Vietnam's *doi moi* achievements. For years, Vietnam practised economic autarky. Production was for domestic consumption and domestic surpluses, if any, were used as exchange for goods that could not be produced locally. Severe trade deficits were recorded yearly. Before 1989 exports only accounted for between one-third and one-half of imports annually. Deficits during this period were covered mostly by grants and concessionaire credits from the former Soviet Union.

However, the collapse of the Soviet Union and the eastern bloc at the beginning of 1989 meant the gradual loss of markets from Vietnam's traditional trading partners. Simultaneously, there was a large reduction in aid to Vietnam from these countries, all of which threatened to disrupt her economy in 1990 and 1991 (World Bank, 1994). In a remarkably short time, however, the country was able to find new export markets in the region. Total exports grew rapidly and earned sufficient foreign exchange to replace the lost assistance.

There are several factors that explain this dramatic success. First, Vietnam was fortunate to have crude oil production coming on line just as the eastern bloc aid was ending. Secondly, the strengthening of property rights in agriculture and the freeing of agricultural prices contributed to the development of an exportable rice surplus. Thirdly, reforms in trade policy, in direct foreign investment regulations and in foreign exchange controls have been important ingredients for developing Vietnam's foreign trade. Large numbers of enterprises have been allowed to maintain trade relations with foreign partners. Vietnam eliminated import quotas and also began to liberalise the system of import permits and licenses. Most important, perhaps, was the unification and major devaluation of the exchange rate in 1989.

Beginning in 1989, Vietnam's exports to the region (mainly Japan, Singapore, Hong Kong, Taiwan and South Korea) and to Western Europe surged. Merchandise export earnings rose 89% in 1989 and, thereafter, grew at about 23% annually. However, as of 1995, *per capita* export is still at a low of US$60 and merchandise exports represent only about 20% of GDP. In 1995, Japan, Singapore and Hong Kong accounted for one-half of Vietnam's exports while Singapore, Japan and Korea accounted for 45.7% of Vietnam's total imports. Singapore plays a major role as a distribution centre for Vietnam. Table 7–1 provides a summary of export and import trade statistics for the period 1989 to 1995 while Table 7–2 identifies major trading partners for 1993.

TABLE 7–1
Foreign Trade Statistics

	1989	1990	1991	1992	1993	1994	1995
Exports (US$ m)	1,946	2,404	2,087	2,581	2,970	3,600	4,700
Imports (US$ m)	2,566	2,752	2,338	2,541	3,415	5,000	6,500
Balance (US$ m)	–620	–348	–251	40	–444	–1,400	–1,800
Share of Export in GDP(%)	23.2	36.0	26.5	29.9	29.5	24.9	31.9
Share of Import in GDP(%)	33.1	45.3	31.6	34.0	38.5	34.7	40.3

Source: Vietnam Central Institute of Economic Management, 1996.

TABLE 7–2
Trade with Major Partners in 1993

Country	Exports to(%)	Imports from(%)
Singapore	28	25
Japan	22	15
Hong Kong	13	10
China	6	7
South Korea	4	18
Total	73	75

Source: Fforde and Goldstone, "Vietnam to 2005, Advancing on all Fronts", 1995.

Major Trade Products

The major export items today are crude oil, textile and garments, seafood and agricultural products (mostly shrimps, rice, coffee and nuts). Compared to 1994, Vietnam's exports are now more diverse. Significant increases have been achieved in key products such as rice and coffee; Vietnam is currently the second largest coffee exporter in Asia and the eighth largest in the world (see Table 7–3).

TABLE 7–3
Major Import and Export Items for 1995

Major exports		Major imports	
Item	**Volume***	**Item**	**Volume**
Crude oil	7,600,000	Petroleum products	5,150,000
Coal	2,800,000	Cement & clinker	2,200,000
Rice	2,500,000	Fertilisers	1,300,000
Coffee beans	200,000	Steel	600,000
Dry rubber gums	110,000	Sugar	200,000
Zinc	4,600		
Textiles & garments	650**		
Aquatic products	650**		

* Volume in tonnes
** Millions of US dollars
Source: Singapore Trade Development Board, *Trends in Vietnam's External Trade*, 1996.

Vietnam can expand as a production centre because regional investors are tapping into Vietnam's educated and low cost labour market. Growth in production is mainly in the engineering, electronics, textiles and garments, and food processing sectors. The textile industry has grown phenomenally in the past few years due to increased sales to Europe. However, imports continue to outpace exports. Machinery, equipment and construction materials accounted for US$2 billion in imports in 1995. Consumer goods imports totalled nearly US$1 billion. Refined petroleum products and fertilisers are the two biggest import items by volume (see Table 7–3). However, these items are expected to decrease when Vietnam starts a second fertiliser plant, and establishes oil refineries and oil chemical industrial zones in Dung Quat in the central part of Vietnam.

Transportation System

Goods are transported to and from Vietnam mostly by ship and air. There are three international airports in Vietnam: Noi Bai Airport in Hanoi; Da Nang Airport; and Tan Son Nhat Airport in Ho Chi Minh City. Air traffic control facilities are not up to international standards, and terminal and cargo facilities require substantial upgrading.

Vietnam has seven international seaports and another five special ports catering only to oil and coal. The chief ports are Hai Phong, Ho Chi Minh City, Da Nang and Can Tho. Saigon (i.e., Ho Chi Minh City) is the main port and it has a capacity of 4.5 million tonnes per year. Hai Phong port, the second largest port, is located 70 kilometres east of Hanoi and it serves the northern region and parts of southern China. These two ports handle approximately 80% of the international traffic and container cargo (Price Waterhouse, 1995).

About 75 shipping companies ply the river and coasts. The largest three shipping companies are controlled by Vinamarine, the Union for Maritime Enterprise. There are three airports with international freight handling capacities, namely at Hanoi, Ho Chi Minh City and Da Nang. Within Vietnam, road and railway are major modes of transportation. These are both in poor condition due to the ravages of war but major investments in transportation have been targeted by the government.

Recent Trends

The government has gradually eased regulations and restrictions relating to trade. A recent decree at the end of 1995 provides for greater clarity in the state management of foreign trade which will continue to focus on export and import-substitution. The sectors that are targeted include food processing, consumer goods, fossil fuel, power, cement, fertilisers, labour-intensive manufactures and electronics.

The entry of Vietnam into ASEAN in July 95 enhances the potential for greater trade between Vietnam and ASEAN members. Vietnam will reduce tariff rates to a range between zero and 5% by the year 2006 to bring its tariffs in line with the rest of ASEAN. Vietnam is currently seeking membership in the larger APEC grouping where the market potential is even greater.

Vietnam is moving rapidly to try and catch-up with its more prosperous neighbours. Having pulled through the era of high inflation and slow growth in the late 1980s and early 1990s, Vietnam is now poised to make fast progress. Many companies are excited by the access to a population of 72 million which needs goods and services in all sectors of the economy.

TRADE REGULATIONS

Despite several rounds of reforms which have been made in the trading environment since 1986, Vietnam is still governed to a large extent by strict regulatory, licensing and documentation requirements, and by tariffs. Both local and foreign traders need to understand these regulations to ensure successful operations.

Licensing

There are three kinds of licenses for import and export trade, namely export-import licenses, quota documents and shipment export-import licenses.

(i) ***Export-import Licenses:*** Export-import licenses are relevant to both foreign-owned and Vietnamese-owned production enterprises. A license allows the company to export items produced by the enterprise and to import commodities (materials, machinery, equipment) to be used in their production regardless of economic sector, level of management and capital capacity.

Wholly Vietnamese-owned trading enterprises can be granted a business license for items that are provided in the decision of establishment of the company and in the business registration certificate, which are issued by the economic arbitration committee or the trade department under the provincial People's Committee (Singapore Trade Development Board, 1996).

An export-import license is granted by the Ministry of Trade. The criteria to be met before being granted a license are:

(a) A legal entity must be established according to law.

(b) The business must have a trade record. Before applying for license, a business must have imported or exported for five years under commissioning contracts with authorised enterprises which have licenses.

(c) The business must have qualified staff to do the export and import business.

(d) An application fee of one million dong (approximately US$91) must be paid.
(e) Working capital of US$200,000 (or US$100,000 in mountainous or difficult areas) is required.

Theoretically, wholly-owned foreign companies or joint venture enterprises can be granted a general trading license with the approval of the Prime Minister on a case-by-case basis. As of March 1996, however, no foreign companies or joint venture enterprises have been granted such a license. A foreign trading company, therefore, cannot establish trading operations in Vietnam but must rely on local counterparts to generate trading activities. This issue is discussed in greater detail below. Export-import licenses have no standard duration of validity and they allow trading in all products except for those goods which are banned and/or are subjected to restrictions.

(ii) ***Quota Document/License:*** These are documents granted by the Ministry of Trade which allows items under control (banned or restricted items) to be exported or imported. This type of license is generally applicable to commodities which have a significant impact on national planning and they are a legacy from the strict controls of a planned economy. For such goods, exports are only allowed when there is a surplus and imports are only allowed when there are shortages as identified by government planning departments and ministries.

(iii) ***Shipment Export-import Licenses (on each Shipment Basis):*** When exporting and importing each shipment, enterprises must apply for a license at the License Issuance Office of the Ministry of Trade. There are six offices in six localities, namely Hanoi, Hai Phong, Da Nang, Nha Trang, Ho Chi Minh City and Can Tho. The shipment license requirement, however, has been removed for many exports since 1 July 1994.

Import and Export Duties

Duties are charged under the *Law of Import and Export Duties*, the first tax law introduced in Vietnam in 1988. Import duties are charged for a wide variety of goods including capital and consumer goods, and on input materials used in the various stages of production. As of the first quarter of 1995, there were about 36 different rates ranging from 0 to 200% most of which are dispersed between 0 to 50%. Rates for basic chemicals and raw materials, intermediate goods and capital goods are generally taxed below 10%. Consumer goods are taxed between 10 to 45% while luxury consumer goods (for example alcohol, cars and finished motorcycles) are taxed at 60% or more (Singapore Trade Development Board, 1996).

To encourage foreign investment, a number of exemptions are given under the laws on import and export duties, foreign investment, and the decree applicable to special export processing zones (EPZ). Generally, foreign investors are exempt from paying import duties for raw materials imported for processing or for the production of exports. Foreign investors are also generally exempt from paying import duties if they are located in an EPZ.

The value of imports for taxation purposes is determined by two methods. The purchase price at the point of importation, including freight and insurance, is used unless this price does not meet certain conditions. Conditions are not met when the purchase price is low relative to the domestic market price and when goods are imported by means other than selling, purchasing or settlement through banks. If the purchase price is not used, then the minimum price is applied from a list which is compiled by the Ministry of Finance in consultation with the Ministry of Trade and the General Department of Customs (GDC) for the calculation of duty payable. This list consists of 18 major commodity groupings of 500 goods. In addition, the GDC establishes the price for an additional 1,500 types of goods. These prices are updated every three to six months and they are made available to the trade community.

In practice, the customs office compares the declared value of the imports against the minimum price list and takes the higher of the two. In cases where the commodity price is not mentioned in the list, the price that is used is settled on a "negotiation basis" between the importer and custom office. Export duties are charged for only a few items and they are basically natural resources such as rice, coffee, crude oil, minerals, forest products and scrap metal. The rates range from 0 to 40%.

Impact of Vietnam Joining ASEAN

In January 1996, Vietnam began a program of reducing tariffs and implementing ASEAN's Common External Preferential Tariffs (CEPT). Under the CEPT plan, all of the ASEAN countries have to reduce the import taxes on goods from other ASEAN nations to between 0 and 5% by the year 2003. Under a separate framework, Vietnam will achieve the target three years later in 2006. Within the next ten years, Vietnam will have to reduce tariffs on about one-half of the current 3,211 groups of import items. The other one-half are already within the 0 to 5% range.[1]

To discourage the import of high social cost products such as cigarettes, alcohol and motor vehicles, Vietnam uses a special consumption tax (an excise tax) in place of high import duties (International Monetary Fund, 1995). For example, the import tariff for new cars is 200% for completely built units (CBUs) and 60% for semi-knocked down (SKD) units with effect from 1 January 1996. But an additional special consumption tax of 100% is imposed on both CBUs and SKD units assembled in Vietnam.

Import and export duties are subject to frequent changes, sometimes as often as each quarter. Various economic and socio-political reasons underlie the frequent rate adjustments. One economic reason is to stabilise prices because of domestic shortages. For example, the import tariff for cement was reduced in November 1995. Rates for unprocessed cement and Portland cement were reduced from 10 to 5% while the rate for other types of cement, such as foam and water resistant cement, were reduced from 18 to 10%. The export tariff for rice was raised from 2 to 3% in October 1995 to slow down exports following domestic reserve shortages.

Customs

The General Department of Customs is responsible for all activities related to imports and exports, as well as immigration and emigration. It has the authority to inspect all imports and exports, including commodities, currency, postal packages and transport or shipments passing through Vietnam.

When undergoing customs procedures, an importer or exporter is responsible for completing a declaration form and submitting it to the customs office. Certain commodities require permits and/or import-export licenses. The party importing or exporting is responsible for paying any duties or fees that the customs office imposes. Once the procedures are complete, the importer or exporter receives a cus-

---

1 Interview with Mr. Do Trung Ta, Vietnam Ministry of Finance, March 1996.

toms declaration certifying that customs procedures have been completed. Tariff rates and duties are subject to frequent change so it is advisable to consult the customs service to confirm current rates and duties before importing or exporting goods.

Ventures established under the *Foreign Investment Law* are exempt from import duties on equipment, machinery, spare parts, production and business facilities, and other materials that form part of either party's contribution to the venture. They are also exempt from import duties on raw materials, spare parts, accessories and other materials imported for export production. If the imported products are sold within the country, the exemption of import duties no longer applies and goods may be subject to sales tax. The *Foreign Investment Law* does not provide specific exemptions for exports; however, at the time of applying to the Ministry of Planning and Investment (MPI) for a business or investment license, an investor can apply for favourable treatment on a case-by-case basis.

Documentation Procedures

Applications for import/export licenses must be made to the Ministry of Trade. Applications must include the identity of a purchaser and supplier, a description of the goods and their market value, and the tariff heading and number code. The General Department of Customs is responsible for the customs entry form, customs invoice and commercial invoice. The certificate of origin and the certificate of value fall under the auspices of the Vietcochamber.

The Vietnam Superintendent and Inspection Company (Vinacontrol) can provide the exporter with a quality control inspection certificate and can provide services in all export ports throughout Vietnam. Health and sanitary certificates are the responsibility of the Sanitary Bureau Office in the Ministry of Agriculture. Insurance certificates are the responsibility of Baoviet (Vietnamese Insurance Company).

To cope with bureaucratic delays, established agents or representatives are necessary to make sure that the goods get through customs and physically off the dock or out of the warehouse. The experience and strong connections possessed by the local trading companies, therefore, are very important.

Role of State-owned and Private Enterprises

As of February 1996, Vietnam had 1,250 companies licensed to conduct export and import activities. Of these, 87% are state-owned companies while the rest are limited liability companies, joint stock companies or cooperatives. Theoretically, all businesses are treated equally by the law but in practice state-owned businesses are granted more favours by government policies because they are considered to play a leading role in the economy.

The following types of state-owned companies participate in foreign trade in Vietnam at various levels.

(i) General State Trading Enterprises: These are companies that operate at the state level and deal with a variety of import/export products.
(ii) Specialised State Trading Enterprises: These are companies operating at the state level that specialise in certain products or industrial sectors, such as agricultural and food products, coal, leather, seafood, electronics and beverages.
(iii) General Provincial Enterprises: These companies operate at the provincial level and deal with a variety of import/export products.
(iv) Specialised Provincial Enterprises: These companies operate at the provincial level and deal with specialised products.

Recent Policies on Import and Export

Vietnam is in the first phase of a classic trade liberalisation program where tariffs are introduced to replace quantitative restrictions (International Monetary Fund, 1995). Import quotas have been eliminated to a large extent and there has been progress with streamlining the system of permits and licenses although these still function as obstacles to trade.

The government policy on import-export commodities is adjustable over time. This policy is managed by the Prime Minister's Office and adjustments or decisions are made annually. The decisions are based on the proposals by the Ministry of Trade (MOT), Ministry of Planning and Investment, and normally through consultation with relevant ministries such as the Ministry of Finance, Ministry of Science, Technology and Environment and the Ministry of Industry.

In 1996, for example, the Prime Minister's Decision No. 864/TTG (on "commodity policy and import-export management for the year 1996" (1995)) stipulated new adjustments to the controlled list of export-import commodities. These are summarised on the next page.

(i) ***List of Commodities Banned from Export/Import***

(a) Banned exports: weapons of all kinds; antiques; opium of many types; toxic chemicals; woods; wild animals and rare plants.

(b) Banned imports: weapons of all kinds; opium of many types; toxic chemicals; depraved and reactionary cultural works; children's toys badly affecting personal education, social order and security; cigarettes; second-hand consumer goods; right-hand drive automobiles; second-hand automobiles and motorbikes including spare parts.

(ii) ***List of Commodities Concerning the Financial Balance (Import Quotas):*** These are imported stocks of commodities in the national economy which affect national planning and the living conditions of the people. The government regulates these commodities by import quotas to ensure that the amount of supplies match domestic demand. If a surplus is recognised for any commodity during the year, then import permission for that commodity is terminated or the commodity is allowed to be exported. The commodities dealt with in the Prime Minister's 1996 decision were:

(a) Petroleum (excluding lubricant oil): The import quota is 5.4 million tonnes for 1996. The import quotas are delegated once in a fiscal year but after six months there are usually amendments.

(b) Urea Fertiliser: The import quota is 1.4 million tonnes for 1996 and applies only to government appointed enterprises that fully meet the conditions for imports and which ensure (rice) production targets for each region.

(c) Cement: The import quota is 1.4 million tonnes of black cement; other clinker and raw material imports are based on demand.

(d) Sugar: There is no fixed quota but imports are only allowed if there is a shortage and the imports do not harm domestic sugar production.

(e) Construction Steel: Quotas are flexible. Items can be imported if they are not produced domestically or there is insufficient volume to meet demand.

(iii) ***List of Commodities Under Regulations on Specialised Management:*** These are special commodities which are controlled by the relevant ministries. Any exports or imports of these specialised commodities must have double approvals from the regulatory ministries such as:

(a) Exports of mineral commodities are controlled by the Ministry of Industry.

(b) Special medicines, addiction causing materials and medical equipment must be imported under regulation of the Ministry of Health.

(c) Imports of media equipment, including telephone sets and fax machines, are controlled by the Directorate General of Post and Telecoms (DGPT).

(d) Imports of banking equipment and machinery are controlled by the State bank.

(iv) ***List of Commodities Managed by Export Quotas***

(a) Rice exporters (only 2 million tonnes can be exported in 1996) together with a list of 15 state-owned enterprises were granted quotas by the Ministry of Trade to export rice.

(b) Textiles and garments exported to the EU, Canada and Norway are governed by import quotas stipulated by the foreign governments. The Vietnamese authorities reallocate these quotas to enterprises (both local and foreign-owned) which have the production capability.

(v) ***Restrictions on Consumer Goods:*** Besides the above control list, import restrictions for consumer goods have also been put in place as follows:

(a) The use of flexible amendments involving different tax rates (these can be changed easily over time) in order to discourage imports of non-essential goods or commodities that are produced domestically and can meet consumer demand.

(b) Trading companies are allowed to import consumer goods up to 20% of their annual export turnover (for example, a firm has to generate US$100 of export turnover in order to import US$20 of consumer goods).

(c) Restrictions are applied to certain consumer goods (luxury or non-essential items) by controlling their quantity or minimum price. Setting a high minimum price deters firms from importing because the import duties are too high.

MONETARY POLICY AND TRADE FINANCING IN VIETNAM

Monetary Policy

The government is trying to control inflation in order to stabilise the exchange rate. The aim is to achieve favourable conditions for the export-import operations of enterprises. Because the country has been experiencing a trade deficit, export-oriented and import-substitution policies are being put in place.

The state encourages export-import enterprises to use foreign currencies and to keep these currencies in Vietnam. Enterprises have the right to deposit foreign currencies at commercial banks to earn interest; to sell their foreign currencies to banks; to sell foreign currencies at foreign exchange centres; or to use them in payment for imports.

Barter

One of the biggest obstacles in selling to the Vietnamese is the inability of Vietnamese companies to acquire foreign exchange to pay for imports. Given their long-standing trading relationship with the former Soviet Union, government-linked firms are traditionally more comfortable engaging in two-way barter trade. The government considers barter as one common form of practice and settlement in international trade. It is required that a barter contract shows the balance of exchange value executed through the banking system.

Types of Financing and Letter of Credit (LC)

Import and export payments through banks are mainly in the form of LCs. In conformity with the contract agreed to by a seller, a buyer normally opens a LC which is irrevocable. In some cases, a seller can request a buyer to open a revocable LC which is confirmed by a third bank. The selection of a confirming bank depends on the creditability awarded by a seller to the bank. At present, a telegraphic transfer remittance (TTR) payment method is widely used in foreign trade, especially if trade amounts are small and trust has been generated between the two parties. Use of a TTR eliminates the high cost of opening a LC account.

(i) ***Back-to-back LCs:*** A back-to-back LC is commonly used to finance orders by middleman. On receipt of the master LC, a trader opens a new LC which mirrors the first one (with some modifications perhaps on the price and delivery time) for the benefit of the factory making the products. A master LC achieves the same result as a transferable LC except that the LC buyer may not be aware that a second LC has been issued against the master LC. Also a second beneficiary (factory) cannot tender their own documents against the master LC, which thereby protects the identity of the actual manufacturer.

When documents do not conform to the credit requirements, delays become inevitable. It is important, therefore, for a middleman to inform a buyer as soon as possible if the manufacturer is unable to comply with the terms of credit so that necessary amendments to the LC can be negotiated. Back-to-back LCs can be used to purchase merchandise from third countries. The LC then should clearly state that a certificate of origin document is required. A bank commission of 0.25 to 0.5% of the credit value is usually paid by the opener of a back-to-back LC.

(ii) ***Deferred Payment LC:*** Under this arrangement, the delivery of the merchandise takes place by accepting the documents and agreeing to pay after a fixed period of time (usually 60 to 120 days after the date on the bill of lading). The issuing bank makes arrangements with the negotiating bank to carry the financing of the transaction. The supplier often discounts the LC with the negotiating bank to obtain funds in advance. On maturity, the opening bank reimburses the negotiating bank for the full face amount of the credit plus the agreed upon interest.

(iii) ***Revolving LC:*** A revolving LC is one that can be automatically restored to its original amount without requiring an amendment. Such credits can revolve in relation to time or value. A revolving credit based on time means that the amount may be automatically available to a supplier during a stipulated period of time. For example, credit may be for US$25,000 for six months (allowing for five incremental shipments). The US$25,000 covers the first shipment, with the stipulation that upon successful negotiation of the documents the credit is restored to US$25,000 for another 30 days to cover the second shipment and so forth for a total of five shipments within six months.

Revolving credit based on value means that the amount of the credit may be automatically reinstated upon utilisation within a specified period of time. The funds are restored to the original amount upon presentation of the documents by the supplier, or after receipt of the documents by the issuing bank, whichever is stipulated.

However, there is considerable risk involved with revolving LCs because not all of the terms and conditions can be stipulated precisely at the time of opening the credit, such as the exact shipping dates or value of the shipments. Consequently, revolving LCs are usually not entered into unless the parties know each other well.

(iv) ***Standby LCs:*** This is essentially a guarantee by another party (or another bank) giving the issuing bank the assurance that payment will be made for the LC to be opened. The main difference between a standby LC and a regular LC is that the former may be drawn against the execution of a simple statement by the beneficiary. There is total risk involved with a standby LC. If anything should go wrong with the shipment, then the buyer and the guarantor are liable for any advance paid to the supplier.

(v) ***Transferable LC:*** A transferable LC allows the second supplier to transfer all or part of the original LC only once to a second beneficiary. This second beneficiary cannot transfer the LC again to a third party. The second party (usually the actual manufacturer) can ship the merchandise ordered and then tender his own documents and invoice (commonly for an amount smaller than the value of the master LC to allow for commission) to receive payment. A transferable LC gives the overseas bank the right to draw documents for the second beneficiary to negotiate the LC straight away in the event that the first beneficiary (the middleman) does not produce, or is unable to produce, the required documents to negotiate the master LC.

The use of transferable LCs is quite common when purchasing goods through a buying agent. Transferability can be restricted by nominating the second beneficiary, if the actual manufacturer is known. Bank commissions and charges, which are currently about 0.25% of the credit value, are usually paid by the first beneficiary of the credit unless otherwise stipulated.

Trade Financing Problems

Foreign trade financing in Vietnam has been constrained by a weak supporting banking system. As of March 1996, Vietnam had 75 banks. Four are state commercial banks, 48 are commercial joint stock banks, four are foreign joint venture banks and 19 are foreign banks branches. Besides these, there are two joint stock financial companies and 182 people's credit funds (*Vietnam News*, March 1996).

All of the local banks, except for Vietcombank, were established quite recently. A large part of foreign trade financing is being done through the Vietcombank which was established in 1963. In the old mono-bank system, Vietcombank provided financing and operating services for many years to support all of the international trade transactions. At the beginning of 1996, the State Bank of Vietnam gave approval to 19 foreign banks to open branches in Vietnam. Since these foreign banks are also allowed to deal in foreign currency, this action should eventually result in increased, and probably better, banking services for foreign traders.

Financing imports is a major problem, however, particularly for local private businesses. Despite reforms, the banking system continues to serve largely as a vehicle for financing the state sector; bank credit to the private sector accounted for only about 20% of the total credit outstanding in 1995 (up from 6% in 1990 and 16% in 1992). The problem is exacerbated by an inefficient payment system. The present form of Vietnam's commercial banking system is very new as it was created in 1990 to replace the mono-bank system. Moreover, not all commercial banks are allowed to operate in foreign currency (in foreign trade transactions), in part because of technical capability considerations.

There are two specific problems with financing imports using the LC mechanism. First, most LCs issued by the Vietcombank and other local banks may require re-endorsement (reconfirmation, or "second bank's signature" as it is referred to in Vietnam, by a foreign bank). Secondly, to minimise their exposure to bad debts, both local and foreign banks require 50 to 100% of the LC value to be deposited in order for the LC to be issued. With the lack of international accounting and auditing standards governing local companies, most banks are unwilling to lower their deposit requirement for LCs.

Not only does the re-endorsement add to the cost of imports but, often, it is difficult to find a second (foreign) bank willing to re-endorse the LC because of historical credibility problems associated with the local bank. Vietnam's largest foreign trade bank, Vietcombank, has reported though that fewer LCs now need re-endorsement as a result of its improved credibility. Also, foreign suppliers are increasingly willing to accept LCs issued by the four state-owned banks.

LCs based on 100% deposit effectively means that imports are financed on a cash basis which clearly constrains import and trade expansion. This is a serious problem that can only be solved through the continual improvement of the local banking system and the use of transparent accounting systems.

PRACTICAL ISSUES FOR THE FOREIGN TRADING COMPANY

Establishing trade relations with Vietnam is not a smooth process, especially if the foreign company intends to establish a long-term presence in the country. Knowing the legal issues and having sufficient finances are not enough. The company must be able to understand the practical operating environment. This section highlights the important practical issues which a foreign company may face and recommends strategies for dealing with them.

The Consumer Market

Vietnam has a population of about 76 million. This is expected to grow to 85.1 million by the year 2002. With a relatively stable government, a booming economy, low inflation and a huge demand for all types of consumer and industrial goods, Vietnam can be considered a foreign trader's heaven. Only ten years ago, buying a motorcycle involved a long, frustrating paper trail of approvals and justification for the purchase. Today, one can walk into any of the hundreds of dealer shops and drive off with a new motorcycle on the same day.

The purchasing power of the Vietnamese consumer is much higher than the official statistics portray. A family earning under US$500 a month was interviewed. They had recently purchased a new motorbike, television, washing machine and a hi-fi. The money came from hoarded family wealth or from undeclared economic activities. The market taste of consumers is also becoming increasingly sophisticated. People are prepared to save for a few additional months in order to purchase an expensive high quality brand rather than opt for the cheaper alternatives. Creating brand and quality awareness is thus very important. The major consumer markets are in Ho Chi Minh City and Hanoi, where unofficial estimates of per capita income are as high as US$1,200 per annum as compared to the official estimate of US$220.[2]

The Correct Form for Foreign Trading Business: The Representative Office

Throughout the *doi moi* reform, the Vietnam government consistently maintained a foreign trade policy which did not allow foreigners to conduct trading or sales activities in Vietnam. The reasons were to control the trade industry and to prevent foreign traders from dominating the market. The government wished to give local trading firms slack in order to build up their experience first before allowing foreign competition.

To exist in the Vietnam market, foreign trading houses have only one legal method and that is to establish a representative office (RO). An RO is not allowed to generate any revenue (i.e., all transactions and contract agreements must be processed by the foreign home office abroad and not by the representative office in Vietnam). In practice, there are always risk-taking players who bend the legal system to conduct trading. These "informal" methods have become accepted as the norm in the market place. They require close co-operation with local counterparts in various configurations.

(i) ***Underground Conductor/Remote Controller:*** In this format, the foreign trader which is usually a small firm, recruits and forms a local staff, such as in sales and marketing, and locates them in local trading companies for contact purposes. These people, although officially under the local company, actually conduct trading in Vietnam under the command of the foreign trading company.

(ii) ***Shadow Company:*** In this case, foreign trading entrepreneurs and overseas Vietnamese often set up a local trading company under the names of local Vietnamese who are trusted friends or relatives.

---

2 Based on interviews with local economists in Hanoi and Ho Chi Minh City, March 1996.

(iii) ***Representative Office Plus:*** This is the most common format among large foreign trading houses. The foreign company establishes representative offices as a base and then it actively sets up trading arms with various local trading companies who have the necessary import-export licenses to conduct trading under the directions of the latter. The difference between the official RO and "RO plus" is the amount of activity that is conducted. Vietnamese regulations on foreign ROs stipulate many restrictions such as no revenue, no sales, no local nominees, no commercial contracts and no sub-leasing of office space or addresses. Generating revenue is explicitly forbidden and trading activity in any form is generally banned. Until such time as regulations on full branches for foreign trading companies are promulgated, most foreign trading ROs are left to operate in unclear waters.

The scope of a foreign trading RO's permitted activities is set out in the legislation of Vietnam's Ministry of Trade. It includes ambiguous terms such as "to speed up the formulation of projects, provide economic and technological scientific co-operation programmes in which the Vietnamese side shall be interested". However, as mentioned above, there are many representative offices which, in practice, stretch the limitations of the legislative envelope provided to them and operate outside the scope of officially permitted activities.

While the RO concept is very restrictive, it is useful because it is the only legal way for a foreigner to gain a footing in the Vietnamese market. The government is expected to liberalise its foreign trade policy further under the scheduled framework of ASEAN and AFTA. Therefore, benefits accrue to those who have a first-mover advantage. Furthermore, many experienced representatives of foreign trade offices indicate that building up competent Vietnamese local staff and establishing local networks are critical to business success. A savvy foreign RO manager, for instance, can make the difference by obtaining prompt and fairly priced utilities, supplies, and services in addition to navigating the usually cloudy waters of compliance with tax, labour and other operating regulations.

Finding Local Trading Partners

The regulatory restrictions have amplified the participating roles of local trade counterparts to foreign traders in Vietnam. These roles range from possessing trading rights (import-export licences), allocating quotas to specific commodities, and handling custom procedures and import-export duty clearances, to organising domestic distributions, gathering market intelligence and managing marketing launches. Local trading companies play the role of direct traders while foreigners play the role of indirect traders. For exports, local trading firms are suppliers and, for imports into Vietnam, they are the primary buyers and distributors. Thus, finding good and reliable local trade counterparts is of utmost importance. As an indirect trader, a foreign company has to rely on local trading companies for on-going business. In the case of consumer products, a foreign company also must co-operate with local distributors to win market share.

Although there are over 1,250 local companies with direct trading rights, very few of them are competent and have strong nation-wide distribution networks. Most of the major Vietnamese trading houses are state-owned (87% of the import-export license holders). Because these entities operate under a central planning mechanism, they tend to conduct business in an inefficient manner.

The emerging private sector has grown significantly since 1990, especially in major cities such as Ho Chi Minh City, Hanoi and Hai Phong. Many provinces, however, are still dominated by state-owned companies. In Ho Chi Minh City, there are approximately 600 new private companies established every month, more than one-half of which are involved in trade and services. In contrast, the numbers of state-owned firms are dwindling because of mergers and liquidation. Given that Vietnam's private company law was promulgated only in 1991, most local private trading firms have been in existence for less than five years and, therefore, few of them qualify for a direct import-export license. To conduct import-export trade activity, they often deal via commission contracts through state-owned trading firms that have trading licenses, and pay commission fees ranging from 1 to 3% of the invoice value. This commission-based system has resulted in some state-owned trading firms showing a very large trade turnover when, in reality, most of their transactions consist of commission contracts.

Each local state-owned or private trader has their own strengths and weaknesses. State-owned enterprises (SOEs) are larger in scale and have longer track records. They are often given more favour for bank guarantees in trade financing and foreign currency exchange. They also have the added advantage of greater access to government approvals including export-import licenses and quotas. However, SOEs are usually complacent and bureaucratic because they are conditioned to getting subsidises and privileges. Moreover, they tend to be less dynamic, less productive and have poorly motivated staff. Their top management positions are government appointed. Internal conflicts within the organisation and changes to appointments are common problems for SOEs. This makes it difficult for a foreign trader to establish a long-term partnership. Under the recent law governing SOEs, which has been enforceable since 1995, most SOEs are of limited liability status and, so, the government can no longer bail them out of bankruptcy.

Private trading firms (PTFs) are mostly new establishments that benefit from the transformation towards a market economy. Foreign traders can usually find PTFs that are bold, highly motivated and dynamic in response to market changes. PTFs tend to have strong connections with downstream distribution networks, and some PTFs also have established strong links with the government for accessing various approvals in trade operations. Many of these companies have been established by former civil servants, SOE employees or relatives of government officials. PTFs often inform their partners of problems related to their financial weakness and low priority for government support (such as quotas, trade licenses/permissions and bank guarantees).

A good partnership mode is to solicit SOEs and PTFs. An active foreign company often nominates local private firms as agents to deal with product distribution and, at the same time, they partner with a local state-owned trading firm to import products and take advantage of export-import licenses and government approvals. From a long-run perspective, PTFs are more likely to succeed given that additional market mechanisms will be established in Vietnam's economy over the next several years.

Recommended Check-List for Evaluating Local Trading Partners

It is difficult to appeal to international accounting standards and credit rating mechanisms for assessing a Vietnamese company because these frameworks are virtually non-existent in Vietnam. Therefore, in selecting local partners, foreign traders often have to rely on their business sense. A recommended check-list for evaluating local trading partners is suggested on the next page.

(i) Examine a company's track record. Evaluate the balance sheet, recent years' financial statements, its experience in trading and the trade turnover recorded (check the amount attributable to direct trade and the amount from commission contracts).
(ii) Determine whether or not the company has an import/export license or if it is trading through commission contracts with another company.
(iii) Determine if it has any links with the government.
(iv) Evaluate its export activities: A company with high export activities is more likely to have access to foreign currency to pay for its purchases.
(v) Check its accessibility to bank guarantees for trade financing and foreign currency exchange.
(vi) Determine its access to distribution networks (wholesale and retail).
(vii) Determine its ability to obtain import and export quotas.
(viii) Examine the background of the managing director/owner (for SOEs, one should also consider the likely successor). Some foreign companies have found that observing the director's personality and behaviour is necessary to ensure that the company is trustworthy.
(ix) Determine the qualifications and experience of the company's trading and marketing staff.

A visit by the foreign company is mandatory for determining the market potential and evaluating prospective partners. An investor must learn about the capabilities of the Vietnamese trading partner. Due to foreign exchange shortages, some Vietnamese companies are more familiar with counter-trade while others are able to open letters of credit. Each company varies in experience. A foreign exporter should begin with small trade amounts to test the trader and the market. Finally, it is also advisable to reconfirm the terms of trade at the time of export, such as the terms of payment, amount of down payment, and the financial ability of the local importer to pay.

Distribution and Retail System

Almost all foreign traders in Vietnam rely on multiple distributors for their products. Similarly, a local distributor rarely distributes for only one company; in fact, it is common for a distributor to sell competing products. The main reasons for this structure are that relationships between foreign and local firms are new and competition is keen; thus, both sides want to spread their risks. Local firms tend to take a short-term view and they will sell anything that can earn a profit. This tendency has become a market norm which a foreign trader simply has to accept at this time.

A foreign trader is handicapped in terms of distribution because the operation is under the umbrella of an RO which is discouraged from being involved in distribution and marketing. The government believes that these functions should be the role of the local companies. The government also does not want foreign goods to be promoted. Therefore, foreign firms can only be involved in distribution if their goods are manufactured in Vietnam. Partnering with local firms that have good distribution networks and warehouses becomes a real competitive advantage for the foreign trader. There are, however, very few local trading companies with nation-wide distribution networks. Each area is dominated by a few players who are strong only in their locality. A foreign firm must deal with several distribution firms in order to market products nation-wide.

Vietnam has few large retail outlets; traditionally, the distributor is king. However, larger retail outlets and supermarkets are now emerging in the big cities and retailers are gaining some influence at the cost of distributors. This is a good sign for international brands and for large foreign retail operators. Nevertheless, foreign retailers are reluctant to jump in because they often have to operate through a local joint venture or go through local companies to get an operation license.

A Suggested Entry Strategy for Foreign Traders

The typical entry steps followed in most countries for trading may be difficult to emulate in Vietnam. This section suggests a strategy which a new foreign trader can consider for entering the market.

(i) ***Evaluate Two Way Trading Potential:*** Given that it has the second largest population in Southeast Asia, Vietnam promises a great market potential for foreign traders in the longer term. Vietnam is evolving with its own development model which seeks to upgrade the infrastructure while selectively fostering the development of import-substitution and export-oriented manufacturing (Vietnam Communist Party, 1996). Observation suggests that sustainable trading should also include importing from Vietnam and/or investing in Vietnam rather than merely éxporting to Vietnam.

(ii) ***Select and Target the Market:*** If exporting to Vietnam is feasible, then the next step is to research the market and determine the product potential, tariff and non-tariff barriers, and the local distribution options. Currently, Vietnam's distribution networks are very limited. Since agency and distributor regulations are disadvantageous to the foreign company, ensuring market access is a challenge.

(iii) ***Learn the Technical and Financial Elements of Exporting:*** Determine the overseas shipping routes, packaging requirements and principal trade terms. Vietnam lacks foreign currency, which makes it very difficult for local firms to purchase foreign products and services.

(iv) ***Assessing Market Entry:*** The traditional options for entering the Vietnamese market exist, such as direct sales to foreign distributors or end users. However, using a foreign agent or representative and relying on an intermediary can be difficult.

(v) ***Determine Product Price and Promotion Strategy:*** To promote the product, traditional strategies such as print advertising, trade and business journals, and catalogues are inadequate. Many foreign firms have found television marketing to be cheap and effective. A company needs to be established in Vietnam in order to promote a self-image through face-to-face interaction and through trade shows and fairs.

(vi) ***Arrange Financing:*** Financing transactions can pose special challenges in Vietnam since the country has limited hard currency. The usual options such as cash in advance, open account transactions, bills of exchange and letters of credit are possible. Barter trade is also used to overcome hard currency limitations.

(vii) ***Get the Product to the Market:*** It is essential to find a trustworthy and reliable partner in Vietnam to ensure that the goods are received, customs documentation procedures are complete, and that storage and transportation are secured.

(viii) ***Modest Initial Sales:*** For a first-time exporter to Vietnam, modest initial sales is the only way to proceed since this allows an exporter to become familiar with the Vietnamese export process while simultaneously limiting the risks.

EXAMPLES OF FOREIGN AND LOCAL TRADING COMPANIES

Case A: Intraco

Intraco is a large government-linked trading company based in Singapore. Its trading activities with Vietnam were established before operations were interrupted by the country's reunification in 1975. Since 1989, it has participated actively in trade missions to Vietnam and in 1992, was among the first few Singapore companies to open a representative office in Ho Chi Minh City. Its trade volume in 1995 with Vietnam amounted to over US$20 million. Most of this was the export of commodities to Vietnam, mainly plastics and petrochemical solvents. It also exports construction materials and consumer products, and imports food products from Vietnam. A second representative office was opened in Hanoi towards the end of 1995 to cater to the increasing trade with North Vietnam (namely Hanoi and Hai Phong) and Laos. The Hanoi office brought in about US$2 million in trade orders within six months of operations.

Intraco has ventured beyond trading and into making investments in Vietnam. In 1995, it established a joint venture with Informatics, which is a publicly listed Singaporean company, to provide computer and education classes in Ho Chi Minh City. The venture is 100% foreign, with Intraco holding 70% of the equity. It also entered into a joint venture with Vietnam Railway to operate a deluxe train service between Hanoi and Hai Phong in the north. Intraco holds 70% of the equity in this venture. The Hanoi office has proven effective in establishing relationships with government officials. This office is critical since approvals for investments have to be obtained from ministries based in Hanoi.

As a trading company, Intraco does not face major trade restrictions. It deals mostly with state-owned enterprises with trading licences, such as Generalimex. The two representative offices serve to facilitate communication between local counterparts and their Singapore headquarters. All orders are made directly with Singapore. Import tariffs are still quite high but Intraco leaves it to the local trading companies to handle customs clearance and duties. Goods are quoted in CIF or FOB prices to customers for delivery at any port of the customers' choice. The local counterpart would then rely on their network to ensure fast clearance and settle import duties. Business operations have generally been smooth. There have been instances when sudden changes in laws, in tariff amounts or in the minimum price for tariff computations have caused clients to cancel orders. In several cases, shipments had to be turned back. Fortunately, such cases constitute an insignificant portion of overall business transactions.

No counter-trading has been used so far. Payments are made by LCs which are accepted by the four state-owned banks and foreign banks. In some instances, telex transfers are made in exchange for bill of lading documents. Prices are quoted in U.S. dollars. Credit is given for up to 180 days to regular customers.

Part of Intraco's success in maintaining low risk and strong orders lies in its careful selection of local counterparts that have good market share and sound financial position. It is not by accident that most of its trading partners are state-owned companies. Private companies who wish to buy from Intraco are directed to one of the state-owned trading companies. Intraco deals with these companies regularly and they act as middlemen in exchange for a modest commission. Another aspect of Intraco's success is a strong network of overseas trade offices which enables it to source timely supplies at good prices. Its long presence in the country also helps in understanding market needs and seasonal demand patterns. However, it is not necessary to provide marketing support for the local counterparts because the majority of products handled are not consumer products.

Intraco recognises that the role of middlemen traders in Vietnam may be limited to another five years after which time Vietnam will have gained the necessary expertise and network to manage trade directly. Therefore, it constantly scans the market in order to identify products that cannot be produced effectively in Vietnam. The company also engages in investment activities to capitalise on its Vietnam network and to ensure a long term viable presence in the country.

Case B: Nissho Iwai Trading House in Vietnam

Nissho Iwai began as a modest one person operation from a hotel room in 1983. Since then, it has made significant progress and turnover has grown from US$7 million in 1986 to a projected US$600 million in 1996. Its business is trade, investments and project financing which has enabled it to build up a reputation as a good long-term partner for the local companies. Its friendly image in the country's development is recognised by both local government and businessmen alike.

The initial years were difficult because Vietnam had not yet fully opened up the economy. Representatives were sent from Japan to meet with the local people and learn about the market. Trade deals were small and few. Despite the restrictions of tight state controls over foreign trade as well as many uncommon business practises in the growing economy, Nissho Iwai has emerged as a powerful trading house in Vietnam.

(i) ***Nature of Business:*** Nissho Iwai is a world-wide trading conglomerate head-quartered in Tokyo, Japan. In Vietnam, it has two official ROs; one in Ho Chi Minh City and the other in Hanoi. These two representative offices have a total local staff of 78 people and ten permanent Japanese expatriate managers that handle various trading activities in three main lines of businesses. These include trade in more than 20 items; investments in industrial zones and in 16 joint venture manufacturing projects; and financing involving syndicate loans to local trading partners. The company's turnover in 1996 is expected to be 43% higher than in 1995. Its trading arms in Vietnam accounts for over 50% of the turnover while exports from Vietnam account for 60% of total trade. The major items exported from Vietnam by Nissho Iwai are crude oil, rice, coffee, textiles and garments, sea food and sports shoes (Nike). Imports include fertilisers, sugar, construction steel, aluminium, cement, petroleum, electric generators, plastics, papers, machinery and equipment, industrial materials, industrial spare parts for the manufacture of TVs, automobiles, motorbikes and various consumer goods.

Nissho Iwai used to have trading branches in Saigon long before they were interrupted in 1975 due to the country's reunification. When the company set up operations again in Vietnam, all of its previous business connections were gone except for some memories of the company's name among the local middle-aged population. In 1983, Nissho Iwai sent a representative to Hanoi to mix with government officials, to evaluate the market, and to establish relationships with some local state-owned trading firms.

Nissho Iwai was one of the earliest foreign companies to operate in Vietnam following *doi moi*, opening the Hanoi RO in 1986 and the Ho Chi Minh City RO in 1989.

Nissho Iwai's initial aim was to exploit vast opportunities in the "honeymoon" period of the emerging economy. It has succeeded in accomplishing this goal. Nissho Iwai's turnover grew rapidly in the period from 1992 to 1996 after some initial problems were overcome (see Table 7–4). It is expecting annual turnover to exceed US$1 billion by the year 2000, with more than 70% being contributed by trading activities.

TABLE 7–4
Growth of Nissho Iwai's Vietnam Trade

Year	1992	1993	1994	1995	1996*
Turnover (US$ mil.)	180	230	360	420	600
Growth (%)	35.2	27.8	56.5	16.7	42.9

* Estimate
Source: Interview with Nissho Iwai, Ho Chi Minh City, March 1996.

(ii) ***The Business Strategy: Generalised Trading:*** "Ultimately we do trading, exports and imports, the very basic two-way exchanges between commodities and money" said Mr. Itoh, the General Director of Nissho Iwai's representative office in Ho Chi Minh City. But what really distinguishes the company according to one marketing manager, is "generalised trading; this is our corporate philosophy".

Generalised trading is the unique strategy of Japanese trading houses world-wide and, in the case of Nissho Iwai, this strategy matched very well with Vietnam's transitional economy. To establish long-term trading in Vietnam, Nissho Iwai provides various kinds of support to the local partners such as trade financing incentives (low interest rate, long-term instalment payments), overseas market arrangements, marketing support and even training. It does this because the local partners usually lack hard currency, know-how and modern equipment. Nissho Iwai's aim is to improve the partners' ability to import large quantities and to enhance the capabilities of the local suppliers to meet high quality standards in the Japanese market with reliable supplies. In the words of Mr. Itoh: "We portray ourselves as a long-term partner. We care about their growth and we expect them to do so in return. We all grow together."

Typically, Nissho Iwai begins operations by importing small amounts of items to Vietnam through a new local buyer. After sustaining a stable relationship, if Nissho Iwai wishes to sell more, then it will work with the local partner on a few issues. Usually these are products which the partner can sell to Nissho Iwai in return for exports so that the partner can generate sufficient hard currency to pay for the imports. Favourable trade financing terms and marketing support to help the new partner secure domestic market share naturally follow.

On the export side of business, Nissho Iwai first works with the local companies on products that they have ready supplied and are familiar with. Once a stable relationship is created, Nissho Iwai then transfers technology and loans for equipment purchases by the local partners so that these can be used to improve production quantity and quality. Free technical advice is provided and experts are invited from Japan at Nissho Iwai's expense to help these companies commence production.

For example, in 1990 one young owner of a private company approached Mr. Itoh and presented his plan for buying modern garment manufacturing machines from Japan. Mr. Itoh was persuaded by the young man's dynamism but doubted his ability to pay for the machines which were worth US$500,000. The young man said he would arrange for loans from his relatives but Nissho Iwai offered to obtain the financing from Japan. The machines would be paid for in five years in the form of finished products. Nissho Iwai also provided the raw materials and technical advice. In return, the local company was to give purchase priority to Nissho Iwai's. This proposition turned out to be a good arrangement because the dynamic young man was able to fulfil the strict quality requirements of the Japanese market and he now has opened three garment factories, a seafood processing plant and various other manufacturing units.

Nissho Iwai has established similar arrangements which include syndicate loans with some 50 Vietnamese companies in various manufacturing industries. Some of these are joint ventures between Nissho Iwai and the local companies mainly in the fertiliser, car, motorcycle, steel, cement and electronic goods industries. These ventures all started with the local company buying from, or selling to, Nissho Iwai first and then eventually progressing toward a solid long-term relationship.

Sometimes, however, wrong judgements were made. For example, a yen-based loan – worth US$20 million at the time the contract was made – was granted to a state-owned Food Company to purchase a rice milling machine worth US$20 million in 1988. The company is unable to pay for the machine to this day due to the appreciation of the yen and poor business management. Fortunately, the amount of bad debts each year account for less than 2% of annual turnover.

(iii) ***Relationship with the Government and Local Partners:*** Vietnam is evolving from a command economy to a market economy but much of the baggage from the command economy still remains. Nissho Iwai carefully tracks government policies and moves along with them. It recognises that the government is pursuing policies aimed at manufacturing for export, import-substitution, and encouraging imports of essential items such as technology and capital goods. Nissho Iwai therefore focuses on trading products and making investments in these categories of items. It is also constantly building up strong government links through participation in government projects such as industrial zones, cement factories, fertiliser factories, and thermo-electric power plants. As a long-term player in the market, Nissho Iwai is careful to play by the rules creatively.

Nissho Iwai judges potential local partners based on business sense. Important considerations are the attitude and behaviour of the private company's owner or the state-owned enterprise's general director. Other than looking at the past performance of the business, consideration is given to factors such as the amount of local influence, business connections, the morality of the partner, and spending habits.

The local buyers of consumer products who are partners do not have sole distribution rights from Nissho Iwai and neither does Nissho Iwai insist on the buyers distributing only its line of products. However, Nissho Iwai fixes the price of its products in a region to prevent excessive competition. For important partners, one year free training is provided to the local company to help it gain market share and the capability to support the product. Nissho Iwai employs experienced local staff to do market surveys on behalf of its local partners. When government statistics cannot be fully relied upon, Nissho Iwai conducts its own market studies.

(iv) ***Trade Finance:*** To help its local partners, Nissho Iwai often negotiates with Vietnam's state-owned banks to be given preferred rates for currency exchange. Even with this advantage, local trading firms are often required by local banks to pay between 50 to 100% deposit for LC assignments. This makes it difficult for the local firms to import from the foreign partner due to their shortage of hard currencies. In these cases, Nissho Iwai either provides or arranges for trade financing to support the local firm. Normally the local firm is given between a one to four years instalment loan and, for expensive equipment, the term can be as long as seven years. This exposes Nissho Iwai to high risks. As a result of a few bad experiences in the past, the company is now careful in arranging loans only to established customers with a good management track record and business potential.

(v) ***Outlook:*** The Vietnam market is promising for Nissho Iwai. The economy is growing rapidly with low inflation but it has become very competitive due to the growing presence of new foreign companies. Nissho Iwai expects to invest more heavily in local manufacturing rather than import from overseas, especially for consumer goods. It also anticipates high demand for industrial, technological and capital goods and is therefore gearing itself for a new phase of growth.

Case C: Ha Thanh Corporation – A Prospering Local Private Trading Firm

Ha Thanh Corporation is a 100% Vietnamese-owned private enterprise. It has four main lines of businesses: real estate and property investment, tourism, advertising and trading. The corporation's trading arm had a turnover of US$21 million for 1995. Ha Thanh is led by an enterprising 28-year old director, Kien, and supported by a 21-person team.

Ha Thanh began its trading and distribution business in 1993. In the initial start-up phase between 1993 and 1995, it traded through licensed state importers under commission contracts with commission fees of about 1% of the invoice value, as it did not yet qualify for an import and export license.

(i) ***Growing Through the Toshiba Group:*** In this start-up phase, one of Ha Thanh's key trading partners was the Japanese Toshiba group. Toshiba supplied air-conditioners and refrigerators to Ha Thanh and Toshiba extended generous credit terms of 60 days. Ha Thanh facilitated the installation of a Toshiba service centre whose costs were fully borne by Toshiba. Although profit margins were slim, Ha Thanh built its distribution network through collaboration with Toshiba. The partnership has been mutually beneficial. Kien attributed much of Ha Thanh's success in the start-up phase to the assistance provided by the Toshiba group.

In February 1995, Ha Thanh secured a three-year import and export license. This is something of a *coup* after only two years of developing a track record. Ha Thanh's business is centred in Hanoi and it is supported by a branch in Ho Chi Minh City and two shared liaison offices in Hai Phong and Da Nang.

(ii) ***Business Strategy and Operations:*** Ha Thanh's current strategy focuses on products with high profit margins. Consumer products which it distributes include refrigerators and air-conditioners of different brands, Naris and Shiseido cosmetics, and Yale locks. The key industrial product distributed is paper used for packing cement. About 65% of its turnover in 1995 came from this product which Ha Thanh imports from China and Russia. Kien hopes to ride on the construction boom in Vietnam and gain a foothold in the distribution of construction machinery and other building materials in the near future. In addition to its distribution and wholesale business, Ha Thanh also maximises the use of its import and export license by acting as a middleman for other companies without such a license. It is also involved in the re-export business; for example, it imports and then re-exports wines and timber.

Ha Thanh's main trading partners are Japan, China, Russia, United States, Singapore, Taiwan and Thailand. So far, it has not engaged in counter-trading because this is more difficult to manage. Ha Thanh has not extended its business to direct retailing. Instead, existing shops are identified which would be successful in selling the products it distributes. Ha Thanh is also responsible for facilitating all of the advertising and marketing functions for products for the trading partner's first year of operations.

The company usually uses the Bank of Foreign Trade and the Bank for Commerce and Industry for trade financing and pays an average charge of 0.2%. Ha Thanh has yet to approach any of the foreign banks in Vietnam for trade financing because their charges are higher. Additional charges (about 0.3%) from Ha Thanh are levied against trading partners if they require additional guarantees from foreign banks.

Ha Thanh conducts market research through staff resources plus information gathered from government officials in relevant agencies. On occasion field surveys are conducted to gauge responses from consumers on potential products.

(iii) ***Problems Faced:*** Ha Thanh complains of frequent changes in government policies which sometimes have a severe impact on the business. For example, the import tax for air-conditioners was suddenly increased from 30 to 40% and this reduced profit margins drastically. It was also doing well by importing instant coffee bags from Singapore until the minimum price was raised overnight from US$2.50 per kilogram to US$10 per kilogram. Thus, government policies can have an extensive impact on business. Frequent changes increase business risks and make planning and forecasting by both local and foreign businesses almost impossible.

Ha Thanh occasionally encounters problems with customs. Import and export taxes are decided by custom officers inspecting the goods. Classification of products is not done according to the 8-digit international Harmonised System but, rather, a 6-digit system is used. The customs officer has full authority to decide which classification the goods fall under and, therefore, what tax is payable. This often leads to inconsistent application of the rules and much unpredictability for Ha Thanh.

(iv) ***Finding its Partners:*** Ha Thanh selects business partners principally on trust. Kien is introduced to potential new partners mainly through the recommendations of reliable friends and business associates. For those without such a recommendation, Kien assesses whether or not he can trust the prospective partner through his intuition and gut feel. The other factors, such as the company's past track record and financial strength, are secondary considerations.

Ha Thanh prefers foreign partners who are committed to expanding the distribution network and increasing volume. This support can be in the form of sharing marketing costs or setting up technical support centres. Kien believes that this commitment is an essential ingredient for successful partnership. He looks for partners with long-term interests rather than single product deals. In line with the market norm, Ha Thanh is free to distribute competing products as well but is not given exclusive rights to any product by its suppliers.

REFERENCES

Editorial, *Vietnam News*, March 1996.

Fforde Adam and Anthony Goldstone, *Vietnam to 2005, Advancing on All Fronts*, The Economist Intelligence Unit, London, 1995.

International Monetary Fund, *Vietnam: Reforming the Tariff and Domestic Consumption Taxes*, Washington, D.C., May 1995.

Price Waterhouse, *Vietnam – A Guide for Foreign Investors*, Vietnam, 1995.

Singapore Trade Development Board, *Trends in Vietnam's External Trade*, Singapore, 1996.

Vietnam Central Institute of Economic Management, *Ten Years Economic Reform in Vietnam – Some Selected Macroeconomic Key Issues*, Hanoi, 1996.

Vietnam Communist Party, *Political Report for the 8th Party Congress* (draft in Vietnamese), Hanoi, 1996.

Vietnam Prime Minister's Decision No. 864/TTG, *Commodity Policy and Import-Export Management for the Year 1996*, Hanoi, 30 December 1995.

World Bank, *Vietnam: Transition to Market*, Country Department, Washington, D.C., 1994.

Chapter 8

Vietnam's Legal Environment for Foreign Direct Investment*

BY
CHIONH Hai Guan
LIM Kah Hock
OH Beng Soon
OW Weng Keong

INTRODUCTION

THE ECONOMIC REFORM programme in Vietnam referred to as *doi moi* is aimed at revitalising the economy and instituting an open door economic policy. Through this programme, the government encourages foreign investment and has successfully attracted billions of U.S. dollars in foreign investment via hundreds of investment projects. The lifting of the U.S. economic embargo in February 1994 eliminated a major impediment to the further development of a favourable business climate. In addition, Vietnam joined ASEAN in July 1995 and this will further boost economic development. Moreover, Vietnam ultimately hopes to become an official member of the World Trade Organisation. All of these external economic linkages should operate to boost trade and attract more foreign investments.

The amount of investment that Vietnam attracts also will be determined primarily by the quality of the investment climate. Vietnam has low cost skilled labour, abundant natural resources, a strategic location within the Pacific Rim and a large potential domestic consumer market. Although these investment attractions are important, foreign investors also need

* The authors are grateful for the guidance and assistance provided by Dr. Choo Teck Min.

stability, transparency and fairness in investment regulations. For example, complexities in the legal system can affect reliability in business transactions and increase investment risks, thereby discouraging foreign investment. However, the general need for developing a legal framework to support market development is recognised by the government.

In Vietnam, as elsewhere, the transition from a socialist planned economy to a market economy requires corresponding changes in the legal framework for business transactions. This is a difficult process for Vietnam. It has to learn the needs of foreign investors and the management elements of private enterprises. Also, the development of a legal framework for a market economy has to be integrated with the socio-economic development of the country and, yet, be able to preserve the values of socialism.

There is now a legal framework for foreign investors to confidently operate in Vietnam. Within the past few years especially, a multitude of legal developments have been implemented in this respect. This chapter examines the current legal system and the various foreign investment methods governed by the *Law on Foreign Investment*. It also focuses on some recent changes in the legal environment which affect foreign investors. Clearly, it is in the interest of foreign investors to understand the effectiveness of law enforcement and the settlement of business disputes in Vietnam. The objective, therefore, is to provide a general overview of the legal environment for foreign investment in Vietnam and, more significantly, examine the changes which Vietnam has made to the legal environment in an earnest attempt to compete for foreign investments.

BACKGROUND

General Legal Framework

Vietnam used the French legal system during the French colonial period. The colonial legal system was abolished and replaced by a Soviet style communist legal system after the communists took over. With the *doi moi* programme, Vietnam modelled itself after the Chinese example, developing its own laws to stimulate the market economy while at the same time maintaining the power of the Communist Party. Vietnam also has a civil law system.

The highest law of the Socialist Republic of Vietnam is the 1992 Constitution. The highest policy-making body is the Politburo of the Communist Party. The National Assembly is the highest legislative body. Its Council of State may enact ordinances when the Assembly is not in session. Executive authority is vested in the government, which also issues ministerial decrees. The National Assembly is charged with enacting laws and ordinances, is elected for a five year term and meets twice a year.

The standing committee of the National Assembly supervises the implementation of the decisions and enactments of the National Assembly. The former enacts ordinances and translates ordinances into "decree" laws. Issuance of legal instruments such as decrees, circulars and instructions is done by the government. The Ministry of Justice coordinates the preparation of legal instruments such as laws, ordinances, decrees and ministerial circulars. The judicial system comprised the supreme people's court, the local people's court and military tribunals. The State Economic Arbitration is the agency for registration of enterprises and companies. The Supreme People's Procuratorate is empowered to supervise the implementation of the law and initiate public prosecutions where necessary (Lovell, 1995).

Vietnam has developed the basic outline of a legal system sufficient to give a degree of confidence to foreigners who are contemplating investment in the Vietnamese market. Foreign investment laws have been introduced which allow for business co-operation contracts, equity joint ventures, wholly foreign-owned enterprises and the establishment of representative offices. Laws have been enacted governing intellectual property, tax, foreign exchange, securities, arbitration, labour, construction, environmental protection, a system of land use rights and land registration, banking, insurance, bankruptcy, civil and commercial law, and the regulation of foreign lawyers. The Vietnamese government has emphasised the need for further development of the legal system as an essential element of the *doi moi* programme.

Similiar to many developing communist countries, the legal infrastructure is incomplete, it is evolving rapidly. Nevertheless, it is often difficult to predict how government bureaucrats or judges interpret and apply these new and untested laws. It thus requires patience and negotiation in order to navigate successfully through the regulatory framework. Government officials have shown an openness and willingness to try and accommodate the needs and expectations of foreign businesses.

The *Foreign Investment Law*

Drawing on the experience of other developing countries, the Vietnamese government has created an environment relying primarily on investment licensing, foreign exchange and import/export controls, tax incentives and restrictions on land ownership to maximise the benefits the country receives from foreign investment.

The *Foreign Investment Law* provides the basic framework for all foreign business activity. This law has been supplemented by detailed provisions for its implementation in a document called "implementing regulations".

As a general rule, foreign investors may invest in any area of the economy except those relating to national security and defence. However, investment is particularly encouraged by tax incentives in those areas that will help the economy to grow the most or earn foreign exchange.

Ministry of Planning and Investment

Due to increasing foreign investment, the government is trying to speed up the flow of foreign investment by reducing the application period. The Ministry of Planning and Investment (MPI) was formed by merging the State Planning Committee and the State Committee for Co-operation and Investment, to provide a "one-stop shop" for foreign investors (Pham, 1996). The MPI is entrusted with socio-economic master planning, management of domestic and foreign investments and drafting laws, ordinances and other legal documents relating to economic management (*Vietnam Investment Review*, November 1995a).

The MPI has been given responsibility for maintaining consistency in the application of laws affecting foreign investors by "giving guidance" to ensure that local governments and local organisations observe national decisions and policies. It is also responsible for controlling outgoing investment by Vietnamese enterprises and has been given a role in the approval process for foreign aid and loans. Lastly, the MPI has been given authority to control organisations offering investment services. The latter power addresses the MPI's concerns regarding the number of local and foreign firms offering unregulated consultancy services (*Vietnam Investment Review*, November 1995b).

In addition to performing its main function of considering and approving projects, the MPI aims to be as helpful as possible in guiding investors through the regulations. It has become easier in the past few years to negotiate joint ventures and to run them efficiently. However, a backlog of applications has developed for the establishment of foreign investment enterprises or representative offices.

Lawyers in Vietnam

There are few Vietnamese lawyers in private practice. In comparison to the west, the number of lawyers authorised to practice commercial law is very limited. Generally, lawyers who were trained in the south before unification, left the country although some lawyers (and other professionals) are now returning in small numbers. Most of these lawyers were trained in French law in the French language. As a result, their knowledge of the new system is sparse.

All international law firms are subjected to Vietnamese restrictions on the practice of Vietnamese law by foreign lawyers. The Ministry of Justice has recently promulgated a regulation which allows foreign lawyers to establish offices by themselves. Foreign lawyers, however, continue to be prohibited from practising Vietnamese law.

Supporting Laws

The business related laws in Vietnam cover general commercial laws, immigration and visas, taxation, business income tax, witholding tax, personal income tax, foreign exchange controls, import and export controls, export processing zones, industrial zones, employment, intellectual property, patents and trade marks, copyright, enforcement, technology transfer and licensing contracts, infrastructure and BOT projects, energy, environmental protection, bankruptcy, banking and insurance. To protect their interests, investors must be cognisant of the appropriate laws.

APPLICATION PROCEDURES FOR FOREIGN DIRECT INVESTMENT

Choice of Investment Form

The establishment of foreign businesses in Vietnam can arise in any of the following four ways:

(i) contractual business co-operation;
(ii) joint venture;
(iii) wholly foreign-owned enterprise; and
(iv) representative office.

The first three types of investment may also be used to establish a build-operate-transfer (BOT) contract. This type of contract was introduced in the *Law on Foreign Investment.*

A BOT contract is an agreement signed between a foreign organisation, or individual investors, and an authorised state agency in Vietnam for infrastructural projects such as roads, bridges, airports, ports and power stations. The foreign organisation or individual, upon completion of the project, manages and exploits the project for a certain period of time in order to recover invested capital and some economic rent. Upon expiry of the agreed period, the foreign organisation or individual then transfers the project to the government without any further compensation.

BOT contracts may be carried out with either 100% foreign capital or in combination with capital contributed by the government and/or Vietnamese organisations or individuals. All foreign investments under the law are required to be approved by the MPI. It is charged with the overall responsibility for matters relating to the investment of foreign organisations and individuals in Vietnam. A joint venture with a local company is the option often recommended for foreign investors. The Chamber of Commerce can assist in putting foreigners in touch with the relevant ministries and people's committees.

Documentation and Approval Procedures

With negotiations successfully concluded, the Vietnamese party together with the foreign party, or in the case of a wholly foreign-owned enterprise, the foreign party itself, prepare the project documentation to be submitted to the MPI. For a joint venture enterprise, this includes:

(i) an application form (including, if applicable, a petition for preferential treatment in relation to taxation, foreign currency balancing, profit calculation and other matters within the discretion of the MPI);

(ii) a joint venture contract;
(iii) a joint venture charter;
(iv) a feasibility study;
(v) evidence of incorporation of the foreign entity;
(vi) an opinion from the investment sponsoring agency; and
(vii) an opinion from the local people's committee concerning the level of land rents.

The opinion from the Vietnamese sponsoring agency provides confirmation of compliance with its policy, determination of the value of the contribution by the Vietnamese parties, and approval of the economic and technical studies relating to the project.

Foreign investments are divided into two categories. Category A investments are classified as: a) those projects involving large scale infrastructure; b) those with an investment of over US$40 million; and c) those which are deemed to be of national importance. Category B investments are all other forms of foreign investment not falling within category A. Examples of category A projects include the following:

(i) projects involving infrastructure, construction for industrial parks, export processing zones and BOT projects;
(ii) projects with investment capital of US$40 million or more in electricity, mining, oil and gas, metallurgy, cement, chemicals, engineering, electronics, sea ports, airports, telecommunications, trade centres, cultural and tourist centres, and real estate business;
(iii) projects involving culture, press and publishing;
(iv) projects involving national defence and security; and
(v) projects using five or more hectares of urban land, or 50 or more hectares of other land.

Within 20 days from the date of receipt of the project documents (category A and B projects), the ministries must forward their opinions in writing to the MPI. If after such time, no opinion is expressed in writing, then all aspects of the projects are deemed to be approved.

The relevant city or provincial People's Committee must submit the written opinion within 45 days from the date of receipt of any project documents to the MPI regarding the following matters:

(i) the legal status of foreign and Vietnamese investors;

(ii) conformity of the objectives of the project and locations of implementation of the project with the socio-economic development plans and strategies of the localities affected;
(iii) land use rights of the Vietnamese parties, use of the land area of the project, land rent rates and compensation plans for site clearance; and
(iv) the value of property (if any) contributed by the Vietnamese party as capital.

If the People's Committee has not expressed its opinion in writing prior to the stated time limit, then the project is deemed to be approved.

Projects submitted through the MPI and classified as category A have to be submitted to the Prime Minister for consideration and approval. The MPI and any other ministries involved must submit proposals to the Prime Minister within 50 days. Where queries raised by the Prime Minister's office are not answered within a specified time allocation, the project is deemed acceptable to the particular ministries concerned. The applicant must be notified of any request for further information or documentation, or any proposed amendment to the project documentation within one month from the date of receipt of the application. Where the applicant does not respond in writing within 45 days of receipt of a request from the MPI, the application is deemed to have been withdrawn.

If the application is approved, the MPI issues an investment license to the applicant. In the case of category A applications, the applicant must be notified within seven days of the decision of the Prime Minister by the MPI. For projects falling into category B, investors must be notified of the decision within 45 days after the project document is submitted to the MPI (*Vietnam Economic Times*, March 1995).

Overseas Vietnamese Investors

The *Foreign Investment Law* implementing regulations make provisions for special treatment to be accorded to overseas Vietnamese. This treatment, which is set out in separate regulations, includes provisions allowing overseas Vietnamese to:

(i) be treated as a "local" partner in foreign investment projects on the condition that they contribute at least 50% of the total investment;

(ii) obtain lengthy tax holidays for their investments;

(iii) obtain a reduction in the rate of withholding tax to 5%;

(iv) obtain a reduction in the rate of profit tax of 20% in the majority of cases;

(v) obtain a rate of 5% for profit transfer tax; and

(vi) have the power to delegate authority as a member of the board of a joint venture to relatives and friends in Vietnam.

DYNAMIC CHANGES IN THE LEGAL SYSTEM FOR FOREIGN INVESTMENT

Necessity for Change

Many foreign investors are concerned about the constantly changing legal environment in Vietnam. Every year there are new guidelines, amendments, supplements and replacements of existing laws, and new laws are enacted to regulate and implement new policy or enhance management of the economic reforms. Sometimes the various legal documents may overlap and mutually annul other existing legal documents (*Vietnam Economic Times*, February 1996). The problem in interpreting the legal requirements for investment is further aggravated by ambiguity and a lack of details in the law. Investors ideally hope for stability and transparency in the investment regulations. However, it is necessary to understand why these changes in the legal environment are occurring, and the long-term goal of these changes.

First, it should be realised that the legislative reform programme in Vietnam only began less than ten years ago. Thus, frequent changes are part of Vietnam's consistent efforts to develop a legal system suitable for international business transactions. Amendments, supplements, replacement of existing laws, and new laws are generated from the process of implementing existing laws and the need to address many legislative issues required in a market economy. Due to the time lapse between promulgations of various laws which cover different areas of the social and economic needs of the country, legal gaps and mutual annulments of certain sections in the laws arise. Also, legal gaps and inefficiencies only become evident after the new laws are promulgated and implementation problems arise. Vietnam is aware of these legal deficiencies and, therefore, is making efforts to fill the legal gaps and clarify ambiguities. Thus, these changes are simply part of the evolutionary process of developing a new legal system.

Secondly, as Vietnam changes from a command economy to a free-market economy, the development of society has to change from one of bureaucratic management to one which manages by the rule of law. The latter is advanced not only to ensure a market-oriented legal framework but, also, to preserve the values of socialism, and harness the benefits of capitalism and foreign investments without selling out Vietnam to foreign interests (Dirksen, 1993). This gives rise to some legislative changes which encourage foreign investments and, also, some which seem to interfere with the conduct of business relating to foreign investment and which seem to protect the interests of Vietnam and the Vietnamese partner. Guidelines are promptly issued to rectify any developments which are perceived as social ills and that are not compatible with Vietnam's national interests and long term goals.

Finally, the Vietnamese laws are often criticised for being ambiguous and lacking in detail. This is due to the many legislative drafters and the lack of experience in legal drafting (*Vietnam Investment Review*, February 1996). Each ministry and government authority drafts its own legal instruments to implement the law, ordinances and decrees. The difficulty in interpretation and implementation of these laws is further compounded by shortcomings in the administrative apparatus. In the process of economic reform, the government is aware of the shortcomings in the operations of the administrative apparatus. Reform of the administrative institutions which enforce legislation and draft regulations speeds up the process of economic reform.

The government has embarked on administrative reforms to streamline the administrative apparatus, clarify the central-to-local relations, define the functions, authorities and organisational structure at various levels and improve co-ordination between the legislature, the government and the various People's Committees in drafting legislation (*Vietnam Investment Review*, February 1996). This could reduce the bureaucratic red tape and create a more efficient business environment for foreign investment. But again, this requires further changes in the legal system to support the administrative reform. All this will inevitably affect investment regulations and the conduct of business.

There is now a legal framework in Vietnam within which foreign investment can operate. It is necessary, however, for investors to know the changes in the *Law on Foreign Investment* and recent legal developments in other areas which also affect the business environment. There is still an ongoing change process, which is necessary to keep up with the rapid economic expansion, social framework and administrative reform in Vietnam.

Changes in the *Law on Foreign Investment*

The *Law on Foreign Investment* in Vietnam was approved by the National Assembly on 29 December 1987. This law provides the framework for legal agreements for the establishment and operation of foreign investment enterprises in Vietnam. The law encourages foreign investment in areas of export-oriented production, labour-intensive industries using domestic raw materials, infrastructure projects and foreign exchange earning services. From the time of its promulgation to the present, the Vietnamese government has made amendments and additions to the law in order to keep up with the country's economic reforms and growth.

In December 1992, amendments to the *Law on Foreign Investment* provided several important changes to the already existing methods of foreign investment, namely the business co-operation contract, the joint venture enterprise and the 100% foreign-owned enterprise. The additions allow for two new methods of foreign investment: the export processing enterprise and the build-operate-transfer contract (Dirksen, 1993). Amendments were made to extend the maximum duration of joint venture and 100% foreign-owned enterprises from 20 years to 50 years, with the possibility of government approval for a duration of up to 70 years. External financing for joint venture enterprises and 100% foreign-owned enterprises was also made easier by an amendment which allows these enterprises to obtain state bank approval to open loan accounts with overseas banks. In the past, preferential tax treatment was available only to joint venture enterprises but this advantageous treatment has now been extended to 100% foreign-owned enterprises (Dirksen, 1993). These amendments were made to streamline the requirements of various investment methods and to make the law more amenable to foreign investments.

Several of the 1992 amendments to the *Law on Foreign Investment* were also directed at Vietnamese partners in projects with foreign investors. The amendment allows private unincorporated Vietnamese companies to join in business co-operation contracts and joint venture enterprises. Thus, foreign investors have a much larger pool of potential Vietnamese partners from which to choose. To enhance the government's efforts to promote parity between the Vietnamese and foreign parties in the equity and control of joint venture enterprises in important economic sectors, amendments were made to allow a gradual increase in the proportion of the Vietnamese party's contribution to the prescribed capital of the joint venture enterprise. Another amendment mandates that Vietnamese business enterprises are permitted to purchase part by part, based on agreement with the foreign owners, the capital of 100% foreign-owned enterprises in important economic sectors (Dirksen, 1993). These changes represent an attempt to enable Vietnamese to share in the benefits of capitalism and foreign investment. The fundamental objective of both the law and the reforms is to improve the standard of living of the nation.

More recent changes to the *Law on Foreign Investment* include decree #191/CP dated 28 December 1994, which details the formulation, evaluation, and implementation of foreign direct investment projects. It categorises the investment projects, streamlines the approval process and establishes guidelines for the valuation of foreign investment projects. These procedures are meant to improve the rate of approval for foreign investments which were deemed to have been held back due to slow processing by the administration.

On 8 February 1995, circular #215 from the then SCCI was issued to provide guidelines for foreign direct investment activities. It replaced 19 previous circulars, decisions and official letters on this subject, thus streamlining this area of the law into one legal instrument. It sets out the procedures to be followed by a foreign investor after their investment licence is granted by MPI and the time limits within which they must attend to those procedures. The circular also regulates many other procedures and transactions associated with business operations, such as the establishment and conduct of management board meetings, the functions of the directors of an enterprise, management companies engaged by the enterprise and various financial issues such as applications to increase the capital of an enterprise (*Vietnam Economic Times*, December 1995). These changes are to clear up inconsistencies in previous decrees and circulars on the implementation of the *Law on Foreign Investment* and to incorporate related requirements by other new laws in the legal system. The state has issued other new laws, such as the *Labour Code, Land Law, Domestic Investment Promotion Law, State-owned Business Law, Bank-*

ruptcy Law, *Law on Taxation* and the *Civil Code* (*Vietnam Economic Times*, November 1995).

A draft of the amended *Law on Foreign Investment* will be submitted to the National Assembly in October 1996. It will have amendments that focus on new policies and measures to attract foreign capital, with a view to perfecting the legal foundation and the investment environment (*Vietnam Economic Times*, November 1995). Amendments to the *Law on Foreign Investment* have been an ongoing process ever since its establishment in 1987 and investors can expect to see more changes developing.

Other Recent Legal Developments

Outside of the amendments and additions to the *Law on Foreign Investment*, other significant legal developments are occurring in Vietnam which are also highly relevant to the foreign investor. In 1994, there were 25 to 30 major pieces of legislation. However in 1995, the figure exceeded 50 pieces of legislation (*Vietnam Investment Review*, February 1996). Many of the changes in 1995 are decrees, regulations and circulars implementing laws and ordinances issued in 1994 or earlier.

The most significant legal development in 1995 is the *Civil Code*, passed by the National Assembly in October 1995. Moreover, the government has passed laws in almost every field including advertising, leasing and hire purchasing, insurance, domestic investment, foreign law firms, bankruptcy and the environment (*Vietnam Economic Times*, December 1995). The following sections focus on some recent major changes in Vietnam's legal environment which are important for foreign investors.

Land Law

This is one of the most controversial regulations, enacted in early 1995, which generated major concerns among investors, financial institutions and Vietnamese land-holders. With respect to the *Land Law* dated 14 July 1993, which stipulates that all individuals and organisations allocated land would be required to pay rent unless the land was used for exempted purposes, several decrees were issued to implement this law. These often cause confusion about the use of the land title as capital for joint ventures and collateral for loans (*Vietnam Economic Times*, December 1995).

Decree #11/CP, dated 24 January 1995, details the eligibility to lease land in Vietnam and the basis on which it can be leased, including prescriptions on the main contents of a lease contract. The Vietnamese party who has contributed the value of the right to use leased land to the capital of a joint venture is the lessee. The land use right certificate, however, is issued in the name of the joint venture instead of issuing it to the Vietnamese party who is the lessee. The concern is that the Vietnamese party as lessee, and not the holder of the land use right, could mortgage the right to use the land upon which the foreign investment project was being developed.

Decree #18/CP, dated 13 February 1995, details the rights and obligations of state and non-state organisations to which the state allocates or leases land. It caused a stir particularly among the Vietnamese land-holders, by stipulating that enterprises which use land for business and production purposes must convert to leasing land from the state. The effect of the decree is to provide a mechanism to calculate the value of the land use right for the purpose of security for lending and contributions to joint ventures. The decree is also aimed at preventing state companies with valuable land use rights in prime commercial areas from profiting by selling or leasing the land (*Vietnam Economic Times*, December 1995).

Decree #56/CP, dated 18 September 1995, regulates the leasing of houses to foreigners. The controversy here is the potential to severely restrict the market for houses available to be leased to foreigners (*Vietnam Economic Times*, December 1995). The government will eventually specify clearer guidelines to clarify these ambiguities, but then business operations will be impeded until such uncertainties are resolved.

The *Civil Code*

In November 1995, the National Assembly approved a civil code which spells out the rights and responsibilities, including issues of inheritance, associated with contract and property ownership. It also addresses such foreign investment concerns as technology transfer, compensation, land use and intellectual property. Chapter 7 of the *Civil Code* deals with foreign individuals and business entities and outlines broad principles which provide a legal base for the fundamentals of a market economy (Phong, 1995). Like the 1992 Constitution, the *Civil Code* reiterates Vietnam's commitment to the rule of law, thus enhancing the legal framework within which foreign investors can operate with confidence.

Other Changes

In 1995, there were other major changes in regulations on arbitration, taxation and law firms. Changes in the regulation on law firms are discussed in the following section on law enforcement issues; and improvement in arbitration channels is discussed in the section on settlement of disputes.

Along with these major changes, there are other rules and decisions issued by the government which should be observed by foreign investors. There are new and revived regulations on approvals for press conferences by companies, increased share proportions of Vietnamese partners in joint venture hotel building projects, and restrictions on multiple bank accounts for foreign invested capital.

There have been constant changes to the *Law on Foreign Investment* and the legal environment. Although these have caused some inconvenience for foreign investors, it is an evolutionary process that Vietnam must go through to achieve a modern legal system conducive to a free market economy. The transition to rule by law will gain efficiency with further administrative reforms, amendments to the legal system clarifying ambiguous laws and more effective enforcement. For sure, there will be more changes in the legal environment as Vietnam continues to plug the loopholes in its legal system.

LAW ENFORCEMENT ISSUES

Judicial System

In addition to the National Assembly and the Standing Committee of the National Assembly, the Ministry of Justice and other ministries are responsible for the preparation of legislative and governmental acts. The State Economic Arbitration arbitrates economic contract disputes and the Procuratorate supervises the implementation of laws.

Ministry of Justice

The Ministry of Justice is the key ministry for making and implementing laws. The main responsibilities of the Ministry of Justice include co-ordination of the preparation of all legal instruments, which include laws, ordinances, decrees and ministerial circulars (Lichtenstein, 1993). The Ministry of Justice is also expected to take an increasing role in the drafting and reviewing legal instruments to support the market economy. It also handles functions relating to the administration of justice (including the courts) as well as training, research and legal education.

Law Enforcement Mechanisms

Given the legal environment currently in Vietnam, there are three main avenues for law enforcement. These are the court system, administrative orders and arbitration orders. The first two are described below while the latter is discussed in a subsequent section on the settlement of disputes.

(i) ***Courts:*** Under the 1992 constitution, and similarly under the preceding 1980 constitution, Vietnam's judicial system is comprised of the supreme people's court, the local people's courts and military tribunals. Courts are required under the constitution to hold public hearings. Lay assessors and judges participate in trials on an equal footing and with equal independence. The constitution also permits the organisation of lawyers' associations to assist defendants and other partners in a case.

Criminal and civil laws are enforced by the judiciary system. Criminal violations involving economic matters are punished through the judicial system, including early action by the economic division of the police. Civil disputes under economic contracts, which include liquidation, company law and private business transactions, are required to be resolved through arbitration.

(ii) ***Administrative Orders:*** As in other legal systems, various Vietnamese laws also provide for the implementing agency to take administrative actions to ensure their enforcement. For example, the state bank has the right to impose penalties for non-compliance on credit institutions under the *Commercial Banking Ordinance* while the *Economic Arbitration Ordinance* can order payment on an award.

To improve on the effectiveness of government administration, the National Assembly passed a government proposal to streamline the administration by merging eight ministries and state committees into three new organisations and reshuffling some members of the Cabinet. These changes have removed a good deal of paperwork and red tape but the implementation of new procedures as described by the government is slow and sometimes it is not taken very seriously.

For example, the National Assembly passed a resolution calling for the establishment of a labour and administrative court. But according to a source close to the law-making body, these new courts will take some time to become functional because the judges have to be trained. To improve the legal environment, the central government has drafted a series of new laws, such as the *Civil Code*, the *State Budget Law* and others. As mentioned by Vice Premier Nguyen Khanh (1995), despite some progress, the building of a new legal institution is lagging behind the renewal process. The law is not seriously observed at all times and violations are occasionally not being detected, judged or punished.

Law Firms and Regulations on Foreign Law Firms

The decree governing the status of foreign lawyers in Vietnam was passed in July 1995 (*Vietnam Economic Times*, August 1995). The main elements of the decree are as follows:

(i) Foreign firms must apply to open up branches in Vietnam and they are allowed a maximum of two branches;
(ii) A branch licence lasts for five years and it may be extended more than once for a maximum of three years each time;
(iii) Companies wishing to employ lawyers in Vietnam should appoint people with a minimum of five years of experience;
(iv) Foreign lawyers will be allowed to provide "legal consultancy services" with regard to foreign and international laws but they are not allowed to provide such services concerning Vietnamese laws. However, they may enter into partnerships with Vietnamese legal consultancies;
(v) They are not allowed to represent clients in Vietnamese courts;
(vi) Payment for services rendered in Vietnam by foreign law firms must be made to an account opened in a Vietnamese bank;
(vii) Foreign law firms are not allowed to hire Vietnamese lawyers but, instead, can accept Vietnamese interns with law degrees (though they are not actually qualified as lawyers). However, on becoming

lawyers, these interns automatically become ineligible to work for the foreign firms that have trained them.

In November 1995, the government ordered tighter controls on legal consultancies by temporarily suspending legal consultation or any legal advisory organisations until the government reviews the organisation and operations of all law firms (*Vietnam Economic Times*, November 1995). The decree says that foreign firms cannot advise on Vietnamese law or hire Vietnamese lawyers as staff. If a client requests advice on Vietnamese law, then the foreign branch must sign a contract with a Vietnamese legal consulting organisation in which a Vietnamese solicitor will provide advice. Essentially, this move by the Ministry of Justice is an attempt to build up strong local law practices similar to neighbouring Asian countries, such as Malaysia, Indonesia and Singapore, where foreigners are not permitted to practice local law. But in these countries there are relatively strong and experienced local law firms which can advise multinational companies and collaborate effectively with international law firms. However, in Vietnam, most of the local law firms are neither particularly well known nor do they have significant international experience (*Vietnam Economic Times*, October 1995).

The spirit of the provision in this decree is to create favourable conditions for domestic lawyers to develop (*Vietnam Economic Times*, May 1995). Although these decisions affect mainly legal circles, they have repercussions on the execution of foreign investment involving huge capital amounts which require very comprehensive legal agreements.

Shortage of Judges

For a long time, legal training in Vietnam has been neglected. The first law faculty in Hanoi was established in 1975. Only one in 10,000 people is qualified with a Bachelor of Law. The Vietnamese President nominated 706 individuals to be judges in 53 tribunals at the provincial and city levels, and 43 as judges in military tribunals. This leaves 412 judges still to be found for provincial tribunals and 29 judges for military tribunals. Clearly, this shows that more qualified judges are needed for the effective enforcement of the law in Vietnam.

SETTLEMENT OF DISPUTES

The Vietnamese have an antipathy towards legal proceedings as do many other Asians. When economic disputes arise, they usually turn to mutual consultation and negotiation. Article 25 of the *Law on Foreign Investment* states that such disputes should first be settled amicably either through negotiation or mutual consultation. If the disputes still cannot be settled then there are two other ways in which to resolve a business dispute; one is by means of judicial proceedings and the other is by arbitration chosen and agreed upon between the parties.

Judicial proceedings can be entered through the economic courts. The standing committee of the National Assembly issued the *Ordinance on the Procedure for Handling Economic Lawsuits* on 16 March 1994. This document sets out guidelines for the conduct of economic disputes in the economic court. The economic court is part of the supreme people's court at the central level and the people's courts at the local level. Economic courts were established by the National Assembly in December 1993 to provide a more specialised forum for resolving disputes and to handle resolution of bankruptcy proceedings with effect from 1 July 1994 (Lichtenstein, 1993). Any disputes have to be brought to the economic courts within a period of six months from the occurrence of the dispute. Failure to do so means the right to legal recourse lapses. Prior to this ordinance, economic disputes involving state enterprises and companies were handled by the State Economic Arbitration Council (SEAC), a state body with ministerial status. SEAC was set up in the early 1960s but was phased out with the establishment of the economic courts.

Economic courts at the district level attend to economic disputes involving less than U.S. $4,600 (Constitution of the Socialist Republic of Vietnam, 1992a). The court proceedings and hearing are held in the defendant's district, that is, the district where he lives or conducts his business (Constitution of the Socialist Republic of Vietnam, 1992b). For contracts involving real estate, the court conducts the hearing in the court where the property is located. Cases involving foreign parties are only heard by higher level economic courts at the provincial level.

Weakness of Economic Courts

One of the disadvantages associated with settlement through the economic courts is that most of the judges do not have sufficient experience in handling cases involving trade disputes especially in speciality areas like shipping, construction laws or indeed any matter outside of domestic laws (*The Vietnam Business Journal*, December 1995). The other disadvantage is that the economic courts do not refer to decisions reached in precedent cases in reaching a judgment. Furthermore, very little information on the outcome of court cases is published as there is no system for reporting the cases. Therefore it is very difficult to make comparisons and different decisions can be reached for similar cases by different judges (Freshfields, 1995).

Arbitration

The other alternative for the resolution of disputes is arbitration. This can be done through the Vietnam International Arbitration Center (VIAC). The VIAC was established in April 1993 as part of the Vietnam Chamber of Commerce and Industry (VCCI), a non-governmental organisation. The predecessor of VIAC are two other arbitration bodies, the Foreign Trade Arbitration Committee (FTAC) and the Maritime Arbitration Committee (MAC). Both of these bodies are also under the jurisdiction of the VCCI. They were set up in the early 1960s to handle arbitration of foreign trade and maritime disputes.

Arbitration can also be done through the Economic Arbitration Centres (EAC) which are set up under the jurisdiction of the Ministry of Justice, the People's Committees and the Justice Departments at both the provincial and city level. The EAC is a body established by decree #116/CP on 5 September 1994. For jurisdiction to lie with an EAC, both parties to the economic contract must agree in writing and all proceedings are in Vietnamese.

Advantages and disadvantages

One advantage to using the VIAC for the foreign investor is that its award is more likely to be enforced. On the other hand, foreign investors can only choose from the VIAC approved list of Vietnamese arbitrators. The hearing is conducted in Vietnamese. Moreover, given the current legal situation in Vietnam, it may not be easy to find arbitrators on the list with certain specific technical skills (Freshfields, 1995).

Arbitration awards are made by a majority vote. The winning party can take the dispute to the people's economic court if the other party does not implement the decision reached in the arbitration process.

Recognition and Enforcement of Foreign Arbitral Awards

Foreign investors viewed positively the enactment of *Ordinance #42-L/CTN*, on *Recognition and Enforcement of Foreign Arbitral Awards* in Vietnam on 14 September 1995. This Ordinance became effective on 1 January 1996 and provides the legal basis for the enforcement of foreign arbitral awards making foreign arbitration more viable.

With the enactment of this Ordinance, which is in agreement with the 1958 *New York Convention*, Vietnamese courts are empowered to examine and allow the implementation of awards of foreign arbitrators from countries with which Vietnam has signed international conventions or on the basis of reciprocal interest. This creates the legal framework for protecting the interests of both Vietnamese and foreign investors and businesses. At the same time, it ensures the recognition of Vietnamese arbitral awards abroad.

This legislation is a welcome development which allows foreign investors to choose a governing law and an independent third party country for the arbitration of disputes. Under this agreement, an award by a foreign arbitrator that is recognised and allowed to be implemented by a Vietnamese court has the same effect legally as a decision by that court. And if a party does not voluntarily implement the decision of the court, then compulsory measures in accordance with Vietnamese laws can be taken against that delinquent party.

In order for the foreign arbitral award to be recognised and implemented in Vietnam, a written request in Vietnamese must be submitted to the Ministry of Justice. The information to be furnished is also stipulated in the Ordinance. It includes the full names and addresses of both parties and the legal representative of the successful party in Vietnam. Certified documents on the award of the foreign arbitrator must also be submitted with this request. The passing of this Ordinance undoubtedly improves the confidence of foreign investors but it will take some time for them to be convinced that the new tribunals are a reliable avenue, not just to settle their disputes but, also, to effectively enforce the tribunal decisions.

If an investor is involved in a dispute, then the success of winning the case still depends on the inclusion of arbitration clauses in the contract with the Vietnamese partner. The partners are required to expressly state the agreed form of arbitration and arbitration tribunal in their contract. The clauses should be clear and sufficiently detailed so that there is no uncertainty of the procedures to be followed. Both the English and Vietnamese language can be used in the legal document with equal validity. It is advisable to state in the contract a clause that clearly stipulates the version of the contract to be used in the event of resolving a dispute (Regional Business Focus, May 1995). During the early part of the negotiation stage, many investors usually leave the finer points to be settled at a later stage but to their detriment. Foreign investors are advised to be as detailed as possible in drafting their contracts even though it is a norm to draft out short agreements on general principles. There are no savings whatsoever in drafting a short agreement that leaves out the details to be worked out at a later date when problems arise.

Causes of Disputes

There have been 150 cases of approved investors who have quit, many on account of irreconcilable differences with their state partners (*Asian Business*, October 1995). Disputes may arise due to a spectrum of reasons ranging from differences in management styles to accusation of partners being involved in dubious businesses. An example of a dispute that put an end to a joint venture involved an Australian mining group, Westralian Sands, which reportedly attributed the reasons for the failure of the project to a falling out with the local partners.

Other reasons that were cited included uncertainty over the ever changing policies and arbitrary treatment meted out to some joint ventures, especially those that fall out with local partners (*South East Asian Monitor*, August 1995). Another reason was the cultural element which is often the case in an international joint venture project. This is especially apparent from the different perspectives adopted by the parties when drafting and interpreting contracts. Problems arising from cultural elements may also be manifested in the different management practices or styles. For example, Vietnamese shareholders, regardless of the amount of equity that they have in the joint ventures always expect a strong voice in the running of the company.

CONCLUSION

Vietnam has developed the basic outlines of a legal system sufficient to give a degree of confidence to foreign investors. However, like many developing communist countries, Vietnam's legal infrastructure is incomplete and evolving rapidly. There are plans to further enhance the Law on Foreign Investment by 1997 in order to accommodate the changes in the legal system and the needs of the business community. It is often still difficult to predict how government bureaucrats and enforcement authorities will interpret and apply new or untested laws.

Foreign investors seek stability and transparency in the investment regulations and the degree of equal treatment for domestic and foreign investments. However, a foreign investor must understand the fundamental structure and spirit of the changes in Vietnam's legal system in order to respond with confidence to the changes. The primary significance of the dynamic changes in the legal system in Vietnam is the consistent progress towards the "rule of law" which eventually will provide stability for foreign investors. As the laws increase in specificity and in stature, the role of political favours and personal influence is diminished. An investor will no longer have to rely solely on high level connections to achieve profit and other goals in Vietnam.

Therefore, as the laws evolve and mutate, which they now do on a frequent basis, it becomes imperative that a foreign investor possesses a working knowledge of the laws which governs his activities. A foreign investor has to understand that the emerging investment laws are changing to accommodate economic and social developments in Vietnam. The changes represent prevalent attempts by Vietnam to bring in the benefits of capitalism and foreign investment while keeping out the negative side effects, so as to preserve the values of socialism.

However, Vietnam must improve its efficiency in the implementation and enforcement of the new laws and the many amendments which are frequently promulgated. If regulations and interpretations of the laws are not consistent at various levels of the bureaucracy and provincial committees, then this leads to difficulties in the enforcement of the legal system. In recognition of these problems, the government has embarked on administrative reforms to streamline the administrative functions, to clarify the central-to-local relations and authority, and to improve coordination between the legislative authority, the government and the various people's committees in drafting legislation. This could reduce the bureaucratic red-tape and propel a more effective enforcement of the "rule of law".

Finally, foreign investors will benefit by understanding that business disputes can be best avoided when an investor has a comprehensive knowledge of the fundamentals of the business law, changes in national policies, the legal environment, the relationship with provincial people's committees and the cross-cultural elements in management issues. Vietnam is a country where the Vietnamese shareholders, almost always, wish to participate actively in the running of the company, especially in joint partnerships. Disputes may arise due to a spectrum of reasons ranging from differences in management styles to accusations of partners being involved in dubious business practices. Business disputes can be resolved by means of judicial proceedings in the economic courts or the various arbitration bodies. Vietnam has also passed the ordinance on *Recognition and Enforcement of Foreign Arbitral Awards* to enhance the confidence of foreign investors. As the Vietnamese tend to avoid legal proceedings to settle disputes, mutual consultation and negotiation are usually the preferred path for settling business disputes.

REFERENCES

"An Introduction to Investment Mode in Vietnam", *Regional Business Focus*, May 1995, p. 4.

"Development Encourages Reform, Interview with Minister Le Xuan Trinh, Head of Government Office", *Vietnam Economic Times*, February 1996, p. 12.

Dirksen Todd E., "Doing Business in Vietnam: The Legal Aspects", *Asia Business Law Review*, 2 July 1993, pp. 4–6.

"Economic Dispute Resolution", *The Vietnam Business Journal*, December 1995, p. 48.

Freshfields (law firm), "Economic Courts", *Guide to Foreign Investment in Vietnam*, London, February 1995.

"Investors Hit Serious Problems with Partners and Officials", *South East Asia Monitor*, August 1995, p. 11.

"Laying Down the Law", *Vietnam Economic Times*, October 1995, p. 30.

"Legal Changes to Help Investment, Interview with Minister Do Quoc Sam, Head of the New Ministry of Planning and Investment", *Vietnam Investment Review*, 20–26 November 1995a, p. 6.

"Legal Update – Cutting Out the Red Tape", *Vietnam Economic Times*, March 1995, p. 38.

Lichtenstein Natalie G., *A Survey of Vietnam's Legal Framework in Transition*, Legal Department, World Bank, Washington DC, 1993.

Lovell White Durrant (law firm), "Legal framework – Vietnam", *Internet*, (http://www.findat.com/lwd/default.htm), September 1995.

"Ministry of Planning and Investment", *Vietnam Investment Review*, 20–26 November 1995b, p. 2.

"News in Brief-Legal", *Vietnam Economic Times*, November 1995, p. 4.

Nguyen Khanh, "Administrative Reform Vital to Development", *Vietnam Investment Review*, 27 November to 3 December 1995, p. 2.

"Ordinance on Procedure for Settlement of Economic Dispute", Chapter 2, Article 13, Jurisdiction of the Courts at Different Level, *Article 91 of 1992 Constitution of the Socialist Republic of Vietnam*, Hanoi, 1992a, p. 1067.

"Ordinance on Procedure for Settlement of Economic Dispute, Chapter 2, Article 14, Jurisdiction of the Courts According to Territory", *Article 91 of 1992 Constitution of the Socialist Republic of Vietnam*, Hanoi, 1992b, p. 1067.

Pham Chi Lan, "Industry-Government Relations in Vietnam", Seminar in Hanoi, 4 March 1996.

Phong Lan, "Code of Conduct", *Vietnam Economic Times*, December 1995, p. 31.

"Regulations on Foreign Law Firms Emerge", *Vietnam Economic Times*, August 1995, p. 6.

"Rule of Law, Interview with Justice Minister Nguyen Dinh Loc", *Vietnam Economic Times*, May 1995, pp. 12–3.

"Troubled Times for Joint Ventures in Vietnam", *Asian Business*, October 1995, p. 32.

"Vietnam's Legal Landmarks", *Vietnam Economic Times*, December 1995, pp. 34–5.

"Vietnam Embraces Legal Evolution", *Vietnam Investment Review*, 5–18 February 1996, p. 52.

Chapter 9

Tax Incentives and Accounting Issues in Vietnam*

BY
Joanne AU YONG L.H.
Karen CHIA L.C.
KU Woei Pin
Nicholas WALSH

INTRODUCTION

ONE OF THE greatest challenges faced by foreign investors when evaluating and implementing their business plans is a country's taxation system. Potential investors must be warned that the tax system in Vietnam was originally designed for a centrally-planned economy. When Vietnam moved into a market economy, however, the government tried to improve the tax laws and investment climate by introducing the *Law on Foreign Investment*. But, since the foreign investment laws were simply added on to the existing tax system, the resulting laws are inadequate to deal with international business. Hence, there is much uncertainty for foreign investors trying to evaluate and implement any long-term business plan.

Similarly, changes in the accounting system in Vietnam followed the *doi moi* process. These changes were implemented in order to align accounting practices with international standards. The government introduced a new Vietnamese accounting system with effect from 1 January 1996, which is primarily a form-driven book-keeping system with a specified chart of accounts. This is the second reform of the

* The authors wish to thank Dr. Choo Teck Min for his valuable assistance and guidance.

accounting system to support a market economy. This new system has also introduced the concept of provision for bad debts and stock obsolescence. Foreign companies can now apply to the Ministry of Finance for approval to use the generally accepted accounting principles (GAAP) as specified by international accounting standards. The objective of this chapter is to highlight the significant accounting issues and tax incentives available to foreign investors seeking to explore business opportunities in Vietnam.

THE VIETNAMESE TAX SYSTEM

According to Irwin (1996), the Vietnamese tax system is simple and yet complicated. It may take only a week to learn the fundamentals of the Vietnamese tax system but the difficulty lies in implementing some of the tax laws due to the existence of many loopholes and ambiguities. The reason is that the Vietnamese tax system is subject to local interpretation and any tax disputes cannot be appealed in the courts. The highest level of appeal at present is to the Ministry of Finance.

The Vietnamese government has recognised the problems in the current system and steps have been taken to make the law more efficient and effective by clarifying and improving the existing tax system. In March 1995, a high level steering committee was established to research on and further develop the tax policy system. Although there has been no announcement as to when the committee will complete its task, the Ministry of Finance issued a report in August 1995 on its views on some of the taxation reforms and recommendations. The proposals in the report covered taxation reforms on turnover tax, special sales tax, profit tax and import-export duties. The main taxes that affect most foreign investments in Vietnam are:

(i) profit tax;
(ii) turnover tax;
(iii) withholding tax;
(iv) export and import duties; and
(v) personal income tax of employees.

The following sections highlight each of these taxes as well as the tax incentives available to foreign investors.

PROFIT TAX

Profit tax is levied on both local businesses and foreign investments but foreigners enjoy a lower tax rate than local businessmen. In the current tax reforms, there is a proposal to replace the existing three rates of domestic profits tax with one rate. However, the proposed domestic rate of 33% is still higher than those applied to foreign investors where the highest rate is only 25%.

Companies that fall under any of the following categories can apply to be taxed under the foreign profit tax rates:

(i) wholly foreign-owned enterprises;
(ii) joint ventures;
(iii) companies operating build-operate-transfer (BOT) contracts;
(iv) a foreign party to a business co-operation contract (BCC); and
(v) branches of foreign banks.

However, companies that are Vietnamese owned, or the Vietnamese party to a BCC, need to apply the domestic profit tax rate. The domestic profit tax applies to a foreigner deriving profits through companies which are not a licensed foreign investment. In this case, the foreign investor is also taxed under the withholding tax laws as elaborated in a subsequent section.

Generally, the basis period for profit tax assessment is on the "preceding calendar year" basis. But an enterprise with foreign invested capital, or a BCC, may apply to the Ministry of Finance to adopt its financial year as the tax year. The determination of the taxable profits is seemingly straightforward; taxable income is the difference between revenue and expenditure in the tax year. However, since the tax law is not clearly defined (for example, the lack of distinction between capital and revenue as well as the definition of revenue itself), computation of the taxable income figure is a complicated process. Although there is a list of deductibles, a foreign investor should resolve the deductibility of any special expenditure that it may have with the tax authorities at the license application stage. The investor should also note that there is no general rule allowing deductions for any business related expenses (Sea, 1996).

Article 27 of the *Law on Foreign Investment* allows for losses of an enterprise with foreign-owned capital to be carried forward to offset against the profit earned in the following year. Joint ventures and enterprises with 100% foreign capital can carry forward losses for up to five years. Other foreign businesses, such as BCCs, should seek approval from the tax authorities concerning carrying forward losses as Article 27 is silent for BCCs. Carry back of losses is not permitted.

For foreign investments, the rates of profit tax applicable are decided during the process of approving the investment license. There are three main categories:

(i) Standard tax rates: 25%
(ii) Preferential tax rates: 10, 15, or 20%
(iii) Other tax rates: above 25%

The standard tax rate of 25% is applicable to all enterprises with foreign capital and foreign partners in BCCs. The 25% rate also applies to investment projects in banking, insurance, accounting, auditing, consultancy services and finance companies. However, companies involved in the exploration and exploitation of oil and gas and other "rare and precious resources" are subject to rates above 25%. For example, under the *Petroleum Law*, the tax rate has been set at 50%.

Preferential tax rates are either 10, 15 or 20% and if a company is able to meet the conditions as given in Table 9–1, then it can apply for any one of the preferential rates. These rates are available for a period of five to ten years commencing in the year following the approval of the investment license from the Ministry of Planning and Investment (MPI). This license was formerly issued by the former state committee for co-operation and investment (SCCI). Once the preferential tax time period has expired, the standard rate of 25% applies. A company can apply to the MPI for an extension of the preferential tax rate time period.

Profit Tax Holidays and Reductions

Joint ventures and wholly foreign-owned companies in Vietnam are entitled to tax holidays in the form of complete exemption from profits tax for a certain period, depending on the preferential tax rate given by the tax authority, beginning immediately from the time the project starts making a profit. This is then followed by a further period where the tax is at 50% of the agreed preferential profit tax rate. Foreign investors should apply to the MPI on a case by case basis to be considered for these benefits. However, it seems that BCCs are not able to seek this tax holiday which is enjoyed by other foreign investments.

Table 9–2 shows the duration of the tax holidays and the rates charged.

TABLE 9–1
Preferential Tax Rates

Tax Rate	Conditions to Qualify
10%	(a) Infrastructure development in mountainous areas and regions of harsh geographical and social economic conditions. (b) Afforestation projects. (c) Projects of prime importance enlisted by the MPI. (d) Projects under BOT.
15%	(a) Other infrastructure projects (not falling under the 10% category). (b) Heavy industrial projects. (c) Industrial crop growing. (d) Projects located in rural areas. (e) Projects which transfer to Vietnamese parties without compensation at the end of the project term (including hotels). (f) Exploitation of natural resources (excluding oil and gas, rare and precious resources).
20%	Projects which meet at least two of the following conditions: (a) Employ at least 500 Vietnamese workers (labour-intensive). (b) Employ qualifying advanced technology (high-tech). (c) Exporting at least 80% of its products (export-oriented). (d) Prescribed capital of any enterprise or the capital contributed to a BCC, is not less than US$10 million.

Source: Vietnam: A Guide for the Foreign Investor (1996).

TABLE 9–2
Tax Holidays for Foreign Investments

Profit Tax Rate	Maximum Number of Years of Tax Exemption	Maximum Number of Subsequent Years at 50% Tax Reduction
10%	4	4
15%	2	4
20%	2	3
25%	1	2
Above 25%	0	0

Source: An Overview of Vietnamese Corporate Taxes (1995).

Since most companies and businesses in Hanoi are still in their infancy, there have been few claims for the tax holidays. However, in Ho Chi Minh City several businesses such as hotel developers and a soft drink manufacturer have been earning profits and are taking advantage of the tax holidays.

Refund of Profit Tax for Reinvestment

If profits derived from Vietnam are subsequently reinvested by the foreign enterprise or individual over a period of three years or more, then the profits tax paid on the profits that are reinvested may be refunded. This would depend on whether the prescribed capital stipulated in the investment license has been fully contributed and whether the reinvestment is in an area encouraged by the government. The application will need to be approved by the MPI.

TURNOVER TAX

All businesses in Vietnam are subject to a turnover tax, which is levied on the gross revenue of the enterprises, regardless of the net position of the company's profit and loss statement. The turnover tax rate ranges from as low as 0% to a high of 40% (see Table 9–3). As the turnover tax is not popular, the government in its reforms is considering replacing the turnover tax with a Value Added Tax (VAT). A pilot scheme has been tested in three sectors. However, as the existing accounting system in Vietnam is not developed enough to support a VAT, the government cannot introduce this straightaway. But steps have been taken in the right direction, such as the introduction of the new Vietnamese Accounting System. Although it is more of a bookkeeping than an accounting system, it is a move in the right direction to be more in line with international accounting standards.

Effective from 1 January 1996, the general definition of taxable turnover is now defined as the total revenue derived from business activities in Vietnam, irrespective of the form of business or whether the business establishment is inside or outside of Vietnam. The National Assembly has introduced with effect from 1 January 1996 the exemption of banks and other credit institutions from Turnover Tax for "credit activities" and the introduction of a uniform rate of 4% applied to construction activities (*Price Waterhouse Newsletter*, February 1996).

TABLE 9–3
Turnover Tax Rates Applicable

Type of Business	Tax Rate (%)
Production Business	0 – 20
Construction Business	3 – 5
Transportation of Goods/Passengers	1 – 4
Commercial Business	0.5 – 25
Restaurants	4 – 10
Services (Other than Special Services)	0 – 10
Special Services*	15 – 40

* Dancing clubs, horse racing, lottery, ship brokers, shipping agents and other agents.

Source: Vietnam: A Guide for the Foreign Investor (1996).

Turnover tax is not applicable in the following cases:

(i) agricultural goods which are subject to agricultural tax;
(ii) goods which are subject to a special sales tax and which are sold directly by the producer;
(iii) goods for export; or
(iv) production of approved import substitutes (but this is normally only a temporary exemption).

At a recent conference, Dr. Nguyen Sinh Hung, Vice Minister of Finance, spoke on several issues including the turnover tax. According to him, newly established manufacturing enterprises can seek a reduction of 50% in their turnover tax for a period of one to two years. There are also reductions available to manufacturing enterprises using advanced technology (Nguyen, 1995).

WITHHOLDING TAXES

Withholding Tax on Repatriated Profit (Profit Remittance Tax)

Foreign investors, after paying all applicable taxes, are allowed to repatriate their profits from Vietnam. The rates of withholding tax when transferring their profits (including income refunded from reinvestment) out of Vietnam vary depending on the level of contributed foreign capital. It can range from as low as 5% for contributions in excess of US$10 million to 10% for contributions below US$5 million.

When a foreign investor transfers profit abroad in the form of finished products, they are not only liable for payment of the export duty but also withholding tax (*Vietnam Investment Review*, 6–12 November 1995). Foreign employees of foreign business enterprises in Vietnam are permitted to remit their earnings abroad after settlement of personal income taxes.

Withholding Tax on Interest Payments

Currently, there is no withholding tax on interest payments but there has been concern among foreign investors because the Ministry of Finance had recently announced a plan to introduce a withholding tax. Many foreign investors raise funds in off-shore centres, such as Hong Kong, due to the relatively undeveloped status of the banking system in Vietnam. Such a tax would increase the cost of debt financing (Irwin, 1996).

Withholding Tax on Royalties Paid for Technology Transfer

A withholding tax of 10 to 15% is imposed on royalties paid. These royalties could be paid for the right to use or for the licensing of inventions, industrial property, designs, trademarks, copyright, technical know-how and supporting services such as technical assistance, and consultancy and technology management services. Where technology transfer forms part of the capital contribution by the foreign party to joint venture enterprises or BCCs, exemption from withholding tax can be obtained.

IMPORT AND EXPORT DUTIES

Import duties in Vietnam generally range from 0 to 50% but maybe as high as 200% for certain products such as liquor, cigarettes and cars. However, with the entry of Vietnam into ASEAN, the government has reduced the import tax from 200% to a maximum of 60%. The government has responded by increasing the special sales tax, resulting in a net increase in tax revenue collected.

All goods entering or leaving Vietnam are subject to import or export duties. The rates for import and export duties vary depending on the nature of the goods. It was reported (*Vietnam Investment Review*, 2–8 October 1995) that although foreign investors are subject to a 200% import tax on cars, there are certain investors who may still be able to import duty-free cars depending on the cost of the project. For example, projects worth at least US$3 million dollars are allowed to import two duty-free cars while projects that are worth more than US$200 million can import up to 12 duty-free cars. Hotels are also able to import a maximum of 12 cars without paying duty.

In addition to the cases of exemption from and/or reduction of import/export taxes as specified under the *Law on Import and Export Duties*, foreign investors are exempt from import duties if the goods are brought in as capital in a foreign investment or where raw materials, components, spare parts and other materials are imported for the production of goods for export. All the imported goods referred to here are subject to a temporary payment of import duties. On the export of the finished products, the tax paid is refunded in a proportion corresponding to the amount of finished products to be exported (*Vietnam Investment Review*, 30 October – 5 November 1995).

PERSONAL INCOME TAX

Personal income tax applies to both local individuals and foreigners who receive personal income in Vietnam. Effective 1 June 1994, an individual living in Vietnam for 183 days or more in a period of 12 months from the date of arrival in Vietnam is treated as a tax resident of Vietnam.

Foreigners who are considered as a non-tax resident in Vietnam (i.e., below 183 days) are taxed at a flat rate of 10% on their Vietnamese source of income. Non-citizens who stay in Vietnam for less than 30 days and derive income from Vietnam are exempted from tax. Table 9–4 shows the tax rates applicable to foreigners.

Two main types of income which are subject to tax are: (1) regular income (salaries, wages, allowances and wage-like bonuses and incentives); and (2) irregular income (gifts in money or in kind, lottery winnings, design or technology transfer fees and other services). There are three exceptions to the tax rates for irregular income: (1) fees received from technology transfer of over VND 2,000,000 for each transaction are subject to tax at 5%; (2) winnings from a lottery in excess of VND 12,500,000 are subject to tax at 10%; and (3) gifts and presents from abroad sent to Vietnam which are over VND 2,000,000 are taxed at 5% tax on the value of the gifts. Table

9–5 shows the tax rates applicable to irregular income and these apply to both Vietnamese and non-citizens.

TABLE 9–4
Personal Income Tax Rates Applicable to Foreigners

Level	Average Monthly Income (VND)	Tax Rate (%)
1	Up to 5,000,000	0
2	Over 5,000,000 and up to 12,000,000	10
3	Over 12,000,000 and up to 30,000,000	20
4	Over 30,000,000 and up to 50,000,000	30
5	Over 50,000,000 and up to 70,000,000	40
6	Over 70,000,000	50

Source: Investment in Vietnam (1995).

TABLE 9–5
Personal Tax Rates on Income

Level	Average Monthly Income (VND)	Tax Rate (%)
1	Up to 2,000,000	0
2	Over 2,000,000 and up to 4,000,000	5
3	Over 4,000,000 and up to 10,000,000	10
4	Over 10,000,000 and up to 20,000,000	15
5	Over 20,000,000 and up to 30,000,000	20
6	Over 30,000,000	30

Source: Investment in Vietnam (1995).

Vietnam has a very high rate of personal income tax. Those earning after tax income exceeding VND 5,000,000 per month need to pay an additional tax of 30% on the marginal income (see Table 9–6 for the tax rates applicable to Vietnamese citizens). This means that for a foreign company to increase its local employee's take home pay by VND 100,000, it would cost the company VND 190,000 (at a top marginal rate of 90% and excluding other taxes). However, there are methods of tax avoidance through paying benefits in kind, for example, paying for the employee's child's education in the U.S.

Foreigners also need to be aware that penalties for non-compliance are provided in the tax laws and they should not be taken lightly. For example, the penalties can range from a fine of VND 500,000 to three times the tax payable for non-compliance. Late payment interest charges at 0.2% per day on the amount of tax unpaid are levied. For serious cases of tax evasion, a tax evader can be prosecuted under Article 169 of the Criminal Code. A foreigner who does not comply with the taxation regulations may face prohibition from leaving the country or the issue of entry permits. However, if a foreigner voluntarily declares non-compliance, then he may request for a waiver from taxes.

TABLE 9–6
Personal Income Tax Rates for Vietnamese Citizens

Level	Average Monthly Income (VND)	Tax Rate (%)
1	Up to 1,200,000	0
2	Over 1,200,000 and up to 2,000,000	10
3	Over 2,000,000 and up to 3,000,000	20
4	Over 3,000,000 and up to 4,000,000	30
5	Over 4,000,000 and up to 6,000,000	40
6	Over 6,000,000 and up to 8,000,000	50
7	Above 8,000,000	60

Note: Vietnamese individuals with after tax income exceeding VND 5,000,000 per month are required to pay an additional tax at 30% of the marginal income.

Source: Investment in Vietnam (1995).

Foreign investors also should be aware of the tax treaties available such as the double taxation agreements between their countries. There are also tax compensation packages for expatriates assigned to Vietnam and it is worthwhile for a company to seek opportunities to structure compensation packages to minimise the taxation burden. (*Vietnam Investment Review*, 25 September – 1 October 1995).

EXPORT PROCESSING ZONES AND INDUSTRIAL ZONES

An export processing zone (EPZ) is a bonded industrial zone specialising in export-oriented production, services or activities. An EPZ offers foreign enterprises a self-contained business and industrial estate with modern infrastructure usually located near a harbour or airport. A substantial lack of infrastructure in Vietnam makes these zones attractive to foreign investors, especially in the manufacturing and services sectors which are export-oriented.

In addition, there are certain locations defined as industrial zones

(IZs) or industrial parks which are concentrated industrial areas established by government decision. Unlike the EPZs, the IZs cater to investors who want to target Vietnam's domestic market as well as produce for export.

An enterprise which is established and operates within an EPZ is called an export processing enterprise and goods exchanged with enterprises in the domestic Vietnamese market are deemed imports and exports. Although the EPZs are subjected to a profit tax, they can also apply for the tax holidays enjoyed by other foreign investments. However, all profits generated from the EPZs that are reinvested for at least three years are eligible for a profit tax refund on the amount reinvested and they also enjoy a lower remittance tax. There is also import duty exemption on equipment, parts, materials and goods imported into the EPZs. Other privileges include simplified customs procedures for imports and exports, immigration procedures and staff recruitment. Table 9–7 shows the various profit tax rates and the tax holidays available to EPZs and IZs.

TABLE 9–7
Profits Tax Rate and the Tax Holidays Available to Export-Processing Zones and Industrial Zones

Zone/Industry Sector	Profit Tax Rate*	Duration of Exemption From Profit Tax After Profitability
Export Processing Zone:		
(a) Production Industry	10%	4 years
(b) Service Sector	15%	2 years
Centralised Industrial Zone:		
(a) Production Industry	18% (12% if 80% of goods exported)	2 years
(b) Service Sector	22%	1 year

* These rates shall be applied throughout the whole duration of the project.
Source: Vietnam: A Guide for the Foreign Investor (1996).

In addition, Prime Minister Vo Van Kiet decreed in May 1995 that production operations and other activities to produce value-added goods in the EPZs would be exempted from turnover tax (*Vietnam Investment Review*, 5–11 June 1995).

INVESTMENT GUARANTEES AND DOUBLE TAXATION AGREEMENTS

The Vietnamese government guarantees fair and equitable treatment of foreign organisations and individuals that have investments in Vietnam. The assets and invested capital of foreign organisations or individuals will not be expropriated, requisitioned or nationalised. *Foreign Investment Law* amendments enable the MPI to protect foreign investors and compensate them for losses due to changes in the Vietnamese law.

To assure foreign investors, and to guarantee their interests, the Vietnamese government has signed agreements on investment protection with the governments of 26 countries and agreements on the avoidance of double taxation with the governments of 19 countries. Singapore entered into a double tax treaty with Vietnam on 1 January 1993 (see Table 9–8 for a list of countries which have treaties with Vietnam).

TABLE 9–8
Vietnam's Tax Treaty Network

Country	Effective
Australia	1 January 1993 (Vietnam) 1 July 1993 (Australia)
Thailand	1 January 1993
France	1 July 1994
Singapore	1 January 1993 (Vietnam) 1994 Year of Assessment (Singapore)
Sweden	1 January 1995
U.K.	1 January 1995 (Vietnam – withholding tax only) 1 January 1994 (Vietnam – other taxes) 1 April 1995 (U.K. – Corporation tax only) 6 April 1995 (U.K. – income and capital gain taxes only)
South Korea	1 January 1995
India	1 January 1996 (Vietnam) 1 April 1996 (India)
Netherlands	1 January 1996

TABLE 9–8 (cont'd)

Country	Effective
Japan	1 January 1996
Russia, Hungary, Poland, Denmark, China, Norway, Romania, Malaysia, Germany	Signed but not in force
Indonesia, Laos, Philippines, Czech Republic, Mauritius, Brunei, Taiwan, Switzerland, Belgium, Italy, Ukraine, New Zealand, Slovak Republic, Canada	Under various stages of negotiation

Source: *Price Waterhouse Newsletter,* No. 8, February 1996.

OTHER TAXES

Tax Incentives for Build-Operate-Transfer Projects

The tax incentives for build-operate-transfer (BOT) projects include a four year tax holiday dated from the first profitable year followed by a 50% cut in profit tax for the next four years after which the eventual full tax on profits is only 10%.

Special Sales Tax

Selected goods are subject to a special sales tax ranging from 15 to 100% which is levied only once. The tax is calculated based on the quantity of goods for sale (including goods for internal consumption) at the selling price at the place of production. Exports are exempt from the special sales tax.

The goods subject to special sales tax include tobacco, cigarettes, spirits, beer and firecrackers. From 1 January 1996, this tax base has been extended to cover imported cars and petrol of all kinds.

For new manufacturing companies, an exemption of 50% of the sales tax is given for a period of one or two years. For companies with losses, they will be able to pay less special sales tax. The exemption amount is in line with the loss but not beyond 30%, and for not more than two years (*Vietnam Investment Review*, 30 October – 5 November 1995).

Social Security Taxes

Local and foreign enterprises must contribute 15% of total wages for social insurance purposes every month while the employee contributes 5%, for a total of 20%. However, expatriates working for foreign-owned enterprises are exempt from this tax.

Health Insurance

Both local and foreign enterprises are required to pay 3% of wages for health insurance premiums to the Health Insurance Office. The employer pays 2 and 1% is contributed by the employee. It is unclear whether this 3% insurance premium also applies to foreigners' salaries but it appears not to be the case in practice.

THE VIETNAMESE ACCOUNTING AND AUDITING SYSTEM

An enterprise with foreign-owned capital licensed in accordance with the *Law of Foreign Investment* in Vietnam constitutes an individual accounting entity and is required to maintain its own accounting records. The laws on accounting for joint venture and foreign-owned enterprises are mainly found in Circular 84 (23 October 1993) issued by the Ministry of Finance. The circular focuses on two main areas: registration of systems and accounting requirements.

REGISTRATION OF ACCOUNTING SYSTEM

Within 180 days of getting an investment license, all joint ventures and wholly-owned enterprises are required to submit details of their accounting system to the Ministry of Finance for approval. The submission must include the following items:

(i) A registration application letter and a copy of the investment license is required.
(ii) Accounting system: Either the Vietnamese or an international accounting policy (subject to approval) may be adopted. When the

Vietnamese accounting system is adopted, the industry sector in which the company operates must be specified. The Vietnamese accounting structure is essentially a book-keeping system with regulations governing the form of the accounts, record keeping, codes of accounts, titles and types of accounts. The latest revision, effective 1 January 1996, incorporates the accrual concept in place of the former cash accounting basis. Further developments are expected as the system moves towards international standards.

If international accounting policies are adopted, then details of the accounting documents, the principal accounting books and records, chart of accounts and financial reports need to be submitted. Almost all joint ventures and wholly-owned enterprises apply for the use of either international accounting standards or the accounting system of the parent company.

(iii) Qualifications of the Chief Accountant are required.

ACCOUNTING LANGUAGE AND CURRENCY

An enterprise may use Vietnamese or another widely used language approved by the Ministry of Finance in the preparation of its accounting records. As for numerals, only arabic numerals are allowed (Foo, 1996).

All numbers in the accounts must be expressed in Vietnamese currency or another foreign currency approved by the Ministry of Finance. In the event that an accounting document is prepared using a different currency, then that currency must be converted to Dong in accordance with the buying exchange rate of the State Bank of Vietnam at the date the transaction occurred.

SAFEKEEPING OF RECORDS

Accounting documents, such as vouchers, books, accounts and other information must be carefully and safely maintained. The accounting information must be classified, filed in original form according to the accounting periods and kept for a minimum period of ten years.

DEPRECIATION OF FIXED ASSETS

The fixed asset depreciation policy for foreign investments in Vietnam is controlled by Circular No. 31 issued on 18 July 1992. Fixed assets covered in the circular include those with intangible form such as expenses for compensation, location clearing, value of right to land use, establishment expenditures and patents. The value of the fixed assets contributed by parties to the joint venture are defined in Circular 379 dated 11 July 1990 by the State Committee for Cooperation and Investment. The value of fixed assets purchased by enterprises is determined according to current international market prices (concerning imported goods) and current prices in the domestic market (concerning goods purchased in Vietnam). One of the important points to note is that the Circular stipulates the maximum depreciation rates for various types of fixed assets. Any rate up to the maximum may be used and any rate higher than that stipulated needs to be approved by the Ministry of Finance. Table 9–9 shows the depreciation rates of fixed assets applicable to foreign invested capital and foreign contracting enterprises as specified in the circular.

Table 9–9
Depreciation Rates of Fixed Assets

Type of Asset	Depreciation Rate
Establishment expenditure	30%
Newly built workshop, construction works	7%
Used workshop and construction works	15%
Generator and equipment	10 to 15%
Machine and equipment used in project	12 to 20%
Road transport	18%
Railway transport	10 to 18%
Water transport	10 to 18%
Oil, gas pipes	10 to 15%
Office equipment	10 to 15%
Perennial industrial equipment	8 to 15%

Source: Circular No. 31, July 1992.

FILING REQUIREMENTS

Quarterly and annual reports of the financial activities and position of the enterprise must be filed. The specific financial statements to be filed are:

(i) The balance sheet;
(ii) The profit and loss statement;
(iii) The Director's report; and
(iv) The audit report (for annual reports only).

AUDIT REQUIREMENTS

The accounting reports of the enterprise must be audited by a professional agency appointed by the Ministry of Finance. A number of international accounting firms have already set up their offices in major cities (Luu, 1996). The auditing standards in Vietnam are also progressing towards international auditing standards. Previous audits meant a 100% check of every transaction. Concepts such as "materiality" and "true and fair" were introduced only recently (Underwoord, 1996). In addition to statutory audit reporting, there is also an audit by the general department of taxes and/or local tax authorities for tax purposes.

CONCLUSION

Although the tax system is very complicated with many different taxes, the Vietnamese government is committed to improving the investment environment to attract more international investors. It has recognised that the current tax policy does not cover all sources of revenue as it seeks to develop a market economy to gradually replace its planned economy. It is also aware that the turnover tax has a negative cascading effect on the manufacturing and sale of goods. With this in mind, the Vietnamese government has a plan to reform and improve the taxation system by introducing a value-added tax law to replace the existing turnover tax law. It also plans to improve the structure of import and export duties to bring them in line with an open external fiscal policy and international practices. These changes are expected to create appropriate conditions for Vietnam to expand its trade relations with other countries.

The reforms in the accounting and auditing systems should also bring about improvements in the accountability and usefulness of financial statements. At present, most of the major foreigń banks in Vietnam are unable to place much emphasis on the local companies' financial statements because the accounts are seen as unreliable (Fang, 1996). In addition, the legal framework is still not very well developed and, hence, there are difficulties in enforcing the guidelines as set out in the accounting standards. Presently, most contractual disputes are settled out of court (Do, 1996).

In the area of auditing, Mr. Dang Van Thanh, Head of the Ministry of Finance's financial and accounting department, admitted that the ministry has not yet issued any clear standards for auditing work. He further claimed that the quality of auditing reports does not meet customer requirements (Dang, February 1996). Indeed, there has been much confusion over the purpose and the responsibility for the audits. According to Mr. Bui Van Mai, Director of the Vietnam Auditing Authority, the main purposes of the audit are to verify the results of performance as well as for tax purposes. This is not in line with the objectives and guidelines of international auditing standards. However, the government hopes that the changes proposed in the tax policy reforms as well as the accounting reforms will encourage more foreign investment in Vietnam (Bui, 1996).

REFERENCES

"An Overview of Vietnamese Corporate Taxes", *Singapore Accountant,* September/October 1995, pp. 41–3.

Bui Van Mai, "New Vietnamese vs International Accounting Standards", Vietnam Auditing Company, Hanoi, Vietnam, 5 March 1996.

Circular No. 31 TC/TCDN, *Providing Regulations on the System of Depreciation of Fixed Assets of the Enterprises with Foreign Invested Capital and with Foreign Contracting Parties*, Ministry of Finance, Hanoi, 18 July 1992.

Circular No. 84 TC/CDKT, *Guiding the Implementation of Accounting Standards for Enterprises with Foreign Owned Capital*, Ministry of Finance, Hanoi, 23 October 1993.

"Clarifying Expatriate Income Taxes", *Vietnam Investment Review*, 25 September – 1 October 1995.

Dang Van Thanh, Editorial, *Vietnam Investment Review*, February 1996.

Do Le Vien, Lawyer, Freehill Hollingdale & Page International Lawyers, Ho Chi Minh City, Vietnam (interviewed 8 March 1996).

Fang I., Chief Executive Officer, Standard Chartered Bank, Vietnam, "Banking Services in Vietnam: Serving an Emerging Market", Hanoi, Vietnam, (interviewed 5 March 1996).

Foo I., Audit Manager, Price Waterhouse, Ho Chi Minh City, Vietnam (interviewed 8 March 1996).

"Foreign Investors to Pay 200 Percent Import Tax on Cars", *Vietnam Investment Review*, 2–8 October 1995.

Investment in Vietnam. KPMG Peat Marwick, Hanoi, Vietnam, Spring 1995.

Irwin R., Tax Manager, Price Waterhouse, Hanoi, Vietnam (interviewed 5 March 1996).

Luu Ngoc Khang, Director, KPMG Peat Marwick, Hanoi, Vietnam (interviewed 4 March 1996).

"On Tax Laws and Investors in VN", *Vietnam Investment Review*, 6–12 November 1995.

Nguyen Sinh Hung, Vice Minister of Finance, Address at the Conference on Recent Developments in Emerging Asia-Pacific Economies in Singapore on "Investment Policies and Incentives to Attract Foreign Investment In Vietnam", Singapore, 24–25 November 1995.

"Premier Lifts Tax on Export Zones", *Vietnam Investment Review*, 5–11 June 1995.

Sea T.S. Jeff, Tax Manager, Price Waterhouse, Ho Chi Minh City, Vietnam (interviewed 8 March 1996).

"Tax Reform – Changes in Turnover Tax and Special Sales Tax", *Price Waterhouse Newsletter*, No. 8, February 1996.

Underwood G., Director (Country Manager), KPMG Peat Marwick, Hanoi, Vietnam (interviewed 4 March 1996).

Vietnam: A Guide for the Foreign Investor, Price Waterhouse Vietnam Limited, 4th Edition, Hanoi, Vietnam, January 1996.

"VN's Import-Export Tax Scheme in State of Flux", *Vietnam Investment Review*, 30 October – 5 November 1995.

Chapter 10

A Synopsis of Vietnam's Regulatory Environment

BY
CHOO Teck Min

INTRODUCTION

VIETNAM HELD ITS eighth National Communist Party Congress in June 1996. At the end of the four-day policy-making Congress, which is staged only once every five years, the Party reaffirmed Vietnam's intention to pursue its open-door policy of economic and social renovation. This was good news for foreign firms which have invested substantial amounts in Vietnam and have a stake in its economic liberalisation programme. But even as more foreign investors enter Vietnam to take advantage of its *doi moi* policy, they have increasingly highlighted the need for greater improvement in Vietnam's regulatory environment. Although Vietnam's *Foreign Investment Law* is regarded as one of the region's most liberal, it still lacks concrete regulations needed to provide a more attractive business climate for foreign investors.

Some laws related to foreign investment have yet to be promulgated, including the commerce and property laws (Dung, 1996). Implementation of the *Land Law* has met with obstacles and difficulties because of different interpretations of the law at different localities and at different levels. Procedures for granting land and land clearance often take one to two years, which is one of the major reasons for delays in projects. Also, a transparent system of taxation still needs to be comprehensively drawn up, and international accounting standards and guidelines have not yet been adopted.

The Ministry of Planning and Investment (MPI) is aware of these regulatory shortcomings, including the lack of stability and synchronisation in the legal system. Amendments to the *Foreign Investment Law* was submitted to the National Assembly in October 1996 for approval, as part of an attempt to further enhance the regulatory and investment environment. The existing *Foreign Investment Law* was promulgated in 1987. Since then, it has been amended twice – in 1990 and 1992. The new statute, after the 1996 amendments, is expected to be put into operation in 1997. It will amend existing regulations rather than introduce an entirely new set of laws (Tilleke and Gibbins, 1996). It will also be more detailed and generate a more competitive business environment by integrating the two existing laws covering foreign and domestic investment (namely, the *Foreign Investment Law* and the *Domestic Investment Law*).

Chapters 7, 8 and 9 provide some insights into the complex regulatory environment that confronts foreign investors who venture into Vietnam. A substantial part of the complexity is due to the fact that Vietnam's laws and regulations are still evolving; thus, investors must be prepared for, and keep up with, the numerous changes that have become a common feature of the regulatory environment. Further, despite its high literacy rate, Vietnam faces critical shortages of the skilled personnel needed to complete its transformation from a rigidly planned economy to a free market. Besides managers, those with skills in law, banking and accounting are in particularly high demand.

Chapter 7 focused on trade regulations in Vietnam, including issues on trade financing, and the market and trading environment in Vietnam. Of particular interest to regional traders is Vietnam's plan to substantially reduce its tariffs and import duties as part of its obligation as an ASEAN member. However, there are still many barriers and obstacles to free trade that foreign trading houses will encounter and these are discussed at length in Chapter 7.

Chapter 8 examined Vietnam's legal environment for foreign direct investment with particular focus on its *Foreign Investment Law*. Legal procedures and guidelines that foreign investors must follow are outlined. Of particular significance, is the discussion on the nebulous nature of law enforcement in the country which the MPI and the Ministry of Justice are working very hard to remedy. The legal and court systems in the country are also elaborated upon in Chapter 8, including insights into the settlement of disputes and arbitration procedures.

Chapter 9 examined tax incentives available to foreign investors in Vietnam and other aspects of the tax regime that they need to be familiar with to conduct business. It becomes clear from this chapter that the lack of a comprehensive tax code in Vietnam limits the effectiveness of the tax incentive packages which the state can offer to foreign investors. In addition, the accounting framework under which financial statements and reports are prepared is discussed. The accounting system currently in use in Vietnam is very rudimentary and needs upgrading before it can meet international standards.

The following sections highlight the most recent developments in the three broad areas of trade regulations, general legislation and tax and accounting issues that Chapters 7, 8 and 9 were not able to incorporate at the time of initial writing. The many changes which have taken place in the short span of a few months are a signal that the government is serious about implementing improvements in economic and investment reforms.

TRADE REGULATIONS

In June 1996, the State Bank issued a directive that local businesses who want to open one-year letters of credit must produce 80% of the value of the credit as a deposit. This move was intended to tighten control over deferred letters of credit guaranteed by commercial banks, but it angered bankers and importers who perceived it as almost a ban on letters of credit (Van, 1996). Barely two months later, in August 1996, those tough regulations were relaxed by the issue of another directive indicating that the 80% requirement is only applicable to imported consumer goods while a deposit requirement on imported production materials will be at the discretion of individual banks. This episode illustrates the fluid nature of regulations in Vietnam.

Chapter 7 highlighted the many restrictions imposed on the operations of foreign representative offices and how some of the more aggressive and risk-seeking players occasionally bend the rules to conduct trading. Even though the latter is fairly common in the market place, a recent case indicates that the government may be clamping down on these activities. In May 1996, the Vietnam subsidiary of the

Hong Kong-based investment company Peregrine Investment Holdings, was put under investigation. The Market Management Control Unit of Ho Chi Minh City has charged that Peregrine was directly engaged in trading activities through 13 Vietnamese private companies. Evidence from these companies pointed to close links with Peregrine in their day-to-day operations. The charge accused Peregrine of setting up domestic private companies with Peregrine money to evade restrictions imposed on foreign representative offices. This case, without a doubt, will be closely watched by foreign trading houses as they try to sort out the actual scope of a foreign representative office's permitted activities in Vietnam .

LEGAL ENVIRONMENT

The Administrative Court and the Labour Court went into operation on 1 July 1996. The Administrative Court handles complaints lodged by individuals and organisations concerning administrative rulings or acts by state agencies. The establishment of Administrative Courts within the country's People's Court system is perceived as a major step forward in protecting ordinary citizens from the abuse of power by state officials and government offices.

The ordinance on labour dispute settlement procedures was passed by the Standing Committee of the National Assembly on 11 April 1996. The ordinance stipulates the procedures for settling labour disputes at the Labour Court of a People's Court, and it officially legalises strikes. The ordinance came into force on 1 July 1996 with the setting up of the Labour Court. It is expected that from now on, labour disputes will be settled in a faster and more effective way, thus protecting the interests of both employers and employees. On another labour matter, the state increased minimum wages in 1996 for foreign invested companies in Hanoi and Ho Chi Minh City to US$45 per person per month from US$35, and to US$35–40 from US$30 in other cities and provinces. Only companies facing infrastructural problems or other difficulties are allowed to pay wages of only US$30–35 per month (Huan, 1996).

Also coming into force on 1 July 1996 was Vietnam's *Civil Code*. Among other provisions, it contains basic provisions for copyright protection. But these provisions are not very specific, particularly on issues of enforcement and penalties. Detailed clarifications of the *Civil*

Code and guidelines for its implementation will be released by the Ministry of Justice at a later date. The Ministry is also working on the new *Criminal Law*, which will be submitted to the National Assembly in 1997.

Article 13 of the 1987 *Foreign Investment Law* requires the consent of all the members of a joint venture's management board on principal matters relating to business objectives, planning, and decisions regarding key personnel. Legislators are proposing amendments to the *Foreign Investment Law* whereby principal matters can be concluded based on a majority decision of the board. The current rule favours and protects the Vietnamese party to a joint venture, who usually contributes a relatively small amount of equity to the business, but who maintains a veto power over all principal matters of the business. The majority rule is considered fairer to the foreign party who has contributed more capital to the business and, therefore, who should have more management power (Tilleke and Gibbins, 1996).

TAX AND ACCOUNTING FRAMEWORK

New draft laws on corporate income tax, personal income tax and the value added tax (VAT) are being proposed by the Ministry of Finance. These are being hailed as a major improvement to the tax system and the foundation for a future comprehensive tax code. At present, there is no codified tax law in Vietnam for foreigners. Such tax provisions are contained in the *Foreign Investment Law*.

According to the draft of the new *Corporate Income Tax Law* (which replaces the current profit tax system), there will be no distinction between foreign and Vietnamese entities – all of them will have to pay a unified tax rate of 33%. There are a few exceptions to the 33% flat rate. Prioritised projects in certain manufacturing, construction and transportation fields are eligible for preferential rates of 15, 20 or 25% over several years. After the incentive period, these companies will also have to pay the 33% rate. For companies that have super-profits, there is an additional 25% tax on their profits. This additional 25% tax rate has been criticised by businessmen as being excessive and a strong disincentive to entrepreneurship (Phu, 1996). Another change under the draft of the new *Corporate Income Tax Law* that is causing concern to businessmen, is the limitation of carrying forward losses for only two years. Currently, foreign enterprises can carry forward their losses for five years for tax deduction purposes.

Foreign investors with existing tax rates written into their investment licenses will not be affected by the 33% across-the-board corporate income tax rate. Any profit tax rates previously specified in their investment licenses will remain valid. A draft amendment on the *Foreign Investment Law* mandates that the remittance tax will be abolished. So new investors will only have to pay corporate income tax while former investors will pay profit tax and remittance tax according to their existing licenses.

Under the new draft of the *Personal Income Tax Law*, tax is computed on the annual rather than monthly income. For foreign residents, the current maximum tax rate of 50% will be abolished under the new draft law. The highest tax bracket will be brought down to 40% and applied only to those foreign residents whose annual income exceeds VND 1 billion. The current highest personal income tax rates for Vietnamese nationals of 50 and 60% will be abolished under the new draft law. The maximum rate of 40% will be applied only to Vietnamese nationals who earn over VND 250 million a year. These changes serve to eliminate the ironic situation where hiring a top local employee used to be more expensive than hiring the equivalent foreigner. The proposed personal income tax rates for foreign residents and Vietnamese are shown in Tables 10–1 and 10–2, respectively. The current rates can be found in Chapter 9.

TABLE 10–1
Personal Income Tax Rates for Foreign Residents (Draft law)

Level	Annual Income (VND million)	Tax Rate %
1	Up to 50	0
2	Over 50 to 200	5
3	Over 200 to 400	10
4	Over 400 to 700	20
5	Over 700 to 1000	30
6	Over 1000	40

The draft law on the value added tax (VAT) has been prepared by the General Department of Taxation under the Ministry of Finance to replace the existing turnover tax. The VAT will be levied on all goods, manufacturing and distribution activities, and on a large number of services including transportation, export-import, trading and catering. Private businesses whose annual turnover is less than VND 600 million will be exempt from the tax. The General Department of Taxation has proposed that the VAT law should come into effect on 1 January 1998.

TABLE 10–2
Personal Income Tax Rates for Vietnamese (Draft law)

Level	Annual Income (VND million)	Tax Rate %
1	Up to 15	0
2	Over 15 to 50	5
3	Over 50 to 100	10
4	Over 100 to 150	20
5	Over 150 to 250	30
6	Over 250	40

The Vietnamese accounting system is still fairly rudimentary even with the improvements that have been introduced in 1996. This has adverse effects on trade financing (as discussed in Chapter 7). Banks are reluctant to lower their deposit requirements for letters of credit to local importers because their financial statements are not prepared and reviewed according to international accounting and auditing standards. The lack of adherence to generally accepted accounting principles (GAAP) also presents a problem to foreign investors when they are trying to assess the financial viability of a potential Vietnamese partner. The degree of reliance that can be placed on locally produced financial statements is minimal at times and it has to be substituted with other means of evaluating the potential partner. Foreign firms can apply to the Ministry of Finance to have their financial statements prepared in accordance with international accounting standards and most of them exercise this option.

CONCLUSION

No one questions the abundance of natural resources that Vietnam possesses. The main issue is whether this business opportunity can be supported by a sufficiently sophisticated legal and commercial infrastructure offering tangible reasons for considering Vietnam rather than

Myanmar, China or other emerging economies in the region. Since 1986 and the advent of the *doi moi* policy, there has been a considerable amount of legislative activity. However, there are many areas of law and administration that need to be upgraded to offer more certainty to foreign investors. Foreign investors who come to Vietnam expecting to find a regulatory system compatible with capitalist expectations will be disappointed. Many pitfalls await firms that are inexperienced in dealing with communist countries experimenting with free market economies.

On the brighter side, Vietnam's tax regime is gradually reacting to the pressures of a developing market economy. The government has set up a programme of comprehensive tax reforms intended to meet the demands of economic industrialisation and modernisation up to the year 2000. The MPI is also proposing many amendments to the *Foreign Investment Law* that are beginning to address and allay the major concerns of foreign investors.

REFERENCES

Dung Nguyen Tri, "Coast and Highlands Made Priority for FDI", *Vietnam Investment Review*, Issue No. 249, 22–28 July 1996.

Huan Hoang Van, "Vietnam Still Needs FDI", *Vietnam Investment Review*, Issue No. 249, 22–28 July 1996.

Phu Nguyen Van, "Super-Tax Could Slug Super-Profits", *Vietnam Investment Review*, Issue No. 246, 1–7 July 1996.

Tilleke and Gibbins (law firm), "Proposed Amendments to *Foreign Investment Law*", *International Financial Law Review*, February 1996, pp. 48–9.

Van Phuong, "New Rules Posted on Letters of Credit", *Vietnam Investment Review*, Issue No. 251, 5–11 August 1996.

TECHNOLOGY TRANSFER

Chapter 11

Telecommunications in Vietnam*

BY
LEE Choon Hong
LOW Kwong Hwee
Phyllis LUM Siu Lin
Daniel POON Heng Wah

INTRODUCTION

UNTIL RECENTLY, TELECOMMUNICATIONS and postal services in Vietnam were provided by a monopoly state-owned enterprise. After years of disappointing results from centralised management, Vietnam tried to learn from the experiences of both advanced and neighbouring countries. The reforms of the telecommunications industry in Vietnam now pivot around two main thrusts: increased private sector participation and market liberalisation.

The central government has since introduced important changes in the structure of service provision and regulation (Fforde and Goldstone, 1995). The Department General of Posts and Telecommunications (DGPT) operated and regulated both telecommunications and postal services until 1993, when the provision of services was separated from the DGPT and a new operating company, Vietnam Posts and Telecommunications (VNPT), was formed. DGPT now has ministerial status and serves as the regulatory and policy-making organisation reporting directly to the Prime Minister's Office while VNPT operates the national telecommunications network.

The effort to introduce private capital into

* The authors are grateful to Dr. Jon Kendall for his guidance and assistance.

the Vietnamese telecommunications market has so far focused more on the need for state-owned enterprises to cope with new telecommunications demands than the willingness to turn the market over to private ownership and management. Through partnerships with large foreign firms that offer the capital and expertise required to develop the infrastructure, the government appears to have found a solution to the managerial, financial and technical problems inherent in business co-operation contract (BCC) arrangements. The benefits have been significant in term of unprecedented capacity development and technological leap-frogging through this private investment, without giving up control of key aspects of the sector.

The DGPT appears reluctant to conclude any type of comprehensive agreement with foreign operators, preferring instead to sign Memorandum of Understanding (MOUs) with many different operators and then play them off against each other in a competitive atmosphere. The current tactic is for the DGPT to select two or three foreign operators to assist it with the development and operation of the public network in several different areas of the country.

Given this background, this chapter analyses the Vietnamese telecommunications industry. It presents the current status of the telecommunications industry in Vietnam and identifies the opportunities available in this industry. The chapter then highlights the factors that may impede industry growth and concludes with critical success factors that summarise the experiences of the more successful foreign companies in Vietnam to date. Since telecommunication technologies span such a wide spectrum, this chapter only considers the fixed line and mobile services in the telecommunications industry.

OVERVIEW OF THE INDUSTRY

Telecommunications Regulatory Structure

The DGPT, Vietnam's telecommunications authority, was originally part of the country's Ministry of Transport and Telecommunications. In mid-1993, the DGPT split off to become an independent ministerial department. At the same time, several subsidiary organisations were created to take charge of planning and operating specific portions of the network.

The DGPT is generally responsible for macro economics level

regulation and planning and takes charge of overall telecommunications policy decisions. It reports directly to the Prime Minister's office. The DGPT has a radio frequency department in each province and the secretary general of the DGPT also serves as the chair of the national frequency committee. Although no restrictions exist on the retail sale of end user equipment, including home user sets, all equipment that is sold must be of the type approved for use with the national system. This approval is available through DGPT's Research Institute of Posts and Telecommunications in Hanoi which generally applies International Telecommunications Union (ITU) standards.

A second organisation, VNPT, serves as the public network operator. Until recently, it has enjoyed a national monopoly with the exception of mobile telephones. In early 1995, the Ministry of Defence-owned Military Electronics Telecommunications Company (METC) was awarded a license to offer civil telecommunications and postal services in direct competition with VNPT. Thus, foreign telecommunications firms now have a choice of either VNPT or METC as local partners when they submit bids for new contracts.

VNPT is composed of the following operating subsidiaries:

(i) Vietnam Telecommunications National (VTN) operates the domestic fixed network.

(ii) Vietnam Data Company (VDC) is in charge of the country's packet switched data network and the provision of data service throughout Vietnam, including the planning and implementation of Internet services.

(iii) Vietnam Telecommunications International (VTI) operates the international communications gateways in co-operation with the Australian carrier Telstra.

(iv) Vietnam Mobile Services (VMS) operates the country's two Global System for Mobile Communications (GSM) systems in Hanoi and Ho Chi Minh City (HCMC). It is also the local partner involved in a recent contract for a nationwide mobile telephone service, worth more than US$300 million, which was awarded to the Swedish firm Comvik International.[1]

---

[1] Although it was announced in late 1994 that VMS will be placed directly in the control of DGPT instead of VNPT, the government redefined the role of the DGPT during 1995 and, at the same time gave full control of cellular systems back to the VNPT. VMS is now an operating arm of the VNPT.

(v) 53 provincial posts and telecommunications companies and an unstated number of factories supply various equipment.

VNPT directs planning and network construction on a more specific level and is responsible for creating and implementing the master plan for Vietnam's telecommunications infrastructure. VNPT falls under the direct supervision of the DGPT and is also responsible for contracting with foreign suppliers for the basic network construction. Since splitting off the organisation from the DGPT, VNPT also serves as the joint partner for foreign firms engaged in local production efforts. Figure 11–1 shows the present telecommunications regulatory structure in Vietnam.

Presently, a new Posts and Telecommunications law is in draft form and is scheduled for approval by Vietnam's National Assembly in 1996. A draft regulation has been submitted to the government concerning operators' rights and duties, and licensing requirements. Many foreign vendors and operators expect that the new law will more clearly define the terms under which foreign firms may participate in network construction and operation.

Telecommunications Industry Profile

After nearly ten years of implementing an open-door policy and developing a market-oriented economy, Vietnam's economic success is clearly shown by a soaring GDP growth rate of around 9.5% in 1995 with over US$4.5 billion in export volume (*Asian Communications*, November 1995). With the buoyant growth in the economy, all sectors of the telecommunications industry are poised to grow during the next several years. Liberalisation, increased access to financing and new technology will fuel this growth. The GDP figure for 1994 was US$14.5 billion with 4.1% coming from the transport/telecoms sectors.

The telecommunications equipment market will be worth an estimated US$786 million by 1998, of which the public telecommunications equipment market will make up US$413.6 million, the mobile market will constitute US$248.1 million, with the remainder from the transmission and telecommunications accessories market. Figure 11–2 shows the market value of telecommunications equipment from 1992 to 1998. Although the high inflation rate (about 12%), rising unemployment rate (around 25%), lack of an adequate legal system and low

FIGURE 11–1
Vietnam's Telecommunications Regulatory Structure

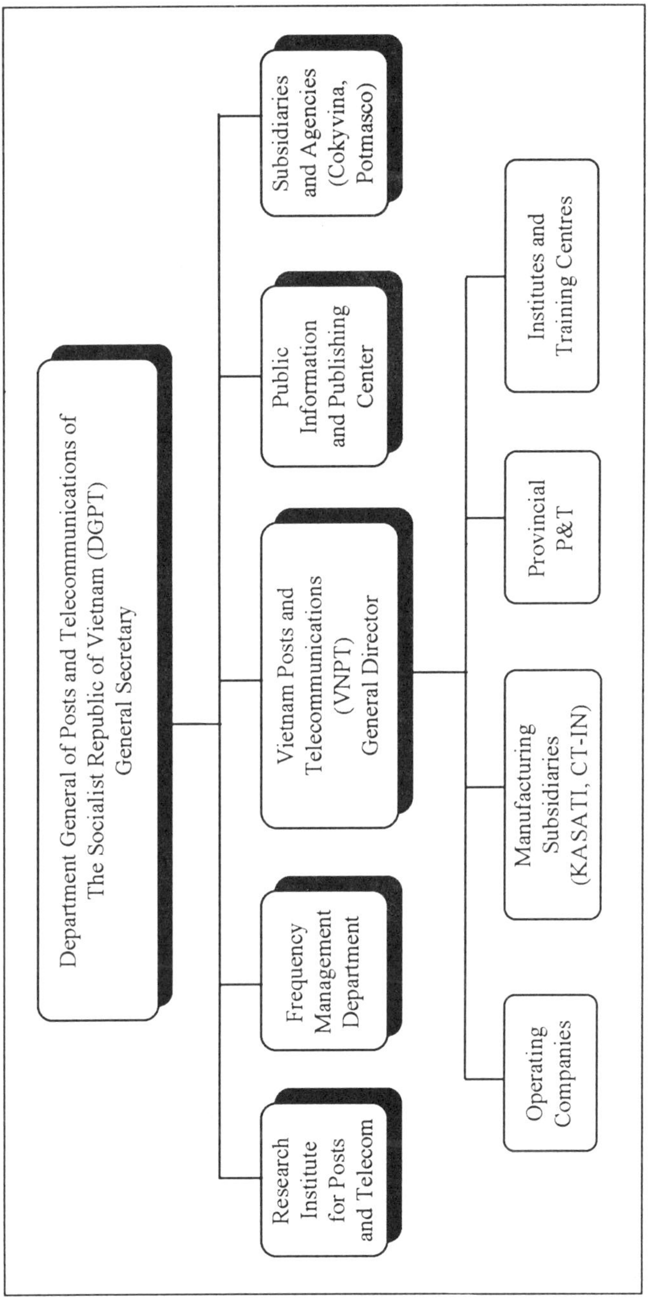

Source: Pyramid Research Report, *Telecoms Markets in Vietnam, Laos and Cambodia*, 1995.

domestic saving rates may deter some foreign investors, the potential of the telecommunications sector has attracted many international firms such as Telstra, Ericsson and Siemens to invest in Vietnam's telecommunications infrastructure projects.

FIGURE 11–2
Market Value of Telecommunications Equipment Market: 1992 to 1998

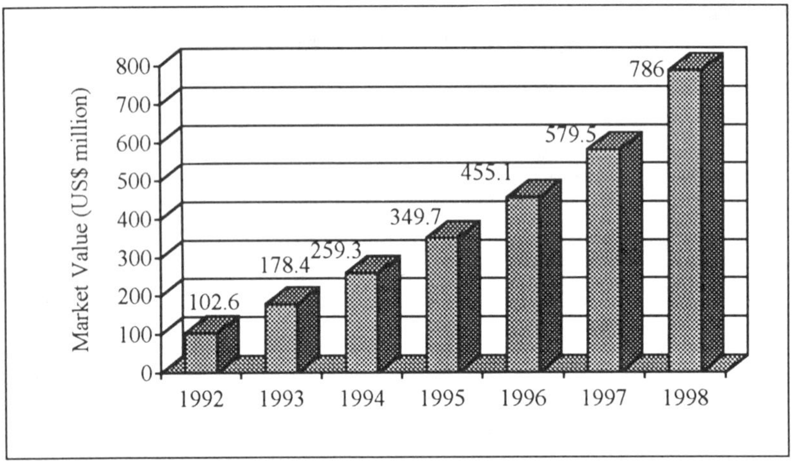

Note: 1995 to 1998 values are estimates.
Source: Pyramid Research Report, *Telecoms Markets in Vietnam, Laos and Cambodia*, 1995.

Table 11–1 compares Vietnam's telecommunications statistics in 1995 with other regional developing countries. With a population of 76 million and a telephone density of only 1% in 1995, the growth potential of this industry is enormous. Table 11–2 shows the estimated telecommunications services growth from 1992 to 1995 while Table 11–3 shows the network capacity of the mobile market in Vietnam during this period. These numbers are translated into penetration rates for the mobile market and projected for the period 1996 to 1998 as shown in Figure 11–3.

TABLE 11–1
Comparison of the Profile of Telecommunications Within Asia (1995)

	Telephone Density (per 100 population)	Telephone Waiting List	No. of Cellular Subscribers	Per Capita Income (US$)[1]	No. of Operators[2]
Singapore	41	573	271,000	16,000	1
Malaysia	11.2	168,681	513,000	2,790	6
Thailand	4.5	1,591,846	1,152,300	2,114	14
Indonesia	2.0	225,713	100,000	821	9
Vietnam	1.0	150,000	8,000	200	5

[1] Numbers indicate 1992 figures.

[2] Numbers include the operators for fixed line, cellular, CT2 and paging networks but exclude satellite and fibre optic operators. These numbers also refer to both state and private operators.

Source: Compiled from market reports in various issues of *Asian Communications* 1995.

TABLE 11–2
Vietnam Telecommunications Services Estimated Growth: 1992 to 1995* (in thousands)

	1992	1993	1994	1995
Main Lines	173	259	420	620
Cellular Subscribers	0.8	4.1	8.3	29.5
Paging Subscribers	3.9	13.8	36.5	63.3
Fax/Telex Users	2.7	5.6	8.2	12.1
Datacom Subscribers	0	0.1	0.2	0.3

* The data are estimates because the sub-categories have never been officially verified.

Source: Pyramid Research Report, *Telecoms Markets in Vietnam, Laos and Cambodia*, 1995.

TABLE 11–3
Network Capacity for Mobile Services: 1992 to 1995

	1992	1993	1994	1995
Cellular capacity	4.5	8.5	15.0	34.1
Digital	0.0	2.0	8.5	34.1
Analog	4.5	6.5	6.5	10.0
Paging Subscribers	3.9	13.8	36.5	63.3

Source: Pyramid Research Report *Telecoms Markets in Vietnam, Laos and Cambodia,* 1995.

FIGURE 11–3
Penetration Rates for Mobile Services: 1992 to 1998

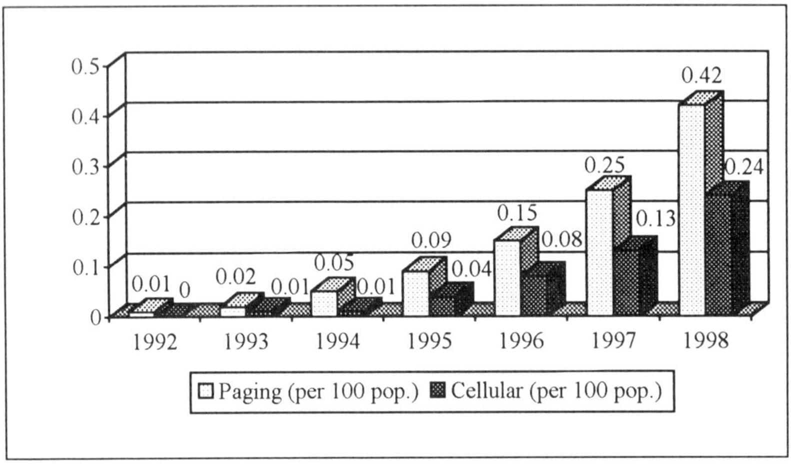

Source: Pyramid Research Report, *Telecoms Markets in Vietnam, Laos and Cambodia*, 1995.

(i) ***Public Networks:*** Vietnam has a very good international network. VTI operates satellite earth stations in Hanoi, Da Nang and HCMC that provide over 500 international telephone circuits to over 15 separate destinations. It is possible to dial direct to over 200 destinations from Vietnam through one of VTI's two digital gateway exchanges. An optical fibre cable linking Vietnam with Hong Kong and Thailand was commissioned in 1995 and provides Vietnam with the ability to carry the most advanced telecommunications services to the world. International services include telephone (automatic and operator), facsimile, telex, telegraph, private leased circuits and international packet switched data services.

The national switched telecommunications network is organised into a four-tiered hierarchy – the international, secondary national, primary transit and local switching levels. There are exchanges at the provincial, district and village levels. Vietnam has 53 provinces and municipalities, 527 districts and 10,000 villages. Digital exchanges have already been installed in Vietnam's 53 provincial centres. In rural areas, 70% of the districts have digital exchanges and about 30% of Vietnam's rural villages currently have telephone service. The country has a 140 Mbps north-south fibre optic backbone and a 34 Mbps digital microwave (DMW) radio backbone for long distance transmission.

On the domestic side, HCMC has a telephone line penetration rate of 2% of the population which is twice the national average. One of the recent infrastructure developments was building a backbone link between Hanoi and HCMC. The backbone consists of a large capacity microwave link in an optical fibre cable that stretches from Hanoi to HCMC. This has vastly improved communications between the two major centres. The backbone will make it possible for provincial centres along the way to become part of the national and international network. The provincial centres along the route have been supplied with digital telephone exchanges.

(ii) ***Cellular and Paging Networks:*** A nationwide digital GSM network was established by VMS. The coverage now includes Hanoi-Haiphong-Quangninh, Da Nang-Hue, HCMC-Vungtau-Dongnai-Singbe, Logan-Cantho and Lamdong (not including the advanced mobile phone system (AMPS) network in HCMC). A nationwide paging network has also been operating since 10 October 1995 (*Conclusions Paper*, *Roundtable with the Government of Vietnam*, 1995). Other services, such as data transmission and pay phones, are currently under development. For the fixed network, 1% telephone penetration or 780,000 subscriber lines are operating in 1995. In HCMC alone, there are four paging networks, one cordless telephone 2 (CT2) network, one analog AMPS network and the digital GSM network. In addition, a recent contract was awarded to Comvik International who will work with VMS to provide a second nationwide mobile network to accommodate 180,000 subscribers by the end of the ten year contract period.

Paging, CT2 and trunked radio services have all been implemented in Vietnam during the previous three years beginning in 1992. There are currently five paging systems in operation in Vietnam. All of them are operated under agreements between local posts and telecommunications (PTs) and foreign operators, and all except one, are operated under informal trial agreements despite promises by local PTs to convert these agreements to full-fledged business co-operation contracts (BCCs). Vietnam's paging subscriber base has increased significantly since the first network was installed in 1992, reaching a total of 63,300 subscribers in 1995. The subscriber base is expected to grow at an even faster rate through 1998. The low cost and instant connections offered by paging networks make them a far more accessible option than cellular telephones for many urban dwellers.

(iii) ***Switching Networks:*** The lack of easily obtainable funding for network development in the late 1980s to early 1990s led Vietnam into a potentially difficult switching supply situation. In an ambitious plan to extend the public network, the DGPT was open to all available suppliers, provided they came with financing. This created a situation where 12 different digital switching products are in Vietnam's network. An estimated 15 different models of analog switching gear are in the network as well, not to mention several types of manually operated exchanges. This diversity will certainly cause problems as Vietnam tries to interconnect various parts of the network and implement network management routines.

OPPORTUNITIES

With the growing importance of telecommunications in the framework of Vietnam's economic reforms, there is tremendous potential for growth in the telecommunications industry. Table 11–4 manifests the projected growth in the telecommunications sectors in Vietnam. Additional information on some of the major telecommunications industry-related announcements made in 1995 is tabulated in Appendix 11–1.

Opportunities in Vietnam exist in public, private and mobile network markets. These opportunities can be evaluated from three very different perspectives, namely those of the network operator, equipment vendor and the equipment manufacturer. To a large extent, the significance of these opportunities and the eligible partners are dependent on the extent to which Vietnam decides to permit foreign participation in public network development.

TABLE 11–4
Projected Growth of Telecom Sectors in Vietnam: 1995 to 1998

Telecommunications by Sector	1995	1996	1997	1998
Private Network Market	43.87	38.11	29.87	35.75
Mobile Network Markets	175.72	35.22	130.85	66.62
Telecom Equipment Markets	34.86	30.14	27.33	23.55
Main Lines in Service	47.62	41.64	32.24	24.38
Cellular Subscribers	257.58	93.56	80.84	80.84
Cellular Penetration	263.64	90.00	77.63	77.04
Paging Subscribers (000)	73.42	73.46	73.41	73.48
Paging Penetration per 1000 population	80.00	66.67	66.67	68.00

Source: Pyramid Research Report, *Telecoms Markets in Vietnam, Laos, and Cambodia*, 1995, Exhibits 1–4, 1–12, 1–14, 1–15, 1–16, 1–17, 1–18, 1–20.

Operating Opportunities

It is unlikely that Vietnam will adopt the model of a full competition approach in the telecommunications operating market over the next five years. Unlike a manufacturer or equipment supplier, opening the operator's market to the entry of an experienced and efficient foreign operator may drive VNPT into financial difficulties. This would then require either fiscal subsidies for its operations or the privatisation of the business. Privatisation of VNPT would most likely lead to job redundancies in the short-term and add greater pressure to the rapidly growing unemployment problem.

To avoid these potentially destabilising developments, the Vietnamese government is holding on to state-owned enterprises (SOEs), such as telecommunications, that are large employers and do not face serious deficits or the risk of bankruptcy. In place of a fully competitive market, the administration appears to have opted for a "controlled" competition approach among state-owned companies.

Finally, the current economic growth and the eagerness of foreign firms to enter the telecommunications market give the government considerable leeway in postponing any radical change. However, long run efficiency demands some convergence on these issues.

Equipment Vendor Opportunities

Digital switching will continue to be an area of intense competition as well as a major opportunity. DGPT has set a goal of installing approximately 300,000 lines per year through to the end of the century but the large number of suppliers already in the market means that competition for contracts will be fierce and profit margins relatively slim. If the DGPT decides to favour selected suppliers, then the field may narrow. If foreign operators are granted an overall network development charter (such as the one France Telecom is vying for), then suppliers with established relationships with current operators are likely to benefit.

The mobile market, which is important for equipment suppliers, will only be open to a limited number of eligible suppliers due to agreements with foreign operators. France Telecom and Comvik of Sweden, both prospective mobile network contractors and/or operating partners with VMS, are likely to continue using their current mobile network suppliers, namely Alcatel and Ericsson, if they participate in network development. There will be additional opportunities for additional suppliers only if other operators are allowed into the market.

Wireless local loops (WLLs) have high potential for growth over the next few years. This is a relatively new market in which there are ample opportunities for suppliers, given the stated interest of DGPT to implement WLL technology in both the rural and urban areas. Over the next few years, rural development will generate steady demand for radio and access line equipment as the country turns its attention to less developed areas.

Equipment Manufacturers

This is the other viable option for investors who wish to capitalise on the growth of Vietnam's telecommunications industry. A joint venture or a totally foreign-owned entity is possible because they meet one of the DGPT's main priorities to increase its local manufacturing capabilities of both communications and information technology products.

The increased employment opportunities, as well as the possibility of technology transfer that comes with such an arrangement, are so significant that the contract with AWA Communications of Australia has been extended several times since 1988 and the current contract is valid until 1997. Above all, new opportunities can always be created if the contractor/vendor can develop better solutions with state-of-the-art technologies, offer more flexible financing, co-develop rural areas, or bundle proposals through a local manufacturing, training and technology transfer arrangement (Pham, 1996a).

IMPEDIMENTS TO GROWTH

There is no doubt that the telecommunications market in Vietnam has great potential for future growth. For the period 1991 to 1995, the telecommunications equipment market grew from US$28.9 million to US$178.4 million which represents an average growth rate of 86%. Although the growth rate for the period 1995 to 1998 is projected to be 27% annually (Pyramid Research Report, 1995), this is still considered to be high by most standards.

However, the bullish development of Vietnam's telecommunications in the past does not imply that it is free of obstacles and that planned development is easily achievable. Education and the availability of skilled manpower, financing of development projects and the investment climate in Vietnam are factors that may hinder the growth of Vietnam's telecommunications industry.

Education and Training of Qualified Manpower

The high growth of the telecommunications industry has resulted in a high demand for qualified personnel. Faced with problems of obsolete equipment and facilities, outdated curriculi and limited access to the latest information on technical and scientific developments, Vietnam's universities are unable to train sufficient manpower to meet the needs of the industry.

(i) ***Equipment and Facilities:*** Funding from the government is limited, and available equipment and facilities for students are inadequate. This decreases the quality of technical education. In addition to being old and outdated, much of the equipment malfunctions. Consequently, university graduates are unfamiliar with the use of the latest equipment; intensive retraining by respective employers is always mandatory (Pham, 1996b).

(ii) ***University Curriculum and Information Access:*** Universities in Vietnam have been out of touch with the international scientific community for several decades and their curriculi do not reflect the latest developments in telecommunications technology. Information on the practical implementation of state-of-the-art technologies, such as "asynchronous transfer mode" and "code division multiple access", are not included in any curriculum. In addition, the link between universities and industry is also weak and there is a lack of understanding between what the universities try to impart and what the industry needs.

Limited access to current information on international scientific and technical developments has also affected curriculum development. The major sources of literature, which came from the Soviet Union and Eastern Europe before 1990, are now cut off. Access to scientific literature from the U.S. and Western Europe is limited by the lack of hard currency (Pham, 1996b).

FUNDING

Funding the ambitious development plan of the DGPT (*Conclusions Paper, Roundtable with the Government of Vietnam*, 1995) is a challenging task. With an estimated US$2.7 billion required for funding, one-third of the bill is expected to be financed by the government and the remainder through external funding (*Vietnam Economic Times*, December 1995). Internal funding comes from revenues generated through existing businesses and the government budget allocated for telecommunications development. External funding will be in the form of soft loans and foreign investment. Soft-loan financing from foreign governments, however, is quite limited due to political differences between Vietnam and many other countries.

Notwithstanding this issue, competition for funds among industries within Vietnam is highly competitive. The development of other infrastructure is equally, if not more, urgent than telecommunications development. Moreover, it is generally more difficult to attract funds from the private sector to develop other infrastructure projects. As a result, funds such as the Overseas Development Agency (ODA) fund made available by Japan are likely to be channelled by the government into the development of other infrastructure areas other than telecommunications development.

The financing model created by Telstra and DGPT is the main funding mechanism now used by most foreign private organisations for telecommunications projects in Vietnam. In this innovative model, vendors supply the equipment and share the operating revenue with their Vietnamese partner (Nguyen, 1995c). This financing model is a high risk option for vendors because it requires a high initial capital outlay and the negative returns will continue for many years. It is therefore evident that the confidence level of vendors on the long-term prospects of the economic and political stability of Vietnam will determine the future success of this financing model.

A changing political climate, slow administrative reforms, immature legal and taxation systems, and shrinking profit margins will affect the willingness of vendors to adopt this financial model (Nguyen, 1995b). In addition, the preference of DGPT for signing MOUs with many different vendors, and then playing them off against each other to achieve competitive agreements, has irritated some vendors who view Vietnam as the only winner in this game (Nguyen, 1995a). If the ill feelings of vendors continue to grow, then it is questionable whether this means of funding is sufficient to address the financing needs of Vietnam's ambitious development. Finally, Vietnam may exacerbate the funding problem by pursuing this type of strategy because other friendly markets in the region are vying for the same pool of global funds.

CONCLUSION

Although Vietnam's future in telecommunications is hindered by potential problems, there are always critical success factors which need to be considered, and managed accordingly, to facilitate the investment process. One factor which is critical to the success of any project is receiving the support of the sponsoring ministry. Equally important is the co-operation of the local People's Committee (PC) (Gatiss, 1995). As with the SCCI (now MPI), officials in the PC are often willing to assist foreign investors in selecting a site, choosing a joint venture partner, and advising them on how to negotiate the bureaucratic hurdles. Co-operation from these officials is crucial in the process of obtaining licenses and permits. Thus, the earlier they are involved in the investment process the better is the chance of success (*Southeast Asia Monitor Newsletter*, 1995).

A second factor deals with the country's national agenda. An investor should look at a proposal from the point of view of the Vietnamese Government and bear in mind the government's perception of the national interest impact from the investment under consideration (Gatiss, 1995).

Many officials and politicians still view the relationship between each project and the interests of the country and its people as a vital criterion even though the authorities have embraced a market system. Hence, changes and reversals of policy, or interpretations of the law, are usually nothing more than a manifestation of the continuing debate on how the national interest can best be served. In the field of telecommunications, where technological changes are rampant, these factors will remain prevalent

A third critical success factor deals with establishing a local presence in telecommunications. Forging a lasting and substantial governmental relationship should be the management goal, and there is no better way to achieve this than by opening an office in the country.[2] It demonstrates intent and commitment. Staff should include experienced managers and engineers and not just sales or marketing people. Correspondingly, the engineering objective is to demonstrate a command of, and access to, the latest telecommunications service and equipment technology, and to share technical information with the local partner.

A local office further facilitates learning the country's business and political practices, helps to gain contacts with the right people, and exposes one to local business etiquette and customs. An established corporate office makes it easier to learn about the environment

---

2 From an interview with Dr. Markus Herlinghaus, Senior Commercial Manager, Siemens AG Representation, Vietnam, March 1996, as well as an interview with Per Karlberg, GM, LM Ericsson International AB, Representative Office, Vietnam, March 1996.

and to liaise in privacy with a third-party counsel who has the experience with the business and political environment. Another demonstrative sign of commitment, and also a distinct advantage, is to have someone on the staff who understands the Vietnamese language, even if most of the local people speak English.

A fourth critical success factor concerns preparation. In view of the length of typical contracts, the importance of thorough preparation cannot be over-emphasised. Getting the technology and the prices right are only a beginning. Investors must develop a thorough implementation plan before submitting bids on tender contracts. This should take the long-term situation into account. In fact, it is important to ensure that the right license for the company is compatible with the long-term situation. Investors must enter contracts with the understanding that things may change over time. For example, Australia, Hong Kong, New Zealand and Singapore all committed to analog cellular service in the late 1980s. However, this technology was soon followed by digital GSM. The latter was relatively inexpensive and created a high demand then but today many of the older systems are taxed to their capacity limits. As a result, a completely new round of bidding in contracts for the latest PCS technology has begun, albeit in some cases more cautiously.

Finally, success depends on an environment of mutual trust and respect. Consultants who have worked in the Asian-Pacific region for many years claim that the element of trust cannot be over-emphasised. Thus, a solid working relationship is fundamental to success.

APPENDIX 11–1
Major Announcements Made in 1995

Month	Foreign Partner	Local Partner	Details	Amount (million)
Jan.	Motorola (U.S.A.)	VMS	Contract for supply of 3,000 mobile telephones to HCMC.	
	Hughes Network Systems (U.S.A.)	VNPT	Letter of intent to supply HCMC with up to 120,000 digital phone lines.	
Feb.	Comvik International (Vietnam)	DGPT	Plan to set up a nationwide network providing 60,000 mobile links and a paging	US$340

APPENDIX 11–1 (cont'd)

Month	Foreign Partner	Local Partner	Details	Amount (million)
Feb.	Industriforvaltings, AB Kirnevik (Sweden)		service. Partners are expected to invest up to US$160 million, including US$125 million for equipment, while the DGPT will provide US$180 million in offices, land and wages.	
	Iridium, Multi-Country Consortium		Invitation to participate in its planned global satellite telecommunications network in a memorandum of understanding presented to the government.	
Mar.			Vietnam is to invest more than US$400 million in 1995 on 600 projects designed to upgrade the country's postal and telephone services. In 1994, the government invested more than US$320 million to install 192,000 telephones, bringing the total to 462,000.	
April	No major announcement.			
May	Ericsson (Sweden) Comvik International (Vietnam)	DGPT	Expected shortly to sign a ten year contract to build a mobile telephone network in Vietnam. The DGPT is likely to retain 50% of the profits for the first five years, and 60% thereafter.	US$300
	Telstra (Australia) Communication Authority of Thailand (Thailand) HongKong Telecom International (Hong Kong)	VNPT	Ceremony to mark the launch of the Vietnamese shore end of the international T-V-H fibre optic network was held in Vung Tau. Expected to be in service in 1997. Cables are from Alcatel while transmission equipment is from Fujitsu. Telstra will finance Vietnam's share.	US$150

APPENDIX 11–1 (cont'd)

Month	Foreign Partner	Local Partner	Details	Amount (million)
May	NTTI International Corp. (Japan)	VNPT	Contract to build a fibre optic telephone network in Hanoi with 25,000 lines.	US$25
	Sprint (U.S.A.)	VNPT	Contract to provide a nation-wide highspeed data network and multimedia system which will connect with Sprint's global value-added network (VAN) and the internet.	
June		VNPT	Inauguration of a microwave communications link stretching 2,500km with a total of 63 transmission stations in 27 provinces along the length of Vietnam from Lang Son in the north to Minh Hai.	US$50
July	Comvik International (Vietnam)		The SCCI has awarded a license to Comvik International Vietnam, a division of the Swedish telecommunications company Industriforvaltnings AB Kirnevik, to invest US$127.8 million in the country's first national GSM cellular phone system. As announced earlier in May, the ten year agreement entitles Comvik to an equal share of the revenues from the first five years of operation with the state-run VMS. The latter five years will see the Swedish partner's share drop to 40%.	US$300
Aug.	Ericsson (Sweden)	VMS/ Comvik	Ericsson announced that the agreement for network equipment had been signed. The new phase is to be installed in Danang, Hue, Haiphong and the Mekong Delta by end of 1995.	US$30

APPENDIX 11–1 (cont'd)

Month	Foreign Partner	Local Partner	Details	Amount (million)
	SCITEC Ltd. (Australia)	CAAV	Communications technology developed and manufactured in Australia has been installed by the Civil Aviation Authority of Vietnam. The four main airports in Vietnam, Ho Chi Minh, Hanoi, Danang, and Quinon, are now able to exchange voice, data and radar communications. Both Cambodia and Laos have also expressed interest in the system.	
	Motorola (U.S.A.)	VNPT	Contract for Vietnam's first nationwide paging system has been awarded to Motorola by VNPT. The system will consist of three Advanced Simulcast Controllers and 28 Nucleus paging stations, operating within the country's 280mhz band.	US$0.8
Sept.	NTT (Japan)	VNPT	NTT is negotiating with VNPT for a contract to design, supply and install a 500,000 line telephone network covering the Hanoi region. Manufacturers from the U.S., U.K., Germany and France are also in the running for the contract. Announcement of award is expected to be at the end of 1996.	US$550
Oct.	Nortel (Canada)	VNPT	Supplied VNPT with DMS-100 switching equipment for the port of Haiphong.	US$6
	Nortel (Canada)	Telstra	Nortel Asia South Pacific has won an order from Telstra to supply a high speed, high capacity 2.5 Gbps synchronous digital hierarchy (SDH)	US$4.5

APPENDIX 11–1 (cont'd)

Month	Foreign Partner	Local Partner	Details	Amount (million)
			transmission system for Vietnam's new 3,000km fibre optic network. This is the next stage of Telstra's US$194 million investment in Vietnam's telecommunications.	US$4.5
	Telecommunications American International (U.S.A.)	Saigon PTS	The PM Office has approved the issue of a telecommunications concession to Saigon PTS Corporation in partnership with the U.S. company TAI. The TAI and Saigon PTS joint venture will operate under the name U.S.A. Telecom. According to the terms of the concession and joint venture agreements, TAI and Saigon PTS will co-operatively develop and manage a cellular telephone network, an international long distance gateway, telephone calling centres and telecommunications equipment manufacturing facilities, as well as cable and broadcast television services in Vietnam.	
Nov.			The Government of Vietnam intends to launch its first satellite by the year 2000. The US$250-300 million communications satellite will be launched by a consortium of American and French firms.	
	Kamematsu Corporation (Japan)		Japan's Kamematsu Corporation has been awarded a contract to provide Vietnam with a radio telephone net-	

APPENDIX 11–1 (cont'd)

Month	Foreign Partner	Local Partner	Details	Amount (million)
			work with a 20,000 line capacity. Kamematsu will supply radio transmitters, receivers and telephone handsets manufactured by Hughes Network Systems, while NEC will provide a telephone exchange. Vietnam intends to order a radio telephone system capable of providing 100,000 lines.	
	Telstra (Australia) France Telecom Cable & Wireless NTT (Japan)	VNPT	VNPT is expected to sign four multi-million dollar deals to develop telecommunications infrastructure in Hanoi and Ho Chi Minh City.	
Dec.	Cambodia and Laos		Announcement from Minister for Post and Telecommunications of Cambodia stating that the three countries will co-operate in enhancing mobile communications, training staff, and managing broadcast frequencies.	

Source: Compiled from market reports in various issues of *Asian Communications,* 1995.

REFERENCES

Bacon Gary, "Looking at the Broader Picture", *Asian Communications*, September 1995, p. 33.

"Cautious Reforming", *Asian Communications*, May 1995, pp. 41–5.

"Clarification on Changes", *Asian Communications*, September 1995, p. 13.

"Conclusions Paper, Roundtable with the Government of Vietnam", Hanoi, Vietnam, 1995.

Fforde A. and A. Goldstone, "Vietnam to 2005 – Advancing On All Fronts", *Research Report*, Economist Intelligence Unit, April 1995.

Gatiss Howard, "Inside View: Avoiding the Pitfalls as an Investor", *Vietnam Economic Times*, November 1995, p. 17.

"Investors Hit Serious Problems with Partners and Officials", *Southeast Asia Monitor Newsletter*, August 1995.

"Market Report on Indonesia", *Asian Communications*, March 1995, pp. 16–7.

"Market Report on Malaysia", *Asian Communications*, February 1995, pp. 16–7.

"Market Report on Singapore", *Asian Communications*, April 1995, pp. 22–3.

"Market Report on Thailand", *Asian Communications*, July 1995, pp. 24–5.

"Market Report on Vietnam", *Asian Communications*, November 1995, pp. 30–1.

Nguyen M., *On Foreign Investment in Vietnam,* State Evaluation Committee, Ministry of Planning and Investment, Hanoi, Vietnam, 1995a.

Nguyen M. T., *Ten-Years Economic Reform in Vietnam – Some Selected Macroeconomic Key Issues*, Central Institute for Economic Management, Hanoi, Vietnam, 1995b.

Nguyen Ngo Hong, *Vietnam – National Network Development and the Role for Foreign Investment*, Vietnam Post and Telecommunications, Hanoi, Vietnam, 1995c.

Pereira Joseph, "A Tumultuous Year", *Asian Communications*, November 1995, pp. 34–42.

Pham Chi Lan, "Industry-Government Relations in Vietnam", Vietnam Chamber of Commerce, Hanoi, Vietnam, 4 March 1996a.

Pham Minh Ha, *Developing Technical Manpower for the Telecoms Industry*, Hanoi Technology University, Vietnam, 5 March 1996b.

"Post-monopoly Interest is High", *Asian Communications*, January 1995, p. 5.

Pyramid Research Report, *Telecoms Markets in Vietnam, Laos and Cambodia*, Pyramid Research, Inc., Cambridge, MA, 1995.

Technical Supplement, *Vietnam Economic Times*, December 1995.

"The Region Advances", *Asian Communications*, September 1995, p. 87.
"Voices on Vietnam", *Asian Communications*, March 1995, pp. 44–7.

Chapter 12

Providing Internet Service in Vietnam: Impediments and Potential*

BY
Jill LEE
Janice LEONG
Shirley LIM
TAN How Choon

INTRODUCTION

THE INTERNET SERVICE industry is at its infancy in Vietnam. Presently, international telecommunication links available from Vietnam are limited and most companies handle their in-country data needs via local area networks. However, with increasing economic growth and accelerated business developments in Vietnam, the demand for new and improved means of data communication services is expected to experience spectacular growth over the next decade.

Internet technology is a possible solution for Vietnam to leap-frog its technological gap in data transmission, and to establish essential connections to the universe of ideas and information available in developed nations. Since 1994, Vietnam has been accessible by electronic mail through Internet. At present, however, the scope of Internet services provided in Vietnam is still limited to only electronic mail-

* We would like to thank the various Vietnamese Government Officials, Singaporean and Vietnamese businessmen who provided sources of information. Most important, thanks to Dr. Jon Kendall for his valuable assistance and advice on the Internet.

ing services. Despite this limitation, the popularity of Internet among companies in Vietnam is growing rapidly, rising from a mere 30 users in late 1994 to approximately 3,000 at the beginning of 1996 (*The Vietnam Business Journal*, October 1995b).

Although the needs of private businesses will continue to drive the growth of Internet in Vietnam, the government also will play a very critical role in accelerating the development of Internet in the country. This will be in the form of setting a well-orchestrated mix of policies and initiatives to promote information technology, developing infrastructure for data communication as well as facilitating data communication both domestically and internationally (Cameron, 1995a).

In policy setting, the Vietnamese government initiated a national programme to promote the development of information technology (IT), including specific directives on Internet. This programme, known as the "Policy and Master Plan on IT Development up to the year 2000" (Socialist Republic of Vietnam, 1995), was formulated to steer the development of the country's information technology to meet the macro economic and business sector needs by the beginning of the 21st century.

In infrastructural development, Vietnam has made substantial progress in telecommunications. Presently, its national system provides 100% digital switching and transmission in cities and between exchanges. One recent infrastructural development is the high capacity microwave backbone link between Hanoi, Da Nang and Ho Chi Minh City. The importance of telecommunications and information technology to the Vietnamese government is evidenced by the recent decision to have the heads of the Directorate General of Posts and Telecommunications (DGPT) and of the Steering Committee for National Programme on IT report directly to the Prime Minister.

Economic growth, fuelled by progress in IT and telecommunications, presents a conducive environment for the emergence of a thriving market for Internet services in Vietnam. However, amidst these optimistic indications of increasing demand for Internet services in Vietnam, foreign Internet service providers entering the country must take heed of certain impediments. Concerns of the Vietnamese government over possible detrimental effects on the country's culture and national security have led to a restriction in the range of services offered by Internet service providers in Vietnam. In addition, foreign Internet service providers can only enter the Vietnamese industry through collaboration with local partners. Service providers are governed by specific contractual terms executed in an emerging commercial legal system.

This chapter analyses the potential for developing the Internet industry in Vietnam, given the government policies and general economic trends. Possible impediments to providing Internet services, as well as business implications for entry into the Vietnamese Internet industry, are also explored.

In this chapter, Internet service provisioning is defined as the supply of Internet services to subscribers, covering full graphical tools like Netscape browser, either in stand-alone mode or connected through a local area network, with routers and firewalls for network security, linked through an Internet backbone to international networks. Internet service providers may provide Internet content publishing, comprehensive information data banks for storage of web pages, billing software facilities, as well as access management functions for proper authorisation of users (Chua, 1995).

The chapter presents a structured analysis of the Vietnamese Internet industry. It explores the supply of and demand for Internet services through an examination of the various key components of the industry and the background influences of the general economic and political environment. A framework based on Michael Porter's model of five competitive forces for industry analysis is the basis for analysis (Porter, 1985). The application of Internet in Vietnam to support communication, information and research, marketing and electronic commerce is also examined (Cronin, 1994). Finally, recommendations on possible focus market sectors and relevant business approaches for potential Internet service providers are considered (Cameron, 1995b).

ENVIRONMENTAL ANALYSIS

Global Trends in the Development of Internet

Dramatic growth in the usage of Internet services is a global phenomena. The availability of state-of-the-art technology has made it possible for emerging countries, such as Vietnam and China, to leap-frog through the rapid modernisation of their telecommunication and information infrastructures. The explosive growth of Internet worldwide is evident by the increase in the number of Internet hosts.[1] Table 12–1 compares the 1994 and 1995 statistics on the number of Internet hosts by region. The present level of Internet usage in Asia is envisaged to increase five-fold in 1996, with rapid growth in demand for Internet services in many Asian countries, especially in Singapore and Malaysia. In Vietnam, the demand for Internet services is expected to experience similar growth as more hosts subscribe to Internet for business communication purposes.

TABLE 12–1
Explosive Growth of Internet Hosts by Region

Region	January 1995	January 1994
North America	3,372,551	1,685,715
Western Europe	1,039,192	550,933
Pacific	192,390	113,482
Asia	151,773	81,355
Eastern Europe	46,125	19,867
Africa	27,130	10,951
Middle East	13,776	6,946
Central and South America	N.A.	7,392
Total	4,842,937	2,476,641

Source: *The Asian Wall Street Journal*, March 1996.

Inherent in the nature of Internet services is the concern by governments worldwide about the infiltration of undesirable information such as pornographic materials and other objectionable articles. It is reflective of technological trends that advances in information security tend to lag behind those of information processing. Along with new developments to improve security within Internet for business and communication, there is a trend towards greater regulation of the use of Internet services and the broadcasting of information. For example, the Chinese government has made it mandatory for Internet users to lodge their personal particulars and to sign a legal undertaking to ensure the upholding of national security when using the Internet. In Singapore, the government is also contemplating the introduction of

1 An Internet host is a permanent connection which can provide some indication of the extent of Internet activity. Currently, there is no precise means of measuring Internet activity globally (*The Asian Wall Street Journal*, 18 March 1996).

some form of legislation to curb the abuse of Internet services. In the context of Vietnam, there is still no legislation on Internet usage but the government presently restricts the range of Internet services supplied by Internet service providers in the country.

Recent technological advances in multimedia technology indicates a possible restructuring of broadcasting and telecommunications industries in the future. In line with this trend, Internet content provision will be based increasingly on an exploitation of multimedia services. This will imply easier accessibility and greater availability of Internet services to more users. With Internet established as an international medium for communication, information and business, it is likely that Vietnam will have to adopt Internet in its entirety to support the needs of a market-oriented economy. Regulation on the use of Internet will increasingly require collaborative efforts and collective legislation by all countries worldwide.

General Overview of Vietnam's Economy

After nearly ten years of implementing an open-door policy and a market-oriented economy, Vietnam has overcome many difficulties. It has transformed itself into a country in the initial stages of industrialisation from a basic agricultural economy. High economic growth rates exist in most of economic sectors, ranging from production, trade, services and tourism to financial markets (*Vietnam Economic Times*, November 1994). Between 1991 and 1995, Vietnam achieved an average annual GDP growth rate of 8.2%, with an impressive rate of 9.5% in 1995 (Nguyen, 1996a).

During the last few years, Vietnam has achieved rapid economic growth despite the imposition of a trade embargo by the U.S. and the absence of foreign assistance to the country. In February 1994, the U.S. lifted its embargo on trade with Vietnam. In July 1995, Vietnam became a member of ASEAN. These developments will avail greater trade opportunities to Vietnam and will further propel her economic growth.

About 80% of Vietnam's 76 million population live in rural areas, and work primarily in agriculture and fisheries. Industrial and commercial activities are primarily located in the major cities of Ho Chi Minh City, Hanoi and Da Nang. Each major city has it own specialisation in key industries and commercial services. Ho Chi Minh City serves as a commercial hub of Vietnam and Hanoi is the capital city of the country where most of the government institutions are located.

Demographically, Vietnam has a very young population with 70% under 35 years of age. It has a high literacy rate of about 90%. In addition, English and French have been implemented as compulsory electives to be taken as a second language in school. There is also an increasing focus on IT education, with a national target of reaching 20,000 IT experts by the year 2000 (Socialist Republic of Vietnam, 1995).

Structure of the Telecommunications Industry in Vietnam

(i) ***Telecommunications Authority:*** The body responsible for the development of telecommunications infrastructure in Vietnam is the Directorate General of Posts and Telecommunications (DGPT). It has relinquished its role as an operator and is now focused primarily on setting telecommunications policy and regulation.

Vietnam Posts and Telecommunications (VNPT) and Vietnam Army Telecommunications Company (Vietel) are the two operators in Vietnam which operate their own independent trunk networks. VNPT's trunk network supports paging services, trunk mobile radio services, cellular mobile telephone services and data services (*Vietnam Economic Times*, December 1994). On the other hand, Vietel primarily supports the requirements of the military sector.

VNPT has licensed one of its subsidiary companies, Vietnam Data Company (VDC), as an independent service operator. VDC is in the process of entering into a joint venture with Sprint International to set up Internet access equipment. The organisation chart of the telecommunications authority in Vietnam is depicted in the Figure 12–1.

Telecommunications Network

Presently, most telephones are concentrated in the cities, with businesses as the main subscribers. Residential ownership of telephones is low and communication in the rural areas is still difficult. Less than 20% of the population in the rural areas have any telecommunication facilities. However, demand for telephone services is expected to rise considerably over the next few years. The forecasted telephone demand by Vietel for the business and residential sector is shown in Table 12–2.

FIGURE 12– 1
Structure of Vietnam's Telecommunication Authority

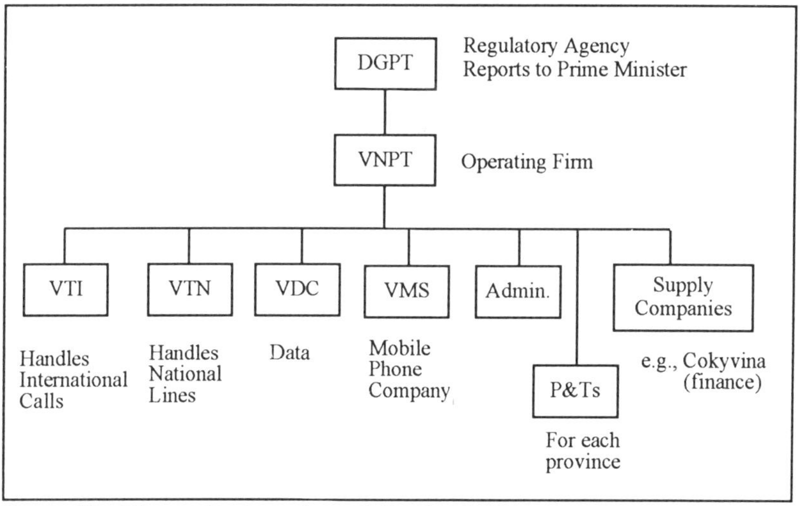

Source: *The Vietnam Business Journal*, October 1995a.

TABLE 12–2
Forecast of Business and Residential Demand for Telephones

	Overall Demand		
Year	**Total**	**Business**	**Residential**
1996	1,160,707	464,283	696,424
1997	1,503,020	563,633	939,387
1998	1,862,123	651,743	1,210,380
1999	2,199,718	736,906	1,462,812
2000	2,463,985	800,795	1,663,190

Source: Vietel, 1996.

Despite the low telephone penetration in the rural areas, Vietnam is taking major steps to accelerate the development of international networks in the cities. The telecommunication networks in the cities are fully digital. There are six earth satellite stations utilising Intersputnik and Intersat systems, and international direct-dial connections, facsimile and data transmission are provided using modern gateway exchanges (Nguyen, 1996b). The recent building of a backbone link between Hanoi, Da Nang and Ho Chi Minh City has also made it easier for provincial centres along the way to become part of the national and international network. These three cities will form the switching hub to the provinces. Figure 12–2 reflects the statistics on the growth of telecommunications services in Vietnam (*The Vietnam Business Journal*, October 1995b).

FIGURE 12–2
Public Network Market (US$ Millions)

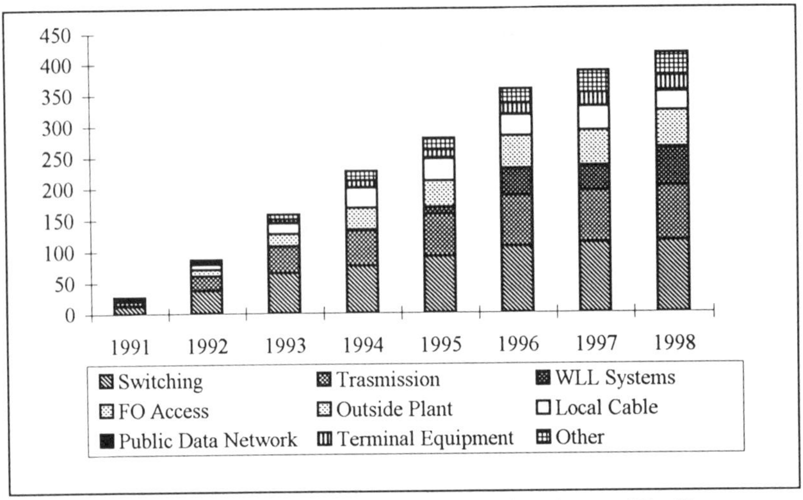

Source: PTT and company reports; Pyramid Research estimates (*The Vietnam Business Journal*, October 1995c).

VNPT and Vietel currently operate two separate telecommunication networks, with gateways in Hanoi, Da Nang and Ho Chi Minh. Each operator is presently responsible for its own gateway. However, it is envisaged that there will be an eventual interconnection of the two networks to facilitate the establishment of a national information infrastructure and to achieve economies of scale. Figure 12–3 shows the modelled inter-connectivity of the two main networks, with links domestically and internationally.

The Government's IT Goals and Policies (Vietnam's IT2000)

The present level of information technology development in Vietnam is low when compared to international standards. There is a low level of effectiveness of IT applications, an absence of an IT industry base, and a serious shortage of IT professionals and institutions embarking

FIGURE 12–3
Future Inter-connection Plan

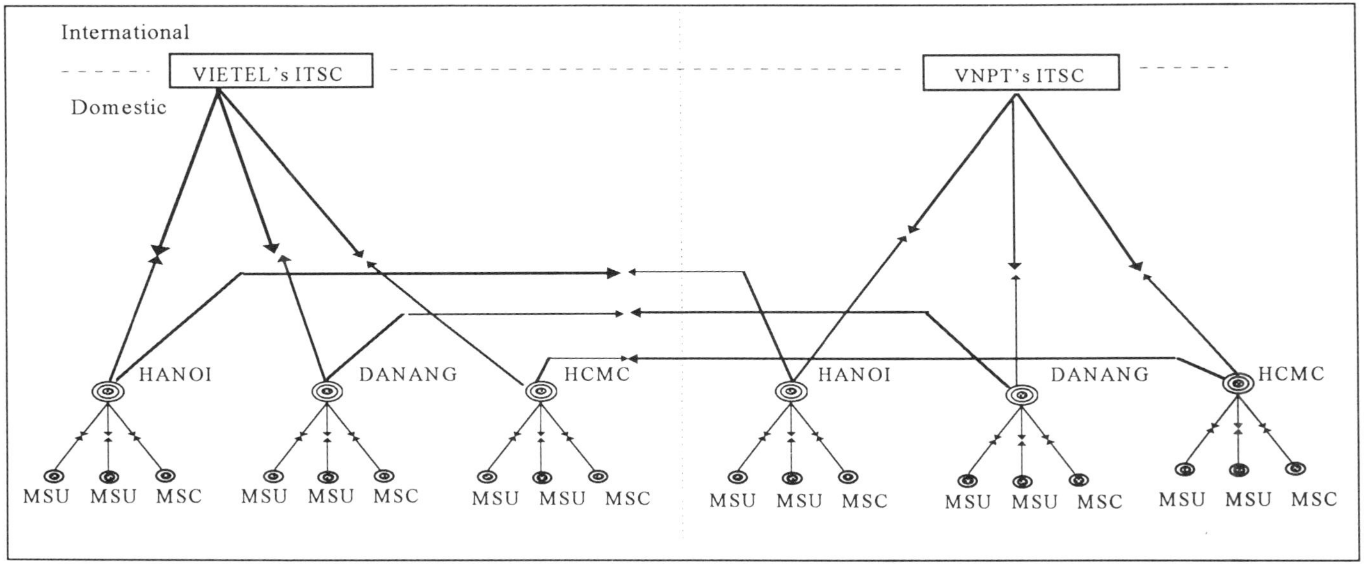

HCMC – Ho Chi Minh City
ITSC – International Telephone Switching Centre
MSU – Modem Switching Unit
MSC – Modem Switching Centre

on IT research and development. One possible indicator of the IT development level is the number of personal computers installed in the country. According to a survey conducted in the first quarter of 1994, there were only 40,000 to 45,000 personal computers installed in Vietnam (Annerstedt and Sturgeom, 1995). This certainly indicates an extremely low usage of personal computers when compared to the country's population of 73 million.

Recognising its lag in IT development, the Vietnamese government initiated a national programme to promote development of IT in 1993 (Sakina, 1994). This national IT plan is a Government Resolution (No. 49/CP/1993) signed by the Prime Minister. All government bodies have been instructed to follow the guidelines and to achieve the objectives stated in this IT plan.

To effect the policies and strategies identified in the government's resolution on IT development, an implementation plan referred to as the "Policy and Master Plan on Information Technology Development Up to 2000" was issued in 1995. It maps the government's objectives on IT infrastructure, cross-sectoral application of IT for state and socio-economic development, building of a national information culture and development of the IT industry in Vietnam. The goal is to increase the country's global competitiveness in IT. Policies, strategies and implementation targets are covered in this IT master plan. A Steering Committee for the National Programme on IT Development, which reports directly to the Prime Minister, has been commissioned with the task of operationalising this master plan. The government's approach to the development of the IT plan is simplified and shown in Figure 12–4.

FINDINGS OF THE PRESENT STUDY

Method

Information on the potential and challenges of providing Internet services was collected from both primary and secondary sources. Prior to the Business Study Mission, secondary information was obtained in Singapore from reports, journals, books and via the Internet. Discussions with major Internet service providers in Singapore were also conducted. During the visit to Vietnam, interviews and discussions were conducted with officials of the Steering Committee for the National Programme on Information Technology (OSC), Vietnam National Administration of Tourism (VNAT), Vietnam Posts and Telecommunications (VNPT), Ho Chi Minh City Hi-Tech Park and several education specialists in Vietnam.

FIGURE 12–4
Development of IT2000 Master Plan

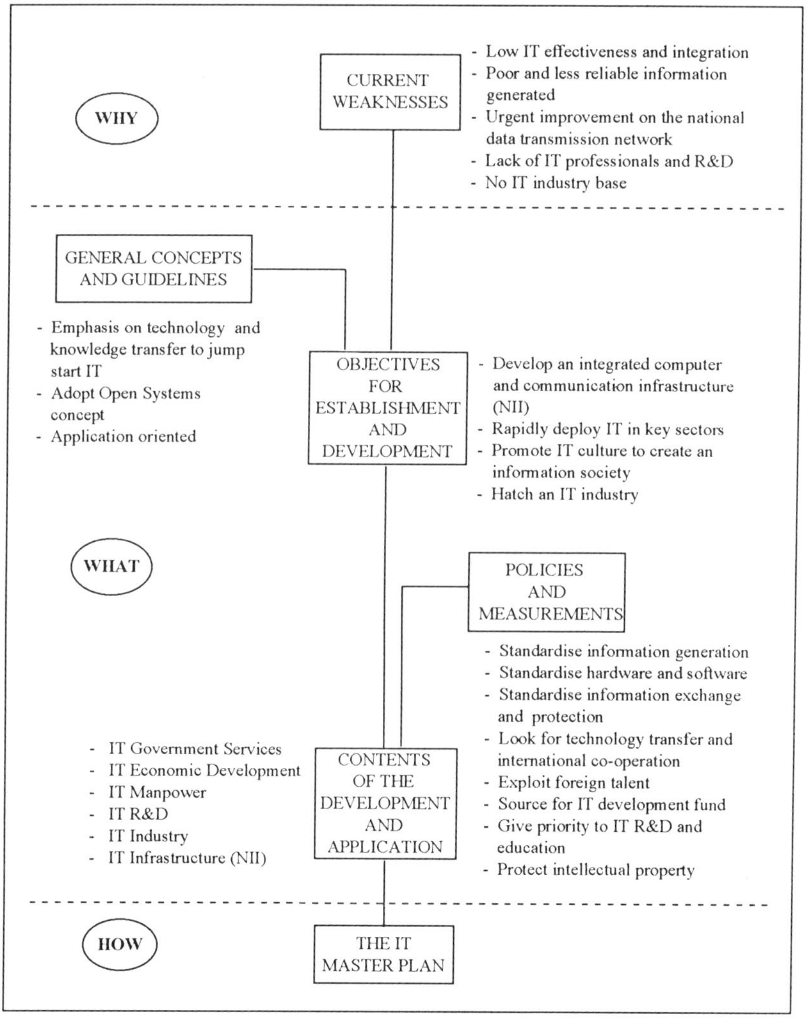

Apart from these, interviews and surveys were also conducted with Internet service providers, several businesses in Vietnam, as well as graduate students and lecturers from universities in Hanoi, Hue and Ho Chi Minh City. For the latter city, focus group sessions were held in Hanoi and Ho Chi Minh City to demonstrate Internet operations (featuring a full spectrum of Internet options) and to obtain feedback on the usage of Internet in Vietnam. Based on the extensive information collected, the potential for, and impediments of, providing Internet services in Vietnam were analysed.

Survey Findings

A survey of Internet usage demand was conducted in Hanoi and Ho Chi Minh City. About 150 survey forms were sent to the business community, non-government organisations (NGOs), institutions and government officials. These forms were distributed throughout the trip and also via the Internet. A total of 92 responded. Table 12–3 summarises the findings of the survey and Table 12–4 shows the composition of the respondents by city and by industry.

TABLE 12–3
Summary of Survey Findings on Internet Usage in Hanoi and Ho Chi Minh City

Survey Feedback	Presently Using Internet	Presently Not Using Internet
Survey Respondents (no. of users)	27	65
Types of services used (present users) or interested to have (non-users) (% of respective survey population)		
Electronic Mail	96%	97%
Information and Research	59%	88%
Marketing and Company Advertising	19%	72%
Business Transactions	4%	31%
Problems faced (users) or reasons for not using (non-users) (% of respective survey population)		
High cost	59%	62%
Not enough training	33%	78%
Limited range of services available	48%	5%
Not safe to use for business	37%	14%
Lack of equipment	15%	48%

TABLE 12–4
Composition of Survey Respondents by City and by Industry

Industry	Hanoi	Ho Chi Minh City	Total
Manufacturing	10%	20%	14%
Hotel/Tourism	13%	5%	10%
Services/Trade (banking, auditing, consultancy, construction, etc.)	62%	58%	60%
Focus Group (university lecturers & graduate students)	15%	18%	16%
Total	100%	100%	100%

From the survey responses, 27 of 92 respondents were current Internet users. There was a slightly higher percentage of respondents using the Internet in Hanoi. This might be due to the fact that Vietnam's first Internet service was commissioned in Hanoi. Another contributing factor could be that most of the non-governmental organisations (NGOs), which are frequent users of Internet, are also located in Hanoi.

Among the Internet users surveyed, 96% use the Internet for electronic mailing and 59% use the Internet for information retrieval and research. There was a relatively low usage of the Internet for marketing, advertising and electronic commerce. Among the non-users, 88% were interested in using electronic mailing services and 62% expressed an interest in using the Internet for information and research. Interestingly, 54% of these non-users were keen to use the Internet for marketing and promotional purposes. This motive may stem from the limited scope of Internet services currently available to users in Vietnam.

Two focus group sessions were conducted, one in Hanoi and the other in Ho Chi Minh City. During these sessions, demonstrations on the use of the Internet (covering the spectrum currently available in Singapore) were conducted for 15 graduate students and lecturers. The participants found the sessions to be informative. Most participants have heard of the Internet but they were unaware of Internet functions beyond electronic mailing. Many questions were raised on the operating costs and business opportunities of setting up the Internet. All of the participants indicated strong interest in using the Internet.

From the findings summarised in Table 12–3, it is clear that the key problems facing Internet users in Vietnam are high costs and a limited range of Internet services. Out of the 27 users, 59% complained of high costs and 48% were dissatisfied with the existing range of services available. Other stated reasons included inadequate security (37%) and lack of training (33%). There appears to be a perception among some businessmen that the Internet is not safe for business transaction purposes.

For the 65 non-users, the reasons for not using the Internet were lack of training (78%), high cost (62%) and lack of equipment (48%). There was also a relatively strong perception among these respondents that the Internet is difficult to use. Nevertheless, 83% of the non-users felt that the Internet would be useful for them.

Interview Findings

(i) ***Interview with VNAT and OSC:*** During a joint interview with the Director of Tourism Information Technology Centre (VNAT) and the Director of the Documentation Centre, OSC, information was collected on the organisation structure of IT authorities in Vietnam, IT-related activities undertaken by the government and the views of some government bodies on Internet.

Due to the importance accorded to telecommunications, the Vietnamese government recently instituted a direct reporting relationship to the Prime Minister for both the heads of DGPT and the Steering Committee for the National Programme on IT. A standing committee, OSC, which reports to the Steering Committee for National Programme on IT, has also been set up to coordinate IT development projects. Investments for all IT related activities must first be submitted to the OSC for approval prior to start-up. The OSC then coordinates with the Ministry of Planning and Investment. The organisation chart depicting these relationships is shown in Figure 12–5.

A pilot project on implementing Internet for selected government ministries, named Experimental Project in IT using Internet, was launched at the beginning of 1996. The responsibility for this project rests with the Steering Committee for the National Programme on IT, VNPT and the Ministry of Domestic Affairs, and it is coordinated by the OSC. In this respect, the Steering Committee for the National Programme on IT is responsible for the choice of software and the type of Internet services to be offered. VNPT will assume responsibility for the choice of hardware and telecommunications medium. Issues pertaining to national security and preservation of traditional values will be under the purview of the Ministry of Domestic Affairs.

FIGURE 12–5
Organisation Chart of IT Management in Vietnam

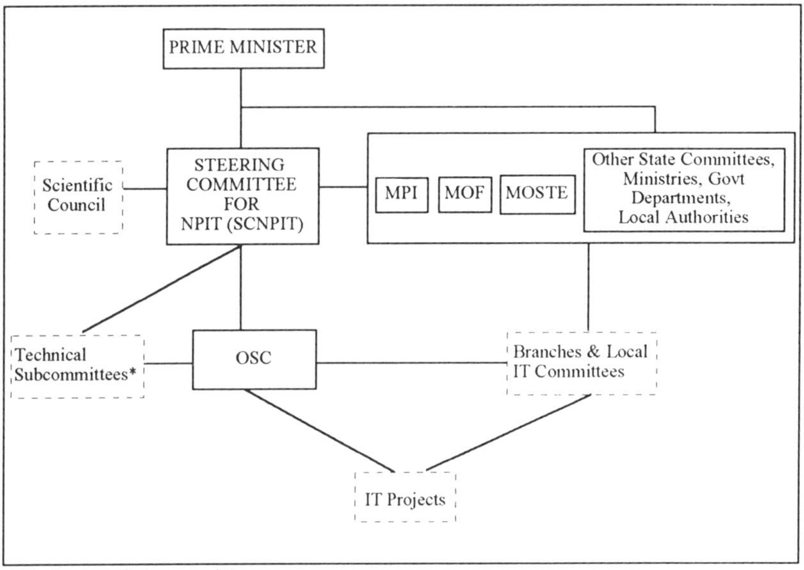

*Technical Subcommittees on:
1. Computerisation in Public Administration
2. Human Resources Development
3. IT Standards
4. Data Communication Networks
5. IT Policies

This pilot project sets up Intranet linkages among five ministries: Science and Technology, Tourism, Education, Domestic Affairs and Finance. Presently, few local area networks are installed in these government ministries. The project will run on the backbone link between Hanoi and Ho Chi Minh City, with nodes in Hanoi, Da Nang and Ho Chi Minh City. Through this project, the Vietnamese government aims to upgrade the administration of its ministries, create an information culture and explore an "open-door" concept to information technology. This pilot project is targeted for completion by the end of 1996. The government hopes to gain experience from this project and to embark on further data communication and information exchange development as identified in its IT master plan for the year 2000 (Socialist Republic of Vietnam, 1995).

Primary among several concerns of the Vietnamese government is the influence of the Internet on the country's preservation of traditional values and its impact on national security. With concerns about possible adverse impacts on the country's social and political culture, the Vietnamese government is taking a very cautious approach to the implementation of Internet. Until it gains experience in the management of a national information highway, the Vietnamese government is likely to opt for Intranet rather than Internet services.

Financing IT development projects is a major hurdle for the Vietnamese government. Infrastructure for telecommunications and information technology requires substantial capital which Vietnam cannot manage on its own accord. Thus far, financial support for IT development has been extended by Canada, Sweden and Australia. In selecting its collaboration partners for telecommunications development, the Vietnamese government places considerable emphasis on the availability of attractive financing from the prospective vendors. In this respect, financing of the experimental Internet project was also a critical limitation. Financing from the World Bank and International Monetary Fund (IMF) is selective and there is very low financial support given to the development of the Internet.

According to the Director of the Documentation Centre, OSC, there is a lack of IT software specialists to support their IT development projects. To alleviate this shortage, some IT personnel have been sent for overseas training; the universities are also expanding their IT departments. With respect to the Internet, there is a strong interest in short-term courses on IT methodology, multimedia technology, networking, windows NT and information association. OSC also has a keen interest to learn from Singapore's experience with the Internet and plans to seek training assistance from Singapore.

(ii) ***Interviews with Internet Service Providers in Vietnam:*** There are two main Internet service providers in Vietnam, namely the Vietnamese Academic, Research and Education Network (Varenet) and Netnam. Varenet was set up by the Institute of Information Technology (IOIT). During the period 1989 to 1992, the United Nations Development Programme (UNDP) provided the IOIT with initial set-up capital. With support from the Australian National University, the IOIT set up VARENET to provide basic electronic mailing services to the research and education communities of Vietnam.

Netnam was established later to facilitate a more participatory and sustainable model for Vietnam's network development (*Far Eastern Economic Review*, 1995). Netnam is headquartered in Hanoi and presently has a second network in Ho Chi Minh City. Netnam was developed by the networking department of the IOIT. The start-up capital was from the government, with assistance from foreign grants. The operation of Netnam is now self-funded and semi-privately owned by a group of entrepreneurs. Its clientele includes international NGOs, government offices, bilateral and multilateral agencies, research institutes, journalists, press organisations and other private users with development interests.

Varenet and Netnam, together, serve about 700 nodes and each node (normally a local area network) may have about 30 to 40 users. With the installation of Netnam's second network in Ho Chi Minh City, the number of users has expanded. The objective is to provide an extensive computer network through the Internet to allow for the easy exchange of electronic mail with any correspondent at a rate of less than one tenth the price of a fax or telex. Netnam operates with a small core group of network and Internet specialists who have been trained locally and overseas. These specialists converse in several foreign languages and provide training, consultancy and technical services to a large number of government offices and international agencies.

A unique feature of Netnam service is "Worldgroup Manager", an on-line service (Galacticomm Inc., 1995). The service is in the form of electronic mail, discussion forums, directory of users, databases and file libraries. Interesting features of the Worldgroup Manager include teleconferencing and drawing-board, as well as polling and questionnaire facilities. These facilities enable commercial users to conduct surveys on their business services, generate statistics on pie charts and graphs, as well as communicate technical designs via Internet. Putting Worldgroup Manager on the Internet will thus enable Netnam's subscribers to resolve designing or manufacturing issues without having to travel long distances.

Access to worldwide web (WWW) is, however, still in the experimental stage. In spite of this, a country profile of Vietnam on CDROM, recently produced by the Department of Tourism, will be available on the WWW services for international access. According to Internet service providers, access to WWW can be made available to their subscribers as soon as the government allows it. Based on observations and the survey findings, there will be a high demand for these services when this occurs.

(iii) ***Interview with a Cyber Café:*** Through a telephone interview, contact was made with a Vietnamese who is currently in the process of setting up a cyber café in Hanoi. This is an entrepreneurial venture modelled after the concept in other countries. Since the vendor presently runs an employment placement agency for new graduates, they constitute the café's initial target group of customers. To complement the services of her employment agency, which includes assisting graduates to prepare their curriculum vitae, the vendor intends to locate her café very near to the employment agency. The café will have five microcomputers with Internet access and should be operational by the end of 1996. The café will also be used to conduct Internet training. The vendor expects the demand for Internet to be good because the café will provide the necessary facilities and services for Internet at affordable prices.

In Hanoi, it was reported that a newly established government-owned hotel was planning to provide Internet services to its clients. The hotel also expressed interest in setting up an Internet Club and a cyber café in the hotel premises as part of its marketing efforts.

AN ANALYSIS OF MARKET SUPPLY AND DEMAND

Suppliers and Interfirm Rivalry

The Internet service industry in Vietnam is still in its infancy, showing characteristics of a low but increasingly growing market demand, and a small but foreseeable growing supplier base. Taking a broad view of the supply chain for Internet services, the supplier base would include providers of hardware for data communications, computer and computer peripherals, and service providers for Internet software and content. Presently, there are a few major local players in the Vietnamese industry, namely VDC and Vietel which provide the data communications infrastructure, and Varenet and Netnam which provide Internet services. Many foreign companies have entered the Vietnamese industry but they are primarily hardware providers such as SUN, Siemens, IBM, Unisys, Sprint and many others. In the case of Internet services, there are also a few international suppliers such as Compuserve, America Online, Genie and Reuters.

Rapid economic growth, modernisation and extension of telecommunications infrastructure, growing IT know-how and increasing government focus on IT are factors that will promote growth in the demand for Internet services in Vietnam. There is certainly room for more Internet service providers in Vietnam. An expansion of the supplier base for Internet services will create greater competition in price and service quality within the industry. This will, in turn, fuel the demand for Internet services, thereby stimulating further growth of the Internet service industry in the country.

The two existing Internet service providers in Vietnam, Varenet and Netnam, are affiliated to the government Institute of Information Technology, and each one supplies Internet services to specific market segments. Varenet focuses primarily on the research and education communities while Netnam provides its services mainly to businesses, government and NGOs. Both Internet service providers currently provide only electronic mailing services.

Although there are foreign Internet service providers supplying Internet services from outside the country, they offer rather limited competition due to the high prices charged to users. Although the range of Internet services which they provide is wider, users subscribing to these services must incur international direct-dialling charges for usage. The high costs deter most businesses and individuals from subscribing to these services and most large multinational corporations use their privately leased lines for data communication.

Vietnamese Internet service providers adopt a tiered pricing system for different customer segments. Businesses and individuals are charged a fixed fee of US$20 for registration and US$30 for a basic monthly connection. Government and NGOs are charged slightly less; US$10 for registration and US$20 for a basic monthly connection. Low income earners are entitled to subsidised charges of only US$20 for a basic monthly connection. The subscription charge for usage is US$0.15 per kilobyte of information transmitted to and from the Internet. Since the Internet service providers are government affiliated, the tiered pricing system ensures affordable services.

Officials from a few Internet service providers and Internet equipment manufacturers in Singapore indicated that the major hindrances in Vietnam are the relatively tight control on widespread Internet availability and the restricted form of business (business co-operation contract) stipulated for foreign investments. These firms are concerned about the readiness of the Vietnamese to manage and control the business undertaking, in view of the low level of know-how and experience in this field in Vietnam.

It is interesting to note that there are entrepreneurs interested in setting up cyber cafés and Internet clubs in Vietnam. If these pioneering ventures are successful in Hanoi, then there will be good intermediary suppliers to create greater awareness and demand for Internet services. However, their main concern is that the range of Internet services offered by local Internet service providers is very limited while the Internet services supplied from overseas is too expensive for most users.

Given these constraints, the Institute of Information Technology needs to consider privatisation through joint venture arrangements as a way for Internet provisioning in Vietnam. A commercial orientation could speed up the development of Internet provisioning in Vietnam. However, it is also necessary for the government to lift its restrictions on the type of Internet services supplied in the country in order to achieve greater benefits from privatisation. An illustration is Pacific Internet in Singapore. Its predecessor, Technet, was originally run as a university network by the National University of Singapore. It was subsequently taken over by a local corporation to offer Internet services commercially. It may be worthwhile for Vietnam to consider this type of model.

Customers

Based on information from primary and secondary sources, there are indications of strong growth in demand for the Internet in Vietnam over the next few years. This is in line with the explosive growth of the Internet worldwide. Demand pull forces will put pressure on Vietnam to provide the full range of Internet services.

In the short-term, the widespread use of the Internet throughout

Vietnam is not expected. The infrastructure to support the Internet is mainly concentrated in the cities of Ho Chi Minh City, Hanoi and Da Nang. Therefore, the potential demand for the Internet is going to be primarily in these cities.

As a target group for the Internet, the market from private individuals is still fairly premature due to low incomes and low computer literacy rate. Apart from business, institutional and governmental demand, there is nevertheless a potential market from private individuals in Ho Chi Minh City. Here, there is a small but growing middle class and the per capita income of the city (close to US$625) is 2.7 times higher than the national average (*The Vietnam Business Journal*, 1995c).

Substitutes

There is no equivalent substitute for the Internet which encompasses communication, marketing, information and research, and electronic commerce. Substitution of Internet services in these application aspects can only be done by the use of separate media.

Since only electronic mailing services are provided in Vietnam, most subscribers of Internet services primarily know and use the Internet as a communication medium. In this context, competing services include international courier services, postal services, facsimile, telex and telephone services. For international courier services, internationally established suppliers such as DHL and Federal Express are already operating in Vietnam. A simple experiment showed that it takes about seven days for inter-city post, three days for intra-city post and two weeks for international post. Due to the concentration of telecommunication services in the cities as well as the high cost, the use of facsimile, telex and telephone services are primarily limited to business users.

Most business organisations use a mix of communication media. However, in the case of sensitive business information, many sources still prefer to use courier services or facsimile for data communication instead of electronic mail services due to security considerations.

Barriers to Entry

Although the Vietnamese government has identified a national programme to implement the Internet, there is still a very strong hesitation to have unregulated access to international information systems.

This stems from concern over the possible erosion of Vietnam's cultural heritage and the adverse impact on the national security of the country. As evidenced from the national IT programme, the government plans to link only some domestic information systems (and not full integration) with international information systems. The IT master plan further specifies that the Internet will focus particularly on education and research and development.

Presently, Internet service providers in Vietnam can only provide country-wide Internet service. They cannot link up directly to the Internet outside Vietnam. Thus, users in Vietnam cannot access, for example, web pages from servers in the United States. Internet users in Vietnam can only gain access to the international systems through connections with foreign Internet service providers and, therefore, they will have to bear exorbitant international direct-dialling charges for usage. As long as the government maintains its restrictions on international linkages, the scope for full Internet access outside of Vietnam will be considerably limited.

In operating networks, DGPT only co-operates with foreign parties in the form of Business Co-operation Contracts (BCC). Under this form of collaboration, foreign Internet service providers provide capital, equipment, technology transfer and technical training programs, while the Vietnamese partner manages, operates and maintains the network. Profits are shared between the two parties based on a mutual agreement until the end of the contract.

DGPT applies five criteria in selecting long-term co-operation with foreign vendors, namely state-of-the-art technology, time-scale, reasonable prices, flexible payment methods and technology (Nguyen, 1996b). In particular, potential entrants to Vietnam for Internet provisioning must be prepared to extend attractive financing and management control to their Vietnamese counterpart. In view of the present state of Internet development in Vietnam, foreign service providers may be reluctant to entrust business control to their local partners at the outset.

Apart from the specific government limitations on Internet provisioning mentioned above, there are also some general difficulties associated with doing business in Vietnam. Bureaucracy, abuse of authority, corruption and frequent changes of government legislation are problems that many investors face in Vietnam. During interviews with individuals from the Steering Committee for the National Programme on IT, it was stated that a period of one year is required for a foreign vendor to obtain a business license to provide Internet services in Vietnam. Some foreign investors also complain of being subjected to business practices different from their domestic counterparts. Foreign investors are sometimes subject to discriminatory pricing (such as higher prices for labour, utilities and other essentials) or are prohibited from entering certain market segments (*The Vietnam Business Journal*, October 1995b).

CONCLUSION

The Vietnamese market holds great potential for Internet service providers. However, prospective investors should consider the likely impediments to the Vietnamese Internet industry.

There is scope for additional Internet service providers in Vietnam. With an increase in the number of suppliers, cost reduction, price differentiation and higher quality services can be expected. Privatisation of the existing government operated Internet services through joint venture arrangements with foreign Internet service providers may be one way to encourage greater competition in the industry. Injecting a commercial orientation could help to hasten the development of the Internet in Vietnam.

In contemplating the mode of entry into Vietnam, foreign Internet service providers should consider strategic alliances or collaboration with existing suppliers who are already familiar with the Vietnamese business environment. Due to the need to operate through business co-operation contracts, the selection of the right local partner can minimise the business risks of foreign vendors. Given the government's priority to improve IT literacy and acquire modern technology, it is advantageous for foreign service providers to emphasise their contribution to the country in terms of IT education and research, as well as technology transfer. Also, they should note that the approval process for IT business start-ups takes about one year from the time of submitting applications to the Office of the Steering Committee.

The initial target market for potential Internet service providers should be businesses and government bodies in the larger cities of Ho Chi Minh City, Hanoi and Da Nang. These are the locations that have the most developed telecommunication infrastructure and the highest concentration of businesses and government departments. In the case of private individuals, there is also a potential market for middle income individuals in Ho Chi Minh City. There is also a growing demand in Vietnam for education services such as Internet training and other IT training courses.

The public sector represents an immediate and large source of demand for Internet services. Upon successful implementation of the pilot Intranet project for the five government ministries by end 1996, it is foreseeable that the government could propagate similar systems throughout the public sector. Opportunities abound for providing consultancy services to the government.

As Internet has evolved into a global phenomenon, the Vietnamese government must carefully weigh the disadvantages of restricting the supply of Internet services in the country. Concerns over the negative social impacts of Internet are not unique to the Vietnamese government. As Internet transcends national boundaries, regulatory efforts governing Internet usage on a global basis may be the only effective means of control.

The Vietnamese government needs to review and deregulate existing policies governing foreign investments on IT projects in Vietnam. The present collaborative arrangement of business co-operation contracts may deter foreign Internet service providers from entering the market. They need to be assured of the readiness of a Vietnamese partner to manage and control the business venture. Since the level of expertise in the Internet service industry is relatively low in Vietnam, most foreign service providers would prefer to have the authority and responsibility to manage Internet services.

REFERENCES

Annerstedt Jan and Tim Sturgeon, "A National Information Infrastructure From LAN and WAN to NII", Chapter 9, *Electronic and Information Technology in Vietnam*, "Http: //www.saigon.com/ ~vacets/it2k/it2k09.html".

Cameron Debra, "Developing a Strategic Plan for Electronic Commerce", Chapter 12, *Implementing the Internet for Business, Computer,* Technology Research Corporation, South Carolina, 1995a.

Cameron Debra, "The Outlook of Electronic Commerce", Chapter 13, *Implementing the Internet for Business,* Computer Technology Research Corporation, South Carolina, 1995b.

Chua Choon Hoe, Internet Service Provisioning, Internet Symposium, Sun Microsystems, Singapore, August 1995.

Cronin Mary J, "Doing Business on the Internet", Van Nostrand, New York, 1994, pp. 54–60.

"Data Transmission – Businesses Find New Ways to Send Data", *The Vietnam Business Journal*, Vol. III, No. 5, October 1995a, p. 36.

"Flame War – Government Firms Battle Over Internet Service", *Far Eastern Economic Review*, October 26 , 1995, p. 23.

Galacticomm Inc., "User's Guide – Worldgroup Manager, Client-side access to Worldgroup Online Interactive Software", Networking Department, Vietnam Institute of Information Technology, *internet: root@hanoi.ac.vn.*, 1995.

"Hello Tomorrow – Telecoms Leap to Vietnam", *The Vietnam Business Journal*, Vol. III, No. 5, October 1995b, pp. 24–34.

"Hooking Up Vietnam", *Vietnam Economic Times,* November 1994, pp. 14–7.

"Network Wizards", *The Asian Wall Street Journal*, 18 March 1996, pp. 7, 10.

Nguyen Mai, "Foreign Investment in Vietnam", Speech, State Evaluation Commission, Ministry of Planning and Investment, Hanoi, March 1996.

Nguyen Ngo Hong, "Vietnam: National Network Development and the Role for Foreign Investment", Speech, Vietnam Ministry of Post and Telecommunications, Hanoi, March 1996b.

"Playing Leapfrog", *Vietnam Economic Times*, November 1994, p. 23.

Porter Michael E., *Competitive Advantage: Creating and Sustaining Superior Performance*, *Free Press*, New York, 1985.

Porter M.E. and V.E. Millar, "How Information Gives You Competitive Advantage", *Harvard Business Review*, July–August 1985, pp. 149–60.

Sakina Dhilawala, *Vietnam – The Commercial and Regulatory Environment,* Datapro International, McGraw Hill, New York, 1994.

Socialist Republic of Vietnam, *Policy and Master Plan on Information Technology Development Up to the Year 2000,* The Steering Committee for the National Programme on Information Technology, Hanoi, 1995.

"The Making of Asian Tigers – Why Should Investors Choose Vietnam?", *The Vietnam Business Journal*, Vol. III, No. 5, October 1995c, pp. 22–3.

Chapter 13

The Measurement of Technology Linker Characteristics in Vietnamese Business People*

BY
Sonnie ANG Chuan Hian
Roger CHUA Yeu Hock
HONG Shaw Chiat
LOW Ngerng Nguang

INTRODUCTION

Technology Linkers

THE TRANSFER OF technology is usually thought of as an imitative process. An underdeveloped nation imports the techniques and tools of more industrially advanced countries; or within a developed nation, one sector of the economy simply adopts a manufacturing process found to be useful in another; or within an industry, a firm copies the products and methods of its competitors (Fish, 1978).

The acceptance or rejection of innovation and technology transfer of any form often de-

---

* *We thank the following organisations and individuals for their contributions: Vietbid, Technology & Investment Consultancy Centre, 138A Giang Vo Street, Hanoi, Vietnam; Mr. Thai Thanh Long (Vice Director) and Mr. Do Thuy Huong (Import-Export Department) of Viettronics Dong Da; Mr. Nguyen Si Hue (Director General Adj) and Mr. Pham Van Nang (Responsable Industriel) of Alcatel Networks Systems Vietnam; and Mr. Tran Ngoc Hang (Deputy General Director), Mr. Nguyen Khac Minh (Manager, QC) and Mr. Dao Duc Thanh (Manager, Technical Dept) of Hanel, Hanoi Electronics Group. Thanks also to Dr. Roger Marshall for his guidance and constructive comments.*

pends very much on the subjective judgement of the decision maker and the people involved. Without a positive motivator, alternately designated as "linker" or "gatekeeper", the completion of the transfer process by actual utilisation is notably diminished. The technology linker is essentially an individual or group of individuals who do exactly what the term implies – they link the source and the application. The human factor is probably the most important element in technology transfer. A linker can be associated with the source or with the user; it also could be somewhere in between or at both ends of the process chain.

A similar phenomenon has been noted in the sociology literature where individuals who pass information from media and original sources to other people in the community are called opinion leaders (Marshall and Gitosudarmo, 1995). Marketing researchers have seized upon this concept and applied it to the process of new product and service introductions rather than to the original scenario, which was typically concerned with the spread of ideas and technology through a community.

Although the original research focused on the spread of new farm technology throughout the U.S., marketing academics have adopted the theory to identify and target opinion leaders in a business' market place through the adaptation of the opinion leadership scale. The objective of this project is to extend this work by developing an instrument to assist companies involved in technology transfer to identify technology linkers.

Several potential applications exist. There may be people in a firm who, though not directly involved in the technology transfer process, may possess the characteristics of a technology linker. These people should be identified and, if appropriate, selected to facilitate the technology transfer process. On the other hand, the company may be in the process of identifying suitable individuals for a new technology transfer effort. A tool, such as the one developed here, will help management to identify who is most suitable for such a role. This applies to both sides of the transfer – the source as well as the recipient.

Vietnam: A Test Bed

After nearly ten years of implementing an open-door policy and developing a market-oriented economy from a planned central economic system, Vietnam has changed from an agricultural economy to the beginning stages of an industrialised nation. About 65% of foreign investment capital is allocated to manufacturing industries and the remaining 35% to service industries.

Although agriculture accounts for 40% of GDP, industrial production output is increasing and growth was 13.5% for the first half of 1995 (*Southeast Asia Monitor Newsletter*, 1995). According to the *Vietnam Business Journal* (Le, 1995), Vietnam's emerging economic role within the Pacific Rim region is likely to be built around four areas:

(i) A source of oil and other valuable natural resources;
(ii) A tourist destination;
(iii) A growing market for consumer durables produced both locally and in neighbouring countries; and
(iv) A low-end assembly and production centre for light manufactured goods.

Hanoi's prolonged delay in setting up a capital market means that Vietnam still relies heavily on foreign investment inflows for capital, technology transfer and other vital inputs to fuel economic growth. Prime Minister Vo Van Kiet and the government of Vietnam have set forth ambitious goals to be met by the year 2000. These goals were laid out as the "socio-economic stabilisation and development strategy to the year 2000" in June, 1991. The strategy implicitly calls for an average growth rate of 9.5% per year and the doubling of per capita income to over US$500. To achieve these objectives, Vietnam will need approximately US$4 billion of investment each year, of which about one-half is expected to come from foreign sources. Foreign investment is targeted to play a central role in the rebuilding of Vietnam's economy. Between now and the year 2000, the government is looking for close to US$15 billion in direct foreign investment (Le, 1995). This emphasis on foreign investment makes Vietnam a near perfect test-bed for the technology linker tool.

THEORETICAL FRAMEWORK

The role of the "linker" in technology transfer projects has been studied and documented, although as discussed below, the existing research is rather old. This project is an application of these established findings to an instrument to identify technology linkers in Vietnam.

Prior Research

One paper which specifically discusses technology linkers is entitled "The Linker Role in the Technology Transfer Process" (Essoglou, 1975). This paper was presented at a 1975 "Briefing on Technology Transfer Projects" organised by the Naval Postgraduate School in Monterey, California. The author was writing more from the perspective of transferring military technology to the private sector rather than the more typical commercial perspective in marketing situations. However, the principles espoused are very similar to the opinion leadership concept well known to marketers (and discussed below), so it is worth presenting the key elements of Essoglou's (1975) paper.

The Information Linker Model

Essoglou comments on a model developed by Creighton *et al.* (1972) and published in a working paper of the Naval Postgraduate School at Monterey. This model suggests that there are both formal and informal factors that influence the transfer of information from a source of knowledge to a recipient of knowledge (see Figure 13–1).

Of all the nine factors highlighted, Essoglou indicates that the linker element is the most significant, suggesting that this human factor is the most important element for technology transfers. The opposite of linker in this context is "stabiliser", a person possessing few linker attributes.

Key Linker Attributes

Essoglou suggests that the following are the key attributes of linkers:

(i) Innovative;
(ii) Willing to accept risk;
(iii) Active in multi-disciplines;
(iv) More information contacts;
(v) High credibility with peers;
(vi) Cosmopolite; and
(vii) Oriented towards outside information sources.

FIGURE 13–1
The Information Linker Model

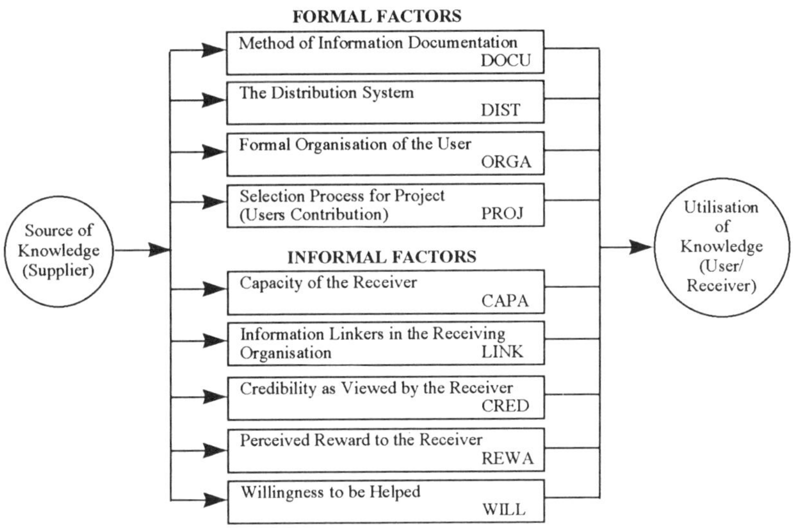

Although these attributes are clearly defined, they are not the only pre-requisites to an individual being a linker. The basis of selection of a suitable candidate for a technology linker-type job may be based on other factors such as availability, language, technical proficiency and experience. The amount of consideration placed on linker attributes may even be minimal. It may be reasonable, therefore, to conclude that not all individuals who are working on technology transfer projects would be effective linkers, and that linkers may typically possess non-personality attributes other than those listed above.

This point may be particularly true in a country like Vietnam, where the ability say, to communicate in English, will pre-dispose an individual to the role of linker. It is important, nevertheless, to establish the tendencies of an individual, whether one is pro-stabiliser or pro-linker, so that this vital role is filled by the most suitable people.

DEVELOPMENT OF THE TECHNOLOGY LINKER INSTRUMENT

Following the research work of Marshall and Gitosudarmo (1995), a survey questionnaire designed to assess pro-linker tendencies was developed. Each of the attributes previously listed were measured using 11 questions with responses recorded on a seven-point Likert-type scale. Adaptation of the Marshall and Gitosudarmo questionnaire centred on rephrasing it to give a technology transfer focus rather than the opinion leadership focus for which the scale was originally designed. The differences are shown below in Table 13–1.

TABLE 13–1
Adaptation of Questionnaire for Technology Transfer

Opinion Leader	Technology Linker
1. I like to talk with people about personal computers.	1. I like to talk with people about new technology (e.g., products or ways of doing things).
2. I give information about personal computers to other people.	2. I give information about new discovery or knowledge to other people.
3. During the past 6 months, I have told at least one person about personal computers.	3. During the past 6 months, I have told at least one person about some new discovery or knowledge.
4. If I were to discuss personal computers with others I mix with, I would be more likely to convince them of my ideas rather than listen to theirs.	4. If I were to discuss new technology with others I mix with, I would be more likely to convince them of my ideas than listen to theirs.
5. I am more likely than most of the people I mix with to be asked for advice about personal computers	5. I am more likely than most of the people I mix with to be asked for information about new technology.
6. I tell people I mix with about personal computers more often than they tell me.	6. I tell the people I mix with about new technology more often than they tell me.
	7. I like to read magazines, attend seminars or watch TV programs regarding new technology and new discoveries.
	8. I feel comfortable working with people from different departments and job functions.
	9. When faced with problems, I like to use solutions recommended by books or experienced people.
	10. There is no need to change the present way of doing things as long as it is working OK.

In addition to rephrasing the original six questions, two additional questions were added to determine the level of interest and participation in acquiring information on new technologies (question 7), and the comfort level one perceives him/herself to possess in cross-functional activities (question 8). Two negatively framed questions (question 9 and 10) were also added to help weed out erroneous responses.

Also, as with the opinion leader questionnaire, a single item validation measure was included (see Table 13–2). This single item gets to the core of the technology linker concept, but it is too "obvious" to be a valid measure of the construct. Furthermore, a multi item scale is inherently more reliable than a single item scale. Nevertheless, this single item should correlate with the scale if they both measure the same thing. Finally, key demographic information questions, including age, gender, job title, job function and years of service, completed the questionnaire.

TABLE 13–2
Adaptation of Questionnaire for Technology Transfer Single Item Validation Measure

Opinion Leader	Technology Linker
How important do you think your personal opinion would be to the people you mix with if they were about to purchase a personal computer?	How important do you think your personal opinion would be to the people you mix with if they were about to purchase a new product or adopt a new way of doing things?

With the help of a Vietnamese national based at the Nanyang Technological University (NTU), the questionnaire was translated into Vietnamese. In Vietnam, this questionnaire was validated for accuracy and intended use by a member of Vietbid, a local investment consultancy company.

SURVEY PROCESS

With the questionnaire translated into Vietnamese, the next task was to identify a local guide to assist in the process of administering the survey. It was necessary to have an individual familiar with local industry and capable of explaining the objective of this survey to employees of the participating companies. Through careful selection, a technology and investment consultancy company called Vietbid provided an individual to assist in establishing meetings with the local companies. Vietbid also examined the questionnaire to ensure that the questions and their intent correlated with the respondent's interpretations, thus ensuring relevancy in the local context.

Arrangements were made to meet with three companies, namely Viettronics Dong Da, Alcatel Network System Vietnam and Hanel. A structured approach was adopted throughout discussions with the management teams. The objectives of the study were first presented followed by a detailed explanation of the survey process. In each case, time was spent understanding the organisation's history, scope of business, organisational structure, technology involved, as well as the source and process of technology transfer.

The original intention was to conduct the survey on-site through gathering several potential respondents together and having them fill in the questionnaire immediately, thus leaving the company with the survey responses in hand. However, due to some "cultural" differences and, perhaps, the need to study the questionnaire in detail prior to responding, questionnaires had to be left at the sites with a promise that the responses would be mailed at a later date. With the purpose of the study clearly established, the questionnaires were left with the management teams who agreed to conduct the survey within their companies and return the completed questionnaires accordingly. They were asked to administer the questionnaires to managers, engineers and supervisors, except direct production workers. In addition, they were to include employees from various functional groups.

COMPANY PROFILES

All of the information and details on the companies were obtained through interviews with the top management staff of the respective organisations. Facts and figures were quoted from company brochures provided by management.

Viettronics Dong Da

This firm is a 100% state-owned enterprise established in 1982 with key businesses in electronics and information technology. It manufactures TVs, radios and radiocasettes as well as components which support these products. A profile of the organisation structure is shown in Figure 13–2.

FIGURE 13–2
Organisation Structure of Viettronics Dong Da

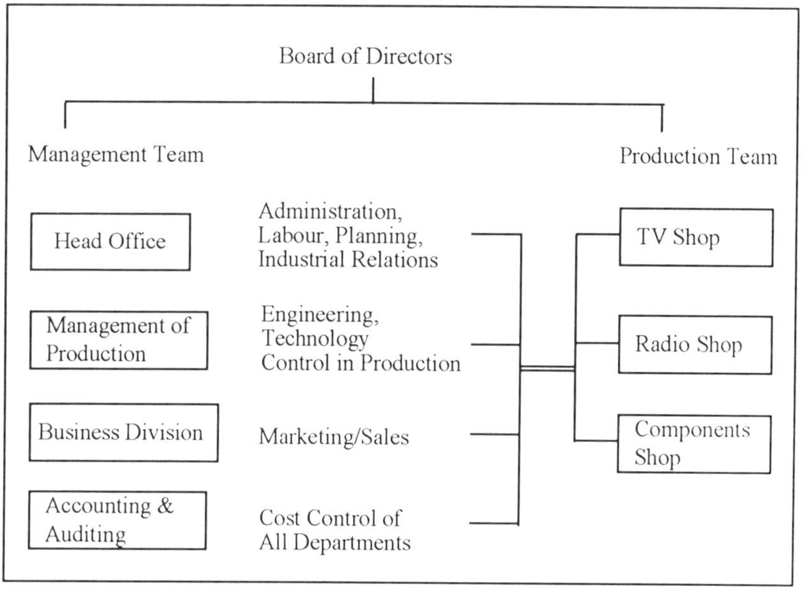

In the TV shop, there are 100 employees producing 100,000 units a year for local market demand. Colour TV assembly started with semi-knock-down (SKD) in 1985 through a joint venture with JVC of Japan. Front-end assembly was done in Japan with the final assembly in Vietnam. A group of engineers from the management team and shop were sent to Japan for training and JVC engineers visited the local factory to assist in start-ups. To facilitate the technology transfer process, a very detailed JVC technology transfer manual was prepared on equipment and various engineering documentation. This was used as a guide during the entire process in Vietnam.

This project was coordinated by a project coordinator from the Board of Directors. Successful completion resulted in moving towards CKD (complete-knock-down) assembly of coloured TVs (CTV) in 1990. Viettronics has a large number of university educated employees and most of them were staff from the research and development division in the Ministry of Science and Technology before 1982. Also noteworthy, is that the primary technology linkers have an engineering background.

Alcatel-VNPT

Alcatel-VNPT is a joint venture between Alcatel of France (51%) and VNPT (49%) which started production in 1995. Its three business areas are Alcatel 1000 switching equipment, software development for Alcatel networks and service/support for both hardware and software. It supplies an internal switching equipment demand of approximately 250,000 per year. The organisation structure is depicted in Figure 13–3.

FIGURE 13–3
Organisation Structure of Alcatel-VNPT

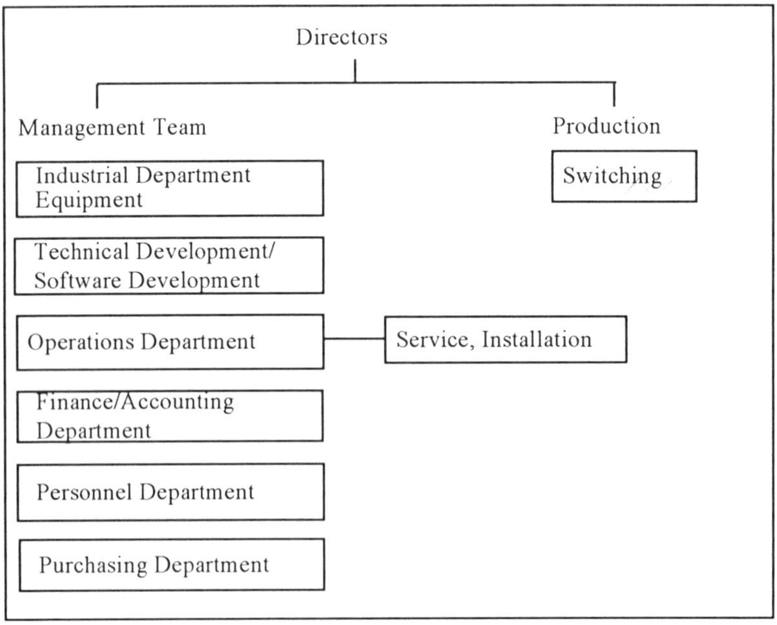

Switching equipment assembly started with CKD. There is a direct link between each department in this joint venture and the technology source department in Alcatel. On the engineering side, there is one Alcatel expatriate "linker" for each department. Training is also provided in Alcatel for the local team. This joint venture has 100 people with about 50% in executive positions and 50% in production.

Hanel

Hanel was established in 1984 and is a conglomerate with businesses in electronics assembly (TV), electromechanical, electronics material, plastics and high-technology industry zone management. It has several joint ventures with foreign partners such as JVC, Toshiba, Samsung and Daewoo. One joint venture is with Orien Electric Co. of Korea in the production of cathode ray tubes (CRTs). The annual output of the joint venture is about 1.6 million units per year. Figure 13–4 displays the organisation structure.

FIGURE 13–4
Organisation Structure of Hanel

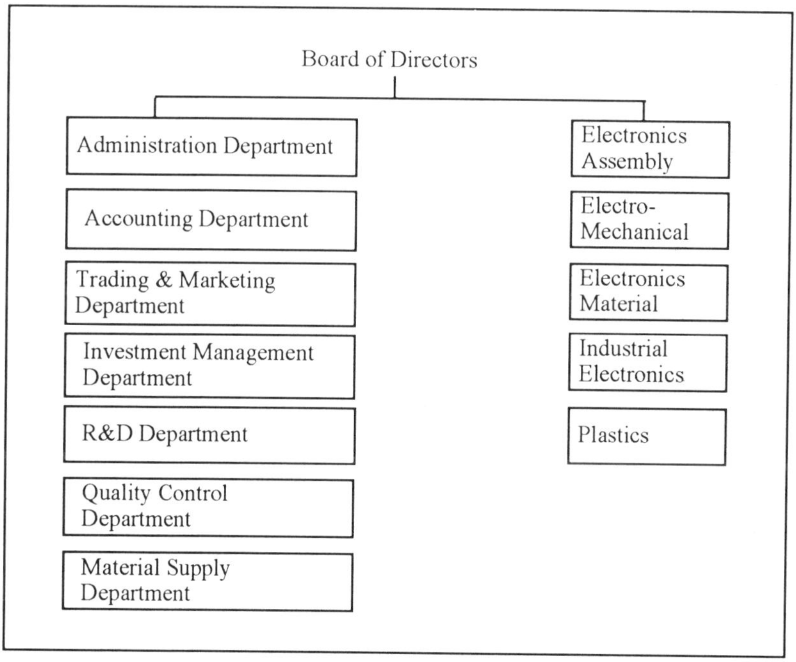

Technology transfer is achieved by sending engineers abroad for training. Joint venture partners also send their engineers to the local factories. Management is all engineering based and, in the opinion of the company, this has provided a significant advantage in its ability to absorb new technology transfers. The most striking common element of all these companies is the predominance of individuals with an engineering background in the linker role.

ANALYSIS AND FINDINGS

Scale Purification

The collected data was first subjected to a reliability analysis. Cronbach's alpha for the ten scale items is 0.48 which is somewhat low. Further inspection revealed that questions 9 and 10 both correlate negatively with all other scale items. These two items were framed negatively so that respondents would not fall into a response pattern. It is evident from the negative correlation that this is exactly what did happen and, thus, the pattern was set by the first eight questions. Items 9 and 10 were removed from the instrument. A subsequent reliability analysis of the remaining eight questions showed a satisfactory alpha value of 0.65. This scale, then, is the one that the following analysis is based upon.

Based on the mean of the first eight questions, a new variable called linker was created. Testing the scale for reliability, as above, is relatively easy but to test the linker scale for validity in Vietnam is far more difficult. Two tests can be readily applied to this end; one is objective and the other is subjective.

The objective statistical test is facilitated by question 11 which is a single item summary question. This question asks each person to rate themselves as a technology linker. However, a single item scale, such as this one, provides an unreliable scale by itself but it is intrinsically valid. Hence, a correlation of the single item with the new, eight item linker scale should provide information about the validity of the linker scale. This procedure has been reported before in the literature (Marshall and Gitosudarmo, 1995). Pearson's coefficient of correlation for the two scales is 0.59 ($p < 0.001$) which provides an encouraging verification of the linker scale. The second way to test validity of the scale in Vietnam is to inspect the distribution of linker scores for the VN sample and compare them to other known linker distributions.

Using a scale from 1 to 7, if the linker score ranges from 1 to 3.5, then the respondent is classified as a technology linker; if the score is greater than 3.5, then the respondent is a non-linker or stabiliser. Figure 13–5 shows the distribution of the technology linkers among the respondents in the Vietnam sample.

FIGURE 13–5
Distribution of Technology Linkers

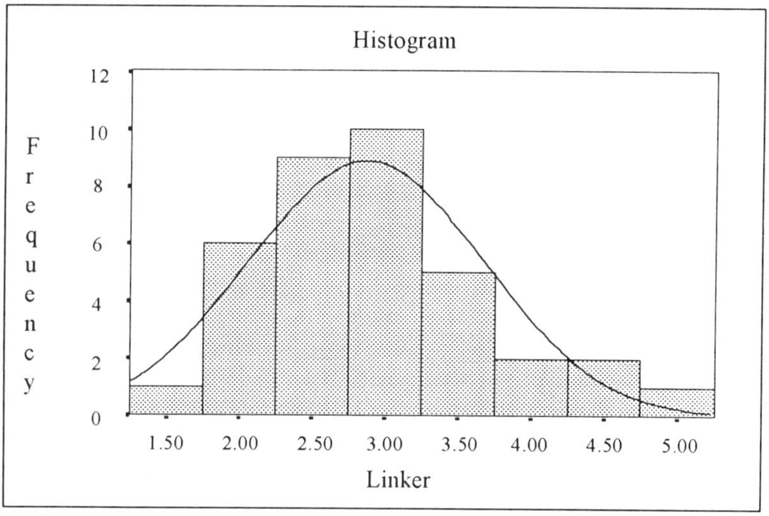

Superimposed on the normal distribution, the distribution in Figure 13–5 shows a mean of 2.87 and a standard deviation of 0.8. A comparison with a similar study of opinion leadership across a number of countries (Marshall and Gitosudarmo, 1995) yields the result in Table 13–3.

It is clear that Vietnamese workers (83%) seem to be more inclined towards an opinion leadership type of character as compared to the other nations. India, though, is also a developing nation and also has a high percentage (65%) of linkers compared to the other, more developed, nations. The similarity between Vietnam and India in terms of both being developing nations may suggest that technology linkers could emerge out of necessity in high growth developing nations.

However, the interpretation of this comparison has to be used with care because the survey on opinion leadership by Marshall and Gitosudarmo (1995) was administered to university students whereas the one for Vietnam covers working professionals.

TABLE 13–3
Comparison of Opinion Leadership Survey Results

Country*	Aus	Ger	HK	Indi	Indo	Kor	NZ	U.S.	VN
O/L	33%	39%	36%	65%	36%	20%	31%	42%	83%
Non-O/L	66%	61%	64%	35%	64%	80%	69%	58%	17%
Mean	4.92	4.63	4.65	3.41	4.79	4.91	5.19	4.48	2.87
Std. Dev.	1.59	1.36	1.56	1.38	1.53	1.14	1.45	1.61	0.8
Skewness	−0.49	−0.28	−0.38	0.46	−0.37	−0.17	−0.42	0.04	0.73
Kurtosis	−0.97	−0.91	−1.1	−0.14	−0.91	−0.49	−1.1	−1.2	0.42

* Aus = Australia; Ger = Germany; HK = Hong Kong; Indi = India; Indo = Indonesia; Kor = South Korea; NZ = New Zealand; U.S. = United States; and VN = Vietnam.

The higher percentage of technology linkers found in the Vietnam sample supports the fact that the linker scale used is a valid instrument to measure technology linker characteristics. This is because the sample population selected in Vietnam is biased towards technology linkers since many of the respondents are actually filling the technology linker's role in their respective companies.

Application of the Scale

Because of the difficulty of collecting the data in the field, the present sample is too small for sophisticated statistical testing (only 36 respondents). Nevertheless, some numeric inferences can be made from further inspection of the cross-tabulated data.

Since 17% of the respondents have more than one job function, the job function scale was re-categorised into "engineering", "marketing" and "both". The job title profile was taken out of the analysis due to the large number of missing data. For the gender variable, the analysis is not valid because out of the 36 respondents only four were female. Similarly, due to the small number of responses the experience variable was also re-categorised into "less than five years" and "more than five years". The age variable was similarly re-categorised into "less than 30 years", "31 to 40 years" and "above 40 years".

Tables 13–4, 13–5 and 13–6 show the re-calculated results for linker versus age, experience and job function, respectively. In Table 13–4, both the younger and older workers show a higher tendency to be technology linkers than the middle-aged staff (31 to 40 years old), as evidenced by the 87.5% and 83.3% of linkers from each of the young (less than 30 years old) and old (above 40 years old) category, respectively.

TABLE 13–4
Cross-Tabulation of Linker Versus Age

	Less than 30 Years	31 to 40 Years	Above 40 Years	Total
Linker	14 (87.5%)	6 (75%)	10 (83.3%)	30
Non-Linker	2 (12.5%)	2 (25%)	2 (16.7%)	6
Total	16	8	12	36

TABLE 13–5
Cross-Tabulation of Linker Versus Experience

	Less than 5 Years	More than 5 Years	Total
Linker	7 (70%)	11 (78.6%)	18
Non-Linker	3 (30%)	3 (21.4%)	6
Total	10	14	24

TABLE 13–6
Cross-Tabulation of Linker Versus Job Function

	Marketing	Engineering	Both	Total
Linker	5 (83.3%)	13 (86.7%)	1 (100%)	19
Non-Linker	1 (16.7%)	2 (13.3%)	–	3
Total	6	15	1	22

In Table 13–5, it seems that people with more than five years of working experience are slightly more inclined to be technology linkers. At first glance, this result may seem to be contradictory with the previous analysis of younger workers being technology linkers. However, if Tables 13–4 and 13–5 are considered together, it simply means that only the group of young workers who have gained at least five years of relevant working experience are able to effectively function as technology linkers as compared to the young and inexperienced workers. Turning to Table 13–6, of the six marketing respondents, 83% were linkers; of the 15 engineers, 87% were linkers. With such a small sample, the difference is not significant and it seems that linker characteristics are equally prevalent among marketers and engineers.

Implication of Results

This project aimed to develop an instrument to measure the presence of technology linker characteristics through the use of a questionnaire survey. To assess the validity of the instrument, a sample of Vietnamese working professionals was selected for the survey. The results from the scale purification confirm that the instrument is both reliable and valid as an indicator of the technology linker score of the respondents sampled.

The instrument was then used to analyse the profile of a typical technology linker in Vietnam. However, due to the small sample size, it was not possible to establish a significant statistical correlation of the profile variables with the linker scale. Despite this limitation, certain trends were manifested. The results suggest that both younger staff (below 30 years old) and older staff (above 40 years old) with at least five years of working experience have a greater tendency to possess characteristics of a technology linker, regardless of their job function.

The above findings were corroborated through interviews with executives and staff of the surveyed companies, as well as by discussions with other business contacts made during the Business Study Mission to Vietnam. It was disclosed that a growing number of young employees attended night classes to study English and were able to converse well with their English speaking counterparts. They are also well-read in foreign publications and news, and many of them have degrees from foreign universities, such as France and Russia, or participate in university exchange programs with Asian universities. Many young executives in Vietnam are now well-travelled throughout Asia, the U.S. and Europe.

This exposure and experience serve to increase their awareness and understanding of international business transactions which, in turn, changes their mind-set and behaviour within the business environment. They are inevitably more suitable for international dealings such as technology transfers, where effective communication and mutual understanding among the project team members is essential. On the other hand, older staff are often considered to be too entrenched in the old way of doing business and seem slower to change their mindset amidst the rapidly changing economic development in Vietnam.

The finding that older executives are also good linkers can be explained by the fact that these executives have had enough time available throughout their career to develop the necessary knowledge base. This advantage, when coupled with the fact that Asians traditionally encourage people to respect and listen to older people, gives them the necessary respectability and credibility to function as technology linkers. On the other hand, the middle-aged group have neither the advantage of respectful years nor the benefits of innovative youth or a modern technological education.

Because of the growing complexity of technology, technical knowledge has become an essential communication language in technology transfers. Thus, technical competency is perceived to be more and more important for technology transfer. One might expect, *a priori,* that marketing skills used in negotiations and persuasion would become less important in such circumstances because engineering people are perceived to be technology opinion leaders in technology transfer matters due to their expert knowledge.

Contrary to this perception, the results here show that there is no difference between these two groups of people with respect to their suitability for the technology linker role. However, people serving in both engineering and marketing functions have a perfect score of 100% linkers. Although the statistical results may not be robust because of the small sample, the results may indicate that multi-functional people are becoming better technology linkers because they possess both technical competencies as engineers as well as the social and communication skills of marketing.

Limitations and Future Directions of the Research

The survey was based on data collected from 36 respondents and, thus, it represents a very small group of companies in Vietnam. However, the selected companies comprise a state-owned enterprise, a local company and a foreign joint venture and, so, the results should be reasonably representative. Unfortunately, due to the low response rate, it is not possible to report statistical significance levels.

The survey was designed in English and then translated into Vietnamese for administration to the various companies. A third party verification of the translated questionnaire was made by a Vietnamese consultant to confirm the accuracy of the translation. Despite the high accuracy achieved through this process, the data could still have been misinterpreted by the respondents. The subtle differences between the two languages could cause responses which are not indicative of the intended question. This is evident perhaps in the failure of questions 9 and 10, which were phrased negatively rather than positively (like the first eight questions), and were generally answered inconsistently.

The data collected to determine linkers were limited to age, gender, title, job function and working experience which is in no way exhaustive. Others factors, such as culture, educational background and social standing, were not taken into consideration. These can be identified and used in future research.

Despite the limitations of the survey, the findings provide some insight into the selection of persons that have a suitable personality to participate in technology transfer projects so that the success of the projects can be greatly enhanced. The survey instrument designed here is also a potentially useful device fcr identifying technology linkers within the company. Management could use this information as a guide for linker-type development programmes.

CONCLUSION

Based on a survey undertaken in Vietnam, the instrument developed here has the potential for effectively identifying linker-type persons. Although the model is clearly applicable in Western countries, the present findings support the validity of the framework in developing Asian countries. It must be noted that in translating the instrument into the language of the country of intended use, care must be exercised so that the original intent is neither diluted nor corrupted. The work undertaken in this project highlights the appropriateness of employing the technology linker model.

APPENDIX 13–1
Technology Transfer Brokers

With emphasis on joint ventures in foreign direct investment (FDI), there is a need to "match-make" foreign companies that have the funds and the technology to the right local partners, who provide land, labour and market opportunity. Such a union has numerous uncertainties and this has led to the emergence of a local industry called "Technology Transfer Consultants" or in our parlance – linkers! To differentiate such consultants from our terminology of linkers we refer to them here as brokers. Brokers seem to link at three levels:

(i) To government agencies so as to facilitate the approval process of a technology transfer joint venture.
(ii) Link up a multinational corporation (MNC) with local partners. Here they can profile local companies for the MNC to select from.
(iii) At the company level, where they facilitate the set-up and transfer technology itself.

With the influx of foreign direct investment, there are now about 20 of these companies, and Vietbid is one of them.. These companies are mostly started by foreign graduates and a key success factor in their operations is their knowledge of the culture and familiarity with local conditions.

APPENDIX 13–2
Sample Questionnaire

NANYANG TECHNOLOGICAL UNIVERSITY
NANYANG BUSINESS SCHOOL
MBA PROGRAMME 1995/1996

28 January 1996

Dear Sir/Madam,

<u>Questionnaire on Technology Linkers for Vietnam Venture</u>

As part of a research project undertaken by NTU in conjunction with the Business

Study Mission to Vietnam, we would like to invite your company to participate in this survey.

In view of the recent developments in Vietnam and the tremendous influx of investments to the country, especially from the Asian countries, there is an urgent need for Vietnam to acquire technologies from other countries. This gives rise to the opportunity for Singapore to transfer our technology and know-how to Vietnam.

As much research has shown that the success of technology transfer depends upon the people involved in the process, there is a need for both the technology source and recipient companies to carefully identify their most suitable candidates to represent them.

The purpose of this survey is to help the technology source/recipient company identify technology linkers within the company who are crucial to technology transfer project. Due to the nature of the survey, we would like to target it to employees who are most likely to be involved in such work. As such, participants should be selected from the executive level and above, e.g., Engineers, Marketing Executives and Plant Managers.

There are only 12 questions to be answered, each by circling a number, and should take no more than 3–5 minutes. A copy is attached for your perusal.

All answers will be kept strictly confidential and the result will only be published when analysed with the combined surveys from other participating companies.

If you are interested in receiving a report on the findings of this study, please write your name and address at the back of the questionnaire, or alternatively, you could request a copy of the report in a separate letter. We will be glad to send you a complimentary copy when ready.

Yours sincerely,

Dr. Roger Marshall	Hong Shaw Chiat	Sonnie Ang	Low Ngerng Nguang	Roger Chua
Senior Lecturer	Manager	Manager	Senior Systems Engr	Supervisor
NTU	Delco Electronics	Compaq Asia	ODE Pte Ltd	S'pore Aerospace

SURVEY QUESTIONNAIRE

	Strongly Agree						Strongly Disagree
1. I like to talk with people about new technology (e.g., products or ways of doing things).	1	2	3	4	5	6	7
2. I give information about new discovery or knowledge to other people.	1	2	3	4	5	6	7
3. During the past 6 months, I have told at least one person about some new discovery or knowledge.	1	2	3	4	5	6	7
4. If I were to discuss new technology with others I mix with, I would be more likely to convince them of my ideas than listen to theirs.	1	2	3	4	5	6	7
5. I am more likely than most of the people I mix with to be asked for information about new technology.	1	2	3	4	5	6	7
6. I tell the people I mix with about new technology more often than they tell me.	1	2	3	4	5	6	7
7. I like to read magazines, attend seminars or watch TV programs regarding new technology and new discoveries.	1	2	3	4	5	6	7
8. I feel comfortable working with people from different departments and job functions.	1	2	3	4	5	6	7
9. When faced with problems, I like to use solutions recommended by books or experienced people.	1	2	3	4	5	6	7
10. There is no need to change the present way of doing things as long as it is working OK.	1	2	3	4	5	6	7
11. How important do you think your personal opinion would be to the people you mix with, if they were about to purchase a new product or adopt a new way of doing things ?	1	2	3	4	5	6	7

12. Please tell us about yourself:

Age: <25 25–30 31–35 36–40 >40 years (Please circle one)
Gender: M/F
Title: ____________________
Job Function: Marketing/Production Control/Design/Manufacturing/Materials/
Others: __________
Working Experience: __________ years (in this same job function)

Thank you very much for your time.

REFERENCES

Creighton J.W., J.A. Jolly and S.A. Denning, "Enhancement of Research and Development Output Utilisation Efficiencies: Linker Concept Methodology in the Technology Transfer Process", Conference Proceedings, Naval Postgraduate School, Monterey, California, June 1972.

"Economic Prospects", *Southeast Asia Monitor Newsletter*, Vietnam, September 1995.

Essoglou M.E., "The Linker Role in the Technology Transfer Process", Conference Proceedings, Naval Postgraduate School, Monterey, California, June 1975.

Fish Howard C., "International Technology Transfer: Ramifications Concerning Communist Bloc Nations", Conference Proceedings, Naval Postgraduate School, Monterey, California, 1978.

Le Luu, "The Making of Asian Tigers", *The Vietnam Business Journal*, Vol. III, No. 5, October 1995, pp. 22–3.

Marshall R. and I. Gitosudarmo, "Variation in the Characteristics of Opinion Leaders Across Cultural Borders", *Journal of International Consumer Marketing*, Vol. 8, No. 1, 1995, pp. 5–21.

Chapter 14

A Synopsis of Technology Transfer Issues

BY
Jon D. KENDALL

INTRODUCTION

ACCORDING TO THE renowned economist, Schumpeter, periods of change create opportunities for investment. If so, then the Vietnamese telecommunications and related sectors provide ample opportunity for investment. The three chapters in this section provide information critical for understanding the telecommunications climate, understanding the opportunities arising from the use of these links, and understanding who in Vietnam can facilitate the technology transfer process required for these opportunities to be realised.

The Vietnamese economy is undergoing tremendous structural change, sparked off by the *doi moi* "renovation". It has moved from its agricultural base to the cross-roads of rapid industrialisation (Nguyen, 1995). Since 1987, links with other economies have yielded US$22 billion for 1,525 licensed projects in Vietnam; around 25% of this amount has been released so far. Since the beginning of 1996 through to August, the government has licensed 198 projects for a total of US$3.36 billion (*Dow Jones News Service*, 9 September 1996). International organisations, such as the World Bank and Asian Development Bank, have agreed to contribute (over the next three years) at least US$4 billion for projects ranging from the Saigon Port project to miscellaneous power projects (*Business Week*, 1 July 1996). All these factors, combined with rising incomes, increase demand for telecommunications-based services.

THE CURRENT STATUS OF TELECOMMUNICATIONS IN VIETNAM

Regulatory Framework

Vietnam's telecommunications sector has experienced recent changes in the nature of regulation and the structure of service provision. Indeed, until mid-1993, the Department General of Posts and Telecommunications (DGPT) regulated both postal services and telecommunications. Previously, it was part of the Ministry of Transport and Telecommunications. In mid-1993, the DGPT became an independent ministerial department, with the head reporting directly to the Prime Minister. The DGPT, as the nation's telecommunications authority, has become the body responsible for the development of telecommunications infrastructure.

Trunk networks in Vietnam are managed by two operators — Vietnam Posts and Telecommunications (VNPT) and Vietnam Army Telecommunications Company (Vietel). Vietel concerns itself mainly with servicing the military sector. VNPT, on the other hand, exercises a virtual monopoly over wire-based telecommunications in the public arena through its numerous subsidiaries, and dominates the wireless market as well. Foreign investors investing in telecommunications must seek approval from VNPT or its subsidiaries. Joint ventures are usually carried out under business co-operation contracts. Such agreements, less well-defined than equity joint ventures, are justified on the grounds of national security (*The Financial Times*, 9 May 1996).

Currently, approval is pending on changes to Vietnam's *Foreign Investment Law* which may increase foreign companies' power in joint ventures. Currently, almost all decisions require unanimous approval of directors on a joint venture's board (*Dow Jones News Service*, 21 August 1996; *The Financial Times*, 22 August 1996). Other changes may also clarify certain legal issues as well as which sectors are vital to national security.

Telecommunications Industry Profile

In addition to providing more detail on telecommunications regulatory structure, Chapter 11 profiles the telecommunications industry. Detailed information is provided about the telecommunications market such as the market value of public telecommunications equipment, mobile market, and transmission and accessories markets. Comparison of telecommunications profiles with other countries in the region reveals that Vietnam has the lowest telephone density in the region, at only 1%.

Investment Opportunities

The low telephone density provides enormous potential in this industry as outlined in Chapter 11. Indeed, Hanoi has ambitious plans to increase the 1% figure to 5% by the year 2000. Over the past year, VNPT has been in negotiations with Telstra (Australian-owned), Cable and Wireless (U.K.-owned), NTT International (Japanese-owned) and France Telecom. These companies form a joint effort to install, as well as to operate, land lines in Hanoi and Ho Chi Minh City. Negotiations are still pending. If successful, then the investment (worth about US$1.4 billion) would be the largest so far by foreigners in telecommunications in Vietnam (*The Financial Times*, 9 May 1996).

Korea Telecom has recently received approval for its US$40 million project in three provinces in northern Vietnam to install and operate telephone lines. Again, this sort of joint venture (with VNPT) will be carried out under a business co-operation contract. Revenue is shared with VNPT for seven years, after which time the equipment will belong to VNPT (*The Financial Times*, 16 May 1996).

Other opportunities are occurring in, for example, the global system for mobile (GSM) telephone networks. VNPT currently runs Mobifone GSM jointly with Comvik of Sweden. VNPT also plans to operate another GSM by itself using equipment worth US$18 million supplied by Siemens of Germany. Mobile telephone ownership passed 35,000 in 1995, a very small fraction of the urban Vietnamese population of 15 million (*The Financial Times*, 25 June 1996).

A new international optical fibre telecommunications link opened early in 1996 allowing the number of simultaneous international calls to double from 11,000 to 22,000. This represents tremendous growth, considering that in 1986, there were only nine international lines to Moscow (*The Financial Times*, 9 February 1996).

Chapter 11 also discusses opportunities for telecommunications operators, equipment vendors and equipment manufacturers. There is a variety of potential for entrepreneurial activity in these fields.

Growth Impediments

Chapter 11 rounds out the discussion on telecommunications by enumerating the obstacles to successful investment. The major impediments include education, funding, a changing political climate, slow administrative reforms, and an unclear and changing taxation system. Indeed, the Communist Party Congress meetings in June and July 1996, in which the old guard showed signs of trying to maintain and consolidate power, dimmed investor hopes that reforms will continue at the previous rate (*Business Week*, 1 July 1996).

Recently, Vietnamese policy makers have been indecisive in completing negotiations with Telstra (Australian-owned), Cable and Wireless (U.K.-owned), NTT International (Japanese-owned) and France Telecom to install and operate land lines (*The Financial Times*, 9 May 1996). Wavering discourages other companies from attempting to enter the market. This may explain, in part, the diminished number of projects licensed (down 38%) for January to August this year relative to 1995 (*Dow Jones News Service*, 9 September 1996).

THE INTERNET IN VIETNAM

The Potential of Internet

Whereas Chapter 11 focused on basic telecommunications issues, Chapter 12 applies Porter's five competitive forces model to analyse Internet service provision. At present, expanding voice, fax, paging, and mobile phone capacity is the main thrust of telecommunications growth in Vietnam. The future will be the network.

The Internet is a recent entrant to Vietnam, and its use is presently limited in scope. From only 30 users in Hanoi in late 1994, now there are more than 3,000 (*The Wall Street Journal*, 6 September 1996). Service provided is limited to electronic mail, linking users to the outside world. However, a local bulletin board serves the business community. Provision for worldwide-web access is under consideration which will create a Vietnam-wide Intranet.

The Internet, with its phenomenal worldwide growth (see Table 12–1) over the past two years, is an added dimension to the expansion of telecommunications infrastructure. Once its telecommunications infrastructure is in place, the Internet has an ability to support communication, information and research, marketing, and electronic commerce faster and at lower cost than competing methods, particularly for technologically advanced small- and medium-sized enterprises (*Far Eastern Economic Review*, 25 January 1996). Moreover, because the information is transported through the use of packet-switching technology, better sharing (and, thus, higher utilisation) of telecom lines can be achieved. Vietnam could be well-positioned to exploit the Internet, both for internal connectivity as well as for facilitating technology transfer.

Surveys and Interviews

Chapter 12 contains very useful and up-to-date information on current and potential Internet uses in Vietnam. Information was collected from surveys as well as from interviews of principals in the industry.

Surveys were conducted in Hanoi and Ho Chi Minh City for a total of 92 respondents. Respondents were classified into those "Presently Using Internet," and those "Presently Not Using Internet." Findings on key problems facing Internet users in Vietnam, based on the surveys, included high costs and limited range of services. Business people tended to perceive the Internet as not secure for business transactions. Non-Internet users found lack of training, high cost, and lack of equipment as major impediments to using Internet. However, most non-users perceived the Internet as potentially useful to them.

Interviews were conducted with principal government IT agencies, Internet service providers, as well as with a business person setting up a cyber cafe in Hanoi. Information relevant to investors was obtained on issues ranging from how the government was piloting an Intranet for selected ministries to problems faced in setting up businesses utilising the Internet.

Market Supply and Demand for Internet Service Provision

Chapter 12 rounds out its discussion with an assessment of the Internet industry using Porter's diamond of five forces. The result is a well-structured analysis, exploring the supply and demand of Internet services.

From the supplier perspective, there is scope for providers of hardware for data communications, computer and computer peripherals, and software necessary for Internet service provision, content, and security. Indeed, a number of companies are joining the rush to enter the Vietnam Internet market. Vietnam's Army Information Company, in conjunction with Sun Microsystems, Grand Pacific and Sembawang Media Pte. (a unit of Singaporean Sembawang Corporation) sponsored a seminar on Internet security. On the agenda was how Sun Microsystem's security software could be used to screen out undesirable information (*The Wall Street Journal*, 6 September 1996).

Other opportunities are arising for suppliers as private companies and even a provincial posts and telecommunications agency has set up local Internet access networks. They hope to be ahead in the game to build up market share. There is speculation that an actual Internet link with the outside world will occur before the end of 1996 (*The Wall Street Journal*, 6 September 1996).

As noted in the surveys and interviews carried out in Hanoi and Ho Chi Minh City, there appears to be demand for Internet services, albeit limited mostly to businesses and a small number of individuals. The market to individuals will remain limited so long as incomes in Vietnam remain low.

Another impediment to the Internet is official hesitancy towards unregulated access to the rest of the world. Indeed, regulations drafted earlier this year by VNPT stipulate registration by users and Internet service providers. They must also report illegal activities (*The Wall Street Journal*, 6 September 1996).

Regulation of the Internet does, however, provide additional opportunities which Sun Microsystems and others are making use of. Internet service providers in Singapore could find an opportunity to provide technical expertise in how to filter out undesirable information.

TECHNOLOGY LINKER CHARACTERISTICS IN VIETNAMESE BUSINESS PEOPLE

The Role of the Technology Linker

Chapter 13 is quite different from the first two chapters as it takes a step back to examine the technology transfer process from developed to developing countries. A key tenet is that acceptance or rejection of innovation and technology transfer depends crucially on the subjective judgment of the decision makers involved. The study draws on a body of literature from sociology which finds that effective technology transfer requires the existence of a 'technology linker' – an individual or a set of individuals whose attributes are likely to range from being innovative to being oriented towards outside information sources.

Technology Transfer and Technology Linkers

Vietnam has ambitious goals for future development which will require enormous technology transfer from developed countries. Thus, Vietnam is an ideal location to test the applicability of the technology linker model. Chapter 13 does just that, conducting surveys on 36 managers, engineers, and supervisors from three different electronics firms. Although the sample set is too small to make meaningful statistical comparisons, it is possible to draw tentative inferences from cross-tabulated data. An interesting result is that both younger (less than 30 years old) and older workers (above 40 years old) with at least five years experience tend to be technology linkers. These findings were collaborated with other evidence from seminars and interviews with corporate executives collected during the Business Study Mission to Vietnam. The chapter explains why this result is plausible.

From an investor perspective, the results, when combined with the collaborative evidence, have tentative policy implications. If one is involved in transferring technology, then s/he should consider technology linker attributes when deciding on the kind of people undertaking implementation of the project in Vietnam.

CONCLUSION

Chapters 11 to 13 form a neat package for an investor interested in telecommunications in Vietnam. Chapter 11 provides a comprehensive overview of telecommunications infrastructure and its investment potential, both current and future, in Vietnam. Chapter 12 deals with Internet service provision in the socialist republic from several perspectives. While the ISP and related markets for individuals will never be sizeable until income levels rise, there is still ample opportunity in business and government. Lastly, Chapter 13 provides tentative advice for firms involved in the actual transfer of technology to Vietnam. Technology linkers may be the ingredient necessary to ensure a successful project in a country undergoing tremendous change.

REFERENCES

Balfour Frederik and Joyce Barnathan, "Is Reform Alive in Vietnam?" *Business Week International Editions*, Hanoi, 1 July 1996.

Chua Reginald and Carey Zesiger, "Vietnam Faces an Internet Quandary: Desire for Data vs. Security Concerns", *The Wall Street Journal*, 6 September 1996.

Grant Jeremy, "Hanoi to Alter Investment Law", *The Financial Times*, London, 22 August 1996.

Grant Jeremy, "Vietnam Opens Fibre Optic Link", *The Financial Times*, London, 9 February 1996.

Grant Jeremy, "Vietnam Plans Second GSM", *The Financial Times*, London, 25 June 1996.

Grant Jeremy, "Vietnam Puts Telecom Deals on Hold", *The Financial Times*, London, 9 May 1996.

Grant Jeremy, "Korea Telecom in Hanoi Deal", *The Financial Times*, London, 16 May 1996.

"New Vietnam Investment Law to Boost the Power of Foreign Cos", *Dow Jones News Service*, Dow Jones and Company, New York, 21 August 1996.

Nguyen Minh Tu, *Ten Years Economic Reform in Vietnam: Some Selected Macro-economic Key Issues*, Central Institute for Economic Management (CIEM), Hanoi, Vietnam, December 1995.

Schwarz Adam, "Proletariat Blues: Both Woeful, Neither Workers Nor Unions Are Top Dogs", *Far Eastern Economic Review*, Hong Kong, 25 January 1996.

"Vietnam Licensed Foreign Investment Down 38% on Year", *Dow Jones News Service*, Dow Jones and Company, New York, 9 September 1996.

SERVICES SECTORS

Chapter 15

Challenges and Opportunities in Vietnam's Banking Sector*

BY
Kimberly TAN
Henry LOH
KER Leh Hiong
CHUNG Thau Hen

INTRODUCTION

THE BANKING INDUSTRY plays an important role in a country's economic development. Its functions are two-fold. First, the industry helps to facilitate international trade and capital flows as well as mobilising investment funds necessary for economic growth. Secondly, an efficient and modern banking system is necessary for the management of monetary growth and inflation which have a broader impact on the overall economy.

The banking sector in Vietnam has undergone significant reform in recent years and this has brought renewed confidence to the financial community. The previous mono-bank system has been dismantled, and commercial and central banking activities are now separated. Interest rates have been adjusted in line with inflation. Since 1992, bank entry restrictions have been greatly liberalised and now there are approximately 60 foreign commercial banks operating in the country. Despite these achievements, however, the industry has a long way to go before reaching the level of development of its ASEAN neighbours.

The pace of the reform, however, is largely determined by the successful implementation of

* The authors are grateful for the guidance and assistance provided by Mr. Peter Low.

new policies and banking practices at individual banks. The latter calls for a pool of qualified and skilled personnel who not only possess a good understanding of the banking business but also the leadership necessary to initiate change.

This chapter examines the state of development of Vietnam's banking system, including the challenges confronting and opportunities available to the banking industry. It looks at the industry from the perspective of the banking and business community and the issues discussed reflect those which are most frequently raised.

Like many developing economies, there are weaknesses in the banking system. The more pronounced areas include the country's payment system, difficulties encountered in fund mobilisation, ambiguities in the legal system, accounting standards which are not in conformity with international practices and a lack of human resource development. Notwithstanding these challenges, the outlook for the industry appears to be favourable for a number of reasons. Vietnamese authorities are currently working closely with the World Bank and central banks of other ASEAN countries to reform its banking system. In fact, a schedule of banking reforms proposed by the World Bank is currently underway. Vietnam's positive economic outlook and strong inflows of foreign direct investment also augur well for the development and expansion of the banking industry.

AN OVERVIEW OF THE BANKING INDUSTRY IN VIETNAM

The State Bank of Vietnam (SBVN) is the central bank and it regulates the banking industry. It has gradually begun to adopt credit and monetary policies along the lines of central banks in market economies since the dismantling of the mono-banking system in 1989. It ceased direct lending to productive sectors in 1991 and terminated direct state budget financing in 1992.

The government effectively eliminated the monopolies of the four state-owned commercial banks (SOCBs) in May 1990 and enacted the *Commercial Banks Decree Law*. This law effectively liberalised banking operations by introducing joint stock commercial banks and popular credit funds (credit unions) as well as allowing the entry of foreign banks (*Vietnam Banking Review*, January 1996). Since 1990, the banking industry has rapidly expanded and, currently, the industry comprised approximately 266 financial institutions made up of banks, credit unions and representative offices. Table 15–1 shows a breakdown of the types of banking institutions in the industry.

TABLE 15–1
Vietnam's Banking System

Types of Banking Institutions	No.	Bank Names
State-owned Commercial Banks	4	Agriculture Bank (Agribank) Foreign Trade Bank (Vietcom Bank) Industrial and Commercial Bank (Incombank) Investment and Development Bank (BIDV)
Joint Venture Banks	4	Firstvina Bank (Vietcombank and Korea First Bank) Indovina Bank (Incombank and Indonesia's BDNI) Vinasiam Bank (Agribank and Siam Thai Bank) VID Public Bank (BIDV and Malaysia's Public Bank)
Foreign Banks	18	ABN Amro Bank ANZ Bank Bank of America Bangkok Bank Banque Indosuez BFCE Banque Nationale de Paris Chin Fong Bank Citibank Credit Lyonnais Deutsche Bank Hong Kong and Shanghai Bank ING Bank Malayan Banking Shinhan Bank Standard Chartered Bank Thai Military Bank United Overseas Bank
Joint Stock Banks	Approx. 50	Names not available.

Source: *Vietnam Review* (1995).

The proliferation of joint stock commercial banks is primarily attributable to the banking industry's low minimum capital requirement. For instance, current laws require a minimum chartered capital of only D70 billion (US$6.4 million) to set up joint stock banks in Ho Chi Minh City, D50 billion (US$4.6 million) in Hanoi, D20 billion (US$1.8 million) in other urban cities/provinces, and merely D3 billion (US$280,000) or less in other rural areas. The minimum initial capital requirement for a joint venture bank is relatively higher at US$15 million.

Foreign banks are allowed to set up representative offices in Vietnam since the banking reforms in 1989. As shown in Table 15–2, the number of foreign banks has more than doubled over the three-year period from 1993 to 1995 due to a further relaxation of the banking laws that permit foreigners to set up branches as well as joint venture banks. This development has had a positive impact on the economy in general and the industry in particular. It has helped to create a favourable investment climate which facilitates international trade and capital inflows. In addition, these institutions also provide opportunities to increase the knowledge of bank management through the employment and training of local staff.

TABLE 15–2
Influx of Foreign Banks

	Representative Offices	Branches	Joint Venture Banks	Total
1 January 1993	8	8	3	19
1 January 1994	22	8	3	33
1 January 1995	32	16	3	51
1 January 1996	40	18	4	62

Sources: World Bank (1995) and Singh (1995).

At the end of 1995, total banking assets were approximately US$6 billion or 36% of GDP. This level of assets is still relatively low if it is compared to other Asian countries such as Malaysia (110%), Thailand (100%), Singapore (95%) or Indonesia (55%), implying that Vietnam remains an "underbanked" country (Zielinski, 1995). SOCBs continue to dominate the industry, accounting for 85% of total banking assets, while foreign banks and joint stock banks, together, account for the remaining 15%.

Current banking activities offered by domestic commercial banks focus mainly on the acceptance of deposits, extension of loans, trade financing and remittances. Mobilisation of funds through the use of savings instruments is still at an early stage of development. According to a World Bank report (1995), resources mobilised from the banking system form only about one-third of the industry's total funding requirement. The remaining two-thirds has to be funded through SOCB's medium-term borrowing (largely trade related) from foreign banks and the SBV.

In tandem with the country's gradual move towards a market economy, there has also been a substantial growth in credit to the private sector since 1990. Although state-owned enterprises (SOEs) are still the dominant users of credit, their share of bank credit fell to 72% in 1994 from an average of 86% in 1991. Credit to the private sector consists primarily of short-term loans (averaging three to six months) to the agriculture and commerce sectors. By and large, long-term financing is scarce and largely extended in foreign currency due to the lack of a long-term funding mechanism. Long-term financing is mainly extended by the SOCBs to SOEs. Foreign currency loans carry lower nominal interest rates than Dong denominated loans but this reduction in financing costs carries the risk of foreign exchange loss.

Despite the increase in the credit extended to the private sector, a recent survey conducted by the Central Institute for Economic Management (Fforde, 1995) shows that considerable difficulties remain for the small- and medium-sized Vietnamese businesses to gain access to bank loans. These difficulties are due to either the lack of collateral or inadequate collateral, coupled with complicated, time consuming procedures imposed by the banks (*Vietnam Investment Review*, October 1995). Approximately 50% of the businesses surveyed were found not to keep funds in bank accounts while 75% did not habitually use banks to settle payments, preferring to use cash instead. Many of the businesses also relied on the informal credit markets, such as money lenders and a variety of rotating savings/credit mechanisms known as the *Hui* system, to meet their funding requirements.

Foreign bank branches are engaged primarily in the financing of major SOEs, Vietnamese commercial banks and joint ventures (Baker & Mckenzie, 1995). Extension of credit to local entrepreneurs has thus far been restrained due to the country's ambiguous legal framework pertaining to commerce, collateral, mortgage and bankruptcy. Most of them choose not to engage in the business of accepting deposits for economic reasons although, technically, they can accept demand deposits amounting to up to 20% of their prescribed capital. The situation has to some extent curbed competition among the many foreign banks, joint venture banks and local commercial banks. Most foreign banks admit that they have yet to fully leverage the US$15 million capital which they brought in as part of the initial capital investment.

CHALLENGES FACING THE BANKING SYSTEM

Weak Payment System

There have been significant improvements in the payment system over the past two years. For instance, the installation of the Society Worldwide Interbank Financial Telecommunication (commonly known as SWIFT) access point stations at SBV and the four SOCBs in 1995 has facilitated fast international payments. Nonetheless, the consensus among users is that more needs to be done to foster an effective and efficient system particularly at the national level.

Presently, there is no national payment service in Vietnam. Although payments within the major cities can now be effected within one to two days, payments between cities, and between cities and other provinces, can take up to two weeks or more. The number of transactions effected is very limited. Government payments between agencies are handled outside of the banking system and so are consumer payments for utilities. There is no electronic payment of payroll, even in the larger companies.

The heavy reliance on cash has a historical basis and this is compounded by the public's unfamiliarity with, and lack of trust in, non-cash instruments. According to a World Bank (1995) estimate, there is four times more cash in circulation in Vietnam than in the other ASEAN countries. The notion of a personal checking account is still new to many individuals and the product has only been available in Hanoi and Ho Chi Minh City since November 1994 and March 1995, respectively. In 1995, there were approximately 20,000 personal accounts outstanding – an amount representing 0.03% of the population.

Checking accounts have not gained wide acceptance because their effectiveness is hampered by a lack of transferability as well as other restrictions. For example, cashing cheques is sometimes delayed due to the bank's inability to pay. Bank branches in the provinces sometimes do not maintain sufficient cash reserves to meet large withdrawals. Consequently, cash remains the preferred mode of payment. This rudimentary form of payment system, and the high reliance on cash transactions, remain two of the major impediments to the development of Vietnam's financial system (Hue, 1995).

Fund Mobilisation Ability

Deposits garnered by commercial banks have increased considerably in recent years. Commercial banks' Dong deposits rose to D12.5 trillion (US$1.1 billion) from a mere D2.3 trillion (US$508 million), and foreign currency deposits grew to D8.6 trillion (US$779 million) from D2.1 trillion (US$454 million) between 1989 and 1994. The rapid growth in Dong deposits *vis-à-vis* foreign currency deposits in this period is mainly due to the increase in the real interest rate on Dong deposits relative to foreign currency deposits. For example, current interest rates average 21% per annum on Dong deposits and 9.5% on foreign currency (mainly U.S. dollar) deposits. The growth in Dong deposits is attributable to three factors: reduction in inflationary expectations; growing public confidence in the national currency; and increasing acceptance of the country's commercial banks.

Despite the above achievements, Vietnamese banks currently lag behind other ASEAN countries and transitional economies in fund mobilisation. Table 15–3 compares the level of financial deepening as measured by the ratio of cash in circulation to broad money.[1] A high ratio suggests that there is a lot of cash in circulation and, hence, a smaller degree of fund mobilisation. As shown in Table 15–3, Vietnam's financial deepening process, as represented by the share of cash to broad money ratio of 45%, is relatively high compared to ASEAN countries and other transitional economies.

However, there are difficulties in fund mobilisation which may be caused by a number of factors. First, besides a weak payment system, the difficulty in making withdrawals from banks also discourages the public from putting their money in bank accounts. In the provinces, it is not unusual to experience delays of two or three weeks when converting funds from a bank account to cash. Secondly, it is estimated that a vast amount of private savings (US$2 to 3 billion in cash and gold) are still being held outside the formal banking system. This is

---

1 Broad money (or M3) is defined as the sum of currency in circulation plus all deposit liabilities of banks.

attributable to the higher return which can be earned in the active informal credit market where interest rates are five to ten times higher than those offered by banks. The lack of trust in the banking system also contributes to this phenomenon. Thirdly, the frequent shortage of currency induces the public to hold currency for a longer period.

TABLE 15–3
Cash to Broad Money Ratio for Selected Countries*

ASEAN	(%)	Other Asian Countries	(%)	Transitional Economies	(%)
Vietnam	*45.0*	China	16.6	Albania	36.5
Indonesia	10.8	South Korea	9.5	Bulgaria	9.0
Malaysia	6.5	Laos	23.5	Hungary	22.9
Philippines	14.7	Mongolia	24.5	Poland	15.9
Singapore	8.2	Papua New Guinea	10.2	Romania	20.7
Thailand	8.0				

* As at September 1994.
Source: World Bank (1995).

Thus, fund mobilisation is an area of concern in Vietnam's economic development efforts which in turn, to a large extent, depend on banks' ability to mobilise and channel funds to finance the modernisation of various productive sectors. Some 50% of the capital needed for the country's development is expected to be contributed by domestic capital. Hence, capital mobilisation is the main thrust under Vietnam's national financial policy. This mobilisation encompasses various forms of savings, credit and bonds (*Vietnam Banking Review*, October 1995).

Ambiguities in the Legal System

In tandem with the move towards a market economy, the Vietnamese government has enacted legislation governing the banking and financial system. The banking and financial legislation defines the organisation and function of the various financial systems (e.g., State Bank of Vietnam, state-owned bank, private commercial banks and foreign banks), the participants and their mutual relationships, as well as their rights and obligations. In addition, the legislation also regulates mechanisms for mobilising funds, such as collateral, mortgage and bankruptcy laws, which are fundamental to lending operations.

While the overall legislation is comprehensive, the need to address myriad new issues over a short period of time has understandably resulted in a lack of cohesiveness and occasional inconsistencies, particularly with respect to cross-referencing between laws and regulations. For instance, foreign participation in banking and finance activities is currently operationalised through three different pieces of legislation:

(i) The 1990 *Commercial Banks Decree Law* which addresses the matter but only in a cursory manner;
(ii) The 1991 *Foreign Banks Legislation* (Decree No. 189-HDBT) issued by the Council of Ministers on foreign bank branches and joint venture banks operating in Vietnam; and
(iii) The amended 1987 *Foreign Investment Law* also contains relevant provisions.

According to the World Bank (1995), it remains unclear which, if any, of the provisions of the *Commercial Banks Decree Law* are applicable to foreign banks and joint venture banks with foreign ownership.

Another common complaint concerns the uncertainty of the legal process itself (for example, the interpretation, application, mechanics and enforcement of specific legislative provisions). Moreover, large portions of the existing legislation is new and has not been tested in court. This is mostly due to the government's unfamiliarity with new legal concepts and practices, a relatively short jurisprudential history, the sheer volume of new legislation and the rapid pace of change. This situation is further aggravated by a shortage of knowledgeable local legal professionals who are familiar with economic contracts and other financial transactions, and who can act on behalf of banks and clients.

Accounting Standards

Vietnam currently does not have accounting and auditing standards that conform to those practised by the international community. While financial records exist for most local companies, they are inconsistent and rarely reflect a reliable financial position. Therefore, it is extremely difficult to assess asset strength or earnings potential for any company. Moreover, it is extremely difficult for banks, in particular foreign banks, to assess the creditworthiness of local businesses.

According to foreign bankers, not much emphasis is given to the financial figures. Instead, they rely on qualitative aspects of credit, such as the reputation and track record of sponsors, industry prospects and intuition in making their lending decisions. Even when they are convinced that a business is creditworthy, foreign banks often face the difficult task of convincing credit committees at the head office to go ahead with transactions because they do not have hard data to support the deal. This dilemma has resulted in foreign banks adopting a very cautious approach in lending to local entrepreneurs.

Development of a Sound Banking System

It is not easy to assess the financial performance of Vietnamese banks because their accounting practices deviate in many ways from international standards. For instance, bank profits are difficult to measure because little is known about their provision policies for bad debts and doubtful account balances. Generally, banks are currently carrying a high proportion of overdue credits owed by insolvent state-owned enterprises as well as private sector enterprises. According to the World Bank (1995), the industry's non-performing assets (delinquencies) are estimated at around five to six trillion Dong. This estimate represents over 25% of current outstanding loans, and twice the aggregate capital and reserves of all Vietnamese banks combined. This implies that the banks would be insolvent if they were to write-off all of the non-performing loans now.

Poor loan asset quality is prevalent due to the inadequate assessment of borrowers' credit standing. At present, most domestic banks extend credit solely on the basis of collateral rather than on the basis of evaluating the borrower's profitability, cash flow, existing debt burdens and capitalisation, which are common yardsticks used in the assessment of debt servicing ability.

Substantial write-offs and recapitalisation are required to "clean-up" the banks' balance sheets, especially if international accounting standards are adopted. This problem is multi-dimensional and it will take time to resolve. Among other things, banks must build up their loan loss reserve by way of providing adequate bad debt allowances, adopting a stringent lending policy and exploring various means of recapitalisation. The latter can be achieved through government support or privatisation.

Human Resources

The challenges mentioned above have overwhelmed the banking sector to the extent that human resource development has become a low priority activity. Typically, human resource policies of local banks emphasise quantity rather than quality in their employees. This is due to the historical requirements of state banks which, apart from their banking functions, provide employment for people. According to Binh (1995), the present Vietnam banking sector employs more than 50,000 people, out of which about 45,000 are employed by the state bank and state-owned commercial banks.

However, there is a general lack of experience in the modern banking system as reported in the *Vietnam Banking Review* (February 1996). The small group of cadres that have accumulated some experience and professional skill will no doubt be attracted to foreign banks which pay better, offer bigger training budgets and provide overseas training opportunities (see Table 15–4). The foreign banks overcome local employees' lack of experience by hiring experienced and professional expatriates (see Table 15–4).

At the national level, education programmes cannot be fully pursued due to budget constraints. Over the past few years, the government's budget expenditure for education has not exceeded 10% of the total budget as pointed out by Le (1996). This is much lower than Singapore's 20% budget allocation to education during the first ten years of independence (Loh, 1985). Vietnam's policy in this respect indirectly affects the quality in the graduates available to the banking sector and possibly, as a result, the relatively stringent entry requirements and emphasis on training by both foreign and local banks (see Table 15–4).

OPPORTUNITIES IN THE BANKING SYSTEM

The challenges discussed in the foregoing section are not peculiar to Vietnam but they are rather typical of the country's radical shift from a closed to a market economy. Despite these challenges, the outlook for the Vietnamese banking sector appears favourable. The influx of foreign banks in recent years is testimony to the international banking community's confidence in the industry's prospects. The factors de

TABLE 15–4
Human Resource Development and Management Among Banks

Banks	Expatriates To Employees Ratio	Entry Requirements	Training Provided	Starting Pay (US$/month)
Foreign banks	5 to 30 (Management level)	English, Computer knowledge, e.g., EXCEL, WORD Degree (Basic) Personal quality like confidence, eloquent	Training budget is 3 to 5% of revenue. On-Job-Training. Local training by overseas trainers. Overseas courses. Expatriates spend 30 to 40% of their time training local staff.	160–200
Local banks	1 to 10,000	Entrance exam on English, banking and computer knowledge Degree (Banking Institute, University of Foreign Language)	Training budget not fixed, allocated when needed. On-Job-Training. Organised seminars.	80–120
Joint venture banks	8 to 70 (Management level)	English Degree (Banking Institute, University of Economics)	Training budget is 1 to 3% of revenue. On-Job-Training. Overseas courses.	140–180

Note: Job-training for local banks focus on computer applications, accounting, and English.
Source: Business Study Mission survey results, March 1996.

scribed below support the favourable long-term prospects of the industry.

Modernisation of the Banking System

The Vietnamese government and SBV are aware of the urgency required in consolidating and improving the banking industry so that it can play a bigger role in funding the country's economic growth. Both parties are currently working closely with various international development agencies such as the World Bank and IMF, as well as neighbouring ASEAN countries, to elevate the country's banking system to international standards (Le, 1995).

The World Bank (1995) calls for reform in many areas of the banking system including legal issues, bank supervision, monetary policy, payment system and financing modes which are to be initiated over a three-year period commencing 1995 (see Appendix 15–1). In November 1995, Vietnam received a US$49 million loan from the World Bank for its payment system and modernisation project which aims to provide a framework for modern payment services. The project represents the first large-scale utilisation of information technology aimed at modernising the banking sector. It comprises the following:

(i) A national inter-bank clearing and settlement system (20% of total project cost) which includes clearing of cheques and electronic payment orders.
(ii) Interbank payment system (67% of total project cost) for six participating banks[2] which aims to facilitate the swift clearance of payment orders between branches of the same institution.
(iii) Strengthening of management practices (12% of total project cost) including a review of commercial banks' modernisation needs, the design of appropriate customer accounting systems, portfolio review and financial audits.
(iv) Project management support (1% of total project cost) for consulting services for the procurement of systems and technical support.

Modernisation of the payment system through the use of infor-

---

[2] Beneficiaries are: State Bank of Vietnam, Vietcom Bank, Incom Bank, Agri Bank, Bank for Investment and Development of Vietnam, Exim Bank and Maritime Bank.

mation technology is an urgent priority in Vietnam's banking reform since it will help to reduce the amount of cash floating on the market, hasten capital flows, increase efficiency in money transfers, and result in greater convenience for consumers. Ultimately, the project will increase consumers' confidence in the banking sector.

In addition, Vietnam has also signed agreements with central banks in the ASEAN countries on bilateral settlements, agency correspondence as well as exchange of information and experiences. While it will take some time for the reform activities to be effected, these measures represent a large step forward in terms of modernising and strengthening Vietnam's banking system.

The Developing Banking Environment

Vietnam's retail banking industry is still in its infancy. Presently, retail banking products are limited to savings accounts and recently introduced (April 1996) credit cards (*Asian Wall Street Journal*, 27 March 1996). However, other retail banking products, such as personal loans, housing loans and life insurance, are currently not offered.

Economists are generally optimistic about Vietnam's economic reform. Political stability coupled with the government's commitment to establish market reforms have contributed to the steady economic growth in the last six years, with GDP growth averaging 7.7% per annum for the period 1990 to 1995. GDP growth is forecasted to reach a high of 9.5% in 1996. This robust economic growth is expected to continue in the near term and it will translate into rising disposable incomes and increased purchasing power for Vietnam's population of 75 million. As with other developing economies, a strong economic performance will naturally act as an impetus for growth in various economic sectors including the demand for banking services (Dang, 1995).

Credit Demand and Infrastructure Spending

The Vietnamese Central Communist Party estimates that Vietnam will require US$50 billion of investment from 1995 to 2000 in order to modernise the country's productive sectors as well as to upgrade its infrastructure, utilities and telecommunications facilities. Domestic and foreign direct investments aside, bank financing and capital market instruments are expected to play a key role in funding the necessary investments (Cao, 1995). This points to a buoyant loan business for both domestic and foreign commercial banks. For foreign banks, opportunities abound especially in the areas of loan syndication, project financing and financial advisory services where they can import their expertise and experience gained from other developing countries. As such, one can expect the rate of credit growth to accelerate once the ambiguities in the legal system are resolved. As previously discussed, this area currently poses a major deterrent for banks engaged in lending activities.

CONCLUSION

Vietnam's banking system has progressed significantly since the dismantling of its mono-banking system in 1989. Over the last seven years the number of banks in the industry has increased gradually, in line with the liberalisation of the industry. Today, the industry comprises more than 250 financial institutions, including branches of many established foreign banks. This development is impressive for the industry and it is testimony to the banking community's confidence in the country's bright future.

Notwithstanding this performance, the banking system is still at a developmental stage and will require some major reforms before it can attain an international standard. The reform effort requires not only the attention of the banking community but also the collective efforts of various government ministries as well as the close co-operation of the business community at large. This is especially true for issues pertaining to legal ambiguities and accounting standards.

Several factors suggest that Vietnam may be able to achieve a modern banking system sooner rather than later. The active involvement of the World Bank as well as collaboration with central banks in ASEAN countries provides valuable expertise for the modernisation of the banking industry. In particular, the experience of the ASEAN countries will be of great relevance for Vietnam since many of them have gone through somewhat similar stages of development. The banking sector is also well-positioned to benefit from the country's strong economic performance. This development will not only boost profitability and capital, but it will also help to provide the much needed funds for investment in modern banking technology and the training of human capital.

APPENDIX 15–1
Proposed Banking Reform Sequence

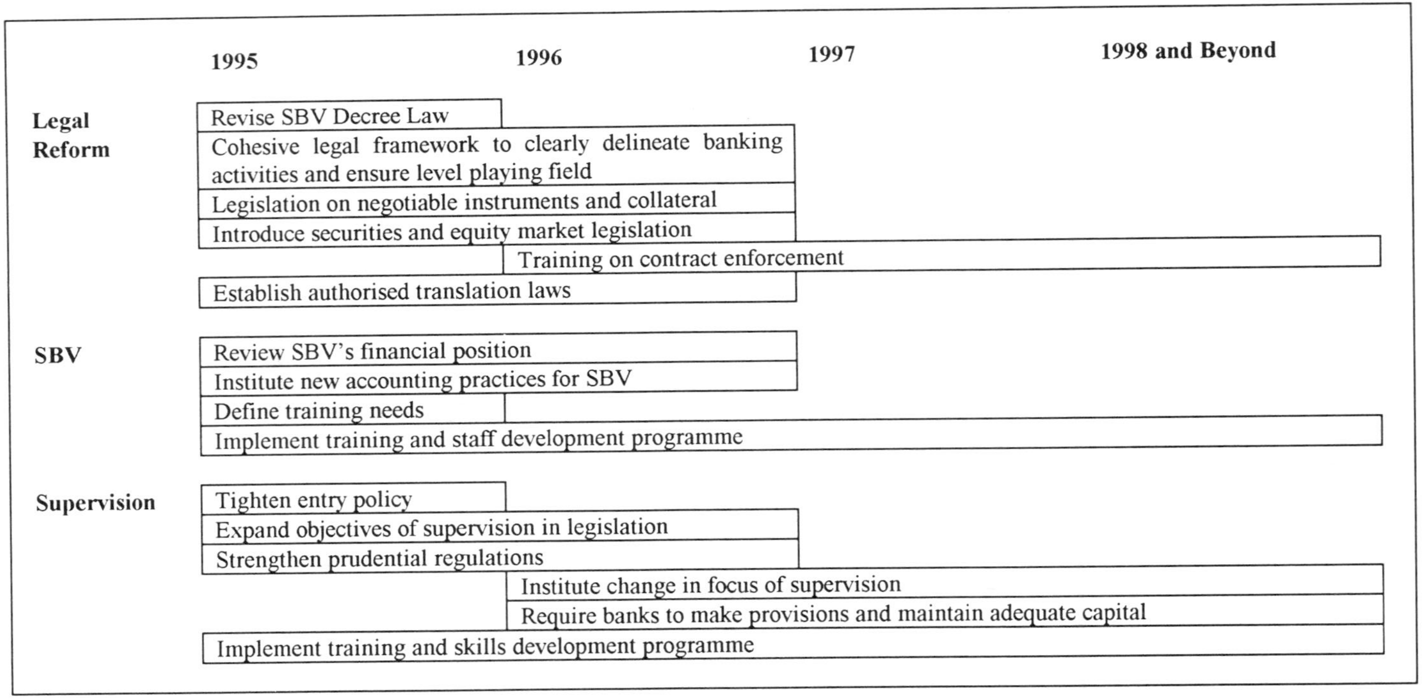

APPENDIX 15–1 (cont'd)

	1995	1996	1997	1998 and Beyond
Monetary Policy	Introduce one minimum deposit rate and one maximum lending rate			
	Revert to earlier policy of unified required reserve ratios			
	Abandon use of excess cash ratios for monetary policy			
	Rationalise use of SBV financing			
	Begin auctioning of T-bills and govt securities			
			Begin open market operations with govt debt instruments and repos	
Commercial Banks	Special audit of all SOCBs			
	Modernise SOCB accounting practices			
		Restructure SOCB management and autonomy Recapitalise SOCBs through govt or private sources		
	Continue staff development through training programmes			

APPENDIX 15–1 (cont'd)

	1995	1996	1997	1998 and Beyond
Taxation of Banking System	Remove turnover tax on banking activities			
		Unify profit tax across commercial banks		
Payments System	Expedite clearing and settlement process			
	Introduce standard technological interconnections			
SOE Restructuring	Settlement of inter-enterprise arrears			
	Settlement of SOE debt owed to banks			
	Institute SOE performance monitoring system			
	Undertake SOE audits			
		Restructuring of key SOEs – financial strengthening and greater autonomy		
		Begin privatisation or corporatisation of SOEs		
Term Finance	Carry out study on ways to improve term finance			
		Implement study finding		

APPENDIX 15–1 (cont'd)

<table>
<tr><th></th><th>1995</th><th>1996</th><th>1997</th><th>1998 and Beyond</th></tr>
<tr><td rowspan="5">Rural Finance</td><td colspan="3">Lengthen the maturities of short-term rural finance loans to nine to twelve months</td><td></td></tr>
<tr><td colspan="3">Encourage rural finance banks to develop operating and strategic business plans</td><td></td></tr>
<tr><td colspan="4">Develop capacity for term lending and savings mobilisation for rural finance</td></tr>
<tr><td></td><td colspan="2">Give rural banks access to SBV refinancing</td><td></td></tr>
<tr><td></td><td colspan="3">Encourage rural banks to develop co-financing arrangements for rural borrowers</td></tr>
<tr><td rowspan="3">Housing Finance</td><td>Remove bias against long-term lending by housing banks</td><td></td><td></td><td></td></tr>
<tr><td colspan="2">Accelerate creation of key markets for housing, assets and inputs</td><td></td><td></td></tr>
<tr><td></td><td colspan="2">Separate subsidy obligations from housing finance</td><td></td></tr>
</table>

Source: World Bank (1995).

REFERENCES

"Banking on Finance Sector Reform in Vietnam", *Vietnam Banking Review*, January 1996, pp. 28–31.

Binh T., "A Personal Strategy is Needed", *Vietnam Investment Review*, Vol. 5, May 1995, p. 17.

Cao S. Kiem, "Making Capital Sources of Society Most Effectively Utilised", *Vietnam Banking Review*, August 1995, pp. 9–11.

Dang Duc Dam, *Vietnam's Economy: 1986–1995*, The GIOI Publishers, Hanoi, 1995.

Fforde Adam, "Vietnam: Economic Commentary and Analysis", Aduki Pte. Ltd., Issue No. 6, April 1995, pp. 12–4.

"Financing Stymied by Collateral Rule", *Vietnam Investment Review*, 23–29 October 1995, pp. 19–20.

"Four Vietnamese Banks to Issue Credit Cards, MasterCard Reports", *Asian Wall Street Journal*, Reuters News Service, 27 March 1996, p. 5.

Fundamental Considerations – Business Forms for Foreign Investors in the Socialist Republic of Vietnam, Baker & McKenzie, March 1995.

Hue Dong, "Cheque for Payment in Vietnam", *Vietnam Banking Review*, September 1995, pp. 4–6.

Le Dang Doanh, Seminar on "Economic Reform and Investment", Hanoi, Vietnam, 4 March 1996.

Le Khanh, *Vietnam Review – Integration into the World Economy,* WI Carr Indosuez Capital, October 1995.

Loh Linda, "Institutional and Policy Measures for Effective Manpower Planning: Singapore Case Study", *Manpower Planning in Asean Countries*, Singapore Regional Institute of Higher Education and Development, 1985, pp. 210–2.

"Several Key Points of Vietnam's National Financial Policy", *Vietnam Banking Review*, October 1995, pp. 30–2.

Singh Vijit, "Commercial Banking in Vietnam – Challenges and Prospects", AIC Conference in Bangkok, 30–31 March 1995.

"Meeting with Citibank Vietnam General Manager", *Vietnam Banking Review*, February 1996, p. 13.

Vietnam Review, Baring Securities, March 1995, p. 25.

World Bank, *Vietnam – Financial Sector Review. An Agenda for Financial Sector Development*, Report No. 13143, Vietnam, March 1995.

Zielinski Robert, *The Alchemy of Asian Banking*, Jardine Fleming Securities, October 1995.

Chapter 16

Development of Education, Training and Investment Opportunities in Vietnam*

BY
CHAN Weng Khoon
Agnes LUI Yim Lin
PEH Chin Sin

INTRODUCTION

THIS CHAPTER EXAMINES the educational system in Vietnam and identifies the business opportunities for private investors that may arise from the current gap between the demand for and supply of education and training in Vietnam.

Education and training are fundamental components of economic development, and they improve both productivity and employability within a nation. However, human capital both influences and is influenced by socio-economic factors, and has to be cultivated and acquired over time. Many of the gains go directly to individuals, with little opportunity for transferability to other users, except where those users themselves become teachers or trainers.

As a consequence, human resource planning is a complex and difficult task for any government, and especially for the governments of transitional economies such as Vietnam. The purpose of this chapter, therefore, is to put Vietnamese human resource development in a proper context.

* The authors are grateful for the guidance and assistance provided by Dr. Ian McGovern.

The chapter begins by describing educational policies and issues relating to developing countries in general. This provides the relevant background for understanding the development of, and potential in, business opportunities in Vietnam's education system. Next, it examines the impact of Vietnam's economic growth on the education system, since economic growth creates different demands on the workforce and these demands must be met through changes in the way people are educated and trained.

Thirdly, the education policies of Vietnam's government are examined, especially the methods by which the government attempts to reconcile the educational and training demands of a rapidly changing economy with a woefully inadequate educational and training system that was designed for a less industrially-oriented workforce. The chapter ends by identifying the opportunities and challenges that may be encountered by private investors in Vietnam when seeking investment opportunities in the education and training sector.

EDUCATIONAL POLICY IN DEVELOPING COUNTRIES

The return on education in any society may differ between the return to an individual and that to society as a whole. From the social standpoint, the benefits are likely to be higher from investment in primary education. This is because primary education can reach a broader base of the population and will increase national productivity since elementary subjects provide factory workers and farmers with the basic technical knowledge to be more productive. In addition, the social benefits derived from secondary and university education are often less than those derived from primary education (Hogendorn, 1992).

For a private individual, the return increases more rapidly with secondary and tertiary education. In lesser developed countries (LDCs), earnings for those with higher levels of education are comparatively greater at every stage than in the developed countries. For instance, private returns to university graduates are six times higher than those to primary school graduates in countries such as Malaysia, Ghana, South Korea, and India; in contrast, the figure is only 2.4 times higher in U.S., Canada, and the U.K. It can be concluded from this that education has tended to increase income inequality in LDCs. In such situations, there will be increased demand for higher education, and this may divert the allocation of resources to higher education in LDCs at the expense of primary education (Hogendorn, 1992).

Education in LDCs is not just likely to be inequitable; it will also be costly due to the scarcity of resources. The scarcity inflates the cost of teachers and the situation is further aggravated by the large amount of subsidies often provided for higher education in LDCs. Compared to primary education, higher education tends to be relatively more expensive in LDCs than in developed countries. Generally, higher education tends to receive a larger proportion of resources and funds than primary education despite the latter's higher social returns. Thus, curtailing heavy subsidies may free resources and funds to the benefit of primary education (Hogendorn, 1992).

Human Resource Planning

A country's human capital development is necessarily affected by human resource (HR) planning. HR planning is an important component in the economic development process since it is through this mechanism that the managers of the economy attempt to balance the longer term changes in demand and supply in the labour market. Some of the major issues involved in HR planning in LDCs are highlighted below.

A major reason for employment difficulties in LDCs is the lack of relevance in the curriculum. The curriculum is predominantly influenced by a country's history, culture, and perhaps religion, and linkages between the curriculum and the needs of the economy are often totally absent (Hogendorn, 1992). In addition, a common trend in LDCs is the deteriorating quality in education which set in during the debt crisis and slowdown of growth in the 1980s. The LDCs have generally put a greater emphasis on the quantity of education rather than the quality, even though the increase in quantity at the expense of quality will not necessarily be beneficial to a country's development prospects (Hongendorn, 1992).

Furthermore, in LDCs there is often a lack of equal opportunities for females in education. In addition to being unfair, this has negative repercussions since education of females carries much greater positive benefits (Schultz, 1981). The prejudice against female education in LDCs broadly hinders the growth of a country's economy since investment in women's education will bring about higher productive returns and is a better form of human capital formation (Schultz, 1988).

However, LDCs are now more frequently looking into the development of vocational training programmes related to job availability (Middleton *et al.*, 1990). The vocational programmes are designed to train labour specifically for employment in those parts of industry where demand for labour is the greatest. There are, however, unavoidable instances where vocationally-trained students can only find jobs in fields for which they are not trained. Such mismatches lead to a preference among both students and employers for a general education at the secondary level whereby the basic foundations are focused upon, so that students remain flexible to fit into a wider variety of jobs. The specific needs of the job can then be met through on-the-job training by employers who better understand the job requirements.

SOCIO-ECONOMIC DEVELOPMENT IN VIETNAM

Before discussing the education system in Vietnam, it might prove useful to briefly mention how the Vietnamese economy has developed in recent years. Vietnam's economy has achieved rapid growth since it underwent a new phase of economic development known as *doi moi* (economic renovation), designed to transform the economy from a centrally-planned to a market-oriented one. The process comprised two stages; economic stabilisation (1986–91) and, since 1992, economic growth (Nguyen, 1995).

In the five years from 1991 to 1995, the average annual increase in GDP was 8.2% and the annual increase of total industrial output averaged 13% (Nguyen, 1995). During this period of economic growth, the most notable achievement was that Vietnam was able to control and bring down its inflation. The high inflation rate of 774.7% in 1986 was down to 14.4% in 1994 (Nguyen, 1995). This was achieved through prudent government control of foreign investment into Vietnam so as to allow the country to absorb the investment without creating high inflation.

In the transition from a centrally-planned economy to a market economy, foreign direct investment has played an important role. By the beginning of 1995, Vietnam had approved licenses for more than 1,500 foreign investment projects. The total registered investment was US$19 billion, of which about US$6 billion has been realised (Nguyen, 1995).

For the years 1996 to 2000, the Vietnamese government has targeted a GDP growth rate of 9 to 10% per annum. To attain this growth, the government has projected US$40 to US$44 billion of investment, of which about US$18 to US$20 billion is expected to come from foreign investment. To further facilitate this inflow, the

Vietnamese government has streamlined and improved the procedures for foreign investment (Nguyen, 1995).

The shift in the economy is towards modernisation and technology upgrading. Specially focused economic zones (industrial zones and import/export zones) have been established, and modernisation and industrialisation programmes will continue to bring about structural change in the economy. The focus will be on the development of industry and away from the current heavy reliance on agriculture. A high priority is to improve the living standards of the rural peasants and poor urban workers. The development plan for the period 1996 to 2000 aims to double the current GDP per capita by the year 2000 (Vo, 1995).

Sectoral Changes

As with all economies, the Vietnamese economy can be broadly divided into three sectors: agriculture, industry and service. The economic structure has changed quite significantly in the last five years and these changes are set to continue, as shown in Table 16–1 below. The reforms, coupled with new foreign investment, are expected to boost industrial sector expansion by an annual growth rate of 13.3%, the services sector by 12.3%, and the agricultural sector by a much lower 4.3%. As the modernisation and industrialisation continues, it is expected that by the year 2000 the industrial sector will account for 35% of GDP while the agriculture sector will account for only 16% (Vo, 1995).

TABLE 16–1
GDP's Sectoral Structure

Year	1990	1995	2000*
Industry	22.6%	31.0%	35%
Agriculture	38.8%	25.7%	16%
Services	38.6%	43.3%	49%

* Projected.
Source: Vo, 1995.

This is a typical pattern of sectoral change for an LDC going through the transition from an LDC to a more industrialised society, though the projected pace of change over such a short period is rather remarkable. A typical LDC (by definition) will have a relatively larger agricultural sector, probably making up the largest share of GDP. The services sector will also be large as people will be engaged in trading, marketing and transportation of goods. Once development occurs, the industrial sector will increase its share of GDP while the agriculture sector will decline. The service sector will grow in support of industry as economic development progresses. (Hogendorn, 1992).

Impact on the Workforce

A key issue in this sectoral change is the accompanying shift in the composition of the labour force. While there would previously have been a high concentration of the labour force in agriculture, the labour force will now begin to shift from agriculture to service and industry as the economy grows (Hogendorn, 1992).

In Vietnam, the labour force composition is about 80% agricultural and 20% industrial and service. This is expected to change over the next five to ten years to about 60% agricultural and 40% industrial and service (*Asiaweek*, 16 June 1995). The emerging industry and service sectors will require a skilled and technically competent workforce, otherwise all the previous sectoral projections will be unattainable.

During the current phase of economic development, Vietnam has attracted much foreign direct investment, and the presence of foreign investors will increase demand in the labour market for managerial/professional staff, supervisors and operatives. In particular, the demand is likely to be heavy for semi-skilled and skilled workers in industries like textiles, construction, electronics, and engineering, while the professionals who will be most in demand will be qualified engineers, business managers, financial experts, and professional accountants (Mai, 1996). In Vietnam, the labour market is not functioning well enough to allocate labour efficiently in accordance with demand and supply (Nguyen, 1995) and, where staff can be found, companies in Vietnam will have to retrain them to fit into organisations (Mai, 1996).

The Role of Education

One of the key factors in the successful transformation of an economy is the efficiency of a country's capital investment programmes (for LDCs this is usually foreign direct investment) which are partly dependent on the education and technical skills of the workforce. Initially, a highly-skilled workforce can attract much needed foreign investment, and subsequent education and training will improve the skill levels of the workforce leading to higher quality investment in the future (Hogendorn, 1992).

In Vietnam, in addition to the shorter term labour market imperfections, the country has a persistently high unemployment rate and a lack of technical personnel. The labour market is unstable and this is compounded by the fact that presently-employed workers could possibly become redundant or unemployed in the near future due to their low level of education and shortage of training (Mai, 1996).

In the agricultural sector, Vietnam (despite increased output) still lags behind China and other countries in the region in terms of productivity (Nguyen, 1995). The training and upgrading of the workforce in this sector is necessary to improve the efficiency of labour and machinery, as well as to absorb new technologies. The new emphasis is on the development of processing in agro-industries, forestry, aqua-products, the development of new crop varieties, improved farm breeding techniques and the intensified development of perennial crops (Vo, 1995). However, none of this will be possible without further training of the rural workforce, both for new jobs in agriculture and in other sectors.

The relationship between basic education and economic development is better understood as a non-linear and interactive process rather than a direct cause and effect relationship. Basic education facilitates the shift of the surplus workforce from agriculture to non-agricultural employment. Focusing the effort in specific areas of basic education will help the workforce to make the transition from agriculture to the industrial and services sectors, and to adapt to new economic opportunities and structures (Manzoor *et al.*, 1991). The current workforce and new entrants will need training and education to meet the new demand in the industrial sector. This new demand will be in the development of information technology; biotechnology; sophisticated consumer goods manufacturing; development of construction material and steel industries; oil, gas and chemical industries; heavy industries; and the mining industry (Vo, 1995).

In terms of investment in education and training, Vietnam invested only 1% of its GDP in 1989 (latest figures). This is much lower than in neighbouring countries such as Thailand (3.5%) and China (3.4%). The average number of school years attended by each person in Vietnam was only 4.5 years (Sloper and Le, 1995). Although the investment in education has increased, it has never exceeded 1% of GDP (Nguyen, 1995). In comparison, the Asian NIEs have been making large investments in education since the 1970s and they are now achieving significant economic growth (Hallack, 1990) which is probably at least partly due to the investment in education.

The number of faculty with postgraduate education in Vietnam's universities amounts to only 12% of all the university lecturers and researchers. This is a low figure since it is generally accepted that a developed country needs a 30% ratio to accelerate the modernisation and industrialisation process (Sloper and Le, 1995). Therefore, given this situation, the Vietnamese authorities will need higher investment in education and training to achieve their projected economic development goals.

In summary, the synchronisation of education with economic development is crucial in Vietnam to bridge the widening gap between business demands and current practices in human resource development. While appropriate education is needed to train new entrants to the labour market, continuous training in advanced technologies for the existing workforce is also crucial to ensure that the workforce has the skills necessary to make a worthwhile contribution to the development of the economy (Sloper and Le, 1995).

VIETNAM'S EDUCATION SYSTEM AND POLICY

Vietnam's Education System

Two significant historical events influenced the culture and educational system in Vietnam. These were the Chinese domination of Vietnam for about one thousand years from 111 BC, and the French colonisation of Vietnam from 1868 to 1945 (Sloper and Le, 1995). During the Chinese domination, writing was in Han – the Chinese classical characters. In the 13th century, the Vietnamese system of writing was developed by combining Chinese characters. Confucianism was also accepted and embedded into the Vietnamese culture. The French colonisation later resulted in the Vietnamese using a Latin script as the basis of the modern Vietnamese alphabet (Sloper and Le, 1995). These two factors have affected both the style and content of current Vietnamese education.

The latest educational reform began in January 1979. The current system stipulates 12 years of basic education from Grade 1 to Grade 12. The five years of primary education commence from the age of six. Secondary education is divided into 2 levels; the lower secondary and secondary level. There are three streams in the secondary level and the foci of each stream is: stream A, mathematics and physics; stream B1, mathematics and technical; and stream C, social science and languages. The education structure is as shown in Figure 16–1 below (Sloper and Le, 1995).

FIGURE 16–1
Education System of Vietnam in the 1990s

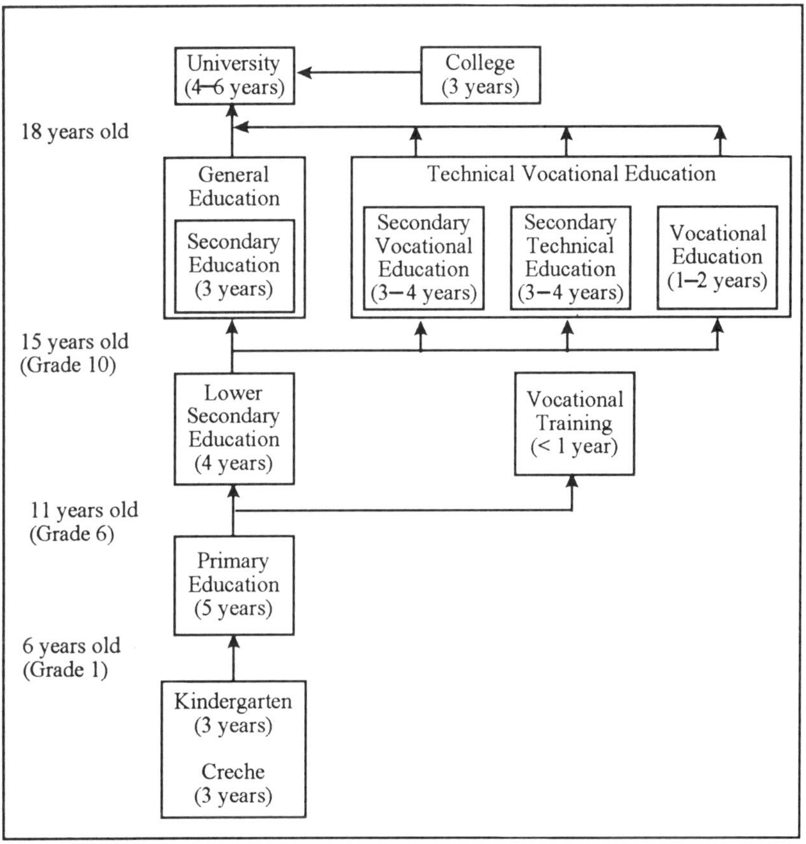

Source: Ministry of Education and Training, Hanoi, Vietnam, 1995.

The bodies responsible for education and training are the Ministry of Education and Training (MOET) in the government, the Culture and Education Commission in the National Assembly and the Committee of Science and Education in the Communist Party of Vietnam. MOET is responsible for all levels of education from pre-school to higher education (Sloper and Le, 1995).

Two-thirds of the teaching institutions, universities and colleges are under the MOET while the remainder are under the administration of other ministries such as Ministry of Health, Ministry of Defence, Ministry of Post and Communication, and so forth. These are usually in specialised fields of studies such as medicine, communications and engineering (Sloper and Le, 1995).

Admission into public higher education can be gained through an entrance examination. Students must also have already completed formal education in either general or vocational education. Only men under thirty-two years of age and women under thirty-five years of age can gain admission (Sloper and Le, 1995).

Presently, about 80% of the children from age six to 11 are enrolled in primary education. MOET has targeted the year 2000 for 99% of the children from the urban areas and about 80% of the children from the rural areas to be in school (Pham, 1996).

Vietnamese Education Policy

The key objective of education and training in Vietnam is to develop and train human resources to acquire the necessary technological know-how needed to foster economic development. The formal education system aims to equip each individual with competent skills and capabilities to find employment in the market economy. As such, the policy on education and training is designed to support economic development. This is manifested in the economic development policies, social policies, foreign policy, investment policy and academic staffing policy (Sloper and Le, 1995). The decision taken by the Central Committee on 14 January 1993 emphasises that:

(i) education and training are the driving force and basic requirement for the realisation of socio-economic objectives;
(ii) the general objectives of education and training are the improvement of the educational level of the population, the training of necessary manpower for development and the creation of the best conditions for the development of talent; and
(iii) education and training should meet the demands of national de-

velopment and follow progressive trends of life-long continuing education in contemporary times.

Although general education forms part of the state's responsibilities, MOET has allowed the establishment of private schools since 1995. In Vietnam, public education up to the university level is heavily subsidised. As for the private schools, the authorities do not provide subsidies but they can assist in providing infrastructural support such as land and buildings (Pham, 1996).

Problems

The challenges for Vietnam in education and training are threefold. The first is how to maximise available resources to more efficiently serve the country. The second is how to expand resources without sacrificing quality. The third is how to address the needs and expectations of industry (Sloper and Le, 1995).

Given these challenges, a key issue is the allocation of the budget for education and training. Although the budget has been increasing, its growth rate is proportionately less than GDP. However, increases in the education budget are limited by the constraints on state revenues (Sloper and Le, 1995).

One of the effects of an insufficient budget is the lack of monetary rewards to academic staff. The salaries of academics are lower than those of their peers employed outside of the education sector. The consequence is that academics are taking additional jobs to supplement their incomes. This has affected academics' morale, satisfaction and attitude towards their profession while the better academics have opted to leave the teaching profession. This has had a considerable impact on the quality of the teaching and on the ability of academic institutions to attract high calibre teachers (Sloper and Le, 1995). At present, only 30% of teachers are considered to have relevant qualifications. At the universities, about 19% of the lecturers possess postgraduate degrees and only 6% have reached the professor or associate professor level (Pham, 1996).

In addition to a shortage of qualified teachers at all levels, there is a high dropout rate at each level of public education. Table 16–2 shows that less than 2% of the student population are in universities or colleges. The high dropout rate after primary school is of concern as these students will enter the workforce without the basic compulsory education and skills.

TABLE 16–2
Education Profile in Vietnam

	1990 ('000)	1991 ('000)	1992 ('000)	1993 ('000)	1994 ('000)
Primary Schooling	11,048.1	8,766.4	9,081.3	9,469.7	9,778.7
Elementary Schooling	N.A.	2,572.4	2,721.9	2,772.8	3,086.7
Secondary Schooling	662.0	524.2	568.2	564.2	703.3
Universities and Colleges	129.6	107.0	136.8	157.1	N.A.
Technical Workers	95.4	63.8	63.2	75.8	N.A.

Source: Vietnam Statistical Yearbook (1994).

In addressing the increase in expectations and demands on higher education, one of the challenges is to ensure that the curriculum is relevant to the country's economic development. The role of education in human resource planning is crucial, yet in Vietnam, the educators and planners have great difficulty in anticipating and projecting the needs and demands of industry. Furthermore, a recent significant development is the changing pattern of students' preferences in the choice of specialisation in higher education. Lately, there has been an increase in the number of students opting for studies in banking, finance and business. This is due to the better salaries and perceived prospects in these areas as compared to engineering. This will inevitably result in a mismatch of supply and demand in the years to come which will hinder the industrial sector's growth (Nyugen and Pham, 1996).

INVESTMENT OPPORTUNITIES IN EDUCATION AND TRAINING

The development of a market economy is creating changes to the Vietnamese socio-economic culture. This has affected the attitude towards work values, the process of socio-economic development and the people's lifestyles (Sloper and Le, 1995). The development of a market economy to replace the previous centrally-planned economy involves the progressive application of advanced modern technology in production, business and management. The sectoral structural changes will require workers at all levels to be trained and competent in many perspectives. Training and education, therefore, assume a pivotal role in the process of economic development.

The present education system in Vietnam is faced with contraints in budget, service quality, resources and the alignment of education to fit workplace needs (*Vietnam Investment Review*, 25–31 December 1995). The cost of financing education, be it public or private, is itself a major issue and international financial aid is limited (Sloper and Le, 1995). Given the current available resources and expertise, and based on the earlier comments regarding the returns to education, the Vietnamese government may be well advised to make general education at the primary and secondary levels a priority.

Though it may still take some time before large scale private sector training/education come into existence, this does not mean there are no business opportunities and potential in this area. International organisations, such as the German Hanns-Seidel Foundation, the Swedish International Development Agency and the Swiss Development Fund, have already established management programmes in Vietnam. These are normally conducted by foreign experts or academics and focus on subjects such as business or economic management. Such programmes, however, are funded with official development assistance (ODA) by the countries concerned and, therefore, are not obliged to run at a profit. Private investment is a different matter altogether.

Role of private investors

(i) ***Higher Education and Professional Training:*** Assuming that basic primary and secondary education will continue to be provided by the Vietnamese government, the role of private training and education would appear to be to complement the role of public education. The business opportunities in private participation, therefore, would appear to lie in higher or tertiary education and training. This would be in the provision of specific commercial and industrial training needed by the economy, and the provision of higher education and professional training courses. As stated earlier, in LDCs, higher education generates better returns to the individual. In this respect, there will always be a strong demand for such education. However, the government, with limited resources, will not be able to meet such demand. Hence, private education can provide the opportunities for those who may not have a chance to enter the government tertiary institutions (although initially the ability to pay for such courses may lag behind demand, this is likely to be a short-term problem). The freed state resources can then be channelled into basic education with its higher social returns.

(ii) ***Vocational Training for School Dropouts and the Unemployed:*** As in most developing countries, private education institutions have played a significant and increasing role in fulfilling the aspirations of those not possessing formal educational qualifications. Being profit-making enterprises, such institutions will need to ensure that the training and education provided meet the immediate demands of vocational students. However, the major problem for the private institution is to find ways of recovering the fees from the students, given that most of them will not have the immediate ability to pay. This is not an insurmountable problem, especially where potential employers can be involved in the training role.

The relevance of such courses is paramount to both students and employers, and here it might be possible to gain some useful insights from the way in which Singapore handles such programmes. The Singapore government has a number of joint development programmes with private institutions and with companies which carry out vocational training roles. These direct links with industry mean that the government is aware of current training needs and, therefore, curriculum changes can be introduced gradually to standard syllabi in the state schools, paving the way for specialised training in the upper secondary schools to meet the demand for skills brought about by industrialisation and market reforms (Low *et al.*, 1991). It must be noted that such a policy would have to be tailored to the needs of the Vietnamese economy. In short, private institutions can carry out their own training and education roles, but any particular role needs to be in support of the government's education and economic objectives.

Forms of Private Investment and Participation in Education and Training

Mention should be made of two types of possible involvement which the private sector might consider, and which would probably be of benefit in Vietnam's education and training drive. These are described in some detail below.

(i) ***Business/Industry Education Alliances:*** Business-industry-education partnerships allow business organisations and industry to tie up with the government educational institutions to provide the necessary training that is required by the market economy. "The alliance between business/industry and education is a natural one based on gearing up for survival, survival of students, business, public education and society....Through creative partnerships with business/industry, schools can improve their programmes, and enhance their student's potential to meet their own and the nation's economic imperative."(Zacchei and Mirman, 1986).

In countries like Singapore, businesses have supported education in a variety of ways for many years. It has been part of many multinational corporations' strategy to provide support for education and training and, thereby, bring forth quicker technology diffusion. Such involvement generates a lot of publicity and goodwill, and it enhances a corporation's image in the host country. The business/industry collaboration can range from small scale *ad hoc* involvement in assisting the set up of technology labs in existing schools/universities, to fully fledged joint venture institutes. Some successful examples in Singapore are the Institute of Systems Science (National University of Singapore and IBM), and the Information Communication Institute of Singapore (AT&T and the National Computer Board) (Low *et al.*, 1991).

One alliance of this nature in Vietnam is the collaboration between Hanoi University of Technology and Inter-regional Development Research Association of France (APDRI) to train Vietnamese lecturers (*Vietnam Investment Review*, June 1996). This project, estimated to cost FF2.5 million (US$510,000), is supported by the French government, the European Union and French companies which have investment projects in Vietnam.

Business involvement in education can take many forms. This ranges from small financial donations (for awards, scholarships, or grants), and materials and equipment (books and computers) to higher collaboration in teacher fellowships, work study programmes and curriculum revision. Most of all, the contribution of human resources, such as speakers, executives-on-loan, scientists, engineers, business managers and so forth, provide effective technology and management transfers that facilitate the transformation of the economy.

According to Zacchei and Mirman (1986), the benefits from business/education partnerships for the company and its employees include the following:

(a) greater consumer understanding of the company's products, services and policies;

(b) quicker diffusion and absorption and usage of its products and services in the host country, particularly if it is of a technological nature like computers, new food processing know-how, and so forth;
(c) improved corporate image through direct involvement in socially responsible activities and participation in the host country's socio-economic development;
(d) solutions for problems such as job training, equal employment opportunities, and entry-level positions; and
(e) improved employee morale.

For educators and the Vietnamese government, the benefits deriving from such partnerships include (Zacchei and Mirman, 1986):
(a) new resources, ideas and commitment to address the education goals;
(b) a broader base of support from industry leaders and the general public;
(c) improved teacher morale through new challenges, experiences, and relationships;
(d) greater opportunities for students to learn about careers, the economy and real world applications of academic subjects;
(e) positive reinforcement of students' self-concept and aspirations through interactions with adults who serve as positive career role models; and
(f) job experience and opportunities for students.

(ii) ***Direct Private Sector Participation:*** Another investment opportunity in Vietnam's education system could be through direct private sector participation in the opening of training institutes or schools to supplement the public education system. Unlike the former business/education partnership, whereby the benefits are more indirect and realisable in the long-term, such involvement is in the provision of education and training as consumer goods/services. One example is the opening of Intraco-Informatics, a Singaporean profit-making franchise partnership offering direct education/training to the Vietnamese public. It seeks to complement the existing public education system by providing the training and education required in a growing economy, and by targeting structural unemployment through retraining in technology and market-oriented management courses.

Other areas of opportunities are semi-boarding schools (*Vietnam Investment Review*, June 1996). These are essentially institutions where primary school students spend a full day, unlike the more prevalent half-day sessions offered by government primary schools. Semi-boarding schools are gaining in popularity, as the nation's increasingly busy parents have less time to look after and teach their children due to socio-economic changes. Such schools are either semi-private (a joint venture with the government) or fully private. Demand for this type of education is so high that the present supply can only meet up to 30% of demand. The Vietnamese authorities have also been encouraging and supportive in such private sector participation. As Nguyen Ke Hao, Director of the Secondary Department at the Ministry of Education and Training said, "The government wants to encourage a diverse number of educational forms. It's policy is to set up a perfect system of semi-boarding schools, otherwise our system will be in danger of falling behind" (*Vietnam Investment Review*, June 1996).

It seems self-evident that educational reforms are needed in Vietnam and the comments of various government spokesmen support this view. The role of private participation in this process, though not widespread at present, is likely to increase in the next few years. The lack of private participants at the moment presents an opportunity for those who are poised to exploit the "first mover" advantage, provided that they are able to manage the business risk and cope with Vietnam's progressing, yet volatile, transition to a market economy.

CONCLUSION

Given that there are investment opportunities in Vietnam's education and training sector, one key concern is the ability of the Vietnamese public to pay for such education. Companies seeking immediate profits may therefore find it difficult (though not impossible) to achieve this objective in the short-term. For those who are patient and seek a long-term return, it may well prove to be a worthwhile venture if they have the knowledge, experience and know-how to provide the much needed training and education.

Private investors may also be able to play a bridging role between the Vietnamese and the more developed educational institutions overseas. This could assist Vietnam to plug into the international network of business. Such linkages with the outside world would likely benefit Vietnam considerably in its task of developing the economy. Overall, it is clear that there is a role for private investment in Vietnam's education and training sector, though that role is yet to be clearly defined by the government. Until it does so, investors are likely to be wary of committing themselves too deeply.

REFERENCES

Editorial, *Asiaweek*, 16 June 1995.

Hallack J., *Investing into the Future – Setting Priorities in the Developing World*, UNESCO International Institute for Education Planning, New York, 1990.

Hogendorn J. S., *Economic Development*, Harper Collins, New York, 1992.

Low L., M. H. Toh and T. W. Soon, *Economics of Education and Manpower Development: Issues and Policies in Singapore*, McGraw Hill, Singapore, 1991.

Mai K. D., *Vietnam's Human Capital Formation, New Focus and The Hanns Seidel Foundation's Training Experience* (Monograph), Vietnam, 1996.

Manzoor A., K. M. Cheng, A. K. Jauluddin and K. Ramachandran, *Lessons from China and India: Basic Education and National Development*, Dryden, London, 1991.

Middleton J., A. Ziderman and A. Adams, *Making Vocational Training Effective*, Oxford University Press, U.K., March 1990.

Nguyen M. T. and M. H. Pham, *Nanyang Technological University's Business Study Mission to Vietnam* (Monograph), Nanyang Technological University, Singapore, March 1996.

Nguyen M. T., *Ten Years Economic Reform in Vietnam – Some Selected Macro-Economic Key Issues* (Monograph), Vietnam, December 1995.

Pham M. H., *Nanyang Technological University's Business Study Mission to Vietnam* (Monograph), Nanyang Technological University, Singapore, March 1996.

Schultz T. P., *Economics of Population*, Addison-Wesley, Reading, Mass, 1981.

Schultz T. P., "Education Investments and Returns" in Chenery and Srinivasan, eds., *Handbook of Development Economics*, Elsevier, Amsterdam, 1988.

"Semi-boarding Schools Struggle to Meet Demand", *Vietnam Investment Review*, June 1996.

Sloper D. and T. C. Le, *Higher Education in Vietnam*, Institute of Southeast Asian Studies, Singapore, 1995.

"Vietnam Colleges Face Cost Crisis" and "First Open University Degrees in Management-informatics", *Vietnam Investment Review,* 25–31 December 1995.

Vietnam Statistical Yearbook, Ministry of Planning and Investment, Hanoi, 1994.

Vo Hong Phuc, "Economic Overview of Vietnam," *Journal of Developing Vietnam*, 1995, pp. 15–8

Zacchei D. A. and J. A. Mirman, *Business-Education Partnership – Strategies for School Improvement*, Blackwell, U.K.,1986.

Chapter 17

Resort Development in Vietnam's Tourism Industry*

BY
Jason ONG
Lim-Low TAY
Kim-Chuan TIEN
Victor WONG

INTRODUCTION

SINCE THE INCEPTION of *doi moi* in 1986, tourism growth has been based on fundamental comparative advantages such as the Vietnamese cultural relics and the unspoiled natural beauty of the beaches spread along Vietnam's 3,444 kilometres of coastline. However, the normal returns from improving the service level in the tourism industry as well as building hotels of international standards have reached a saturation point.

The 15-year Tourism Master Plan outlines various strategies to enhance the tourism industry. One of the main objectives is to build a minimum of six world-class resorts located in strategic places such as Ha Long Bay, Da Lat and Da Nang. These resorts will serve as "regional destinations" for tourists who visit the Southeast Asia region. Moreover, they will serve as part of the hardware in the concept of "tourism unlimited". This is a concept that is being actively promoted by the Singapore Tourist Promotion Board (STPB) which will allow countries such as Singapore and Vietnam to co-operate at a regional level. This co-operation is intended to enhance the value of the investment in these resorts.

* The authors are grateful to Dr. Luu Trankiem for his guidance and assistance.

This chapter discussess the rationale underlying the tourism unlimited concept within the broader context of Vietnam's tourism industry. Examples of projects in Da Lat and Da Nang are utilised to illustrate the opportunities of resort development in Vietnam and to highlight some of the challenges faced by foreign investors.

BACKGROUND

Vietnam is one of the fastest growing economies in Asia. Since *Doi Moi* in 1986, the country's economic growth has been phenomenal. Part of this growth has been spurred on by a significant amount of foreign direct investment (FDI). It has been one of the major forms of investment capital since 1986 (see Figure 17–1). The next few years should yield a significant increase in FDI from Southeast Asia. Following Vietnam's inception into the Association of Southeast Asian Nations (ASEAN), Vietnam has been heralded by many economists and analysts as another Asian "tiger" in the making. The comparative advantages that Vietnam offers are low cost skilled labour, an abundance of land and inflation rates that now are almost identical to Malaysia and Thailand.

FIGURE 17–1
Foreign Investment by Years

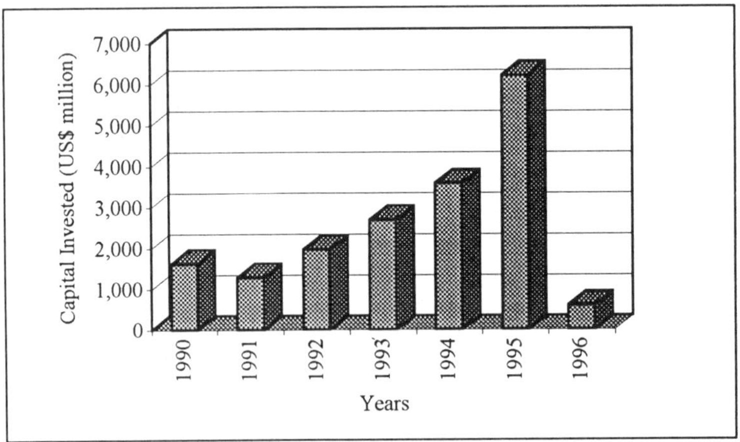

Note: 1996 capital invested includes only January and February 1996 figures.
Source: Luu (1996).

One of the main sources of economic growth is tourism products and services (see Figure 17–2). The tourism industry in Vietnam features a prevailing culture and ancient heritage that date back centuries. This attraction has captivated many tourists, both domestic as well as international. Moreover, the natural landscapes of Ha Long Bay and Lang Co Beach (near Da Nang) have also played a complementary role in sustaining double-digit growth in the tourism industry. The growth rates in the member of tourists for 1994 and 1995 are shown in Figure 17–3 as well as the projected rates for 1996 and the year 2000.

FIGURE 17–2
Foreign Investment by Sectors

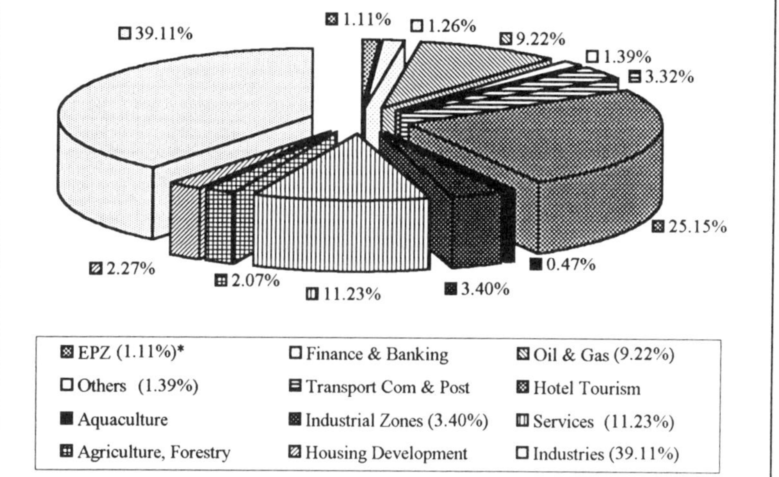

* clockwise, selected percentages.

Source: Luu (1996).

There are many coupling effects from the tourism boom in Vietnam. One of the most important areas is the boom in hotel rooms (Brady, 1996). However, FDI in this form (i.e., building hotels and restaurants) has now reached the point of diminishing returns. This effect is undesirable for investors, the tourism industry and Vietnam's economy. Also, environmental issues and the negative impact of tourist resorts/hotels near conservation areas (Tripathi, 1995) are serious areas of contention. There is, therefore, a need to sustain tourism growth in a creative manner in the next decade. Simultaneously, this need must also create long-term value for both local and foreign investors.

FIGURE 17–3
Growth Rate of Tourist Visits

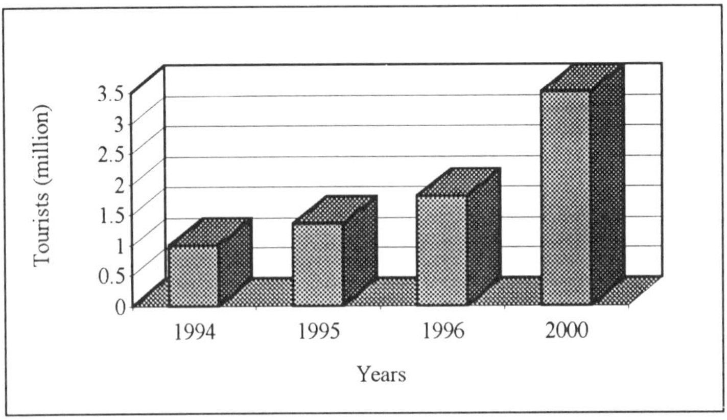

Source: Bui, 1996.

The Tourism Master Plan, detailed in 1995, outlines some critical areas of concern. A major goal is in the area of resort development, with the aim of elevating Vietnamese tourism to a level of sustainable competitive advantage. This advantage cannot be achieved by Vietnam alone. Therefore, it must continuously seek assistance from other countries and, in particular, its ASEAN neighbours (Nguyen, 1995). The idea of regional tourism which emerges from co-operating on issues of resort development and related operations can lead to Vietnam and Southeast Asia capturing substantial growth in the international tourism market.

THE TOURISM INDUSTRY IN VIETNAM

Vietnam's tourism industry has been undergoing some significant changes as a result of the liberalisation of the economy. Investment has been targeted at two areas. One is infrastructural and includes the building of international standard hotels while the second is service level training.

The growth in the number of hotel rooms has been phenomenal. The demand and supply of hotel rooms have been erratic in moving toward short-term equilibrium. This is primarily due to the difficulty of obtaining accurate information on the demand for hotels. Efforts to improve the service and skills of restaurant and hotel personnel also have contributed to the industry's growth. However, these two areas of development have reached a point of diminishing returns as alluded to earlier. Therefore, there is a need to develop Vietnam's untapped competitive advantages.

Two of the most important advantages, and attractions, in Vietnam are its geographical landscape and culture. Within Southeast Asia, Vietnam has the largest number of ancient tombs and pagodas; citadels number in the hundreds and scenic places are plentiful. Beautiful Ha Long Bay, the cooling highlands of Da Lat and the immense vastness of the Mekong Delta captivate most tourists.

There are substantial efforts in progress to develop these opportunities. One example is the Heritage Hotel at Ha Long Bay which was opened by a Singaporean in September 1995 and thus far has occupancy rates above 80% (Chan, 1996). However, there are also examples of more difficult joint ventures. Australia's Bulk Materials (Coal Handling) Pte. Ltd. was building a US$11.1 million plant near Ha Long Bay to process anthracite coal until Hanoi became concerned that the facility might be too close to a neighbouring resort. Even after the company obtained environmental clearance, the Quang Ninh Province People's Committee decided against the plant's location (Tripathi, 1995). This is a prime example of the necessity for the government to manage issues pertaining to environmental conservation with industrial needs. It also suggests that investors need to be particularly careful about choice of location and, if necessary, anticipate weaknesses in government planning.

The Tourism Master Plan and Resort Development

Despite the odd exception, over the past ten years of steady growth, Vietnam has realised the need to critically plan its growth in tourism for at least the next 15 years. In May 1995, the government presented the latest 15-year Tourism Master Plan for Vietnam which details the necessary development both in terms of hardware and software. Mr. Bui Xuan Nhat, Vice Chairman of Vietnam National Administration of Tourism (VNAT), firmly acknowledged the need to provide a legal framework to manage tourism. Plans to create fundamental tourism laws could help in the realisation of the hardware goals set out in the master plan.

The master plan's key development strategy is in resort development. There are a minimum of six resorts being developed over the next five years. These resorts are located in Ha Long Bay, Hai Phong, Hue/Da Nang, Vung Tau, Da Lat and the Mekong Delta (Phu Quoc Island). These places have been chosen because of their comparative advantage. The resorts will be large scale investments, in the region of hundreds of millions of dollars.

Ha Long Bay is one of the most scenic places in Vietnam. It is recognised by the United Nation's Education, Scientific and Cultural Organisation (UNESCO) as one of the world's heritage sites. The scenic beauty of over 3,000 islands has awed tourists both domestically and internationally (Centre of Information Marketing, 1995). The government's plan is to have a resort in this region but it must be able to capitalise on the natural and scenic beauty, and portray the unique features of Ha Long Bay. There are currently several feasibility plans under study. For example, the Singapore Tourist Promotion Board is in the process of helping to plan the development of the Ha Long Bay area (Goldstein, 1995).

Another resort location is in central Vietnam between the cities of Hue and Da Nang. Within the city of Hue lies one of the world's legacies of cultural relics and heritage. As the ancient capital of Vietnam, Hue still possesses the unspoiled beauty of many citadels, tombs and pagodas. Da Nang is located about 120 kilometres south of Hue. Within the vicinity of Da Nang lies Hoi An, another ancient city which holds many historical and cultural attractions. Accessibility to Da Nang is enforced by an international airport. Finally, Lang Co Beach is part of the 120 kilometre stretch of coastline between Hue and Da Nang.

Da Lat Dankia Resort is destined to be another world-class resort which will enable Vietnam to draw international tourists. Currently in the feasibility study stage, and well supported by both the governments of Singapore and Vietnam, this resort will encompass an area of 500 hectares. Golf courses, hotels, wildlife parks, entertainment centres and family/fun theme parks of international standard, which may even rival that of Disneyland or Ocean Park, will be located within this US$700 million resort.

The Mekong Delta is another region with high tourism growth

potential. The resort located here will be able to exemplify the idea of regional tourism with other Indochinese countries. Sharing common natural resources, such as the Mekong river which flows through the six Mekong states, provides a platform for economic co-operation in areas such as the development of tourism, generation of hydro-electricity and telecommunications.

The Role of Vietnam National Administration of Tourism (VNAT)

Vietnam's tourism body is represented by VNAT. Its key role is to develop tourism policies, manage and administer tour agents, and work with ministries such as Ministry of Planning and Investment (MPI). VNAT's role has been very important in the past few years because of tourism growth. It has served the critical role of communicating the country's tourism objectives to foreign counterparts such as the Singapore Tourist Promotion Board (STPB). In developing the concept of regional tourism, the fundamental ideas need to be collated and disseminated internally and externally and, thus, it has been working with the STPB for the past four years. During this period there has been a cross-training of Vietnam's tourism personnel in Singapore. VNAT also has co-operated with Nanyang Technological University on research involving investment and development opportunities at the regional level.

INTEGRATION INTO THE ASEAN TOURISM INDUSTRY

Fully aware that the development of tourism will bring in much needed foreign exchange and generate employment, Vietnam's government is now planning carefully so as to benefit from the growth of tourism in Southeast Asia. This region is forecasted to experience the highest growth rate of tourism in the next decade (Hobson, 1994). If the development of the Vietnamese tourist industry is successful, then it will benefit Vietnam and the region. One clear path to success is to integrate the Vietnamese industry into the larger, regional tourism industry. One of the most direct and effective ways to foster this integration is to take part in joint marketing efforts with neighbouring ASEAN countries. This alternative will be enhanced if the complementary features of Vietnam's tourist resorts *vis-à-vis* her ASEAN counterparts are developed.

The Tourism Unlimited Concept

Tourism unlimited is a concept that the STPB has been promoting to neighbouring countries in recent years. In an announcement in February 1996, Mr. Tan Chin Nam, Chief Executive of STPB, revealed five areas emphasised in the STPB plan (Dhaliwal, 1996). One aspect concerns repositioning Singapore as a tourist destination where the STPB will work with governments in the region on joint marketing programs. Another aspect deals with facilitating investments by Singapore businesses in regional tourism activities.

Under this concept, Singapore can borrow the attractiveness of other countries to enhance the attractiveness of Singapore in a win-win situation. Tourists from other parts of the world could visit other countries in the region as part of their tour plan in addition to visiting Singapore for a few days. In Singapore, tourists can shop and visit theme parks on the island before they continue with the remainder of their journey in neighbouring countries featuring other cultural attractions and natural scenery. It is a concept that combines the strengths of Singapore as a modern state and the beautiful scenery of neighbouring countries. By doing this, an attractive tour package can be created that could boost the tourism industry in the region by increasing tourist traffic. Tourists from other parts of the world would have the opportunity to explore the region in total, with each location providing a different and rewarding experience.

Vietnam features both a cultural and a natural heritage. However, it has a limited infrastructure in terms of links with the rest of the world. Therefore, it cannot receive tourists from other parts of the world as easily as Singapore. Singapore, on the other hand, has a world-class communication and transportation infrastructure that links it to the rest of the world. It also possesses successful experience in tourism development. Therefore, both countries are complementary to each other. Vietnam can capitalise on this broader concept because it now views tourism as a total business which includes development, conceptualisation and training. STPB's plan to facilitate investments by Singaporean businesses in regional tourism activities can also provide Vietnam with the needed capital to develop tourism.

Learning from the ASEAN Experience

Vietnam can learn from the experience of its ASEAN neighbours in tourism development, thus avoiding major mistakes detrimental to the long-term growth of its booming tourism industry. Moreover, it must avoid paying huge social costs for the sake of tourism development.

Another area for consideration is the preservation of its culture and natural environment while developing the tourism industry on a large scale In many countries, tourism has developed at the expense of the environment. Tourism development must respect and preserve the unique beauty and characteristics of the area and the quality of the environment. Fortunately, Vietnam's tourism strategy is addressing these issues by emphasising the nation's rich cultural and natural heritage, and focusing on the conservation of the country's culture and environmental assets for sustainable growth in tourism. If the Vietnamese authorities adhere to this strategy, then tourism development will be in harmony with their long-term economic potential (Bui, 1996).

OPPORTUNITIES AND CHALLENGES IN RESORT DEVELOPMENT

Vietnam's ambitious Tourism Master Plan offers many opportunities for foreign businesses and governments to establish a presence in the industry because of its potential as a world-class tourist destination. However, businesses face challenges when operating in Vietnam. Unfortunately at this juncture, it has both an under-developed infrastructure and an evolving legal system. These areas especially impact resort development which involves significant capital outlays and vast land use. Moreover, these types of projects require high level approval, intense feasibility studies and careful planning. Some of these problems, and corresponding strategies for overcoming them, are featured below with the cases of Da Lat, Hue and Da Nang.

Resort Opportunities in Da Lat

The city of Da Lat is located 300 kilometres north of Ho Chi Minh City (HCMC) in the southern area of Vietnam's central highlands. It was created by French settlers in the late 19th century as an alpine retreat because the cool, pristine environment was an ideal place for

Europeans to relax and recuperate from the searing heat of the coastal areas. The average temperature in Da Lat is only 18°C and the humidity is relatively low.

Hundreds of villas featuring the French architectural style have been built during the 20th century. Even when the French were ousted from Indochina, Da Lat served as a popular retreat for the south Vietnamese administration and U.S. officials. After reunification in 1975, Da Lat remained a favourite retreat for top government officials and it has become a popular destination for Vietnamese tourists.

Da Lat, with a unique pine forest environment that is unmatched in the region, is like a European city in the tropics. Within the Da Lat region, there are also villages of ethnic minorities. Their culture and heritage is a potential tourist draw which can add to the attractiveness of the area. There are also two lakes in the Da Lat vicinity; Dankia Lake is 250 hectares in size and Suoi Vang Lake covers 50 hectares. The two lakes not only add to the beauty of the area but they also have the characteristics of an ideal development site with water sports facilities.

There are limited domestic flights available from HCMC to Lien Khuong airport, which is 30 kilometres south of Da Lat. The other airport that is near to Da Lat is the Camly Airport which only has a runway of approximately 1400 metres and, therefore, is not suitable for any commercial aircraft. Da Lat is also connected to HCMC by National Route No. 20. However, the highway is not very well maintained and it can take up to seven hours to complete the 300 kilometre journey between the two cities. This trip is rather uncomfortable due to bad road conditions which are probably not acceptable to the kind of middle-class tourists that Vietnam hopes to attract. Therefore, for Da Lat to develop into a tourist attraction, establishing a good basic infrastructure that links Da Lat to the outside world is an essential part of the overall development plan. The next challenge is how to develop the area on a large scale and, yet, preserve the natural and cultural heritage of the region.

A Singapore consortium is currently working with the Vietnamese tourism authority to develop a 500 hectare hill resort 25 kilometres northwest of Da Lat, within the Dankia and Suoi Vang Lake area. The investment project is estimated to involve approximately US$700 million (Mehta, 1995). The consortium is a joint venture with the state-owned firm Lam Dong Tourist Service to develop a resort with a built-up area of 430 hectares. The proposal by the Singapore consortium has been approved by Vietnam's tourism authority and the People's Committee of Da Lat, which is the local government. The project includes building a luxury hotel, a tourism and entertainment centre, theme parks, a golf course and golf club.

The Singaporean side also will be renovating one of Da Lat's airports. It is likely to be Camly Airport which is only about 10 kilometres northwest of Da Lat. The Singaporean consortium initially wanted a 70-year lease on the property but finally agreed to a 65-year lease after negotiations with the Vietnamese tourism authority. However, these plans are still subject to approval by the Ministry of Planning and Investment (MPI) and the National Assembly.

This development by the Singaporean consortium provides an opportunity to implement the tourism unlimited concept between Singapore and Vietnam. With a flight time of about two hours to Vietnam, a tourist visiting Singapore for a shopping and sight-seeing tour can relax in the tranquil environment of a highland resort at the Da Lat golf course a short time later.

Resort Opportunities in Hue and Da Nang

The city of Hue is located in Thua Thien Hue province, which lies in the north-central part of Vietnam. Hue has a population of about one million. Da Nang is in the province of Quang Nam – Da Nang, which is adjacent to Thua Thien Hue province in the south. Da Nang has a population of about 1.9 million. These two cities are discussed simultaneously because of the strategic strengths that each draws from the other. Hue is home to a fascinating cultural heritage while Da Nang provides access as well as a scenic and beautiful natural setting (Centre of Information Marketing, 1995).

The People's Committee of Thua Thien-Hue has drafted a plan for their province up to the year 2010 (Nguyen Van Me, 1996). Nguyen Van Me, Chairman of Hue's People Committee, described the positioning of Hue tourism in the national Tourism Master Plan and the goals and strategy underlying Hue's tourism development. According to the plan, Thua Thien-Hue province is the centre of the tourist zone in north-central Vietnam. Hue was the royal capital of the Nguyen dynasty where the Forbidden Purple City (Tu Cam Thanh) and many royal tombs and pagodas are located.

Besides cultural heritage, Hue and Da Nang have long stretches of beautiful beaches such as Lang Co in Thua Thien Hue and China

Beach in Da Nang. These definitely have the potential to be developed into high standard tourist destinations. There are domestic flights linking Da Nang to Ho Chi Minh City, and Hue is linked to Da Nang by State Highway One and a railway (Nguyen Thu, 1996).

Travelling north to Hue from Da Nang, the highway passes through Hai Van Pass before reaching Lang Co. This is a peninsula of palm-shaded sand with a crystal clear blue lagoon on one side and many kilometres of beach facing the South China Sea on the other side. Nguyen Van Me further stated that a feasibility study, involving European parties, is currently looking into the potential of a resort in Lang Co that may amount to US$300 million. In addition, there is a joint venture between BBI of the U.S. and the state-owned Non Nuoc Seaside Tourist Company which commenced an eight-year, US$234 million effort in August 1995 to develop Da Nang's China Beach into a resort attraction (Goldstein, 1995).

There are many unspoiled beaches along the coast line between Da Nang and Hue and many of them also have great potential for development. Canh Duong is one of them and it has a deep-water seaport to harbour huge cruise ships. When combined with the national forest and mountains along the coast, there is potential for tourism products such as mountain tracking, sea tours, cruise and adventure voyages, and so forth. All of these opportunities await foreign capital.

CONCLUSION

Amidst the challenges that investors face, one common complaint is the lack of infrastructure in Vietnam. This problem has been one of the main concerns of investors in most industries. In the area of resort development, this issue could very well turn out to be an opportunity for foreign investors. Developing resorts requires large scale funds and multiple equity holders. This infusion of funds is usually headed by government bodies.

For example, in developing the Song Be Vietnam-Singapore Industrial Park and the resort in Da Lat, the joint ventures were mooted at a governmental level. The investment of such large funds usually means that the infrastructural support decisions must be resolved when the original concept is formulated. This forces the negotiation process to resolve any infrastructural barriers and simultaneously adds value to the entire development process. For example, building highways and airports to serve large scale resort development not only provides accessibility to tourists but also stimulates growth and productivity throughout the entire infrastructural chain.

Resort developments via joint ventures are usually undertaken on the basis of build-operate-and-transfer schemes. The operational duration of large scale resorts is usually 50 years. This mandates a need for foreign partners to manage the operations of the resorts. The operational issues facing investors are manpower development, hotel management skills, and general service and retail industry skills. However, these challenges can easily be managed via linkages among VNAT and various foreign government bodies, such as the STPB, and tourism schools such as the Nanyang Business School in Singapore.

All of the above challenges are significant and they apply with equal validity to resort development in Da Nang and Da Lat, and other potential sites for that matter. In summary, it is imperative for potential investors to understand the complexity of the economic, social and cultural dimensions at the earliest possible planning stage in doing business in Vietnam's tourism industry.

REFERENCES

Brady Diane, "Hoteliers Invade Hanoi, Promising More Choices", *The Asian Wall Street Journal,* Hong Kong, 26 March 1996.

Bui Xuan Nhat, "The Master Plan for Vietnam Tourism Industry", A Presentation to 12th MBA Business Study Mission – Vietnam, Hanoi, Vietnam, March 1996.

Centre of Information Marketing, "Ha Long Bay" in *Vietnam Culture and Tourism*, Published by Department of the Ministry of Culture and Information, Ho Chi Minh City, Vietnam, June 1995.

Chan Seng Wah Anthony, "Tourism and Hospitality Service Projects", A Panel Discussion during 12th MBA Study Mission – Vietnam, Hanoi, Vietnam, March 1996.

Dhaliwal Rav, "STPB Plans to Make Singapore More Attractive to Visitors", *The Straits Times*, Singapore, 30 January 1996.

Goldstein Tally, "Vietnam: Asia's Next Tourism Frontier", *Vietnam Business News*, Singapore, November 1995, pp. 8–12.

Hobson Perry, Vincent C.S. Heung and Kye-Sung Chon, "Vietnam's Tourism Industry: Can it be Kept a Float", *The Cornell H.R.A. Quarterly*, October 1994, pp. 42–9.

Luu Trankiem, "Vietnam in the ASEAN Era", Paper presented to the Nanyang Business School Alumni Association, Singapore, May 1996.

Mehta Harish, "Singapore Group Gets Hanoi Nod to Develop $1 Billion Resort", *Business Times*, Singapore, 28 November 1995.

Nguyen Sinh Hung, *Investment Policies and Incentives to Attract Foreign Investment in Vietnam*, Paper presented at the Conference on Tax and Investment in the Emerging Asia-Pacific Economies, Singapore, November 1995.

Nguyen Thu, "Da Nang Port", *Vietnam Southeast Asia Today*, Published by the National Centre for Social Sciences and Humanities, Institute of Southeast Asian Studies, Hanoi, Vietnam, February 1996.

Nguyen Van Me, "Some Main Features of Tourist Planning of Thua Thien Hue Province Up to the Year 2010", Speech given during the MBA Business Study Mission, Hanoi, Vietnam, March 1996.

Tripathi Salil, "The Last Dragon", *Asia Inc.*, Hong Kong, April 1995, pp. 24–31.

Chapter 18

A Synopsis of the Service Sector

BY
Roger
MARSHALL

INTRODUCTION

AS ECONOMIES MATURE, their structures shift away from agriculture towards manufacture; then, we see a further shift to the development of the service sector. This is so first, because a vigorous manufacturing sector demands a high level of service support and, secondly, because individual consumers in the population demand more and better services as their income levels rise. This structural shift is apparent in Vietnam as elsewhere, and it is all the more noticeable and critical because the speed of development within the country is so rapid.

The three chapters preceding this synopsis deal with specific aspects of this shift toward services. They not only highlight the problems faced by potential investors in Vietnam (both in manufacturing with its dependence on services and in services themselves) but, also, and more importantly, the inter-relationship of services within industrial and social development.

While the three chapters deal with different specific topics, they all share the same fundamental concern of how to ease the path of development and guide it down a route acceptable to investors, the government and the population at large. All three chapters are also similar in that they are deeply concerned with human capital. Although this is always the basis of economic development, it is more obviously so in the case of services where the good being marketed is, to a large degree, embodied in people. One chapter deals directly with this aspect, within the scope of education and training. The other chapters are less directly related to the issue but, nevertheless, they are actually concerned with it. The banking sector has specific problems, but its major challenge concerns the training of an educated workforce. Resort development also confronts specific challenges, but ultimately governmental approval of projects will often hinge upon the impact that a particular proposal will have upon the long-term enhancement of the human capital of the local population.

The purpose of this brief chapter, then, is not so much to reiterate or repeat what has gone on before, but to draw a thread through the three chapters that anchors them securely to the underlying problems of economic development discussed above. Each chapter is discussed in sequence, beginning with banking and finishing with the educational issue.

DEVELOPMENT OF THE BANKING SECTOR

The more Vietnam's economy grows, the closer the nation moves toward the rest of the world. As trade develops, indeed for trade to develop, elements of the infrastructure must fall into line with the dominant practices of the international business community. Thus, unless the form of accounting practices and financial institutions, and the procedural behaviour of local business partners are all familiar to prospective investors and acceptable to their governments, the growth of commerce will be seriously impeded.

A number of fundamental changes in the banking system are required and some are actually occurring. That these changes are of such a large magnitude is because the recent history of Vietnam has been communistic, so the attitudes and institutions have been a reflection of the belief in a centralised economy. Not only is it monumentally difficult to break the grip of the state-owned enterprises and banking institutions, but it is also difficult to change the mind-set that first looks to government rather than to private sector solutions. It is also evident that changes made too quickly will be altogether too disruptive, but that changes that lag too far behind the demands of the emergent economy will create a serious impediment to its growth.

An example can illustrate this dilemma. It is not uncommon in other countries in ASEAN that the population clings to cash as the preferred medium of exchange. There are probably several reasons for this behaviour. The perceived security of receiving cash rather than a cheque or electronic credit is probably one of the most quoted reasons, allied to the complaint that the cost of the technological infrastructure required to use non-cash methods is exorbitant. These costs are not justified in the face of the low wage structures of the extra people necessarily employed to handle the large amounts of cash required in cash-economies. There is also an "unofficial" argument that taxation audit trails are harder to follow when transactions are in cash.

At least for now, the biggest single factor mitigating against the use of electronic funds transfer is attitudinal. Indonesia, for instance, is largely a cash economy at a consumer level and, yet, its population commonly uses cellular telephones linked to a sophisticated satellite communication system, without eyebrows being raised. It is quite clear to even a casual observer that the operations of the small businesses (those that form 80% or so of that nation's companies) would be vastly more efficient if the sophisticated funds transfer systems available to the larger international traders were extended to these small companies. But this has not happened, even in a country that has had ample opportunity, through a steady, slow, planned growth pattern, to institute such a system. Changes in attitudes, then, are probably the key to the type of changes that are required in Vietnam, and actual attitude changes usually lag behind requirements for change due to the fundamental, psychological unwillingness of individuals to change their value sets.

Chapter 15 discusses the requirements of the changes that are necessary to create a system of banking that will spur rather than rein-in the economy. Much is already in place but the chapter repeatedly points out that these changes are happening in spite of, rather than because of, several negative environmental influences. The first of these is the law and the second is the lack of human capital enhancement in the major banking institutions.

Laws are a reflection of the values and aims of a society. For a law to change appropriately, certain requirements or, perhaps, a combination of requirements, are fundamental. A ground-swell of popular support for a change is often the forerunner of a new law or an amendment to an existing one. Isolated voices are rarely enough, an over-loaded legislature will only respond to a voiced opinion if a cry is loud enough to be heard amidst the clamour of competing demands. Isolated voices can carry the day, however, if they come from individuals or organisations that are important enough to the legislators. In the case of the financial system, there are a number of individual local and overseas multinational companies, as well as a ground-swell of opinion from smaller companies, all insisting that major change is required.

A second requirement for appropriate change is that the legislators, themselves, really need to understand the issue that the legislation is supposed to address. This is hard to satisfy in this case because the issues are not only complex, but they are also very new and under almost constant flux. The legislators in Vietnam are ill-equipped to accomplish this task satisfactorily even if the target was not moving; it is little wonder then that, as mentioned in the chapter, some of the new financial laws still need clarification.

An additional requirement for appropriate change is that the new laws must be manageable in terms of implementation. This is even more difficult to accomplish. To create an unrestrained, competitive banking system too quickly would be to doom the state banks. This is not to be thought of, as not only do they form the keystone of the present system, but they are also major employers in their own right. Slow change, then, is occurring, and international banks are being allowed to compete more and more, although the playing field is necessarily not yet level. These thoughts lead back again to one of the major themes of this chapter and that is the need for enhanced human capital.

One of the most important comments in Chapter 15 concerns the lack of human resource training and adequate reward systems in the state banking sector. A cycle is set in motion whereby poor rewards lead to a drain of the better staff, which makes training more necessary but harder and, therefore, more expensive; this, in turn, leads to more staff turn-over as new employees reach private sector competency levels. Again, it is an attitudinal change that is required. State banks (and state-owned enterprises for that matter) must abandon the central-planning attitude which assumes that individuals will be politically or socially motivated to work for them and, instead, embrace the profit motive that will attract better people to their ranks.

DEVELOPMENT OF EDUCATION

This topic is thoroughly covered at a specific level in Chapter 16 and, therefore, the comments here are more general. The efforts of Vietnam's government to achieve education goals is admirable. Here again, though, the issue is not as clear as it first appears. The comments within Chapter 16 are of real interest and value, namely that there is a clearer national benefit from concentrating on a wide general education than there is from offering specific tertiary courses. The immediate returns to productivity are swift and significant if the education level of the mass of individual workers is raised so that most of them can read instructions clearly. Alternatively, the tertiary educated masses not only cost a great deal but they are often lured away from the country by the prospect of enhanced wages and lifestyle overseas. Unfortunately, educational infrastructure takes time to build and it must be constructed with great care so that the output meets the needs of both a rapidly-changing industry and a persistent cultural need.

Bold first steps are being taken, at the elementary level by the government and at the tertiary level by private institutions. The cost of developing and delivering this tertiary education, however, is so high and the returns (to non-government suppliers) so low that it is only in the rare case of MBA degrees perhaps, or more commonly with the assistance from supportive overseas governments, that any progress is possible.

At the risk of repetition, the point is made (indirectly) in Chapter 16 that a partial solution, at least, may be found when the education plans are laid alongside the plans for general investment-driven development. It quickly becomes clear that, in the frequent cases where government-to-government contact is involved in setting up investment projects (such as the Singapore Tourism Unlimited plan), then educational assistance should become part of the package. Moreover, private investors should also be guided to include education as part of the system of building local capacity.

THE TOURIST INDUSTRY

Chapter 17 is interesting, as much for what it leaves unsaid as for what it says. This does not imply that the contents are unimportant or uninteresting; it is just that the descriptive approach taken skirts around two of the most difficult and possibly most controversial issues in the topic area – government development priorities and (again) human resource development. The problem is that these issues cannot be dealt with in the same prescriptive way that Ong *et al.* adopt to dispose of the problems surrounding resort development. First, then, what they address is examined here in a more objective light. Then the two larger, undeveloped issues are raised again in more detail in order to clarify them.

The sheer physical beauty of Vietnam, allied to a rich history, should be eloquent enough to convince a thoughtful investor of its tourism potential. However, the substantial infrastructural development necessary to access the various attractions of the country is not quite so readily understood and the authors point out, very sensibly, that there are opportunities here for investment that are unconnected to specific tourist development projects.

The descriptions of current efforts to develop a number of resorts are interesting, too, mainly because they illustrate one method, *inter alia*, of achieving the development goals of the industry despite an internal shortage of capital. The "Tourism Unlimited" concept designed by the Singapore Tourism Development Board, described in the text as the driver of the development of the Da Lat resort and others, is a bold, interesting initiative that typifies such an approach.

Tourism Unlimited means that investment in Vietnamese tourism will be more attractive to potential investors because a united, regional approach will be adopted rather than a strictly national one. The rationale is that the larger attraction of a complimentary, cross-national package can prove to be a stronger drawing-card than a lone hand played by one nation in a region competing with its neighbours. The advantages for (in this case) Singapore, over and above any profits that might accrue from the specific capital investment, are significant. With its limited list of national attractions, this tiny island would find it impossible to compete in the long-run with her more richly-endowed ASEAN neighbours. On the other hand, if Singapore can become the region's gateway city, then her own tourism value is leveraged.

For Vietnam, there are also advantages. There is little local capital to develop the country's tourist attractions and even less expertise. Furthermore, the tourist infrastructure is weak in terms of the financial systems to support payments and the physical, logistical support systems needed by a service-intensive industry such as tourism. By teaming up with Singapore, capital can flow more easily and, with good management, the tourism technology will be transferred. Most importantly, the budding tourism industry in Vietnam would be "kick-started" with an almost immediate influx of tourists and their dollars.

There are players in the market other than just Singapore, of course, and there are other ways to boost the fledgling industry within Vietnam. The method described in Chapter 17 is, nevertheless, an attractive one that seems promising at this stage of its development.

The above discussion leads nicely to one of the larger issues referred to previously and that is the human capital issue. The question of transferring tourism technology is of central importance because without this transfer the Tourist Unlimited arrangement (and other, similar schemes) merely become exploitive. One of the fundamental purposes of such joint ventures is that they should revolve around the training and development of a strong core of local senior and middle managers who can lead the industry into its subsequent, more independent, phase of development in the next century.

Another aspect of this issue is the danger that Vietnamese resorts could be developed simply into more "international" resorts rather than as vehicles for the preservation of the national historical heritage and development of the living Vietnamese culture. The experience of many ASEAN areas stands as a warning about what can happen. International resort development brings so many people who are doing the same things that they do in other international hotel resorts that the local culture is seriously threatened.

Examples of this phenomenon abound. Resorts now dot the coastline of Malaysia but many local people cannot afford to use them, and it would be a challenge to know what country you were in if you were randomly set down in one. Bali is another sad example. Nearby Lombok Island is now being touted as the "new Bali" and more international resorts (indistinguishable in all but their name from any others) are being rapidly built there. Indeed, Singapore itself, which presents an enviable model of tourism development, often struggles with cultural identity problems in this regard.

This issue is dealt with in Chapter 17 through mention of the 15-year Master Plan for Tourism, where government objectives are clearly laid out. However, it seems ominous that the descriptions of the resort at Da Lat which follow a discussion of these Master Plan objectives, speak of a theme park, a golf course and a huge hotel. To hold in check any deviations from the spirit of the expressed desire of the Vietnamese government to enhance rather than destroy the local culture requires neither legislation nor even master plans, but thinking, sympathetic, and trained local managers and executives working in the industry.

A second unspoken and knotty problem is raised in a circumlocutory way within this very interesting chapter. There is mention of a coal mine being forced to close because it threatened the environment of a nearby resort. There is at least a strong implication here that tourism is a more desirable industry to develop than coal mining, and that tourism is less damaging to the environment. Undoubtedly, the Vietnamese government will do its homework thoroughly before any final decisions are made, but it is not clear that the long-term environmental effects of a coal mine (if it is properly managed and filled in after its useful life) are worse than a hotel golf resort. Certainly the coal mine would have a much smaller cultural impact. A tourism plan is important, of course, but its value only becomes really evident when it is treated as an integral part of a total development plan. This is a large question, however, and it is well out of the scope of Chapter 17 as it stands.

SUMMARY

The three chapters discussed here deal with the development of the service sector in Vietnam. Many useful guidelines for potential investors are drawn up and several warning flags are waved. The topic is complex and a deep political/economic analysis is not called for here; after all, the important investment and business procedure information dates very quickly in any case. Nevertheless, a careful reader is provided with much food for thought. Moreover, admiration for the way in which the Vietnamese government has handled the transition from a centralised economy to a free market mechanism thus far may be mixed with trepidation concerning how it will meet the challenges that lie in wait over the next, critical decades of development.

BUSINESS ATTITUDES AND BEHAVIOURAL ISSUES

Chapter 19

Changing Business Attitudes in the Emergent Vietnam Marketplace*

BY
TAN Kee Cheong
Jimmy TAN
William KU
Michael CHANG

INTRODUCTION

THE OBJECTIVE OF this chapter is to investigate whether cross-cultural differences exist in the way business ethics is viewed as between northern and southern Vietnam. Business ethics are rules, standards, codes, or principles which provide guidelines for morally right behaviour and truthfulness in specific situations (Abratt *et al.*, 1992). Ethics is a function of the cultural influences imposed on a subject. This chapter investigates whether differences in these influences are translated into different ethical standards in individuals from two cultural settings in Vietnam.

Many cultural differences between the north and south are primarily due to their social and political past. The north has been dominated by the Vietnamese Communist Party since 1954 and the south by the French since 1883, with a strong American influence from 1965 to 1975. After the fall of Saigon in 1975, the country was finally reunified in 1976 to become what is now known as the Socialist Republic of Vietnam in 1976.

These different historical experiences have

* *The authors wish to thank Dr. Roger Marshall for his valuable assistance.*

had an impact on the lives and attitudes of the northern and southern Vietnamese. Knowing more about this phenomenon can help foreign investors adopt the appropriate ethical behaviour in different parts of Vietnam. This is significant in two areas. First, international managers can obtain a better understanding of the cross-cultural differences within Vietnam and, therefore, be better positioned to make ethics-related business decisions. Secondly, there are implications for the relative competitiveness and productivity of the Vietnamese in different regional, age and gender groups.

RELEVANT PRIOR STUDIES

Early theorists studied ethics from a normative perspective. They were concerned with "constructing and justifying the moral standards and codes that one ought to follow" (Vitell and Hunt, 1986). On the other hand, a positivist perspective of ethics attempts to describe and explain how individuals actually behave in ethical situations (Tsalikis and Fritzche, 1989). In general, these studies can be grouped under three main ethical value systems namely, the utilitarian approach, ontological ethical analysis and a distributive justice approach.

The utilitarian approach is where moral standards are applied to the outcome of an action or decision; it is ethical if the results are good. For deontological ethical analysis, an act or decision can be judged to be "moral" only if everyone faced with similar circumstances performs the same act or makes the same decision. Lastly, a distributive justice approach is where moral standards are based upon the primacy of a single value called justice. Thus, an action is considered ethical if the results of the action are deemed fair and just to all stakeholders. In the harsh world of business, an utilitarian approach is almost always observed; therefore, the present study takes this less judgmental approach.

There are also four factors that influence ethical behaviour in a business context. These include situational, organisational, demographic and cultural influences, with the last two providing the focus for this study.

Situational

Studies have shown that personal, ethical and moral standards may be compromised in the face of situational demands. Weiss and Adler (1984) believed that personality characteristics will likely have a greater impact on organisational processes given low situational constraints than under high situational constraints, which produce more uniformity in responses. In a sense, this aspect can either be considered as standardised for business situations worldwide, or contingent on the cultural aspect which is described below.

Organisational

The influence of the organisation on ethical behaviour is often illustrated and argued in academic papers. For instance, the achievement of organisation goals is believed to have a significant influence in this respect (Carroll, 1975). Wahn (1993) found that the more highly dependent an individual is on the organisation, the more likely that the individual will succumb to the pressure to compromise personal ethical values. However, this is not the only causal variable. Wahn (1993) also acknowledged that other factors, such as the level of moral reasoning and personality (Bommer *et al.*, 1987; Stead *et al.*, 1990), attitudes (Murphy *et al.*, 1992), peer group behaviour (Zey-Ferrell *et al.*, 1979), and organisation, industry and cultural norms (Dubinsky and Loken, 1989), are also influential.

It is also interesting to note a phenomenon known as the "Bathsheba Syndrome" within a business management context. This phenomenon refers to the fact that ethical standards appear to be influenced by certain "dynamics of success", such that the individual involved is lured into a false sense of power and security which, in turn, may lead to participation in unethical behaviour (Ludwig and Longenecker, 1993). This implies that the degree to which managers are prepared to deal with success is a major determinant of ethical behaviour, regardless of their moral and ethical character. Since the issue here is with business ethics, it seems reasonable to assume that this influence should not vary significantly between managers in northern and southern Vietnam.

Demographics

Age and gender were found to be the most significant predictors of ethical attitudes in separate studies by Serwinek (1992), and Tse and Au (1995), respectively. They found that as age increases, the subjects appear to become more conservative in their ethical attitudes. Moreover, females tend to be more ethical than males. Although there is no corroborative evidence to support this hypothesis, these outcomes may reflect the Bathsheba phenomenon in that more mature people have come to grips with success and, perhaps, their behaviour is more ethical as their position in life is accepted.

Cultural

Cultural differences can cause wide variations in business practices. This common sense observation was supported empirically by England (1975) in a study of achievement motive in different countries. England also believes that the upbringing of people in different cultures results in their acquiring different values and ethical beliefs.

THE PRESENT STUDY

The main concern of this study is business ethics in two regions of Vietnam, the north and south. It seems probable that business-related ethical standards will differ in a quasi cross-cultural manner, given the differences in the recent social histories of the two regions.

A second area of interest is to explore the attitudes of Vietnam's future business leaders who are presently undergraduate students. Also, since the role of women in society is changing rapidly, and more and more of them are entering the executive ranks of business, the difference in ethical attitudes between males and females is explored.

It is important to note that there is no intention here to be judgmental with regard to ethical standards; what is considered unethical in one country may be quite acceptable and ethical in another. Rather, the purpose is to investigate the standards that different subsets of the Vietnamese population have regarding certain business-related ethical issues.

Research Overview

A questionnaire was designed and translated into Vietnamese and then self-administered by the respondents. Factor Analysis (a statistical method to reduce many variables into a few significant factors) was used to tease out the underlying factors followed by an analysis of variance (ANOVA) which attempts to explain the observed differences.

Sample

A sample of university students and business people was drawn by convenience to represent the north and south of the country. A total of 204 responses were collected. A profile of the sample is shown in Table 19–1.

TABLE 19–1
Profile of the Sample

	Business			Student			Totals		
City	**Fem**	**Male**	**Sum**	**Fem**	**Male**	**Sum**	**Fem**	**Male**	**Sum**
Hanoi	11	24	35	29	23	52	40	47	87
Hue	43	33	76	31	10	41	74	43	117
HCMC*									
Totals	**54**	**57**	**111**	**60**	**33**	**93**	**114**	**90**	**204**

* Ho Chi Minh City.

Questionnaire

The questionnaire used in the study is based on one used during a data-gathering exercise commissioned by the Independent Commission Against Corruption (ICAC) of Hong Kong. The original questionnaire was deemed too lengthy to be administered and, thus, a series of data reduction techniques using Factor Analysis were employed to condense the questionnaire into a more manageable and practical form (a two-sided one sheet form, reproduced in Appendix 19–1).

Steps were also taken to reduce the ambiguity of statements in the questionnaire by rephrasing or changing ambiguous sentences and rewording leading statements. Culturally sensitive words were replaced with ones that have a universal meaning.

The questionnaire consists of three sections in a structured, undisguised form. A seven-point Likert scale (where **1** represents strong disagreement with the relevant statement and **7** represents strong agreement) is used throughout all three sections.

Section A consists of 16 general statements that make up the constructs to be tested. Section B consists of five situational statements that address five different issues: self interest, loyalty to friends, bribery, job switching (loyalty to company) and risk aversion. Since respondents are unlikely to reveal their true attitudes in terms of ethical conduct when the latter is referred to directly, indirect statements are used such as "your neighbour" instead of "you". Section C is designed to determine the relative importance of a number of possible influences on respondents when they make ethical judgements.

To reduce any possible bias due to the arrangement and numbering sequence of the statements, two versions of Section A were used with one ordered in a different sequence from the other. Sections B and C were unchanged as it was considered that there were too few statements to invoke any order bias. The final three items on the instrument sought information on gender, age and nationality.

In order to facilitate administration, the questionnaire was translated into Vietnamese for this project. During the process of translation, care was taken to ensure that the equivalence of related concepts and meanings across cultures were maintained through a technique of back-translation.

Procedure

Student respondents are from various universities in three cities (Hanoi, Hue and Ho Chi Minh City). Business people sampled are from the companies invited to participate in the business study seminars and also from the contacts made during our visit to the three cities. The respondents were asked to fill out the self-administered questionnaire and return them to the research team.

Results

Raw data from the survey forms were compiled, coded and entered into the SPSS PC+ statistical software package. The first step in the analysis process was to factor analyse the 16 questions in Section A to see if they could be reduced to a smaller number of variables to facilitate the north-south comparison. (An appropriate test[1] established that the data set is indeed amenable to factor analysis.) A principal component analysis revealed five factors that represent more than 50% of the variation (see Table 19–2). Note that items **A11** and **A12** were dropped because they do not load on to any of the five factors produced and they add nothing to the explanatory power. The five factors extracted thus seem to represent the underlying variables indicated in Table 19–2 satisfactorily. Therefore, these new variables (**AF1** to

---

1 Barlett's Test of Sphericity yielded a score of 366.29 ($p < 0.001$).

AF5) were constructed by taking the mean of the variables loading on to each factor.

TABLE 19–2
Five Factors Extracted From Questions in Section A

Factors	Items loading on to Factors	Eigen-value	Cum. %
AF1 (Relationship with Co.)	A6, A7, A15, A16	2.89	18.1
AF2 (Marketing tactics)	A3, A4, A5	1.54	27.7
AF3 (Importance of money)	A9, A13, A14	1.41	36.5
AF4 (Personal ambition)	A1, A2, A8	1.18	43.9
AF5 (Retribution)	A10	1.07	50.6

The second stage of the analysis used an analysis of variance (ANOVA) to provide a comparison of the ethical "score" among gender, generation and geographic region. The dependent variables in this analysis are the five factors extracted above from the questions in Section A and the questions from Sections B and C. The independent variables in each analysis are gender, work status (student or executive) and north-south. Table 19–3 presents a summary of the significant main and interactive effects identified by the ANOVA procedure.

A detailed analysis of the results and findings are presented in Appendix 19–2. The following discussion extracts and summarises the significant facts from that analysis.

DISCUSSION

From the analysis, respondents in Vietnam seem to espouse fairly low, absolute ethical standards overall as compared to respondents from other countries such as Singapore, China, New Zealand and Australia (see for instance, Ang *et al.*, 1996, and Lim and Tay, 1996). The latter scores on the seven-point Likert scale are generally higher than the scale mid-point with respect to the relationship with the company, marketing tactics, importance of money, personal ambition, loyalty to friends, bribery and job switching (see Appendix 19–2). Thus, a generally low ethical standard of business behaviour is implied. The data also suggests that most Vietnamese overtly consider their individual interests to be more important than other individuals even if this means degrading colleagues in order to increase their chances of promotion.

TABLE 19–3
The Main and Interaction Effects for Each Factor

				Significant Interaction Effect			
Factor	**N–S***	**Gender**	**Work**	**N–S and Gender**	**N–S and Work**	**Work and Gender**	**3-way**
AF1							
AF2	Yes				Yes		
AF3			Yes			Yes	
AF4		Yes			Yes		
AF5	Yes	Yes					
B1					Yes		
B2							
B3							
B4	Yes					Yes	
B5	Yes	Yes		Yes	Yes		
C1A					Yes		
C1B							
C1C		Yes		Yes		Yes	
C1D	Yes						
C1E	Yes						
C1F						Yes	
C1G	Yes						
C2	Yes						
C3	Yes						Yes

* N-S = northern versus southern Vietnam.

Female respondents were found to be more ethically inclined in terms of their relationship with the company, importance of money, personal ambition and job switching than were male respondents. The results also suggest that people from the south are more ethically inclined in the areas of relationship with the company, marketing tactics, implications of money, self-interest and bribery than are those from the north. Students generally seem more ethical in the areas of relationship with the company, marketing tactics, implications of money, self-interest, loyalty to friends, bribery and job switching than are businessmen.

Implications for Academics

Conducting a survey of business ethics of this kind has certain limitations. The limited sample of 204 people from different social groups in just three cities reduces the generalisability of the findings. However, the study is not without its merits since the results, although more indicative than conclusive, can still be of interest to many businesses in search of opportunities in Vietnam. The implications of the study for business people are discussed below.

In an academic sense, it has not been established rigorously here that the high absolute scores on the seven-point scale truly represent respondents' feelings or whether there is a national tendency to score high on such scales. Thus, a shift of the "natural average" of the scale may have taken place in practice and the scores may simply represent a scale artifice. On the other hand, the results do have face validity in that one would expect ethical standards to be more flexible in this emerging economy. However, the challenge of conducting a truly cross-cultural study remains to be undertaken.

Implications for Business

The purpose of this study was not to make value judgements about countries or individuals because ethical standards are bound by cultural values. It is not realistic for a Singaporean to condemn an American, for instance, for having a standard different from his or her own because these standards are individualistic and unique to a culture rather than universally held. However, it is important to understand how these standards differ between countries or social groups so that international managers can assess the skills, behaviour and productivity of their workers in different cultural contexts.

There are some implications for productivity and motivation here. It seems as if "money rules" and that the best way to get loyal and motivated staff is to pay them. At a minimum, a company cannot expect to receive loyalty unless it is seen to be actively supporting the self-interest of the staff. This is probably true in most markets to a certain degree but the high absolute scores evident in Vietnam suggest that this trait is even more applicable in Vietnam than it is in many other and more developed markets.

Competitors should also be cautious because it seems that Vietnamese business people are unscrupulously competitive. There is indeed a frontier in terms of open markets and the business population seems hungry and very determined to succeed (Fforde and Goldstone, 1995). This statement has even more weight in the newly opened markets of the north rather than in the slightly more settled southern region. Getting the job done is apparently important and if international conventions regarding business behaviour have to be adapted to succeed locally, then so be it.

It appears that northern Vietnamese have more of a sense of retribution and a greater fear of getting caught than do those in the south. This not only makes sense in light of their recent history but, also, it makes for a difference in their attitudes. For instance, northern business people appear to have a more positive attitude towards risk than do their southern counterparts. It also seems, in spite of the general concern about the ethics of the youth of the country, as if the older people are morally tougher and more unscrupulous than the younger ones. This suggests that market behaviour will settle down into a pattern which is more typical of a developed country model in the next decade or so as the younger generation of people assume more senior roles in business.

APPENDIX 19–1 BUSINESS ATTITUDE SURVEY

Section A

Please indicate whether you agree or disagree with the following statements. Since there are no right or wrong answers, please circle the number that best reflects your attitude.

		Strongly Disagree						Strongly Agree
1.	Survival of the company is paramount and is more important than behaving ethically.	1	2	3	4	5	6	7
2.	In society and the workplace, one should strive to make no mistakes rather than attaining success.	1	2	3	4	5	6	7
3.	For all good and evil deeds, there will be retribution.	1	2	3	4	5	6	7

4. It is acceptable to take away office stationery for personal use.	1	2	3	4	5	6	7
5. Money is all important.	1	2	3	4	5	6	7
6. Those who do not take care of their own interests can only perish.	1	2	3	4	5	6	7
7. It is acceptable to make an unauthorised copy of computer software without paying any money.	1	2	3	4	5	6	7
8. It is acceptable to obtain sick leave to handle personal matters.	1	2	3	4	5	6	7
9. As long as a person achieves his/her goal, it does not matter how he/she does it.	1	2	3	4	5	6	7
10. In the event of pressure from above, it is acceptable for a salesperson to recommend low quality goods to customers.	1	2	3	4	5	6	7
11. It is acceptable to promote a manager who is capable, and at the same time a close friend, to the position of vice president even if there is another more capable person for the post.	1	2	3	4	5	6	7
12. It is acceptable to fix a price at as high a level as possible no matter what financial position your target market is in.	1	2	3	4	5	6	7
13. As long as an advertisement provokes enough attention, it does not matter if the advertisement is deceptive and misleading.	1	2	3	4	5	6	7
14. Respondents need not be told that hidden hardware devices (such as hidden tape recorder) are used in market research in order that meaningful data can be collected.	1	2	3	4	5	6	7
15. So long as it does not jeopardise one's work, it is acceptable to handle personal matters during the office hours.	1	2	3	4	5	6	7
16. Even if it means that a colleague is fired and the money involved is a small amount, one must report theft to the supervisor.	1	2	3	4	5	6	7

Section B

Please circle the chosen answer for each of the following situations.

	Strongly Disagree						Strongly Agree
1. It is acceptable for your neighbour to be involved in a business deal which will result in him/her earning a large sum of money but his/her company will make losses.	1	2	3	4	5	6	7
2. Your neighbour strongly desires to be promoted to a vacancy which is also being sought by his/her colleagues. It is acceptable for your neighbour to degrade his/her colleagues in order to increase his/her chance of promotion.	1	2	3	4	5	6	7
3. Your neighbour is a hairdresser in a salon. It is acceptable for him/her to treat customers who give him/her tips better than those who do not.	1	2	3	4	5	6	7
4. Your neighbour's company pays for him/her to go overseas to work for a year. Two weeks after he/she comes back, another company offers to recruit him/her with a higher salary. It is acceptable for him/her to switch jobs.	1	2	3	4	5	6	7

5. Imagine that you are given the following two choices:

   Choice A: An instant cash prize of $500.
   Choice B: Enter into a game to win $100,000.

   What is the minimum probability of winning the game before you will select Choice B?

   Minimum winning probability (0% – 100%): __________%.

Section C

1. Please rate the level of importance of each of the following as a guide when you judge whether an action is ethical or not.

   (Unimportant 1 2 3 4 5 6 7 Important)

   Religion _____

Acceptance by society	_____
Personal morality	_____
Overall benefit to society	_____
Contravention of the law	_____
Disloyalty to your employer	_____
Fear of getting caught	_____

		Strongly Disagree						Strongly Agree
2.	My country's youth has high ethical standards.	1	2	3	4	5	6	7

3. Is an ethics-related subject compulsory in your current university course, either as a full subject or as a significant part of it?

   Yes/No

Background Information

1. Gender: ________ 2. Age: ________ years

3. Nationality: _______________

THANK YOU FOR YOUR KIND CO-OPERATION

APPENDIX 19–2
DETAILED RESULTS AND FINDINGS

In the following discussion, each of the relationships identified in Table 19–3 is analysed in more detail to highlight the differences found.

SECTION A

Relationship With Company (Factor AF1)

Table 19–4 shows the means for factor AF1. This factor has connotations for productivity since it mainly deals with the way in which an individual uses company resources for personal use. Note that a seven-point scale was used, where a score of one indicates a very positive attitude towards what is generally considered to be ethical behaviour while a score of seven indicates a positive attitude towards "unethical" behaviour. In this instance, there is no main effect (which means that there is no overall difference in attitude between the north and south, between gender or between work status) but there is an interaction effect. In the north, students are more ethical than their seniors while in the south the opposite is true. In both cases, the mean score falls somewhat above the mid-point of the scale which indicates an overall willingness to appropriate company time or property for individual use (see Table 19A–1).

TABLE 19A–1
Mean Scores of Factors for Each Category in Section A

	Overall	Geographic		Gender		Work Status	
Factor	**Rating**	**North**	**South**	**Fem**	**Male**	**Stu**	**Bus**
AF1	4.09	4.06	4.12	3.96	4.26	4.02	4.15
AF2	5.11	4.90	5.25	5.14	5.06	5.01	5.18
AF3	4.18	4.15	4.21	4.11	4.27	3.93	4.39
AF4	4.78	4.75	4.79	4.64	4.94	4.81	4.75
AF5	4.45	5.02	4.03	4.01	5.00	4.34	4.53

Note: A seven-point Likert scale was used where 1 = strongly disagree and 7 = strongly agree.

Marketing Tactics (Factor AF2)

This factor is mainly concerned with the scrupulousness that individuals would apply to marketing tactics; for example, fixing price levels high and using misleading advertisements. In this instance, there is both a main effect (for north-south) and an interaction effect concerning working status and student women. Northerners have few scruples, as suggested by a mean score of over five. Southerners also score high on this factor in absolute terms but significantly lower than their compatriots. The interaction effect shows that northern women are less ethical than are northern men, whereas the reverse is true in the south. Again, all scores clearly fall on the "unethical" side of the scale.

The Importance of Money (Factor AF3)

This factor deals with the importance that sample respondents placed on money, both indirectly as expressed in their desire to make sure that the company survives even if ethical standards are strained, and rather more directly in their expressed agreement that their own personal interests must be given paramount importance. The scores are high in absolute terms for all groups, although not as high as for the previous factor. The main effect here is between students and executives. It is perhaps understandable that the latter should be much tougher in their stance because they have been through tougher economic and social times than has the younger generation.

Personal Ambition (Factor AF4)

This factor deals directly with ambition as expressed in the desire to achieve goals by any means, the acceptability of recommending low quality goods to customers and the reporting of co-workers' theft to supervisors. Males have higher agreement scores than females; thus, the former group is apparently less ethical than the latter group.

Retribution (Factor AF5)

This factor is concerned with the belief in retribution for all good and evil deeds (A10). It is believed that the more a respondent agrees with the existence of retribution, the more likely he or she would behave ethically. The findings suggest that northerners have a stronger agreement on the likelihood of retribution for unethical behaviour than southerners, and that males, in general, have a stronger agreement than females. The male businessmen in the north scored particularly high on this factor, with a mean score of 5.83 versus an overall mean of 4.45.

SECTION B

The following analysis relates to the scenarios that respondents were asked to judge in Section B of the research instrument. Responses from each question were treated as the dependent variable in an analysis of variance and the independent variables from Section A above again are utilised. The first two questions showed no significant main or interactive effects but the overall scores are of interest and they are shown in Table 19A–2. Scenario B5 is dealt with separately because it is concerned with a different aspect from the first four scenarios.

Scenario B1, Self-interest

For scenario B1 (self-interest), the mean scores are consistently above five for all groups. This indicates that most Vietnamese overtly care about their own self-interest more than they do about other people's self-interest.

TABLE 19A–2
Mean Scores of Factors for Each Category in Section B

Factor	Overall Score	Geographic		Gender		Work Status	
		North	South	Female	Male	Stu	Bus
B1	5.11	5.03	5.17	5.06	5.18	5.05	5.16
B2	6.32	6.32	6.31	6.29	6.34	6.18	6.42
B3	4.73	4.57	4.85	4.92	4.49	4.59	4.85
B4	5.00	4.58	5.31	4.89	5.14	4.88	5.1

Scenario B2, Loyalty to Friends

Contrary to all preconceptions, every group expressed almost full agreement for B2 (disloyalty to friends). The mean scores greater than six indicate that friendship is not a consideration when it comes to competing for a job or promotion.

Scenario B3, Tipping

For scenario B3, female students expressed a higher acceptability of bribery (tipping) than did male students. It could be argued that the question of tipping a hairdresser in a salon may be more relevant to females than males and, thus, they may have a stronger tendency to agree about tipping the hairdresser so as to get better service. However, there is little chance of bias in this question because there is no significant difference observed between the scores of businessmen and businesswomen, or between the scores of males and females in general.

Scenario B4, Job Switching

In the case of the scenario on job switching (scenario B4 in Section B), southerners expressed stronger agreement for job switching for a higher salary than did northerners. A difference also exists between northern and southern students.

Scenario B5, Risk Aversion

Scenario B5 deals with risk aversion. People from the south are more risk averse than those from the north, and females are more risk averse than males. On the other hand, southern females are more risk averse than northern females. Interestingly, looking at the north-south/work status interaction, northern students are more risk averse than southern students but southern businessmen are more risk averse than northern businessmen.

SECTION C

There are three questions in Section C. The main emphasis in this section is on the guiding factors used for ethical decisions and behaviour.

Question C1: Important Factors Guiding Ethical Behaviour

Each respondent was asked to indicate the importance of each of the seven sources of ethical guidance suggested below:

(i) C1A Religion;
(ii) C1B Acceptance by society;
(iii) C1C Personal morality;
(iv) C1D Overall benefit to society;
(v) C1E Contravention of the law;
(vi) C1F Disloyalty to your employer; and
(vii) C1G Fear of getting caught.

There were no main or interaction effects observed for items C1A or C1F. For item C1B, however, male businessmen find acceptance by society more important than do male students. An analysis of item C1C indicated that female respondents depend more on their own personal morality as a guide than do male respondents. An interesting interaction in north-south/gender was also observed with respect to this item. Northern students graded this factor higher than did northern businessmen but the reverse was observed in the south. For item C1D, respondents in the south graded this guide more important than did those in the north. People from the north think that it is more important not to contravene the law (item C1E) than do people from the south, although female students graded this item higher than did businesswomen, and male businessmen graded it higher than did male students. On the last item, C1G, people from the north appear more concerned about getting caught than do those in the south.

Question C2: Ethical Standards of Youth

This question was simply a rating of the ethical standard of the nation's youth. The responses produced the lowest mean score (3.28) from among all of the questions answered. This result suggests that the respondents are very cognisant of the currently perceived low ethical standard of young people. In fact, northerners expressed a stronger dissatisfaction about the ethical standards of the younger Vietnamese than did the southerners. On the three-way interaction check, northern female students expressed the strongest dissatisfaction of any group.

Question C3: Ethics Course in University

Given the responses to question C2, it was somewhat surprising to discover that northerners believe that an ethics-related subject should not be compulsory in university courses.

REFERENCES

Abratt R., D. Nel and N. S. Higgs, "An Examination of the Ethical Beliefs of Managers Using Selected Scenarios in a Cross-Cultural Environment", *Journal of Business Ethics*, Vol. 11, 1992, pp. 20–35.

Ang C. T. L., K. J. S. Chng and S. L. J. Yeo, "A Cross-Cultural Study of the Ethical Standards of Business Students", Nanyang Business School, Singapore, 1996.

Bommer M., C. Gratto, J. Gravander and M. Trittle, "A Behavioural Model of Ethical and Unethical Decision Making", *Journal of Business Ethics*, Vol. 6, 1987, pp. 265–80.

Carroll A. B., "A Survey of Managerial Ethics – Is Business Morality Watergate Morality", *Business and Society Review*, Issue 13, Spring 1975, pp. 58–60.

Dubinsky A. J. and B. Loken, "Analysing Ethical Decision Making in Marketing", *Journal of Business Research*, Vol. 19, 1989, pp. 83–107.

England George W., "Personal Value Systems of Managers – So What", *Personnel Administrator*, Vol. 20, Issue 2, April 1975, pp. 20–3.

Fforde A. and A. Goldstone, "Vietnam to 2005: Advancing on All Fronts", *EIU Research Report*, The Economist Intelligence Unit, 1995.

Lim S. X. and C. M. S. Tay, "An Exploration into the Ethical Attitudes of Singapore University Students and Their Parents", Nanyang Business School, Singapore, 1996.

Ludwig D. C. and C. O. Longenecker, "The Bathsheba Syndrome: The Ethical Failure of Successful Leaders", *Journal of Business Ethics*, Vol. 12, 1993, pp. 265–73.

Murphy P. R., J. E. Smith and J. M. Daley, "Executive Attitudes, Organisational Size and Ethical Issues: Perspective of a Service Industry", *Journal of Business Ethics*, Vol. 11, 1992, pp. 11–9.

Serwinek P. J., "Demographic and Related Differences in Ethical Views Among Small Businesses", *Journal of Business Ethics*, Vol. 11, 1992, pp. 555–66.

Stead W. E., D. L. Worrel and J. G. Stead, "An Integrative Model for Understanding and Managing Ethical Behaviour in Business Organisations", *Journal of Business Ethics*, Vol. 9, Issue 3, March 1990, pp. 233–42.

Tsalikis J. and D. J. Fritzche, "Business Ethics: A Literature Review With a Focus on Marketing Ethics", *Journal of Business Ethics*, Vol. 8, 1989, pp. 695–742.

Tse A. C. B. and A. K. M. Au, "Are New Zealand Business Students More Unethical Than Non-Business Students?", *Journal of Business Ethics*, Vol. 14, 1995, pp. 1–6.

Vitell Scott J. and Shelby D. Hunt, "A General Theory of Marketing Ethics", *Journal of Macromarketing*, Vol. 6, Issue 1, Spring 1986, pp. 5–16.

Wahn J., "Organisational Dependence and the Likelihood of Complying With Organisational Pressures to Behave Unethically", *Journal of Business Ethics*, Vol. 12, 1993, pp. 245–51.

Weiss H. M. and S. Adler, "Personality and Organisational Behaviour" in B. M. Staw and L. L. Cummings (eds.), *Research in Organisation,* JAI Press, Greenwich, CT, Vol. 6, 1984, pp. 1–50.

Zey-Ferrel Mary, K. Mark Weaver and O. C. Ferrel, "Predicting Unethical Behaviour Among Marketing Practitioners", *Human Relations*, Vol. 32, Issue 7, July 1979, pp. 557–69.

Chapter 20

Joint Venture Strategies in Vietnam: A Non-economic Analysis*

BY
Scott LAM Theam Fatt
NG Kam Tong
WONG Wai Hoong
CHAN Wai Keong

INTRODUCTION

IN A CLIMATE of intense international competition, many corporations are exploring investment opportunities beyond their borders. However, investing in an unfamiliar environment involves risks not normally encountered in a simple investment evaluation. Often, these risks are non-economic in origin such as political instability, social reaction to perceived encroachment by foreign cultures, lack of a well-defined legal framework and law enforcement, or simply, inadequate physical infrastructure in telecommunications, roads or flood controls (Kobrin *et al.*, 1980). In general, political uncertainties can be categorised by flows of capital, payments, technology, people, policies that directly constrain local operations, and policies relating to ownership or managerial control (Root, 1968).

Recent examples of non-economic environmental issues affecting foreign investments include changes in government policies affecting foreign investments in consumer products as a result of the newly installed government in India, and the recent clamp down on foreign

* The authors are grateful for the comments and assistance provided by Mr. Peter Low.

advertisements and commercial presence in Vietnam just prior to an important local political congress. In any case, evaluating potential investments in a foreign country is incomplete without a careful assessment of the non-economic environmental factors.

Among the ranks of the world's established multinational corporations (MNCs), Singapore-based MNCs are relative newcomers. Nonetheless, following in the steps of Japan and Taiwan, Singapore has already made its presence felt as a significant investor in the Asian region. For instance, Singapore was the top ASEAN investor in Vietnam in 1995 and the fourth largest foreign investor after Taiwan, Hong Kong and Japan. Singapore ranked ahead of the U.S. and France (see Figure 20–1).

FIGURE 20–1
Ranking of Top Ten Countries: 1988 to 1995

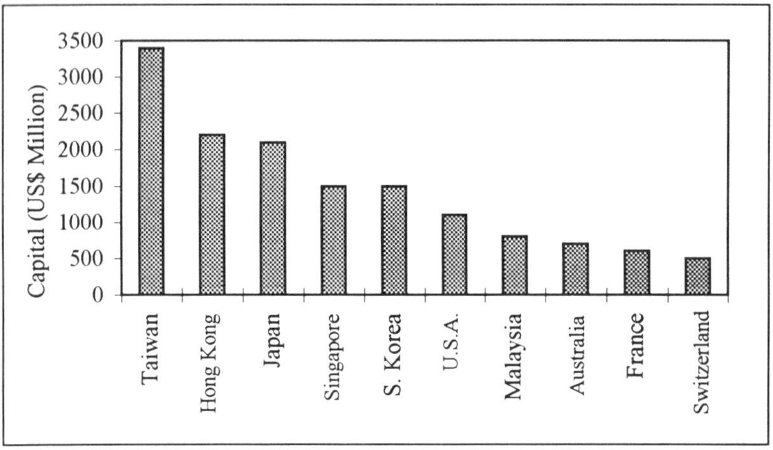

Source: *Vietnam News*, March 1996.

This chapter describes an exploratory study of the non-economic risk assessment activities of 32 major companies in Singapore with respect to their investments in Vietnam. For expediency, and to be consistent with previous studies, this chapter regards politics as an aggregate of the non-economic environment. Political risk includes the current and potential impacts of a non-economic environment on the operations of a firm.

The present study was conducted at two levels. At the corporate head office level in Singapore, the study focused on the overall management framework in conducting a non-economic assessment of firm activities. At the subsidiary or joint venture level in Vietnam, the study examined the practicality, implementation and effectiveness of these assessment activities. Specifically, sources of information in Vietnam, their reliability and significance, the type of analysis and frequency, and their reporting framework were examined. Notwithstanding the social/political assessment that was undertaken, the study also highlights some of the common problems encountered and the key success factors that are unique to investing in Vietnam.

Relevant Prior Studies

Kobrin's (1979) definition of politics, in terms of "power and authority relationships exercised in the context of society at large", can be usefully distinguished from economics. In their classic research, Haendal *et al.* (1975) on the other hand, studied the concept of political risk in considerable detail and offered the following operational definition: "... political risk in international business exists when discontinuities occur in the business environment,... these changes in the business environment must have the potential for significantly affecting the profit or other goals of a particular enterprise."

In general, the results of previous surveys of corporate assessments and the evaluation of foreign political environments are consistent over time. Kobrin *et al.* (1980) concluded that the assessment and evaluation of the non-economic environment was emerging as a management function in U.S. international firms involving several factors. First, political stability and risk are considered major, or even dominant, factors in the direct foreign investment decision. Both Aharoni (1966) and Basi (1963) found that political stability is the first factor considered in a foreign investment decision.

Secondly, the process of assessing and evaluating the non-economic environment appears to be relatively unsophisticated and unstructured. Kobrin *et al.* (1980) concluded that one-half of their respondents had institutionalised the responsibilities in assessing and evaluating the non-economic environment in the form of a group (or groups) concerned with environmental analysis. Root (1968) conducted a pioneering study of U.S. businesses abroad and observed that none of the surveyed firms had any systematic method of assessing the impact of non-economic risk factors on company operations.

Behrman *et al.* (1975) noted that executives react to environmental developments rather than "anticipating them through systematic forecasting". This behaviour was confirmed by Kobrin (1979) who also concluded that the assessment and evaluation of non-economic environments tends to be reactive rather than active. Typically, the need for companies to assess and evaluate environmental events arose from either some dramatic event (for example, war or shifts in government policies) or a change in strategic plans. Moreover, few instances of environmental analysis were being routinely conducted and updated.

The assessment process was frequently "bottom-up", and it lacked strategic direction from top management. In many instances, aspects of the environment, or events to be analysed and reported, were left to the discretion of the host country management or staff analysts. These decisions invariably led to *ad hoc* evaluations, making comparisons across projects, countries or regions difficult and meaningless.

A third factor is that information about the external environment comes from general rather than specific sources. The single most important source of information is internal to the firm and it comes from managers stationed abroad or those in company headquarters with international responsibilities. For instance, Aguilar (1967) reported that subordinates, peers and superiors account for 32% of the important external information gathered. Zink (1973) and Keegan (1974) both confirmed Aguilar's finding that the most important external information sources are banks and the public press. Behrman *et al.* (1975) and Aguilar (1967) both contend that managers rely heavily on networks of interpersonal contacts for information about the external environment.

Kobrin (1979) also concurs that the network of host country managers, who are often local nationals, is one of the primary sources providing essential information to an international firm. However, local managers are likely to be members of the local elite, and while their contact with the existing regime may be excellent, their position makes it difficult to maintain communication with, or understand the position and potential strength of, opposition groups. Thus, it may not be reasonable to expect an objective and unbiased analysis of the social and political factors in the context of a recommendation or proposal that a local manager is attempting to sell.

A fourth factor is that evaluations of foreign non-market environments tend to be subjective and often ethnocentric. Root (1968) found that subjective and general perceptions of instability were important determinants of managers' attitudes toward the security and profitability of an investment. Kobrin *et al.* (1980) noted that the environmental assessment process in most firms developed a subjective "feel of the political situation".

Lastly, integrating environmental assessments into decision making in a more systematic and objective manner has been relatively absent. Kobrin *et al.* (1980) concluded that the resulting evaluations served as a context in which investment decisions were taken. Few attempts were made to use non-economic evaluations as direct input into a decision-making process such as capital budgeting.

In summary, despite the importance of information on the political environment which would allow investors to convert uncertainty into a risk that is at least potentially "measurable, insurable and avoidable", current practice dealing with non-economic environmental assessment and evaluation does not facilitate rigorous planning or decision making.

THE PRESENT STUDY

Sample

A sample of 32 Singaporean companies was selected on the basis of their investments in Vietnam. The corporate headquarter offices of these firms were located in Singapore. Each firm had a joint venture partnership and, thus, a representative subsidiary office in Vietnam. In view of the sample size, there was no attempt to stratify the companies on the basis of industry classification. The sample firms included property developers, contractors, banks, hotels, logistics and trading companies. In total, 65 managers and executives were surveyed and interviewed during February and March of 1996.

Method

The present study closely follows the method of data collection used by Kobrin *et al.* (1980) in their pioneering U.S. research on non-economic risk analysis as well as Low *et al.*'s (1989) Australian study. Thus, in the first phase of the survey, senior managers in the Singapore headoffices were interviewed with the aid of a questionnaire which is presented in Appendix 20–1. The purpose for gathering information in this phase was twofold: first, to determine whether the

Singaporean companies surveyed had established any formal system for assessing and evaluating non-economic (for example, social and political) risk factors; and, secondly, to examine those responsible for assessing and evaluating these risk factors, including the number and types of activities involved in their assessment.

In the second phase of data collection, a follow up procedure was carried out in Vietnam. The purpose here was to gauge the extent to which non-environmental analysis policies and objectives which were initiated from corporate headquarters in Singapore became effectively implemented. The senior officers in the Vietnamese subsidiaries of the Singaporean corporations were interviewed regarding the issues and questions noted in the first phase of data collection.

The data collected via the questionnaires was tabulated and the information gathered through interviews was content analysed. To facilitate the presentation and discussion of these results in the following section, the findings are grouped under the following seven sub-headings:

(i) Organisation of the assessment function;
(ii) The context: when are environments assessed;
(iii) Sources of information;
(iv) The process: assessment methodologies;
(v) Integration into decision making;
(vi) Problems encountered; and
(vii) Non-economic key success factors in investing in Vietnam.

RESULTS AND DISCUSSION

Organisation of the Assessment Function

All respondents from the head offices in Singapore reported having a group within corporate headquarters that reviews overseas political and social factors when new investments are proposed. Table 20–1 shows that the business development unit (65%) takes the corporate lead in this activity followed by the international division (20%) and the marketing division (10%). Furthermore, the same groups monitor the existing or eventual operation in Vietnam. Thus, they are formally responsible for monitoring and assessing existing as well as potential projects. These groups, however, vary in size and composition in terms of seniority, contingent upon the magnitude of the proposed investment. However, they are normally far more established and formally structured in those firms which have large projects.

TABLE 20–1
Location of Assessment Responsibilities

Location in Firm	Percentage of Respondents
Business Development Unit	65
International Division	20
Marketing	10
Planning	5
Legal	NA
Product Line	NA
Corporate Economist	NA
Public Affairs	NA
Finance	NA

Monitoring existing operations, however, is usually delegated to the most senior representative in Vietnam, but this is accompanied by frequent visits to the project by the person who is responsible for the overseas operation. The frequency of visits varies with the size and complexity of the investment. Since most Singaporean investments are relatively new in Vietnam, the top management from every organisation interviewed seemed to be directly involved in assessing all proposals and existing investments. The environment surrounding existing operations, however, is monitored only informally. There are no specific guidelines or procedures emanating from head office for this kind of activity among the sampled organisations. Finally, the management team in the Singaporean subsidiaries in Vietnam appear to enjoy a harmonious working relationship with top management at the corporate headquarters in Singapore and feedback regarding the Vietnamese operations frequently is given on an informal basis.

The Context: When Are Environmental Risks Assessed?

The assessment and evaluation of the social and political environment seem to be reactive rather than proactive in nature. The process is typically initiated by an internal event such as a new investment proposal or some reported major event which might affect the organisation. Environmental risk assessment is rarely conducted to anticipate environmental trends that may present threats or opportunities to the companies beyond the immediate projects at hand.

Environmental risk analysis tends to be carried out on "demand". The frequency of environmental analysis is significantly related to the magnitude of investment in Vietnam. Given the essentially reactive nature of the assessment process, it follows that environmental analyses are likely to be utilised in conjunction with a "specific action". As indicated in Table 20–2, the majority of respondents confirmed the use of environmental risk analysis in conjunction with an initial investment (65%), reinvestment (25%) and strategic planning (7%). In fact, virtually no managers (1%) indicated that assessments are systematically carried out on a regular basis. However, assessments are normally carried out in conjunction with financial risk analysis.

TABLE 20–2
Activities Where Environmental Analysis is Systematically Utilised

Activities	Percentage of Respondents
Initial investment	65
Reinvestment	25
Strategic planning	7
Divestment	2
Repatriation and other exchange operations	0
Day-to-day operations	1

Sources of information

The results on sources of information are consistent with previous research. The source of environmental information that is considered most important by the majority of firms is internal to the firm. Table 20–3 shows that 85% of the respondents rely on their subsidiary managers in the field. Banks are also very important sources of information; 75% of the respondents indicated reliance on them for the latest events and used them to substantiate information provided by their own subsidiary managers. Also, 35% indicated reliance on publications from the Singapore Trade and Development Board (TDB) and the Singapore Economic Development Board (EDB), among other international publications on the risk assessment of countries, to update their information on Vietnam.

TABLE 20–3
Relative Importance of Information Sources

Information Sources	Percentage of Respondents
Subsidiary managers	85
Regional managers	55
HQ personnel	35
Banks	75
Consultants	40
Business periodicals	25
Other firms	15
Agents and outside counsel	5
Singapore Embassy	15
Domestic Agencies (EDB, TDB)	35
Professional Journal	10
Trade associations	2
Newspaper, radio, TV	3

In addition to the subsidiary managers, senior executives from headquarters tend to rely on colleagues in other companies, banks and impressions emerging from trips to the joint venture operations. In cases where projects in Vietnam are already in progress, subsidiary managers are relied upon by headquarters for information about risk assessment. Reports from the former are normally forwarded to head office for additional proposals and strategic planning.

Subsidiary managers normally seek information regarding risk assessment *via* their personal networks. Networking with Vietnamese government officials, the local Singaporean business community and other expatriates is essential for gathering information and resolving administrative problems. There is little doubt that subsidiary managers prefer to obtain these environmental assessments from people whom they know and trust.

It seems that anecdotal evidence is the most common type of information. Often it is the only available information that provides some indication, however limited, of future political developments in the country. Other types of information are not available because information on political matters is highly sensitive in Vietnam (*The Straits Times*, 15 April 1996). Firms which are larger, international, or which have institutionalised the environmental assessment process to some degree, are more likely to engage consultants on a regular basis.

It is important to note that, in most cases, environmental risk analysis is a bottom-up procedure. Subsidiaries and regional managers not only prepare the assessments but they generally decide on what aspects of the environment merit coverage.

The Process: Assessment Techniques

Table 20–4 shows that 75% of the respondents carried out some form of preliminary research coupled with an inspection tour by a team of management staff. Depending on the circumstances, local leaders are contacted and meetings are held with government officials and local businessmen. A decision to proceed with an investment is made after the political landscape is surveyed together with an estimate of costs.

TABLE 20–4
Summary of Assessment Techniques

Assessment Techniques	Percentage of Respondents (Routine Use)
Any method	47
Quantitative	5
Investment model	3
Statistical analysis	2
Structured qualitative	40
Checklist	28
Scenario development	12
Delphi (e.g., BERI)	13
Grand tour	75
Old hand	20

In many instances, organisations try to acquire area or country expertise from seasoned educators, diplomats, journalists or business people. These experts are asked to assess the objectives and personalities of a country's leadership, the strengths and weaknesses of competing political groups, and the likelihood of any new legislation.

The obvious drawback to the "old hands" approach is that organisations tend to place explicit faith in the judgment of outsiders. However, it can provide an improved understanding of the political dimension and 20% of the respondents in this study resorted to this approach.

Delphi techniques are some of the more systematic approaches used by a small proportion (13%) of the organisations sampled (see Table 20–4). Typically these techniques first try to identify selective variables which influence a nation's political destiny. Next, they are weighted and ranked. Finally, the ranked variables are aggregated into an overall measure or index of political risk by a panel of experts.

However, these same respondents also indicated that they rely on independent research organisations which have already developed political risk indices such as the Business Environmental Risk Index (BERI) or the Business International Index of Environmental Risk (BIIER). BERI assesses the business environment in a country from the view point of investments which are six months to a year in the future (Haner, 1975).

Table 20–4 indicates that 40% of the respondents utilise some form of structured qualitative methods including checklists and scenario development. Only 5% of the respondents reported that structured quantitative methods are used. These methods include modified forms of investment models and statistical analysis, or a combination of both. Although there are inherent limits to aggregate quantitative analyses, as there are with the Delphi techniques, they do provide a basis for a systematic and rigorous assessment of the political environment.

Integration into Decision Making

From discussions with managers in Vietnamese subsidiaries, a formal, systematic and objective integration of the political and social evaluations into the decision-making process is more an exception than the rule. These managers tend to focus on environmental events that have a direct impact on their business operations. Table 20–5 reveals that the more significant aspects of Vietnam's environment included changes in land use rights (85%); taxation (35%); employment policies; restrictions on imports and exports, profit remittance and exchange controls (45%); administrative procedures and local regulations (85%); and the government's attitude towards foreign investors (75%). In general, these non-economic environmental events and other information are not actively acquired nor carefully assessed for their risk implications beyond the immediate future.

Notwithstanding the findings in Table 20–5, the managers sampled agreed on several decision-making functions and the importance of attaching these functions to environmental risk analysis. For instance, 60% of the respondents thought that combining the latter with the planning and investment decision is essential (see Table 20–6). In addition, the five decision areas listed in Table 20–6 and their linkage with the environmental analysis function were considered potentially useful by a majority of the respondents. The least important role of the environmental analysis function is in recruitment; 50% of the respondents deemed this linkage to be unnecessary.

TABLE 20–5
Most Important Aspects of the Vietnam Environment

Aspects of Environment	Percentage of Respondents
Political stability	65
Foreign investment climate	65
Profit remittance and exchange control	45
Taxation	35
Expropriation	20
Political party attitude towards foreign investors	75
Labour strike and unrest	5
Administrative procedures/local by-laws	85
Public sector industrial activities	2
Public image of company	3

TABLE 20–6
Importance of the Environmental Analysis Functions

Analysis Functions	Percentage of Respondents		
	Essential	Useful	Unnecessary
Integrate analysis with planning and investment decision	60	33	7
Relate analysis to operational problems	32	50	18
Modify recruitment	8	42	50
Establish better guidelines for provision of relevant information	8	64	28
Modify relative weights assigned to political and economic factors	10	61	29

Non-economic Environmental Problems Encountered

Apart from environmental risk assessment and information acquired by the Vietnamese subsidiaries, the following problems were identified by the respondents.

(i) *Excessive Bureaucracy:* Despite efforts by the government to streamline approvals for investments, long delays are the norm for doing business in Vietnam. Delays arise not just from government hierarchy and the agencies involved in the decision-making process, but also because the decisions of the central government in Hanoi do not always coincide with those of local administrations. Excessive bureaucracy seems to result in lengthy delays during the application approval stage.

(ii) ***Inadequate Infrastructure and Telecommunication:*** Most roads in Vietnam are in critical need of repair. The existing transport system is inadequate in linking Vietnam to outside markets and in providing a network for integrating the national economy. The speed and adequacy of telecommunication facilities in certain provinces also needs to be improved.

(iii) ***Inadequate Technology and Managerial Skills:*** Although Vietnam has a high literacy rate and a good supply of professionals in a number of areas, the country is lacking in technical knowledge. In particular, many technical cadres lack knowledge in modern technology and international practices. This situation creates problems in a rapidly growing economy, and substantial upgrading of skills and an increasing understanding of international business practices are required.

(iv) ***Absence of Reliable Market Data:*** There is insufficient market information. Statistical information, if available, is often outdated when it is published. Operational and managerial planning are often done on an *ad hoc* basis. Frequent changes in commercial rules and regulations also frustrate businessmen, particularly traders whose operations are highly exposed to constant revisions in export and import requirements.

(v) ***Problems in Communication:*** A language barrier is not an issue in communicating with the Vietnamese, although a few foreign investors claim that some of their local staff do not understand English very well. The crux of the problem is simply that the country has been cut off from the non-communist world for so long that people are unfamiliar with the rituals of capitalism and modern business. Therefore, it is necessary for foreign businessmen to clarify their intentions. For example, documentations such as letters of credit and invoices necessitate meticulous explanations to the Vietnamese partners and employees.

(vi) ***Inadequate Legal and Accounting Standard Frameworks:*** In the past, an inadequate legal framework for business transactions has hampered foreign investors. However, serious efforts are underway to rectify this problem. Also, a lack of transparency in financial regulations, tax laws and ownership of assets by state-owned partners of overseas investors is slowing down the disbursement of Vietnam's US$18 billion of licensed foreign investment. Furthermore, international accounting standards need to be established and disseminated throughout the country rapidly to enhance the prospects of a viable stock exchange.

Business Implications

Respondents suggested that foreign firms must be cautious and sincere in approaching the Vietnam market. At all cost, they must contain their high expectations and avoid apparent short-cuts. Similar to China in the 1980s, a sober approach to the market is required. News about contracts signed, licenses issued, or other market issues requires a sensible interpretation and should be carefully validated.

The common advice from investment advisors that the careful selection of a local partner is of paramount consideration for any foreign firm wishing to establish a joint venture or business co-operation contract in Vietnam was confirmed by many of the respondents. Among the criteria to be considered in this crucial selection process are: the condition of the plant and the validity of any land use rights; the capability of the workforce and the vision of management; the local partner's established network (both political and business) plus knowledge of the local by-laws and regulations; and the receptiveness of the Vietnamese partner(s) to foreign inputs that can best harness the synergy between them.

Respondents also referred to a government business report published in late 1993 which examined why 14% of all joint ventures failed to commence operations even after a licence had been granted. Three categories of problems appear to explain the 100 or so aborted joint venture projects.

First, local partners failed to understand the scope of the proposed joint venture project in terms of cost, time scale and possible profits; lacked sufficient knowledge, especially in marketing; under estimated the financial resources required; and they could not recruit capable staff. Secondly, the foreign partner was unable to provide the pledged amount of capital; encountered conflicts revolving around the culture and style of the local partner; and produced a feasibility study that did not accurately reflect the local partner's capabilities.

Thirdly, outside influences, such as the decline of a particular market, an increase in costs, currency fluctuations, impending increases in taxes and tariffs, insufficient local credit and profit repatriation limits, doomed approved joint venture projects.

CONCLUSION

The findings from the present study suggest that companies use a wide variety of techniques to reduce risk and cope with the uncertainties in many areas of business operations prior to investing in Vietnam. Opinions about the impact of politics on local operations in Vietnam appear superficial and based almost entirely on subjective perceptions. In addition, there is no systematic approach to gathering data for environmental risk analysis. Information is mostly gathered to prepare for any forthcoming changes, or for reinvestment and strategic planning. Moreover changes in government policies and regulations are likely to occur in the midst of economic reform in Vietnam which clearly suggests the need for foreign firms to adopt a formal and systematic approach to analysing political risk.

Responsibility for collecting risk information seems to rest mainly with a company's senior representative in Vietnam. Crucial sources of information for head office executives mainly originate with banks, and informal networking with government officials and the business community. In general, there is a preference for information pertaining to changes in government policies and regulations over other aspects of the environment. Finally, most managers' understanding of the political risk concept, their assessment and evaluation of politics, and the manner in which they integrate political information into their decision-making, are all rather general, subjective and superficial.

APPENDIX 20–1
Non-Economic Risk Assessment Interview Questionnaire

This survey seeks to understand the current practices of Singaporean firms in evaluating the non-economic environment for purpose of investing in Vietnam.

1) Did your company review Vietnam's political and social factors when the investment was proposed?

   Yes _____ No_____

2) Was this done formally with any group or groups being assigned formal responsibility?

   Yes – One group ________
   No, done informally ________
   Yes – More than one ________

3) The assessment and evaluation of the non-economic environment are undertaken by:

   Junior analyst – One _________
   Middle Manager/Consultant _________
   Senior Manager _________

4) From which functional organisational units are these group/ groups located (please check accordingly)?

Business Development Unit	
International Division	
Marketing	
Planning	
Legal	
Product Line	
Corporate Economist	
Public Affairs	
Finance	

5) Under which of the following circumstances are environmental analyses systematically utilised (please check accordingly)?

Initial investment	
Reinvestment	
Strategic planning	
Divestment	
Repatriation and other exchange operations	
Day-to-day operations	

6) For investments in Vietnam, please select the top four considerations in the environmental analysis and rate the relative importance on the source of information about social and political factors affecting the firm's planning, investment and operation decisions by giving 1 for the most important item and 5 for the least important item.

Subsidiary managers	
Regional managers	
HQ personnel	
Banks	
Consultants	
Business periodicals	
Other firms	
Agents and outside counsel	
Singapore Embassy	
Domestic agencies (EDB, TDB)	
Professional journals	
Trade associations	
Newspaper, radio, TV	

7) Do the assessment groups employ the following techniques routinely for assessing the non-economic environment (please check accordingly)?

Any method	
Quantitative Investment model Statistical analysis	
Structured qualitative Checklist Scenario development	
Delphi (e.g., BERI)	
Grand tour	
Old hand	

8) For investments in Vietnam, the four most important aspects of non-economic environmental risk to your company (please check accordingly)?

Political stability	
Foreign investment climate	
Profit remittance and exchange control	
Taxation	
Expropriation	
Political party attitude towards foreign investors	
Labour strike and unrest	
Administrative procedures/local by laws	
Public sector industrial activities	
Public image of company	

9) In evaluating non-environmental risk, which of the following objectives are the two most important (i.e., essential) and which ones are considered unnecessary (please check accordingly)?

	Essential	**Useful**	**Unnecessary**
Integrate analysis with planning and investment decision			
Relate analysis to operational problems			
Modify recruitment			
Establish better guidelines for provision of relevant information			
Modify relative weights assigned to political and economical factors			

10) Were the two most important objectives identified in question (9) above fulfilled for the investment in Vietnam (please circle accordingly)?

1. Totally fulfilled
2. Somewhat fulfilled
3. Not fulfilled
4. Not applicable

11) Which of the following individuals receive any environmental risk analysis (please check accordingly)?

Chief Executive Officer	
Chief Financial Officer	
Director of Planning	
Legal Counsellor	
General Manager, International Division	
Corporate Economist /Corporate Affairs	
Director of Public Affairs	
Director of Government Affairs	

REFERENCES

Aguilar Francis Joseph, *Scanning the Business Environment*, MacMillan, New York, 1967.

Aharoni Yair, *The Foreign Investment Decision Process,* Division of Research, Graduate School of Business, Harvard University, Cambridge, MA, 1966.

Basi R. S., *Determinants of United States Private Direct Investment in Foreign Countries,* Kent State University, Ohio, 1963.

Behrman Jack N., J. J. Boddewyn and Ashok Kapoor, *International Business Communications: U.S. Structures, Actors and Issues,* Lexington Books, Lexington, 1975.

Haendel Dan H., Gerald T. West and Robert G. Meadow, *Overseas Investment and Political Risk,* Foreign Policy Research Institute, Philadelphia, 1975.

Haner F. T., "Business Environmental Risk Index (BERI)" *Best's Review (Property/Liability ed.*), July 1975, pp. 47–50.

Keegan Warren, "Multinational Scanning: A Study of Information Sources Used by Headquarters Executives in Multinational Companies", *Administrative Science Quarterly*, September 1974, pp. 411–21.

Kobrin S. J., "Political Risk: A Review and Reconsideration", *Journal of International Business Studies*, Spring/Summer 10(1), 1979, pp. 67–80.

Kobrin S. J., J. Basek, S. Blank and J. L. Polombara "The Assessment and Evaluation of Non-Economic Environments By American Firms – A Preliminary Report", *Journal of International Business Studies*, Vol. 11, 1980, pp. 32–47.

Low P. S., B. W. Stening and K. Stening, "The International Political Risk Assessment Activities of Australia Corporations": *International Internal of Management*", Vol. 6, No. 4, 1989, pp. 341–9.

"Obsession With Secrecy Hurts Vietnam Economy", *The Straits Times,* 15 April 1996, p. 17.

Root Franklin, "Attitudes of Business Executives Towards Foreign Investment Opportunities", *Economics and Business Bulletin,* Temple University, January 1968, pp. 14–23.

Vietnam News, March 1996.

Zink Dolph Warren, *The Political Risk for Multinationals Enterprises in Developing Countries,* Praeger Publisher, New York, 1973.

Chapter 21

Managers' Expectations of Hotel Management Trainees in Vietnam*

BY
LOO Chuen Yew
Stephen SUM Ngai

INTRODUCTION

THE PURPOSE OF this chapter is to identify the key competencies required of new recruits entering management training programmes in Vietnam's hotel industry. Job competencies are those activities and skills which are considered necessary to perform the duties of a specific position. Competence in the performance of these duties is based on one's ability to accomplish specific job-related tasks and assume the role associated with the position.

At a time when the hotel industry in Vietnam is becoming more competitive, human resource issues are also becoming increasingly critical in influencing business profitability and competitiveness (Bailey and Hunt, 1990; Wain, 1993). It is important that graduates of programmes in hotel management are able to function effectively as management trainees and attain the relevant competencies in specific areas that make for effective managers (Tas, 1988).

The present study replicates two similar studies carried out in the U.K. by Baum (1991b) and in the U.S. by Tas (1988). The

* The authors are grateful to Mr. Peter Low for his valuable assistance and helpful comments. Thanks also to Wilbert Monforte and Teng Ann Boon for their assistance and comments on earlier drafts of this chapter.

replication of the Tas and Baum studies in Vietnam can contribute to understanding the critical competencies required from management trainees for successful hotel operations and management. A detailed comparison of the responses from the Vietnam, U.S. and U.K. managers is undertaken and tentative conclusions are drawn about cultural variations and the implications for employment within the hotel industry. Knowledge of these differences can have important implications for business as well as educational programmes in this field.

THE CURRENT STATE OF HUMAN RESOURCE MANAGEMENT IN VIETNAM'S HOTEL INDUSTRY

In 1991, the World Tourism Organisation (WTO) conducted an industry-wide survey of business practices in Vietnam and found, among other things, that private or public hospitality schools for training hotel employees do not exist (World Tourism Organisation, 1991; Hobson *et al.*, 1994). Moreover, by March 1996, the hospitality training environment had not improved significantly. Only a few small-scale operations, predominantly located in Hanoi and Ho Chi Minh City, had been set up by the government.

However, Vietnam's National Tourism agency plans to build three major hotel and tourism schools in its effort to upgrade hospitality training and deal with tourism growth. Currently, it is the subsidiaries of foreign hotels operating in Vietnam that are most likely to train their employees. Employees are typically trained on the job. Occasionally, those on the "management track" are sent abroad to parent hotels for advanced training.

Hotels without formal training programmes are forced to rely on competitive wages to attract trained staff. If they are unable to compete with the wages offered by international hotels, then they must seriously consider formalised training as a means of upgrading their service standards. As a strategic thrust for Vietnam's hotel industry, government and industry need to institutionalise hotel skills and management training. Moreover, this training must focus on generic competencies that reflect hotel industry demand.

Presently, foreign hotels operating in Vietnam must comply with the *Decree on Labour Regulations*. Foreign hotels have to supply the Foreign Service Bureau (FSB) with the job description of every expatriate employed. These expatriates normally are employed on a contractual basis. Most hotels have plans to replace expatriates eventually with local Vietnamese staff. Hence, it is in the interest of the hotels to have training programmes for upgrading the skills of their workers and to groom potential management trainees for higher management positions.

The lack of standardisation in the hotel training curriculum of universities adds to the difficulty in the recruitment and selection process. The critical competencies identified in the present study could be a benchmark for the recruitment and selection of potential hotel managers throughout Vietnam.

PRIOR STUDIES

In a pioneering study in the United States, Tas (1988) analysed and determined the most important competencies required of a graduate management trainee. These were identified and rated by the general managers from large U.S. hotels. Tas identified a list of 70 competencies from a literature search that might be needed by hotel management trainees. This list of competencies was then examined by two separate review panels (consisting of hotel school professors and hotel general managers) for clarity and content validity. A list of 36 items emerged after this review and selection process.

The Tas study identified six essential competencies for hotel manager trainees focusing on the following human relations skills: managing guest problems; professional and ethical standards; professional appearance and poise; effective communication; positive customer relations; and positive working relationships. The analysis by Tas focused on recommendations from specific hotel management training programmes that were effective in developing these key competencies.

Baum (1991b) replicated the Tas study in the United Kingdom. Baum's study essentially compared the two sets of data. The checklist used by Baum was identical to the one used by Tas in the U.S. Baum found a high correlation (0.88) between the results of the U.S. survey and the U.K. survey. Both surveys gave high ratings to the human relations-related competencies. The U.K. managers gave higher ratings (mean = 4.02) than their U.S. counterparts (mean = 3.76). According to Baum, the difference in mean ratings, as well as other major differences between the two studies, can be attributed to cultural differences.

THE PRESENT STUDY

Research Overview

Tas (1988) expressed the view that the study of hoteliers' expectations of their management trainees should be extended to the larger international context. The objective of the present study, therefore, is to extend the work by Tas (1988) and Baum (1991a; 1991b) to a less developed country, namely Vietnam, by examining whether the expectations of Vietnam's hotel managers differ from those found in the U.S. and U.K. studies.

The general managers of 30 hotels in Vietnam were surveyed via a questionnaire on their perceptions of job competencies. The objective was to identify the competencies required of management trainees in Vietnam. In this study, competencies are defined as activities and skills that are essential to perform the tasks of an assigned position in the hotel. The general managers were asked to indicate their perception of the importance of 36 competencies listed on the questionnaire. The responses were compared with the studies by Tas (1988) and Baum (1991b).

The approach in this study adhered as closely as possible to the methodology and instruments used by Tas and Baum in order to facilitate a direct comparison. However, the survey approach in the present study differs from the two prior studies in the way the questionnaire responses were collected. Due to the limited number of larger hotels existing in Vietnam in early 1996, a majority of the responses data was collected directly through site visits and interviews with the hotels' general managers. This approach was preferred to collecting responses by mailing the questionnaire which would lower the response rate. The direct interview method also provided an opportunity to gain valuable additional information which was useful in interpreting the survey findings.

Sample

Tas (1988) and Baum (1991b) surveyed over 400 medium-to-large size hotels in their respective studies. They were able to gather a large sample because the hotel industry in the U.S. and U.K. is in the mature stage of development. However, the hotel industry in Vietnam is in the early stage of development and, thus, there are a small number of hotels. Therefore, only 30 foreign and state-owned hotels were sampled. This yielded 14 small hotels, ten medium-sized hotels and six large hotels.

Questionnaire

The questionnaire used in the survey was a modified version of the one used by Tas (1988). The questions were retained in order to facilitate a comparison with the results of the Tas and Baum studies. The chief executive officer of each hotel was administered a structured questionnaire and asked to respond to 36 statements pertaining to their subordinates' jobs. The complete survey questionnaire is presented in Appendix 21–1.

Results

The respondents' scores from each competency statement were averaged to yield the mean level of importance for that item. The average score for each statement was then tabulated (see Table 21–1). These values are categorised according to the following range of scores on each item, which is consistent with what was done by Tas and Baum.

Essential:	Over 4.50
Considerably important:	3.50 to 4.49
Moderately important:	2.50 to 3.49

The overall mean score for the 36 items for the Vietnam study is 3.90 which is between the U.S. mean of 3.76 and the U.K. mean of 4.02 (see Table 21–2). General managers in Vietnam rated four individual competencies as essential whereas there were six essential competencies in the U.K. study and eight essential competencies in the U.S. study.

The rank order correlation coefficients among the Vietnam, U.S. and U.K. studies are shown in Table 21–3. The correlations between the Vietnam study and the U.S. and U.K. studies, (0.68 and 0.76) respectively, are lower than the correlation between the latter two studies (0.88). This suggests that fewer high scores from the Vietnam sample are associated with high scores on items from the U.S. and U.K. results.

TABLE 21–1
Perceptions of Competencies Across the Vietnam, U.S. and U.K. Hotel Industry

Ranking	Description	Mean Scores (Ranking)		
		Vietnam	U.S.	U.K.
	Essential			
1	Manages guest problems with understanding and sensibility.	4.82	4.80(1)	4.81(1)
2	Follows hygiene and safety regulations to ensure compliance by organisation.	4.79	4.61(3)	4.61(3)
3	Communicates effectively both written and orally.	4.61	3.99(13)	4.71(2)
4	Develops positive customer relations.	4.59	4.60(5)	4.55(6)
	Considerably Important			
5	Motivates employees to achieve desired performance.	4.33	4.44(8)	4.52(8)
6	Follows established personnel management procedures in supervision of employees.	4.31	4.33(9)	4.23(14)
7	Maintains professional and ethical standards in the work environment.	4.22	4.69(2)	4.40(9)
8	Follows the legal responsibilities associated with hotel operations.	4.21	3.90(14)	4.54(7)
9	Assists in the development and control of departmental employee productivity.	4.10	3.75(18)	3.87(23)
10	Strives to achieve positive working relationships with employees.	4.02	4.52(6)	4.57(4)
11	Demonstrates professional appearance and poise.	4.00	4.61(4)	4.56(5)
12	Identifies operational problems.	4.00	4.00(12)	4.24(13)
13	Manages employee grievances effectively.	3.99	3.87(15)	4.12(17)
14	Assists in the development and maintenance of budgets for each important element of the organisation.	3.99	3.24(31)	3.77(25)
15	Uses front office equipment effectively.	3.98	3.31(29)	3.58(30)
16	Assists in the development of a balanced program of preventive security.	3.97	3.19(32)	3.44(33)
17	Prepares weekly, monthly and annual financial statistical reports.	3.97	2.96(36)	3.65(28)

TABLE 21–1 (cont'd)

Ranking	Description	Mean Scores (Ranking)		
		Vietnam	U.S.	U.K.
18	Develops reliable revenue and expense tracking systems.	3.97	3.16(33)	3.77(25)
19	Knows personnel policies which govern supervisory activities.	3.96	4.15(10)	3.97(19)
20	Possess needed leadership qualities to achieve organisation objectives.	3.96	4.48(7)	4.40(9)
21	Uses past and current information to predict future departmental revenues and expenses.	3.92	3.75(18)	4.31(12)
22	Effectively manages life-threatening situations.	3.92	3.75(18)	4.31(12)
23	Uses past and current information to predict future reservations.	3.92	3.61(23)	4.06(18)
24	Delegates responsibility and authority to personnel according to departmental objectives.	3.91	3.84(16)	4.14(16)
25	Analyses weekly, monthly and annual financial and statistical reports.	3.90	3.49(25)	3.95(20)
26	Assists in establishing organisational objectives and their priorities.	3.90	3.67(21)	3.92(22)
27	Develops workflow patterns to meet specific operational requirements.	3.89	3.57(24)	3.79(24)
28	Analyses past and present business information to effectively predict marketing strategies.	3.87	3.39(28)	3.57(32)
29	Analyses factors that influence the controllability and level of profits.	3.85	3.73(20)	4.19(15)
30	Conducts an informative and valid interview with prospective employees.	3.85	3.47(26)	3.94(21)
31	Appraises employee performance.	3.84	3.67(21)	3.67(27)
32	Inspects services, hotel rooms according to standard operating housekeeping procedures.	3.80	3.76(17)	3.58(30)
33	Assists in operational and strategic planning.	3.79	3.31(29)	3.59(29)
34	Assist in establishing organisational objectives and their priorities.	3.21	3.03(35)	3.26(36)
35	Processes hotel arrivals and departures.	3.00	3.05(24)	2.95(30)
36	Promotes a co-operative union-management relationship.	1.90	3.45(22)	3.11(29)

TABLE 21–2
Comparative Overall Averages Among Countries

Mean Scores	Vietnam	U.S.	U.K.
Average rating of competencies	3.90	3.82	4.02

TABLE 21–3
Rank Order Correlation Among Countries

Rank order correlation between Vietnam and U.S.	0.68
Rank order correlation between Vietnam and U.K.	0.76
Rank order correlation between U.S. and U.K.	0.88

A more useful display of the major differences among countries is presented in Tables 21–4 and 21–5. In the former, there is agreement or correspondence on seven out of the top ten items in the Vietnam sample compared to the U.S. results. Likewise, Table 21–4 indicates that two items from the U.K. results are not in the top ten echelon for the Vietnam sample.

TABLE 21–4
Similarities of U.S. and U.K. Perceptions Relative to the Top Ten in Vietnam

Item	Vietnam Ranking	Correspondence	
		U.S.	U.K.
1.	Guest problems	Yes	Yes
2.	Hygiene and safety regulations	Yes	Yes
3.	Communication skills	No (13)*	Yes
4.	Customer relations	Yes	Yes
5.	Employee motivation	Yes	Yes
6.	Follows rules	Yes	No (14)
7.	Professional and ethical standards	Yes	Yes
8.	Legal responsibilities	No (14)	Yes
9.	Employee productivity	No (18)	No (23)
10.	Superior-subordinate relationship	Yes	Yes

* Numbers in parentheses indicate the relative ranking within each study, respectively.

TABLE 21–5
Exceptions to the Top Ten Ranking in Vietnam

Item	Vietnam Ranking	U.S. Ranking	U.K. Ranking
11.	Professional appearance	4	5
19.	Personnel knowledge	10	n.a.
20.	Leadership qualities	7	9

Of interest are the items ranking in the top ten for the U.S. and the U.K. samples which are not listed in Table 21-4. Table 21–5 shows the items which ranked in the top ten in the U.S. and U.K. studies but which did not rank in the top ten relative to the Vietnamese sample. There are three items from the U.S. sample and two items from the U.K. sample.

DISCUSSION

The results in Table 21–4 suggest a strong correspondence between managers' expectations in Vietnam hotels as compared to their counterparts in the U.S. and U.K. hotel industry. However, relative to the U.S. findings, communication skills, legal responsibilities and productivity issues are more important in Vietnam's hotel industry. Moreover, relative to the U.K. findings, work-to-rules and productivity issues are more important in Vietnam.

With the exception of productivity, these differences may be attributable to cultural differences among the three countries. However, Vietnam is distinctly different than both the U.S. and U.K. on the productivity issue which suggests a difference in the philosophy of managerial expectations in the Vietnam context. Further insight on this issue emerges from the exceptions noted in Table 21–5. Leadership qualities ranks in the top ten for both the U.S. (ranked seventh) and the U.K. (ranked ninth) studies while for the Vietnam sample it ranks 20th.

Collectively, these results suggest a profile for operational managers in Vietnam which follows a rigidly efficient, productive, customer-oriented and co-operative set of competencies. At the same time, however, this image is constrained by the hierarchy and rules of the organisation. In particular, leadership skills are much less important than following organisation procedures, and professional appearance is of less concern in Vietnam than getting the job done effectively and efficiently.

Implications

Given the emphasis on the importance of "soft" or human relations associated competencies, such as guest care, employee relations, customer relations and communication skills, a standard package of training dealing with these areas can be applied throughout Vietnam. It is perhaps irrelevant whether it is delivered in-house or via government sponsored programmes, including university training. The important message is that the essential competencies are not materially different from global standards anywhere (based on comparisons with the U.S. and U.K. studies).

More importantly, technical competencies appear to be more important than leadership qualities or decision-making skills on the part of operational managers. Therefore, at this juncture in the development of Vietnam's hotel industry there is little need for hotel-specific programmes, which would only be appropriate within the unique corporate personality of each individual hotel. These priorities were substantiated in discussions with many senior managers from the sample of hotels interviewed.

It is not difficult to appreciate why these priorities currently exist in the Vietnam sample of senior managers. First, many of the hotels which were sampled have only been in existence for approximately one year, and in some cases, not even for that long. Thus, the expectations of senior managers may be influenced by start-up difficulties which, of course, would impact any business in terms of priorities. Secondly, there is a dearth of well-trained operational managers combined with the reality that almost everyone in any given hotel is new and unfamiliar with other employees. Naturally, while interpersonal relations are important, it is critical that hotels get the job done effectively and efficiently. The best way to achieve this objective in the short-run is to rely on established procedures and the technical qualifications of managers. More flexibility in decision-making and leadership can be emphasised at a future time.

Another factor to be considered in importing training programmes into Vietnam is the discrepancy in salaries offered between foreign-owned hotels and state-owned hotels. Senior managers from the latter in Hue, for instance, commented on the difficulty of training managers and retaining them given the higher wage structure in foreign-owned hotels. Notwithstanding this problem, two Singaporean general managers in Hanoi expressed concern over their ability to add responsibility, via leadership and more decision-making authority, because of the practice of fixed salary increments in the country. According to Vietnam's labour laws, hotels are bound to award the same annual salary increment to every employee. This tends to place additional pressure on stressing fundamental, technical competencies and nothing more.

CONCLUSION

The hotel industry in Vietnam is in its infancy and offers much potential to educators, consultants and experts in the field of hotel management. As Thornhill (1993) acknowledges, management education and training necessitates a consideration of cultural diversity. Interestingly, the hotel industry in Vietnam appears to demand a set of essential competencies which are remarkably similar to those found in Western nations such as the U.S. and U.K. Thus, providers of these skills have a significant and growing market in Vietnam. At the same time, however, it is important for these suppliers to realise that higher-order training, which emphasises more flexibility in the leadership and decision-making aspects of operational managers, is not the first priority in Vietnam's hotel industry at this stage of its growth cycle.

APPENDIX 21–1
Management Expectation Survey

A Hotel Management Study of Managers' Expectations of the Importance of Subordinate Tasks

Please rate the following statements that relate to your management trainees' tasks on the scale from (1) least important to (5) most important.

STATEMENTS	Least Important				Most Important
1. Manage guest problems with understanding and sensitivity.	1	2	3	4	5
2. Follow health and safety regulations to ensure compliance by the organisation.	1	2	3	4	5
3. Communicate effectively both written and orally.	1	2	3	4	5
4. Strive to achieve positive working relationships with employees.	1	2	3	4	5
5. Demonstrate professional appearance and poise.	1	2	3	4	5
6. Develop positive customer relations.	1	2	3	4	5
7. Follow the legal responsibilities associated with hotel operations.	1	2	3	4	5
8. Motivate employees to achieve desired performance.	1	2	3	4	5
9. Possess needed leadership qualities to achieve organisational objectives.	1	2	3	4	5
10. Maintain professional and ethical standards in work environment.	1	2	3	4	5
11. Effectively manage life-threatening situations.	1	2	3	4	5
12. Use past and current information to predict future departmental revenues and expenses.	1	2	3	4	5
13. Identify operational problems.	1	2	3	4	5
14. Follow established personnel procedures in the supervision of employees.	1	2	3	4	5
15. Analyse factors that contribute to fluctuations in level of profits.	1	2	3	4	5

16. Delegate responsibility and authority to subordinates according to departmental objective(s).	1	2	3	4	5
17. Manage employee grievances effectively.	1	2	3	4	5
18. Use past and current information to predict future hotel reservations.	1	2	3	4	5
19. Know personnel policies which govern supervisory activities.	1	2	3	4	5
20. Analyse weekly, monthly and annual financial and statistical reports.	1	2	3	4	5
21. Conduct an informative and valid interview with prospective employees.	1	2	3	4	5
22. Assist in establishing organisational objectives and their priorities.	1	2	3	4	5
23. Assist in the development and control of departmental employees productivity.	1	2	3	4	5
24. Develop work flow patterns to meet specific operational requirements.	1	2	3	4	5
25. Develop reliable revenue and expense tracking systems.	1	2	3	4	5
26. Assist in the development and maintenance of budgets for each important element of the organisation.	1	2	3	4	5
27. Appraise employee performance.	1	2	3	4	5
28. Prepare weekly, monthly and annual financial statistical reports.	1	2	3	4	5
29. Assist in operational and strategic planning.	1	2	3	4	5
30. Use front office equipment effectively.	1	2	3	4	5
31. Inspect serviced hotel rooms according to standard operating housekeeping procedures.	1	2	3	4	5
32. Analyse past and present business information to effectively predict future marketing strategies.	1	2	3	4	5
33. Assist in the development of an effective energy management programme.	1	2	3	4	5

34. Assist in the development of a balanced programme of preventive security.	1	2	3	4	5
35. Promote a co-operative union-management relationship.	1	2	3	4	5
36. Process hotel arrivals and departures.	1	2	3	4	5

REFERENCES

Bailey Murray and Jill Hunt, "Travel and Tourism Opportunities in Vietnam: A Blueprint for Development", *Business International*, Hong Kong, 1990.

Baum T., "Management Trainees in the Hotel Industry", *Journal of European Industrial Training*, Vol. 15, No. 2, 1991a, pp. 3–8.

Baum T., "The U.S. and the U.K.: Comparing Expectations of Management Trainees", *The Cornell Hotel and Restaurant Administration Quarterly*, Vol. 12, No. 4, 1991b, pp. 18–21.

Hobson J.S.P., V. Heung and K.S. Chon, "Vietnam's Tourism Industry: Can It Be Kept Afloat?", *The Cornell Hotel and Restaurant Administration Quarterly*, Vol. 16, No. 2, 1994, pp. 222–7.

Tas R., "Teaching Future Managers", *The Cornell HRA Quarterly*, Vol. 9, No. 1, 1988, pp. 41–3.

Thornhill A.R., "Management Training Across Cultures: The Challenge for Trainers", *Journal of European Industrial Training*, Vol. 17, No. 10, 1993, pp. 43–51.

Wain B., "Paris Meeting Formalises Vietnam's Rebirth", *Asian Wall Street Journal Weekly*, November 1993, p. 14.

World Tourism Organisation, *Vietnam 1991 Tourism Development Master Plan, Summary Report*, Geneva, 1991.

Chapter 22

A Synopsis of Managerial Attitudes and Behavioural Issues

BY
Peter Isac LOW

INTRODUCTION

IN DECEMBER 1987, Vietnam introduced the *Foreign Investment Law* which represents the single most important policy manifestation of *doi moi*. It has virtually transformed the nation from a closed centrally-planned economy, in which the private sector was deemed illegal, to a market economy based on incentive, profit motive and encouragement of private enterprise. Vietnam now has the most liberal foreign investment code in the region. Global response to Vietnam's "open-door" policy has been swift and unprecedented investments are pouring into various sectors of the country.

However, the pace of economic development has not been without problems. Cash strapped Vietnam lacks the infrastructure, and also the management and technical expertise to cope with the burgeoning growth of its economy. Foreign investors have also had their share of problems, mostly attributable to hasty investment decisions and also a failure to understand Vietnam (Robinson, 1995).

Much has been written about *doi moi* from the economics perspective and, apart from Deloitte *et al.*'s (1993) work on the business profile in Vietnam, little else has been documented about Vietnam's venture into capitalism from a management perspective.

Thus, this section explores some aspects of management in Vietnam business with respect to three studies that were recently conducted in Vietnam. The first study, in Chapter 19, focuses on Vietnamese business people's stance on ethical standards. The nature and the manner in which country risk is assessed forms the subject matter of Chapter 20. Finally, Chapter 21 examines management development and training in the hotel industry in Vietnam. The significance of these management issues, along with their ramifications for doing business in Vietnam, are discussed next.

ETHICS AND BUSINESS ATTITUDES

The study of ethical behaviour is often complex, to say the least. The concept of ethics is amorphous and frequently subjective because the phenomenon is difficult to measure. Data is not always consistent, and more issues seem to be raised as a result of examining any single issue. In spite of these problems, every effort should be exercised towards a better understanding and appreciation of ethical behaviour in business, particularly today when the call for "transparent" practices are more vocal than ever.

The findings on ethical behaviour in Chapter 19 provide some insight into the Vietnamese respondents' stance on ethical behaviour. Given its exploratory nature, it is probably more meaningful to discuss the practical implications using an organisational shared value framework, thus avoiding "pointing the finger" judgments.

According to Posner and Munson (1981) and Seibert and Proctor (1984), ethical behaviour may be better understood from an organisational perspective when it is considered in conjunction with a framework. For example, when managers' values are compatible or congruent with the values of the organisation, their personal lives are in better harmony, and their approach and attitudes to their jobs are healthier. Hence, the greater the compatibility or congruency, the higher the shared value (between the individual and the organisation). Posner and Munson (1981) found that a positive relationship exists between value-sharers and ethical behaviour. For instance, high sharers are more likely to resign than carry out some action that they feel is unethical. Also, they are (as might be expected) much more certain than low-sharers that their organisations are guided by highly ethical standards. Low-sharers, on the other hand, are much more likely to attribute unethical behaviour to organisational policies.

What can be learned from the respondents to the Vietnam study on ethical behaviour and the organisation literature is that more attention needs to be given to the power of values and organisational culture in promoting and inculcating ethical behaviour in the workplace. For instance, Robbins *et al.* (1986) suggest that this can be achieved via a committed and ongoing socialisation process and also a "transparent" organisational culture. Although results, whenever they are formulated, may seem as tentative and elusive as capturing a river in a bucket, the subject is so significant that it warrants continual monitoring.

COUNTRY RISK ASSESSMENT

In general, a country's risk may be defined as the possibility of exposure to the loss of an asset or a business caused by events that are, to some extent, under the control of the government of that country, but are beyond the control of foreign asset owners and business managers (Negandhi, 1987). Moreover, Kobrin (1979) suggested a typology in which two alternative methods might be appropriate for assessing country risk. One method evaluates country risk on the basis of economic (quantitative) factors while the other assesses it using non-economic (qualitative) factors. The Vietnam study reported in Chapter 20 applies the latter approach.

Essentially, the Vietnam study looks at the international social and political risk assessment activities of Singaporean corporations. Specifically, it focuses on the organisational and process aspects involved in the function of monitoring and evaluating country risk.

The study highlighted several key issues that are associated with the Singaporean corporations' assessment of the risks they face in Vietnam. While the small sample necessarily demands that caution be exercised in drawing conclusions, the results of the study point to two fundamental areas of concern. First, the majority of firms exhibit a fragmented and ad hoc system in assessing country risk. The second area of concern raises the question of how efficacious are the means by which the Singaporean firms obtain information on the country risk assessment function. Evidence of over-reliance on informal and internal sources of information on the part of the firms studied suggests intelligence systems that are narrow and short-term oriented, as well as inefficient in dealing with the Vietnamese environment, one that is both dynamic and volatile.

Foreign firms with interests in Vietnam recognise that an essential component of effective management is the capacity to decipher the important external forces at play. An efficient country risk assessment that takes into account the firm's unique features/interests, and its adaptive ability, is the first step towards developing this capability. Only then can the critical task of an appropriate strategic response be considered.

In conclusion, a couple of observations are noteworthy in the spectre of Singapore's globalisation drive. First, Singapore is a "new kid on the block" insofar as global expansion is concerned. It is likely that Singaporean corporations will seek opportunities in new emerging Asian markets, so-called "transition" economies. These environments necessitate constant monitoring with sophisticated methods. While the evaluation of country risk in the Third World has never been easy, it is daunting with respect to transition economies because their path to development is without precedent. One might imagine this task as akin to criss-crossing a river blind-folded and moving forward on one stone at a time.

Secondly, Singapore is in the hub of a Southeast Asian region that manifests both challenges and opportunities. These days, global political conflicts and confrontations occur without warning (i.e., the recent China-Taiwan confrontation; the current Palestinian-Israeli conflict; and U.S. sanctions on Myanmar). Reverberations from these events affect not only Singaporean business interests, but all other global investors as well. While hard economic factors will form the basis for corporate investment decisions, at the same time, firms can ill afford to underestimate the vital importance of the non-economic aspects of the countries in which they operate. Environmental analysis must be recognised as an integral part of an international investor's decision-making. Apart from the special case of transition economies and the impact of their dynamics on the global economy, the ever-changing global environment and global relationships in the last two decades also raises the imperative to constantly review and update the methodological and country-specific aspects of the country risk conundrum.

MANAGEMENT DEVELOPMENT AND TRAINING IN THE HOTEL INDUSTRY

If statistics are anything to go by, Vietnam can claim to be on the threshold of a tourism boom; the predictions are extremely positive with forecasts of 1,000 hotels to be built in Ho Chi Minh City alone by the year 2000. Tourist arrivals of six million a year are expected (*Vietnam Business News,* 1995). Indeed, the country is gearing up to meet the onslaught of tourism growth. For now, at least, the hospitality industry is faced with obstacles such as infrastructure problems, acute shortages of skilled manpower, low levels of service and the need for professionalism in the industry (*Vietnam Business News,* 1995).

Chapter 21 examines the expectations that senior hotel managers have of their subordinates. Two caveats regarding the methodology are noteworthy. First, the vast majority of the hotels surveyed are generally small in size (less than 100 rooms). Secondly, at least one-half of the chief executive officers (CEOs) interviewed are expatriates and, therefore, their views are not necessarily representative of Vietnamese managers. However, despite these limitations, the study provides some useful observations as well as contributing to the knowledge of hotel management.

The most significant result is that the vast majority of the CEOs regard "soft" human relations factors (for example, handling guest problems, motivating employees, and communication skills) as the top priority over "hard" competencies (for example, financial and technical skills). This finding appears to be consistent with research previously conducted in the United Kingdom and also the United States. However, caution is advised in interpreting the Vietnam results. For instance, since the survey sample consisted of a large number of small hotels, it may be argued that they are smaller, family-type establishments and, hence, such housekeeping skills are associated with them (Baum, 1990).

Interestingly, more than one-half of the respondents ranked legal procedures and policies among the top ten priorities they expect of their subordinates. Baum's (1990) literature review revealed that most hotel CEOs, even in advanced countries, placed much lower emphasis on such competencies than did the Vietnamese respondents. These results may indicate that the Vietnamese sample is generally more ethical and professionally oriented than their counterparts in advanced nations. The study of business attitudes in Chapter 19 disclosed that the Vietnamese are actually less ethical than their counterparts in more developed countries. One possible interpretation for this difference may be attributed to the timing of the study. Many of the sampled CEOs attended hospitality professionalism seminars held in conjunction with the MBA Business Study Mission trip and thus responses could be biased.

CONCLUSION

In summary, the results of the study are useful in guiding hoteliers to develop performance benchmarks by which hotel employees may be appraised and nurtured in their career paths. Designers of hospitality curricula need to keep abreast of research and industry practices to provide the latest training methods in hospitality schools. Thus, the contents of Chapter 21 contribute knowledge in the area of hotel management and guidelines in curricula development as well.

REFERENCES

Baum T., *Responses to the Human Resource Dilemma in the International Hospitality Industry*, Proceedings from the hospitality research development conference, Washington, D.C., August 1990.

Deloitte, Touche and Tohmatsu, *Vietnam Business Profile*: Deloitte, Touche and Tohmatsu International, Hong Kong, 1993.

Kobrin S. J., "Political Risk: A Review and Reconsideration", *Journal of International Business Studies*, Spring/Summer 10(1), 1979, pp. 67–80.

Negandhi A., *International Management,* Allynand Bacon Inc., Boston, 1987.

Posner B. Z. and J. M. Munson, "Factorial Validity of England's Personal Value Questionnaire", *Educational and Psychological Measurement,* Vol. 41, 1981, pp. 243–54.

Robbins S., P. S. Low and M. P. Mourell, *Managing Human Resources,* Prentice-Hall International, Australia, 1986.

Robinson J. W., *Doing Business in Vietnam,* Prima Publishing, Los Angeles, 1995.

Seibert D. V. and W. Proctor, *The Ethical Executive: A Top CEO's*

Program for Success with Integrity, Cornerstone, New York, 1984.

"Vietnam: Asia's Next Tourism Frontier", *Vietnam Business News*, November 1995, pp. 1–12.

SINGAPORE'S INVESTMENT INITIATIVES

Chapter 23

The Vietnam–Singapore Industrial Park*

BY
Ambar AGUSTONO
Pranjal GUPTA
KOH Eng Kheng
GOH Wee Liam

INTRODUCTION

THE REMOVAL OF Singapore's trade and investment sanctions in 1991 and the U.S. embargo in 1994 (Lee, 1995) has induced interest in Vietnam among foreign investors keen on developing a large untapped market with low cost manpower resources. The economic reforms in Vietnam have given its economy a much needed boost and enabled GDP to grow steadily at approximately 8 to 9% per annum from 1992 to 1994.

An ASEAN member since 1995, Vietnam does not yet have the most favoured nation (MFN) status nor a generalised scheme of preference (GSP) treatment. However, with the formal recognition of Vietnam by the U.S. in July 1995, the likelihood of these trade privileges being conferred is appealing to investors. Realising these privileges will permit investors in Vietnam to reach out to the international market.

These factors, coupled with the emerging economic eminence of the Asia-Pacific region in the world economy, make Vietnam an extremely viable investment location. By the end of 1995, for instance, 1,470 licenses had been

* The authors are grateful to Dr. Luu Trankiem for his comments and assistance.

granted for foreign investment projects with a total registered capital of US$19.3 billion (*The Straits Times*, 31 March 1996).

One form of investment which is emerging involves the concept of an industrial park. This chapter explores the viability of investing in Vietnam through the structure of industrial parks. It first evaluates the challenges that a prospective investor might face in Vietnam, and then it suggests how industrial parks may overcome some of these challenges. To explain the nature of an industrial park, the Vietnam–Singapore industrial park (VSIP) is used as an illustration. The chapter then evaluates the extent to which an industrial park can assist foreign investors in overcoming the potential challenges of establishing a business in Vietnam.

INVESTMENT CHALLENGES IN VIETNAM

Vietnam represents a vast opportunity to foreign investors. However, because it is a transitional economy, there are obstacles to overcome in the business and commercial environment that may daunt even the most astute investor. These include the inadequate infrastructure, vague land use rights and labour recruitment.

Inadequate Infrastructure

Unfortunately, Vietnam's infrastructure is in poor condition (Glinow and Clarke, 1995). Years of war have taken their toll on the country's infrastructure. Investors must contend with an infrastructure which can barely support the country's business aspirations. Transportation networks, telecommunication systems, office and factory space, power and water supplies, and port facilities are minimal and underdeveloped. Several infrastructural projects are currently being undertaken in Vietnam by international aid organisations and private institutions. However, these efforts alone are incapable of meeting industry demand.

Land Use Rights

Vietnamese law states that all land belongs to the people but it is under the sole administration of the state. Foreign-owned enterprises are allowed to use land for residential or business purposes. When an investor has identified a plot of land for business use, he needs permission from the owner and the local People's Committee. However, considerable ambiguity exists as to who is the owner of the "land use rights", which leads to inevitable business delays and substantial costs.

Bureaucracy and Red Tape

In a recent study conducted in Singapore (Neo *et al.*, 1995), a sample of Singaporean investors in Vietnam rated bureaucracy and red tape as the most frustrating problems facing foreign investors. The problem of bureaucracy is acknowledged even by Vietnam's Prime Minister Vo Van Kiet: "Although our administrative system has contributed greatly to the achievements of the *doi moi* policy, it has many flaws which need reform and rectification" (*The Saigon Times*, 13–19 July 1995).

The administrative mechanism can be extremely bureaucratic and cumbersome in the application process for an investment license. To obtain an investment license in Vietnam, a foreign investor has to pass through 13 different doors, including 36 intermediary phases. In addition to this, after the license is obtained, nine other licenses are necessary before plans can actually be implemented (*The Saigon Times*, 13–19 July 1995). This process is being improved with the creation of the new Ministry of Planning and Investment.

Recruitment and Training of Labour

Many foreign companies come to Vietnam seeking a low cost and literate workforce. However, the recruitment of labour in Vietnam must be done through the Service Company for Foreign Missions, which is also known as the Foreign Service Company (FOSCO), or through a labour supply investment service company. Only if the manpower supplied by these agencies does not meet the requirements of an enterprise, may the latter advertise and recruit its own staff. Even then, it needs to submit the names of the proposed staff to FOSCO. Clearly, these requirements and procedures complicate recruitment.

Business Practices

Although difficult to verify, many investors acknowledge that unethical dealings take place. A report prepared by the Hong Kong based Political and Economic Risk Consultancy Ltd. (PERC) stated that corruption within Asia is most worrisome in Vietnam, alongside Indonesia and China (*The Straits Times*, 24 April 1996). In 1995 alone, the

Vietnamese courts indicted more than 1,000 people on corruption charges and about 800 people were sentenced to jail terms (*The Straits Times*, 23 January 1996).

Political and Economic Risks

Even though Vietnam is opening up its economy to the world, it remains a communist country under the governance of the Central Communist Party. Thus, there is some anxiety concerning the government's sustained receptiveness towards foreign investors. The PERC report ranks Vietnam as Asia's highest in terms of systemic and socio-political risk. Moreover, despite the Vietnamese government's guarantee of repatriation of profits and non-expropriation of assets, these issues largely remain empirical.

INDUSTRIAL PARKS

An industrial park is a designated area for the production and provision of services in support of industrial activities. An industrial park in Vietnam is distinct from an export processing zone (EPZ) in that the latter is an area designated specifically for export-oriented production. Imports of equipment and raw material, and exports from the EPZ, are allowed to flow through the zones duty free. Investors in an EPZ can take advantage of preferential tariff and taxation levies on the manufacture of goods. An example of an EPZ in Vietnam is the 750-acre Tan Thuan EPZ on the Saigon river which is downstream from central Ho Chi Minh City. Production in an industrial park on the other hand, does not have to be export-oriented. Thus, companies within an industrial park can produce for the local market. However, it is possible to have an EPZ within an industrial park.

Industrial parks provide investors with the facilities, infrastructure and services necessary to commence and operate manufacturing or other industrial activities. These usually include ready-built factories or prepared land lots for lease; utilities such as power, water, sewage and telecommunications; and support facilities such as canteens, post offices, clinics and shops. It is common for an industrial park to be served by a network of roads that connect it to seaports or airports.

In addition to providing infrastructural support, the management of industrial parks may also assist a prospective investor in applying for a license to set up operations in Vietnam. As discussed previously, the process that an investor must go through to obtain a business license in Vietnam can be quite daunting. This difficulty is exacerbated by a recent announcement that Vietnam's Ministry for Planning and Investment is going to be more selective in approving foreign-investment projects (*The Straits Times*, 31 March 1996). The management board of industrial parks can provide a one-stop service to potential investors. Investors only need to submit an application for an investment license through the Management Board, thus eliminating the task of seeking approval from the various individual government agencies.

There are several sites in Vietnam which have been designated for the development of industrial parks. These include the high-tech industrial parks in Hanoi and Ho Chi Minh City, and the Vietnam–Singapore industrial park in Song Be province. Discussions with government officials in Thua Thien Hue province in central Vietnam revealed that it also has plans for a high-tech park in Phu Bai town. The following section focuses on the development of the Vietnam–Singapore industrial park in Song Be district, near Ho Chi Minh City.

THE VIETNAM–SINGAPORE INDUSTRIAL PARK (VSIP)

Singapore's Regionalisation Drive

The small size of Singapore's domestic market and the upsurge in economic activity in the Asia-Pacific region have motivated Singaporean companies to regionalise operations. With large populations generating growing disposable incomes, countries such as China, India, Vietnam, Indonesia and Thailand present huge investment opportunities to Singaporean companies. This opportunity was recognised by the Singaporean government and personally endorsed by Senior Minister Lee Kuan Yew in a speech at the Singapore Business Awards on 9 January 1993 where he encouraged Singaporean entrepreneurs and business people to venture abroad in order to stay competitive.

The Singaporean government encourages local investors to operate in the region and overseas to maintain their competitiveness in the international market and to develop a "second wing" to Singapore's economy. This is a farsighted policy which recognises that as worldwide telecommunications and transportation improve, and trading becomes more global, the world's markets will be open to everyone. Thus, all Singaporean businesses are urged to explore and seize opportunities in the region for tapping new product and service markets.

According to the Economic Development Board (EDB) of Singapore (EDB, 1995a),

> The strategic intent of the regionalisation programme is to build an external economy that is closely linked to, and which enhances, the domestic economy by participating in the growth of Asia. This programme seeks to form a network of strategic zones in key markets with emphasis on building good linkages among our regional projects and domestic clusters.

The EDB provides various incentives to Singaporean companies in planning their regional investments. One example is the co-investment scheme whereby equity partnerships between the EDB and individual companies helps to spread risks in regional investment by utilising the former's information services. These efforts by the EDB are reflected in Singapore's overseas direct investments which reached a high of S$28 billion in 1993, a 25.5% increase over 1992. In 1994, the EDB facilitated 217 outward investment projects, an increase of 40% over 1993 (EDB, 1995a).

However, Senior Minister Lee also cautioned in October 1994 that companies should conduct a careful analysis of their management resources before jumping on the bandwagon (*The Straits Times*, 12 October 1994). He stressed that effective management expertise was necessary for any company investing overseas because regional business environments are more difficult to cope with than the local Singaporean business environment.

The Vietnam–Singapore Industrial Park (VSIP) is a result of the working synergy between business and government leaders from the two countries. The idea of building an industrial park was raised by Prime Minister Vo Van Kiet when Singapore's Prime Minister Mr. Goh Chok Tong visited Hanoi in 1994. The vision that led to the development of the VSIP grew out of a spirit of ASEAN co-operation and a strengthening relationship between Vietnam and Singapore. The vision was also prompted by Vietnam's desire to improve its economy and the livelihood of its people (EDB, 1995b). The Singaporean government's direct involvement in the park is driven by a desire to assist Singaporean-based companies expand their reach beyond the island's borders to create an external wing for the economy.

Following Prime Minister Goh's visit to Hanoi in 1994, a private sector consortium of experienced and well-capitalised companies from Singapore and Vietnam embarked on the development of the VSIP. Intensive studies and planning were conducted in Singapore and Vietnam in preparation for the park's development. The US$52.9 million industrial park has received an investment license from the Ministry of Planning and Investment (*The Straits Times*, 11 March 1996).

The VSIP is a joint venture between a consortium of Singaporean companies and a Vietnamese partner. The Singaporeans have a combined 51% stake in the 50-year project with the Vietnamese partner, Song Be Commercial Import-Export Company (Becamex), holding the remaining 49%. The partnership is a synergy of diverse strengths and contributes a range of expertise and experience in property development, engineering, construction, property management and investments in emerging economies.

Leading the project from the Singaporean side is Sembawang Corporation, a leading engineering industrial group with business interests in the Asia-Pacific ranging from infrastructure development to marine-related areas. The other shareholders are JTC International (a subsidiary of the Jurong Town Corporation), the KMP Group, LKN Construction, Temasek Holdings, United Overseas Bank and Japan's Mitsubishi. Becamex, is a state-owned enterprise belonging to the Song Be People's Committee, one of Vietnam's most successful state enterprises.

The VSIP is located in Song Be, 20 kilometres north of Ho Chi Minh City, the industrial and commercial hub of Vietnam (see Figure 23–1). This location gives companies easy access to the international airport at Tan Son Nhat and the bustling seaports around Ho Chi Minh City. Song Be is also connected by highway to the deep seaport in Vung Tau on the south coast.

FIGURE 23–1
Location of the Vietnam–Singapore Industrial Park

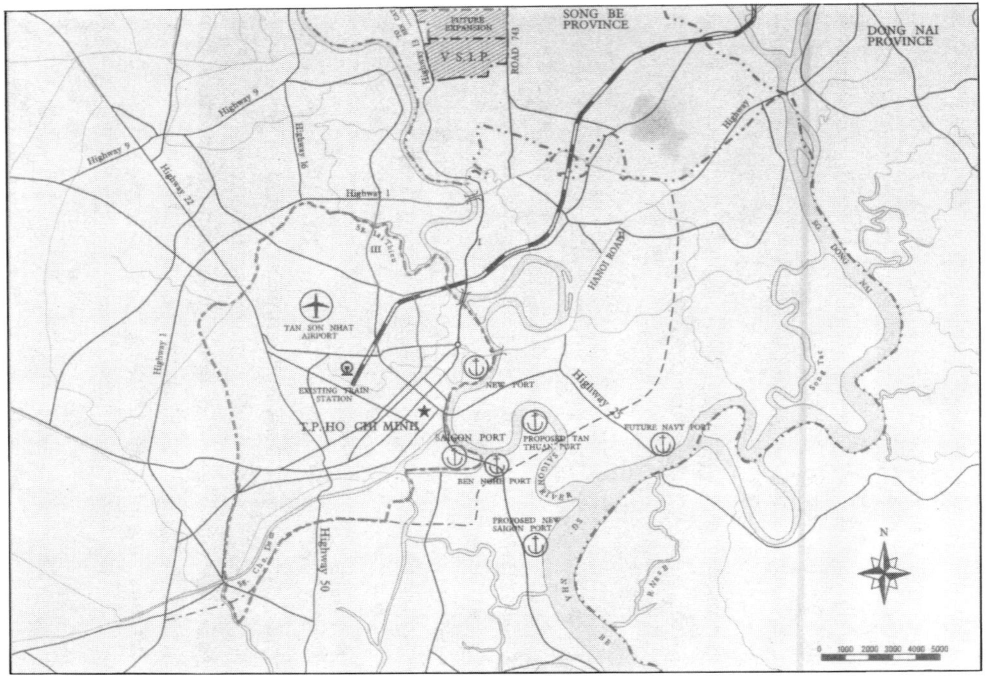

— · · — Province Boundary — — · — Ho Chi Minh City Boundary

Within a 15-kilometre radius of VSIP is a working population of over 200,000 people which provides a ready pool of labour. In addition, investors can draw upon the skilled labour in Ho Chi Minh City. The VSIP will span an initial area of 500 hectares when developed with options for another 500 hectares. Construction of the first phase, which will cover an area of 100 hectares, began in May 1996. The first factory is expected to be fully operational in early 1997. The VSIP offers manufacturing tenants the best of two worlds: management expertise and a reliable infrastructure patterned after a Singaporean style industrial park, combined with a highly productive work force and competitive cost structure in Vietnam.

Infrastructure

Within the park, a network of roads will ensure a smooth flow of goods and traffic. Tenants can look forward to a supply of reliable and sufficient power since the park is building its own power station. In addition to this, tenants will also have access to other utilities such as water, sewerage and telecommunications which will be provided by the province of Song Be. A comprehensive drainage system within the park guarantees that investments are safe from flooding. Prepared land plots are available for lease for up to 50 years and investors can buy ready-built factories for very quick start-ups. Moreover, there will be amenities such as canteens, shops, a clinic and a post office to support manufacturing activities.

Administrative Support

A powerful management board for industrial parks, formed by the Vietnamese authorities, will approve and issue investment licenses. Outside the industrial park, investors must go through a time consuming process to secure investment licenses. The process requires investors to obtain at least 13 seals which means that an application has to go through 13 doors. On average, an investor outside the VSIP has to wait for six months before an investment license is approved.

The VSIP offers potential tenants a one-stop service for the application of investment licenses for projects worth up to US$40 million. This substantially reduces the amount of administration and legwork that goes into the application process. The park's management is also optimistic that licenses can be approved within two months of the submission date.

The VSIP will also provide advice on investment proposals, management and accounting, factory design and construction, labour recruitment, training and logistics. With a reliable infrastructure in place and support provided on operational issues, potential investors only need to make decisions specific to their businesses.

Investment Incentives

Various types of investment structures, including 100% foreign-owned enterprises, joint ventures and local enterprises, are allowed in the park. Companies may export their production output or sell it in the domestic market. There are also plans for an EPZ within the park. Tenants in an industrial park such as VSIP enjoy an exemption from profit tax for a period of two years from the first year of profit. In addition, the preferential profit tax rate of 12 to 18% is lower than the normal profit tax rate of 25% outside the industrial park. Tenants also have the advantage of concessions on withholding tax, as well as on import duties on equipment and raw materials.

Investors can tap the abundant supply of high quality labour at very competitive costs in the immediate vicinity. To enhance the talent pool, the Singaporean consortium will support the Vietnamese authorities in setting up a technical training centre close to the park. Tenants of VSIP will have first priority in hiring graduates from this training centre.

Target Industries

The VSIP is targeting companies in the following industries as potential tenants: consumer electronics; electrical products; automotive components; machinery and metal fabrication; food and beverage; supporting industries in plastics, metals, moulds and packaging; and other light industries. Tenancy in the VSIP is not restricted to Singaporean or Singapore-based companies. Enterprises from any country may apply to set up operations in the park.

SINGAPORE'S EXPERIENCE IN INDUSTRIAL PARKS

Jurong Town Corporation

A key contribution that Singapore brings to the VSIP is experience and expertise in the development and management of industrial parks. The first one established was the Jurong Town Corporation (JTC) of Singapore on 1 June 1968. The JTC evolved out of Singapore's EDB, the statutory board charged with promoting investments on the island. In 1961, the EDB was faced with the development of a 6,500 hectare site in Jurong as the location for Singapore's first industrial estate. The foundation stone for the first factory was laid in September 1962. Within a year, 24 factories had been established. By 1968, some 1,500 hectares of land had been developed. With this accomplished, the EDB then delegated the planning, development, leasing and management of all industrial estates to the newly incorporated entity called JTC on 1 June 1968.

JTC's primary objective, then, was to help spearhead Singapore's industrial development by conceptualising, planning, developing, leasing and managing industrial sites on the island. As a newly emerging economy, Singapore was experiencing a rapidly growing population. Labour intensive industrialisation was identified as the main strategy to absorb the expanding work force. The first industries, therefore, were mainly low technology and low skill operations which helped to provide employment for the population entering the work force each year.

JTC provided a wide range of facilities including prepared industrial land, standard factories, flatted factories, and business parks for integrated manufacturing and commercial operations. The prepared industrial land helped to provide essential infrastructure such as electricity and water. Standard factories helped investors to shorten their start-up time by providing permanent concrete premises which were ready for immediate occupancy and operation. Flatted factories catered to those investors who needed relatively smaller sites by providing multi-storey buildings which could be sub-divided into smaller units to suit their needs. Finally, business parks provided comprehensive facilities to support the operations of investors. All of these facilities were established with the objective of kick-starting Singapore's industrialisation drive.

China–Singapore Suzhou Industrial Park

Singapore's success with the JTC prompted the government to replicate its experience in neighbouring countries, especially in response to Senior Minister Lee Kuan Yew's call for Singaporean companies to regionalise. So far, the Singaporean government and various companies have been actively involved in the development of industrial parks in Batam and Bintan in Indonesia, Bangalore in India, and Suzhou and Wuxi in China. Singapore's experience in developing these parks should serve as a yardstick against which the VSIP can be evaluated. The VSIP can also benefit from the experiences of the Suzhou industrial park in China's southeastern province of Jiangsu since both projects are attempts initiated by the Singaporean government to set up industrial parks in previously closed economies featuring idiosyncratic commercial environments (*The Sunday Times*, 5 May 1996). The essential features of the Vietnam and Suzhou industrial parks are highlighted in Appendix 23–1.

ASSESSING THE VSIP'S EFFECTIVENESS: A SUMMARY

To be effective, the VSIP must offer prospective tenants and, hence, investors advantages that would not otherwise exist. This section summarises the benefits that can accrue to potential investors.

To begin with, businesses contemplating investment in Vietnam may be deterred by the lack of adequate infrastructure to support business activities. However, the VSIP's power, water, sewerage, transportation and telecommunications systems guarantee potential investors a reliable infrastructure. This advantage is further enhanced by the availability of amenities such as training facilities, canteens, shops, clinics and post offices within the park.

Secondly, the park offers investors prepared land plots and ready-built factories which can be leased for up to 50 years. This feature overcomes the problem of acquiring land use rights on an individual basis. Furthermore, businesses which constrained their alternatives to joint ventures with Vietnamese partners because of the need to acquire the rights to use land, now have a new option with the industrial park. Opting for the latter means that they only need to deal with the park's management for the lease of the land or factory.

Thirdly, one of the distinct advantages of setting up operations within the VSIP is the administrative support offered by the park's management. Applications for investment licenses can be made through the park's management board. This one-stop service reduces the amount of transaction costs and administration required to obtain a license. Furthermore, it is likely that by initiating applications through the park, the waiting time for approval will be substantially reduced. The intention, ideally, is for investors to be absolved of all concerns about the administrative and infrastructural support necessary to operate. *De facto*, time and effort can be devoted to business decisions and operations.

Fourthly, the VSIP's plan to establish a technical training centre and give priority to park tenants in hiring graduates of the centre is a distinct advantage. This arrangement decreases the reliance on tedious recruitment efforts through the Foreign Service Bureau or other approved labour agencies.

Fifthly, investors in the VSIP can benefit from the strong connections between the park's management and Vietnamese government officials. Any business dealings which involve interaction with government officials, such as investment applications and customs clearance, can be made through the park's management. This administrative support provided by the VSIP guarantees high operating standards without investors having to ask for favours from local officials or getting involved in unethical business practices.

A sixth advantage, and one that is often overlooked, concerns the diversity of tenants. The type of investors being targeted for tenants in VSIP is quite broad, in terms of industries and nationalities. A wide representation of nations can bring about stability in the park's ongoing operations in Vietnam. There is less chance that the Vietnamese government will intervene or take over the regulation of the park as such action would invite criticism from the home governments of the various tenants. Therefore, joining the VSIP reduces the sociopolitical risk of investing in Vietnam.

Finally, one of the most important attributes of an industrial park that an investor must carefully evaluate is the management. Invariably, this includes the reputation, expertise and experience of the park's management in establishing and operating an industrial park. The VSIP brings together a consortium of companies which have considerable experience in planning, developing and managing industrial park projects. The presence of a Singaporean style management in the VSIP may well be the critical factor that attracts investors who are interested in long-term security and safety in a stable environment.

CONCLUSION

The idea behind setting up industrial parks in Vietnam is to enhance the country's policy objectives on industrialisation and modernisation. Industrial parks certainly can promote the invigoration and development of the technological base of Vietnam's industries. The performance of the parks, and the entities within them, will have a direct impact on the economic performance of the country. For example, employment is enhanced from both within and outside the parks; foreign exchange is generated from foreign direct investments, taxes, wages of workers, exports and import substitution; and the average per capita income is likely to increase. Moreover, the involvement of various global companies in the parks promotes international co-operation in industry, science and technology.

The establishment of industrial parks also results in multiplier effects on the country's economy. For example, transportation, utilities and communication infrastructures become improved; the transfer of technology is facilitated; and, generally, support activities such as training, education, and recreation flourish.

Industrial parks also serve as a magnet which attracts the country's intellectuals, science and technical experts, thus preventing a brain drain or a waste of intellectual resources. In return, activities within the parks help to develop highly trained and qualified personnel, who then serve as catalysts to perpetuate Vietnam's industrialisation. Industrial parks represent a viable means by which investors can establish a presence in Vietnam. They assist investors in overcoming some of the challenges which exist in a transitional economy.

APPENDIX 23–1
The Vietnam and Suzhou Industrial Parks

	Vietnam–Singapore Industrial Park	China–Singapore Suzhou Industrial Park
Company:	Vietnam Singapore industrial park (VSIP)	China–Singapore Suzhou industrial park Development Co. Ltd. (CSSD)
Partners:	Singapore Consortium (VSIP Pte. Ltd.) Sembawang Corporation; Jurong Environmental Engineering; LKN Construction; KMP Group; Temasek Holdings; Sembawang Engineering; United Overseas Bank; Mitsubishi Corporation.	Singapore Consortium (Singapore–Suzhou Township Development – SSTD) Keppel Corporation; Sembawang Corporation; Wing Tai; City Developments; Temasek Holdings; KMP Group; Samsung Corporation; Mitsui–Mitsubishi JV; Rodamco NV.
	Local partner Song Be Export-Import Trading Company (Becamex)	Local partner China National Cereals, Oils and Foodstuffs Import and Export Corporation; China National Chemicals Import and Export Corporation (Sinochem); China Ocean Shipping Company (Cosco); China Huaneng Group Co.; China Great Wall Industry Co.; China National Technical Import and Export Co.; China Energy Conservation Investment Co.;

APPENDIX 23–1 (cont'd)

	Vietnam–Singapore Industrial Park	China–Singapore Suzhou Industrial Park
		China Central Television (CCTV); Bank of China Trust and Consulting Co.; Jiangsu Provincial Investment Co.; Suzhou industrial park Economic Development Co.
Location:	Song Be province, Vietnam	Suzhou, China
Size:	500 hectares (with option for another 500 hectares)	70 square kilometres
Expected Development Period:	eight years	15 to 20 years
Nature of Development:	Industrial and commercial	Industrial, commercial and residential
Investment:	US$52.9 million Singapore Consortium – 51% Vietnamese Consortium – 49%	US$28 billion Singapore Consortium – 65% Chinese Consortium – 35%
Investment License application:	One-stop service for projects worth up to US$40 million.	One-stop service for all projects with no upper limit on investment size.

REFERENCES

Economic Development Board, *The EDB Yearbook*, Singapore, 1995a.

Economic Development Board, *Vietnam Singapore Industrial Park*, Economic Development Board, Singapore, 1995b.

Editorial, *The Saigon Times*, 13–19 July 1995.

Fernandez Warren, "Go Regional Only if You Have the Resources", *The Straits Times*, 12 October 1994.

Glinow Mary Ann and Linda Clarke, "Vietnam: Tiger or Kitten", *Academy of Management Executive*, Vol. 9, No. 4, (1995).

Lee Kim Chew, "Sound Reasons for Formalising U.S.–Viet Ties", *The Straits Times*, 14 July 1995.

Neo Ling Sim, Tang Puay Keng and Yew Huey Fern, *Singapore Direct Investments in Vietnam: Opportunities and Challenges*, Nanyang Technological University, 1995.

Pang Gek Choo, "Poll: Singapore Least Stressful Asian Nation to Work In", *The Straits Times*, 24 April 1996.

"Singapore-Viet Park Venture Gets License", *The Straits Times*, 11 March 1996.

"Stricter Rules for Investors in Vietnam", *The Straits Times*, 31 March 1996.

"Suzhou Park Vies for Place in the Sun", *The Sunday Times*, 5 May 1996.

"Vietnamese Official Flees With $700,000", *The Straits Times*, 23 January 1996.

Chapter 24

Problems in Vietnam's Construction and Building Development Industries*

BY
LOW Wing Kong
Kelvin LIM Kian Pheng
SIM Moh Wee
WOON Ming Hwa

INTRODUCTION

VIETNAM IS AN emerging market of great opportunities and challenges. It is predominantly the cost factor of low wages that has lured many investors into the country since the economy opened up in 1988. The prospect of reaping higher returns in a new frontier has yielded a long list of Singaporean businesses ranging from construction, manufacturing and telecommunications to property development and electronics among others (State Committee for Co-operation and Investment, 1995).

After years of neglect as a consequence of war, Vietnam is now building infrastructure and developing quality hotel, office and residential properties. According to a September 1995 government report, about US$20 billion will be spent on infrastructure construction in the country between 1996 and the year 2000 (Chotrani, December 1995/January 1996b). Mr. Pham Si Liem, Vice Minister of Construction, stated that "More than two-thirds of this amount will have to come through foreign financing."

However, amidst all of the euphoria and

* The authors wish to thank Dr. Luu Trankiem for his valuable guidance and comments.

enthusiasm, doing business in Vietnam is beset with problems (Le *et al.*, 1995) and many investors only realise this after making the initial commitment. Vietnamese Prime Minister Vo Van Kiet, in his recent opening address in the National Assembly, called for swifter economic reforms to overcome deep-rooted problems of bureaucracy and corruption. He further noted that the Vietnamese government needed to consider its "shortcomings and mistakes". Also, shortages of domestic savings, confusing tax policies and a financial system unable to keep pace with developments in the economy, are hindrances to economic growth (Nguyen, 1996). In a constantly changing environment, the Vietnamese government is striving to improve its policies in order to induce future injections of foreign investment into the country (*Asian Business*, January 1996). However, problems in setting up operations in Vietnam still persist.

Given the existence of these problems, the purpose of this chapter is to examine several fundamental issues that bear on investing in Vietnam with an emphasis on the construction industry and the related building development industry. Specifically, the following issues are explored: (a) the supportive nature of the financial infrastructure and tax system; (b) the legal and administrative systems; (c) the management of human resources and technology; and (d) support and logistics problems emanating from the existing infrastructure.

In gathering data to assess these issues, questionnaires and interviews were utilised through a sample of Singaporean companies that have operations in Vietnam. Sharing the views and experience of these firms can potentially benefit global investors who are considering investments in these industries and, perhaps, other industries as well.

SOME RELEVANT ECONOMIC BACKGROUND

Impact of ASEAN on Vietnam's Economy

Ever since the normalisation of relations between Vietnam and ASEAN in 1989, trade, foreign direct investment and official/commercial links between the two sides have been thriving. ASEAN's reciprocal trade with Vietnam rose from US$163.2 million in 1989 to US$1,643.8 million in 1992 – a tenfold increase. Among the ASEAN countries, Singapore is by far Vietnam's largest trading partner followed by Thailand, Malaysia, Indonesia and the Philippines, respectively (Development Bank of Singapore, 1995). Although not in same league as some of the major investors such as Taiwan and Hong Kong, ASEAN countries, nonetheless, have increased their stake in direct investments in Vietnam. Cumulative investment commitments rose from US$179.2 million in December 1991 to US$1.2 billion by the end of 1993. In terms of total direct investment, this reflects a doubling from 7% in 1991 to 15.5% in 1993. This growth has persisted and by early 1996, foreign direct investment exceeded US$19 billion (Luu, 1996).

Within ASEAN, Singapore and Malaysia have led the way in setting up business operations in Vietnam. As of June 1994, Singapore had 60 projects worth US$567 million while Malaysia had 26 projects amounting to US$50 million (Development Bank of Singapore, 1995). Singapore's investments in Vietnam are diversified, ranging from manufacturing and power plants to hotel projects. Malaysia's interests are mainly concentrated in plantations, oil and gas, banking and the hotel sector.

Vietnam's ASEAN membership signals a new era in the relationship between the two sides. Numerous treaties and high level official visits prior to entry, and since, have helped seal the growing links. Singapore's growing economic links with Vietnam have been further bolstered by the signing of a shipping agreement and a trade treaty providing for most favoured nation status and arbitration. Moreover, a "memorandum of understanding" to provide assistance on land transportation, which will be funded by the Singaporean government's US$10 million Indochina assistance fund, has also been signed. Another major project undertaken by the Singaporean government is the Vietnam-Singapore Industrial Park in Song Be.

Infrastructure and Construction

Vietnam's low wage labour force, large population, abundance of natural resources and developing economy have attracted the attention of investors. Increasing foreign investment, a growing expatriate community and the tourism industry have created a large demand for office, residential, hotel and industrial space of international quality. Severe shortages have greatly increased the cost of office and residential rental accommodation and have limited the growth of the tourism industry. These shortages should be alleviated in the next several years with a number of projects due to be completed. For example, the number of available international hotel rooms in Ho Chi Minh City will increase to 9,000 units by 1999 and office space will grow exponentially to 300,000 square metres by 1999 (Chotrani, December 1995/January 1996b).

In transportation development, the focus is on meeting present requirements as well as long-term development demands – defined in terms of scale and technical needs, as well as modernisation goals. Besides domestic transportation, Vietnam must respond to international needs. Thus, proposed projects include upgrading Noi Bai, Tan Son Nhat and Da Nang airports to international standards; upgrading and building several international transit seaports; and international rail links and a highway system which extends to Phnom Penh in Cambodia and other Mekong river countries (The Economics Conference, 1995).

This brief background indicates that construction and building development are important areas of economic development. Furthermore, these areas will remain dominant in Vietnam's economic expansion plans well into the 21st century. These factors thus provided the rationale for examining current problems and challenges facing companies now doing business in Vietnam.

THE PRESENT STUDY

The Sample

A total of 50 questionnaires were distributed to Singaporean firms operating in the construction-related industry in Vietnam. The construction and building development industries are defined as those businesses directly or indirectly related to infrastructure and building construction works. This includes activities undertaken by property developers, contractors, suppliers of material and equipment, consultants and so forth. The questionnaires were sent directly to the managing directors of the operations in Vietnam and 25 responses were received for a response rate of 50%. As a follow up, interviews were conducted with selected responding firms in both Singapore and Vietnam. The interviews in Singapore were done on a convenience basis depending upon the availability of executive managers since all of them could not be interviewed in Vietnam due to time constraint. This resulted in seven interviews in Singapore and six interviews in Vietnam. The size of companies in the overall sample of 25 ranged from small entrepreneurs to large publicly listed firms on the Singapore Stock Exchange.

The Questionnaire

The questionnaire was designed to be open-ended in order to solicit responses appropriate to the specific issue of concern. Eight different topical areas were covered in the questionnaire; namely, finance, tax, laws, human resources, infrastructure, government bureaucracy, technology and logistics. For each area, the questions were phrased to highlight any problems or apparent difficulties that impeded doing business in Vietnam, with particular reference to companies operating in construction-related industries. In some cases, leading questions were asked to invoke agreement or disagreement from the respondent.

Method

To facilitate discussion and presentation of the results, the responses were aggregated across questions and then presented as a percentage of the total usable sample. The interview data was used to confirm or elaborate upon the responses to specific questions contained in the questionnaire. Again, to facilitate the presentation of the results, each of the eight areas of concern is addressed separately in the following section.

RESULTS

Finance

Four questions dealing with financial matters were presented to managers: these included questions on the money market, foreign exchange, banker's guarantees and repatriation of profits. The financial environment in Vietnam continues to present difficulties. The high agreement rating of 88% in Table 24–1 suggests that the money market is weak, especially in the area of raising funds. Difficulties in assessing credit ratings of potential borrowers and, hence, the associated credit risks were mentioned in interviews, and these factors add validity to the findings. All Singaporean companies in Vietnam raise required capital through their parent companies in Singapore. The latter either arrange loans with local banks in Singapore or finance the Vietnam operations via retained earnings.

Foreign exchange is another main concern of foreign investors. Many respondents acknowledged that foreign exchange facilities in Vietnam are not easily available. Moreover, 64% of the firms sampled felt that conducting business in Vietnamese Dong exposes them to foreign exchange risks. Presently, the conversion of large amounts of Vietnamese Dong to U.S. dollars is difficult, and this problem is likely to continue because there are insufficient foreign funds to facilitate a large volume of currency exchange. Furthermore, foreign exchange is controlled by Vietnam's central bank and, because the Vietnamese Dong is pegged at a fixed exchange rate to the U.S. dollar (Development Bank of Singapore, 1995), any exchange exposure faced by foreign companies is that of their own currency against the U.S. dollar.

Financial instruments, such as bankers' guarantees (BG), are required in most construction and development projects. Thus, BGs are quickly becoming one of the emerging banking products in Vietnam. While Vietnamese banks are able to provide such facilities, most clients prefer those BGs which are raised through foreign banks. However, this requires parent companies in Singapore to provide corporate guarantees. Also, given the limited financial position of most Vietnamese banks, it is not surprising that 80% of the surveyed companies encountered difficulties in obtaining BGs (see Table 24–1).

TABLE 24–1
Survey Results on Finance Issues

Description	Percentage of Respondents Perceiving Difficulty
Money market	88%
Foreign exchange risks	64%
Raising of bankers' guarantees	80%
Repatriation of profit	72%

Finally, exporting profits from Vietnam is perceived to be problematic by 72% of the surveyed companies although many have yet to act on the repatriation process. At the same time, profits cannot be repatriated at the full amount because of the mechanism implemented by the Vietnamese government to encourage reinvestment of profits in the economy.

Despite these concerns, it is important to point out that construction and property development investments in Vietnam are in their early stages. The interviews revealed that many investments are still in the construction phase and they have not yet generated profits. However, most managers acknowledged the uncertainties and difficulties that may surface over profit repatriation in the future.

Tax

The corporate tax system and structure pose difficulties for some foreign companies in Vietnam. One of the problems is the frequent changes that have been made to the tax system over a relatively short period of time, even though these were done with the good intention of improving the tax system (Development Bank of Singapore, 1995). Such changes are inevitable, especially in a newly emerging economy, because the tax authority is continuously reforming the tax system in an effort to have a better system. Nonetheless, these changes have caused confusion for foreign companies. Until the Vietnamese tax authority is able to generate an optimal tax system, foreign investors will continue to be frustrated.

As shown in Table 24–2, 64% of the respondents agreed that the Vietnamese tax system is not clearly defined. The present system is a mixture of many imported tax systems and most tax consultants in Vietnam admit that the tax system is still evolving and has some poorly defined elements. It is not surprising, therefore, that just over one-half of the companies indicated that they have difficulties in complying with the tax requirements (see Table 24–2).

TABLE 24–2
Survey Results on Attractiveness of Tax System

Description	Agree
Poorly defined tax system	64%
Difficult to comply with tax requirements	52%
Attractive corporate tax system	12%
High corporate tax bracket	60%

There are numerous taxes imposed on organisations such as the turnover tax, land tax, profit tax, profit remittance and withholding tax, among others. A majority of respondents (60%) agreed that the tax rate is high while only 12% agreed that the corporate tax structure is not an obstacle to attracting foreign investments (see Table 24–2). Apart from corporate tax, some of the difficulties faced by expatriates stationed in Vietnam are related to personal income tax. This tax is relatively high compared to Singapore. Therefore, after tax-considerations become important in the Vietnamese context.

Legal Problems

Since Vietnam embarked on its market economy in 1987, the state has constructed a fairly complete economic legal system. The *Law on Foreign Investment* in Vietnam is prerequisite knowledge for foreign investors before they start any ventures in Vietnam. However, despite efforts to make the legal system more conducive for foreign investment, a number of law-related problems persist.

Table 24–3 shows that 48% of the respondents encountered legal problems in setting up their ventures in Vietnam, and 52% of them found it difficult to form companies and joint ventures. In addition, 44% of the respondents felt that the legal framework in Vietnam does not provide sufficient information to foreign companies while 52% thought that there are inadequate provisions for bankruptcy and dissolution. Finally, 72% of the respondents believed that the laws in Vietnam do not adequately protect foreign companies in the event of a dispute.

TABLE 24–3
Survey Results on Legal Problems Faced by Singaporean Companies

Description	Percentage of Singaporean Companies Affected by Legal Problems
Setting up business	48%
Formation of companies and joint ventures	52%
Information on Vietnamese companies	44%
Bankruptcy and dissolution	52%
Protection by Vietnam laws in the event of litigation	72%

Certain interviewees highlighted that the laws, decrees, policies, procedures or guidelines may change on short notice, and without much consultation from the relevant departments nor any consideration given to affected investors. For example, the new leasing law strips state bodies of their right to lease real estate to foreign bodies (*Vietnam Business News–2*, December 1995/January 1996). This will nullify many existing leases as the government has set out to regain control of vast amounts of state-owned property (*Vietnam Investment Review*, 4–10 March 1996).

A big problem in the past has been the inability of investors to be fully aware of all the laws that might apply to a given project. It is common for a single submission to require approval from more than one authority and the processing time can take years. In some cases, investors have to seek approvals individually from each respective department (Chotrani, December 1995/January 1996b).

However, there are increasing efforts to amend the laws on foreign investments which, to some extent, have eased worries about the legal problems. Investors need to realise that this is an on-going process (*Vietnam Investment Review*, 4–10 March 1996). Furthermore, 14 foreign law firms were recently granted branch status, thus giving investors better access to legal advice (*Vietnam Investment Review*, 26 February – 3 March 1996).

The law on dispute resolution is also changing. Vietnam has signed the New York Convention, which means that judgments from abroad can now be enforced in Vietnam. In terms of domestic arbitration, foreign companies can approach the Vietnam International Arbitration Centre (VIAC) that has been formed to hear grievances (*Vietnam Investment Review*, 4–10 March 1996).

Government Bureaucracy

Table 24–4 summarises the responses on several factors in the government system which influence business operations. Interestingly, 96% of the respondents agreed that the government is too bureaucratic. Most of the companies agreed that corruption within the government rank and file hinders business organisations.

TABLE 24–4
Survey Results on Factors in Government System Influencing Business Operations

Description	Percentage of Singaporean Companies Affected by Government System
Bureaucracy	96%
Connection with government authorities	92%
Corruption	68%
Political Stability	80%

The interviews revealed that government policies and procedures are not considered comprehensive. Some policies have not been updated to reflect the latest developments in economic reform. Also, procedures used by one government authority may not be consistent with those adopted by another. In addition, approval requirements often turn out to be vague. Even where requirements are explicit, it is not clear which government authority will be the approving body.

Other comments revealed that, although the Vietnamese government has drawn up certain investment guidelines, serious inconsistencies have taken place during implementation. Changes and poorly thought out plans have created confusion, even among various government departments. One example is the conflict that arises between policies aimed at maximising land use returns and preserving agricultural land. Another example is the change in the location of an oil refinery, from a viable economic location to a less suitable location in response to environmental concerns. Of course, there is also the perennial conflict of interest between the provincial governments and the central government.

Problems related to ascertaining the actual positions of lot boundary lines have also led to land rights disputes. Various government departments adopt different points of reference for conducting their land surveys. A given lot of land can thus end up having different boundaries that do not coincide leading to land rights disputes between neighbouring parties.

In a majority of joint ventures, the Vietnamese parties generally provide land as their contribution to the shareholding structure. The valuation of the contributed land allows the Vietnamese parties to be only minority shareholders in most instances. However, the Vietnamese law stipulates that even with a minority shareholding, the local party has the controlling vote. This discrepancy is a major point of contention for foreign investors who see this structure as an unfair deal.

Resettlement related problems also create serious difficulties for investors in Vietnam. Even when development plans have been approved by government authorities, tenants tend to take a long time to vacate the development sites. There have also been instances of clashes between tenants at such sites and the authorities (*The Sunday Times*, 19 May 1996).

The government recently combined the State Committee for Cooperation and Investment (SCCI) and the State Planning Committee

(SPC) to form the Ministry of Planning and Investment (MPI) in order to provide a one-stop approval service. MPI is now considering sweeping changes to amend and improve the *Foreign Investment Law* (*Vietnam Investment Review*, 4–10 March 1996).

Human Resources

Human resource issues can be approached from a variety of perspectives. However, in this section the focus is on two areas. First, several characteristics relating to the work force and labour supply are discussed. Secondly, some typical problems associated with expatriates are considered.

(i) ***Labour and the Work force:*** Although low cost labour is one of the major advantages overarching the decision to invest in Vietnam, the experiences of foreign business entities with the local labour force have often been labelled problematic. To be sure, basic flaws in the labour supply framework have caused uncertainty for Singaporean companies in Vietnam.

To begin with, problems can be encountered in recruiting personnel in Vietnam. Over and above the shortage of highly qualified people in engineering and technical fields, it is difficult to source capable, well-rounded individuals who are able to assist in management, business development and so forth. Foreign investors must realise the need to train and develop their local staff in order to facilitate operational effectiveness.

Also, because of the short period of time in which the Vietnamese market has been opened to foreign influence, it cannot be assumed that well-trained Vietnamese personnel can be sourced from existing foreign companies. It is generally understood that the Vietnamese people are very loyal to these employers, who take considerable effort and time to develop their skills. Furthermore, most Vietnamese are interested in long-term careers rather than short-term gains.

These tendencies appear to be supported by the sample responses which are shown in Table 24–5. A majority of respondents considered the local labour force easy to employ (72%), abundantly available (64%), and cheap and competitive (56%). At the same time, however, less than 20% of the respondents held the view that labour is generally skilled and productive.

In the interviews, firms also expressed concern about the delay which arises when security checks are done on prospective employees. An individual employee must reside within the geographical locality of the firm to be eligible for employment at that particular firm. For example, an employee must have a resident permit for Ho Chi Minh City to work there.

TABLE 24–5
Survey Results on Labour and the Workforce

Description	Percentage of Respondents in Agreement
Easy to employ	72%
Abundantly Available	64%
Cheap and Competitive	56%
Skilled and Productive	16%

(ii) ***Expatriate Issues:*** Table 24–6 presents a summary of responses affirming the existence of problems associated with expatriates in Vietnam. For instance, 80% of the companies sampled agreed that recruiting expatriate staff from Singapore to be stationed in Vietnam is difficult; 92% of those surveyed agreed that they have problems with their children's education; and 88% agreed that they have language problems. An interesting survey finding is that problems related to obtaining work permits and being exposed to relatively high personal income tax rates, as well as difficulties in adapting to the Vietnamese lifestyle and housing are perceived as relatively much less significant than the former group of problems.

TABLE 24–6
Summary of Survey Results on Singaporean Expatriates

Problem type	Percentage Affirming Existence of Problem
Recruiting personnel	80%
Work permit	16%
Personal income tax	44%
Lodging/housing	32%
Children's education	92%
Language	88%
Adapting to local lifestyle	40%

Compensation and benefits for local staff have increased considerably with the influx of foreign firms. Due to a variety of cultures and business ethics associated with the mix of foreign investors, the pay structure of these companies tend to differ. As a result of their vastly different corporate strategies inflated salaries are causing an increase in staff turnover.

Technology

Approximately US$20 billion will be spent on construction in Vietnam between 1996 and the year 2000. A large portion of this amount will be allocated to building the country's infrastructure. The task of meeting these development goals has underscored the shortage of skilled workers. While substantial effort has been made to train the local work force – as evidenced by the establishment of vocational schools in Ho Chi Minh City that train about 700 people each year for the construction industry – more needs to be done (Chotrani, December 1995/January 1996a). Another factor inhibiting the growth of skilled labour is the lack of good quality facilities and experienced teachers.

Equally important, and serious, is that a shortage of funds has prevented importing the necessary modern equipment for construction. This shortage has simply added to the obstacles that suppress the improvement of technology in the country. No doubt it will take several more years before the local Vietnamese work force can attain standards comparable to international ones in terms of both skills and technology.

The responses reported in Table 24–7 confirm that many firms have had to come to terms with these deficiencies. A majority of firms (84% of the companies) agreed that necessary skills and know-how are lacking. In addition, 96% of the companies felt that the necessary equipment required for operations is not easily available.

TABLE 24–7
Experiences of Singapore Companies on Technology

Description	Percentage of Respondents in Agreement
Necessary skills or know-how are lacking.	84%
Necessary equipment required for operations are not easily available.	96%

Presently, Singaporean companies in Vietnam are bringing in more expatriate staff to handle their operations, or else they are sub-contracting jobs to foreign contractors. In addition, the Singaporean firms are expending more effort to train their Vietnamese staff. To solve the equipment problem, most companies import the necessary items from overseas. Clearly, these options translate into a higher investment cost in the short-run and potential investors, therefore, need to factor these costs into their project forecasts accordingly.

Infrastructure

Not unexpectedly, infrastructure is problematic in any developing country and Vietnam is no exception. The survey results summarised in Table 24–8 show that firms overwhelmingly view infrastructure in Vietnam as problematic. For example, 84% of the companies agreed that the road transportation system is poor and inadequate. This view holds because roads which are considered good (i.e., that are pebbled, paved or covered in asphalt) constitute only 30% of the total roads in Vietnam. Further, most of these better roads are located in the bigger cities. Since all construction and development projects rely on the regular delivery of building materials and supplies, the condition of the road is a key determinant for prompt deliveries. To counter this problem, companies need to advance their lead times for delivery. They may even have to resort to larger inventory holdings so that material is available when it is needed.

TABLE 24–8
Results of Survey on Infrastructure

Infrastructure Affecting Business Operations	Yes	Neutral	No
Roads	84%	8%	8%
Airports	76%	24%	0%
Telecommunications	68%	20%	12%
Utilities	88%	12%	0%

Air travel is a concern and 76% of the companies felt that it was inadequate. Currently, there are only three international airports: Noi Bai near Hanoi; Tan Son What near Ho Chi Minh City; and Da Nang on the coast in central Vietnam. Collectively, these airports are able to handle a total capacity of 15 million passengers per year. With the level of air transport growing by 15 to 20% per year over the past few years, companies are experiencing increasing difficulties in booking flights into Vietnam from major cities in Asia and vice versa.

A large proportion of respondents (88%) felt that utility services are insufficient and that this posed a problem to their operations. An unstable power supply and power cuts were cited as the main problems. Since power supply is critical only at certain stages of construction, some companies purchase stand-by generators to overcome this problem.

In the area of telecommunication facilities, 68% of the respondents agreed that such facilities are inadequate. However, interview comments painted a rather different picture. A majority of interviewees indicated that they have no difficulty installing a telephone or fax machine. Interviewees also noted that poor connections at times, especially for international calls cause inconveniences. Moreover, they observed that the cost of using the telephone or fax is much higher in Vietnam. But generally, such services are viewed as acceptable, and the cost of such services constitutes only a fraction of total operating costs in Vietnam.

Telecommunications in Vietnam has witnessed drastic changes in the last few years. Many experts and professionals believe that Vietnam's communication system has reached the same level of technical and hi-tech development as other countries in the region and, in some aspects, it has approached international standards.

Logistics

Another concern is the difficulty faced by companies in arranging the logistics to support construction or development projects. In fact, the success or failure of any project often is contingent on a company's ability to marshall together all of the essential information and resources (labour, materials, information on Vietnam's construction laws and so forth) and organise them sufficiently to execute the plan effectively.

Table 24–9 shows that 72% of the companies agreed that raw materials are difficult to obtain in Vietnam. In fact, many essential materials needed for construction either are not available or the locally sourced items are of poor quality. For example, cement would be in grave shortage were it not for four joint venture manufacturing plants that have obtained licenses to start production early in 1996. Also, high tensile steel of 460 grade quality has to be imported. Other necessary imports include bricks for load bearing application, anti-corrosion paints, granites and ceramics, to name a few.

In addition, 84% of the companies agreed that custom duties on imported goods affect their logistical operations. Most companies need to import building materials (reasons cited above) for their projects. Currently, a construction license can be used to waive import duties on building materials for projects. To qualify for a waiver, a firm must above all clearly spell out the raw materials it will import when applying for the license. Otherwise, high import duties are levied on the imported raw materials (*Vietnam Business New–4*, December 1995/January 1996). Table 24–10 shows the tariff rates for some selected building materials.

TABLE 24–9
Results of Survey on Logistics

Description of Logistic Support	Agree	Neutral	Disagree
Difficulties in obtaining raw materials	72%	18%	10%
Problematic custom clearance on materials	84%	16%	0%
High import duties on building materials	80%	16%	4%

TABLE 24–10
Import Duties for Building Materials

Items	Tariff (%)
Cement	10 – 20
Most steel for construction	30
Most glass products	30
Doors and windows	15
Ceramic tile	35
Granite and marble blocks/slabs	2
Finished granite and marble	20

Source: Steve Reid, Indochina Building Supplies, Vietnam.

The interviews also highlighted difficulties in getting imported building materials through customs. Generally, it can take as little as two weeks or as long as several months to clear customs. Relating this problem to the poor road system discussed earlier is an additional reason for investors to factor extended lead times into their project schedules.

CONCLUSION

This study has presented the views from senior managers of Singaporean firms operating in Vietnam with respect to eight major areas of concern when doing business in Vietnam. Although the sample is limited to the construction and related building industries, the solicited views and opinions of these particular firms may be extended, albeit with caution, to other potential business opportunities in Vietnam.

Clearly, different industries and individual firms have somewhat unique, but yet common, operating environments which may not present some of the difficulties elaborated upon in the present chapter. Nonetheless, the message to potential investors is that acquiring information and learning from the prior experience of existing companies in Vietnam can substantially reduce envirnomental and operating risks associated with their investments in Vietnam.

To the extent that changes in various laws and bureaucratic regulations are occurring constantly, the findings from this study need to be altered accordingly. For certain, there is no substitute for actual visits to locations of interest and acquiring the best legal advice available. But then, higher risks are normally associated with higher returns, and this is an axiom that global investors can fully appreciate. Vietnam is currently a land of opportunities which simply need to be managed properly and with due care.

REFERENCES

Chotrani R., "Foreign Technology Badly Needed!", *Vietnam Business News–1*, December 1995/January 1996a.

Chotrani R., "Property Development in Vietnam: Paradise or Nightmare", *Vietnam Business News–3*, December 1995/January 1996b.

Development Bank of Singapore, "Vietnam: New Links With ASEAN", Pacific Economic Development Report, Economic Research Department, Singapore, 1995.

Editorial, *The Sunday Times*, 19 May 1996.

"Foreign Law Firms Get Branch Status", *Vietnam Investment Review*,

26 February–3 March 1996.

Le D. A., J. Vong and R. Kanesan, *Strategies, Problems and Solutions for Doing Business in Vietnam*, Nanyang Technological University, Singapore, 1995.

Luu Trankiem, Speech on "Vietnam in the Asean Era", Singapore, 4 May 1996.

"New Vietnam Leasing Law Worries Investors", *Vietnam Business News–2*, December 1995/January 1996.

Nguyen Minh Tu, *Ten Years of Economic Reform in Vietnam*, Paper presented at the Business Study Mission Seminar, Hanoi, Vietnam, March 1996.

"Raw Material: Import or Source Locally?!", *Vietnam Business News–4*, December 1995/January 1996.

"Scepticism Over Ministry Merger", *Asian Business*, January 1996.

State Committee for Co-operation and Investment, *Guidebook for Foreign Investors in Vietnam*, Investment Transaction Centre, Hanoi, May 1995.

"Steady Legal Changes Clearing Investors' Path", *Vietnam Investment Review*, 4–10 March 1996.

The Economics Conference, *The Third Roundtable with the Government of Vietnam*, Vietnam, November 1995.

Chapter 25

Management Practices and Work-Related Values: Vietnamese Firms Versus Singaporean Firms*

BY
QUAH Chee Yong
Steven SIM
HO Sook Hwa
SOH Lay Kuan

INTRODUCTION

THIS CHAPTER COMPARES two different sets of firms, Singaporean companies operating in Vietnam and local indigenous Vietnamese firms, in terms of their work-related values and management practices.

Since Singapore and Vietnam both have been influenced by Chinese culture, there may be a tendency to view their work-related values and, hence, managerial practices as fundamentally similar. The different political and economic evolution of both countries, however, could lead to different approaches in management styles.

This chapter explores several managerial and organisational aspects of enterprises located in Vietnam. Specifically, it assesses Vietnamese and Singaporean managers' perceptions of work-related values and managerial expectations as important factors in the management of their organisations. The values identified by the two groups of managers in relation to various organisational goals, organisational stakeholders and personal traits are examined. From this assessment of work-related values, the chapter

* The authors wish to thank Mr. Peter Low for his valuable guidance and assistance.

further examines how management practices of the two groups of firms differ in terms of planning, organising, controlling, leading and staffing. Discovering significant similarities or differences could enable potential investors and managers to understand, manage and assimilate into Vietnam's business environment more easily.

RELEVANT PRIOR STUDIES

Past studies have shown that personal values impact management behaviour (Posner and Low, 1990). Since values are at the core of individual behaviour, they can influence the style of management which is practised in business operations. Comparative management is a distinct field of research concerning the way management is practised in different countries. According to Negandhi and Estafan (1965), comparative management research helps to foster an understanding of other cultures and societies where different ways of doing business are often observed.

The significance of comparative management studies has grown in recent years as a result of the expansion and the spread of global markets, intense international competition and increased multinational business. As more subsidiaries of multinationals are set up overseas, more needs to be understood about their operations in foreign environments, particularly with respect to the inter-relationship of the parent corporations and their counterparts in host countries. In the future, therefore, the ability of some companies to compete successfully in worldwide markets may be dependent not only on how well they apply established management know-how but, also, on the extent to which the influence of cultural factors, driven by personal values, is recognised (England, 1987).

Due to increasing international trade and multinational business, many people realise that different cultures need to be managed differently. The assumption of universality in management practices is no longer a valid depiction of reality. Skill transferability from developed countries to third world countries often does not work because the skills are either culturally irrelevant or even dysfunctional in the context of other countries. When management practices are transferred from one country to another, chances of success depend to a large extent on the similarity of the value systems between them (Sekaran, 1984). As a result, there is a growing effort on the part of educators to identify clusters of countries which share similar individual values and value systems.

The impact of personal values on managerial behaviour continues to generate attention from practitioners (e.g., Seibert and Proctor, 1984; Peters and Waterman, 1982) and academics (England, 1975; Posner and Munson, 1979; Posner and Low, 1990). The reason for this interest is that values are at the core of individual behaviour. Values influence the choices that are made, the people that are trusted, the appeals that are responded to, and the way time and energy is invested. In turbulent times that are fraught with conflicting views and demands, values can give a sense of direction.

At the meta level, values are the bedrock of an organisation's culture (Dean and Kennedy, 1982). They provide guidelines for how employees can expect to be treated and, in turn, are expected to behave. Transparent unless challenged, values provide the scaffolding for hundreds of decisions that are made at all levels of an organisation every day. Options that run counter to the company's value system are often never even considered.

Since the *doi moi* reform in 1984, Vietnam has attracted an increasing amount of investment, particularly from countries in the Asia-Pacific such as Korea, Singapore, Malaysia and Hong Kong. The companies behind these investments have brought their own managerial styles and practices to Vietnam. However, little has been done to determine whether or not the managerial styles and practices of foreign firms are different or similar to their foreign subsidiaries operating in Vietnam. A review of the literature reveals that, while comparative management studies have been conducted in many parts of the world (e.g., Low, 1984; Yeh, 1985), little work has been done on this topic in Vietnam. Most of the research on comparative management practices covers areas such as normalisation of the organisational structure, specialisation, planning, authority and feedback systems, the use of staff and committees in major policy decisions, human resource management, performance appraisal systems, training and development.

THE PRESENT STUDY

The objective of this exploratory survey is to examine the management practices and organisational values of managers in subsidiaries of

Singaporean firms operating in Vietnam and managers in local indigenous Vietnamese companies. Singaporean subsidiaries are defined as firms that have 50% or more ownership in the Vietnam operation.

Sample

A questionnaire was sent out to 80 companies in Vietnam and the sample composition and response rate for the study are shown in Table 25–1. In total, 53 responses were collected for a response rate of 67% which is substantially higher than normal response rates for survey type research.

TABLE 25–1
Sample Characteristics

Nationality	Number of Firms	Number of Responses	Percentage Response of Total Firms	Percentage Response of Sub-Sample
Vietnamese	50	34	43%*	68%
Singaporean	30	19	24%*	63%*
Total	80	53	67%	N/A

* Rounded.

Demographics

While this study does not attempt to cross-tabulate demographic characteristics to various organisational characteristics, a schematic profile of the two groups of firms surveyed is presented. The two groups generally share similar characteristics in terms of the nature of the company (consumer manufacturing), functional areas of work (manufacturing) and the position of managers (supervisory levels). However, a large percentage of Vietnamese companies are small in size and employ less than 100 people.

The Singaporean managers sampled tend to be somewhat younger than their Vietnamese counterparts and they also have more education than the Vietnamese managers. Finally, a higher percentage of female and non-married managers comprise the Singaporean subsample relative to those in the Vietnamese sub-sample (see Appendix 25–1).

Questionnaires

The questionnaire used to assess work-related values is reproduced in Appendix 25–2 while the questionnaire used to gather data on management practices is reproduced in Appendix 25–3. The two groups of companies were matched as closely as possible according to the nature of the company and functional areas of work. The questionnaires that were sent to the Vietnamese firms were translated into Vietnamese and assessed for content validity by Vietnamese scholars working in Singapore.

The questionnaire pertaining to organisational and personal values comprised five sections. Section A is designed to determine the importance of 11 selected organisational goals. Section B consists of 16 groups of stakeholders. Respondents were asked to assign what they believe to be the degree of importance of these stakeholders to the organisation. As for section C, respondents were asked to assign the degree of importance to ten personal traits. A seven-point Likert scale was used to measure responses for sections A to C (where **1** represents little or no importance and **7** represents very important).

In section D, respondents were asked to choose three out of ten values (personal qualities or characteristics) that they admire most in their subordinates, colleagues and superiors. Section E consists of a series of questions about the respondent's job and organisation. Respondents were asked to indicate the extent to which each of the questions best describes their job and the organisation. For example, respondents were asked to what extent doing the job well contributed to recognition and respect. A seven-point Likert scale was again used in section E (where **1** represents very little and **7** represents very much).

The questionnaire for management practices was divided into six sections pertaining to organisational structure, controlling, planning, communication, leadership styles and staffing (see Appendix 25–3).

Data Analysis and Method

The results were analysed using the Statistical Package for the Social Science (SPSS) and descriptive statistics were used to facilitate discussion of the findings. The means from various questions for each sub-sample of firms are compared for significant differences using independent t-tests.

RESULTS

Previous studies have shown that there is a close link between personal and organisational values and that a manager's ability to identify with corporate values can lead to increased effectiveness (Posner and Low, 1983; England, 1975). Thus, the following section describes the relative importance of personal and organisational values revealed in the two samples of firms operating in Vietnam.

Organisational Goals

Figure 25–1 compares Singaporean and Vietnamese managers' ratings of the importance of various organisational goals. Singaporean managers rated the importance of organisational growth, efficiency, strong organisational leadership, high productivity and budget stability higher than did Vietnamese managers. One possible explanation for this outcome is that Singapore has a relatively stronger influence of western corporate culture brought in by multinational corporations (particularly from the U.S.) than does Vietnam.

An interesting outcome displayed in Figure 25–1 is that organisational stability is rated the highest from among all of the organisational goals for the Vietnamese managers. This preference may have roots in Vietnam's colonial past. Historically, Vietnam has experienced turbulent times. The country was colonised by the French (1869–1954) and was at war with the United States in the 1960s and 1970s. Given these events, the Vietnamese may have become imbued with a desire for peace and stability at all levels of society. It is probably this feeling of wanting security and peace that is reflected in their ranking of organisational stability as the most important organisational goal.

The overall average across all of the organisational goals for Singaporean managers is 5.72 while for the Vietnamese managers it is 5.31. This difference is marginally significant statistically ($p < 0.072$).

Organisational Stakeholders

Figure 25–2 compares Singaporean and Vietnamese managers' ratings of the importance of various organisational stakeholders. There is a considerable difference between the two groups of managers. White collar employees, owners and "myself" were assessed much higher scores by the Singaporean managers than by the Vietnamese managers. On the other hand, Vietnamese managers perceived craftsmen,

FIGURE 25–1
Importance of Various Organisational Goals

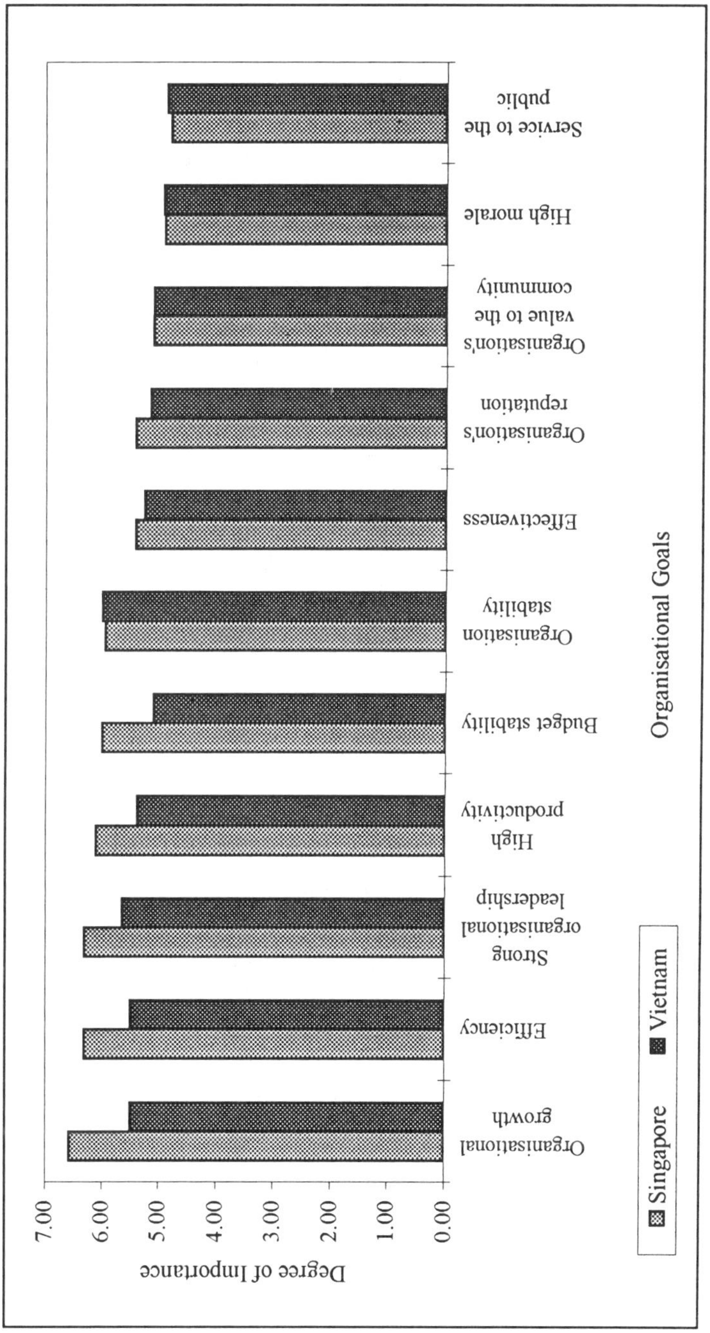

FIGURE 25–2
The Importance of Various Organisational Stakeholders

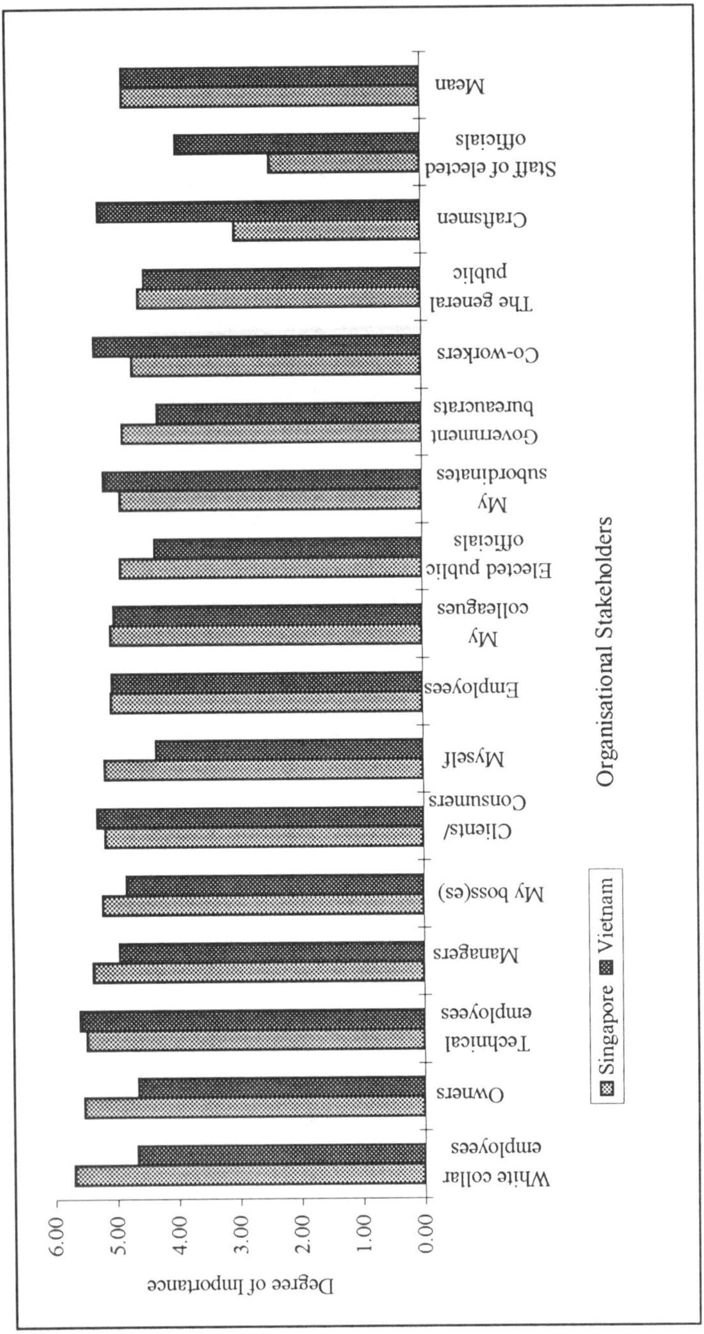

staff of elected officials, co-workers and subordinates as considerably more important than did the Singaporean managers. It may be that under communist influence, the Vietnamese people were generally taught to revere the idea of equality and, therefore, they do not perceive superiors and white collar employees as more important than craftsmen and co-workers.

Personal Traits

Figure 25–3 shows that Singaporean managers tended to place more emphasis on competitiveness, ability, skill, ambition, achievement and success. These characteristics are consistent with the business environment in Singapore. Given the stringent competitiveness in Singapore, managers have to be highly efficient, competitive and success oriented (Chong, 1987). The Vietnamese managers, on the other hand, placed more emphasis on creativity, flexibility and co-operation than did the Singaporean managers. Overall, there is no significant difference between the two groups on all the characteristics considered collectively. The overall means are 5.63 versus 5.72 for Singaporean and Vietnamese managers, respectively.

Work-related Expectations of Managers

Table 25–2 shows the percentages of both Singaporean and Vietnamese managers who considered the various work-related values expected of subordinates, colleagues and supervisors to be among the three most important. More Singaporean than Vietnamese managers expected their subordinates, colleagues and superiors to be competent. A larger percentage of Vietnamese managers, on the other hand, preferred their work force to be co-operative. Singaporean managers also tended to be more self-reliant in that they did not appear to need dependable and co-operative supervisors, which may indicate more decisiveness on their part in terms of decision-making.

Job Factors and Organisation Climate

The results pertaining to job factors and organisation climate are depicted in Table 25–3. Columns 3 and 4 show the means for the Singaporean and Vietnamese sub-samples on items (**a**) through (**o**). Column 5 reports the p-values from independent t-tests on the means for each item. Both groups agreed that they get insufficient feedback on their efforts (see item **d**). Lack of feedback is an important organisation factor that contributes to poor morale, resulting in an unhealthy organisation climate. The means for both groups on the adequacy of feedback are relatively low (less than the scale's midpoint) and show no significant difference. Three other items (**i, m** and **n**) also show no significant difference between the means of the two groups.

FIGURE 25–3
Importance of Work-related Personal Traits

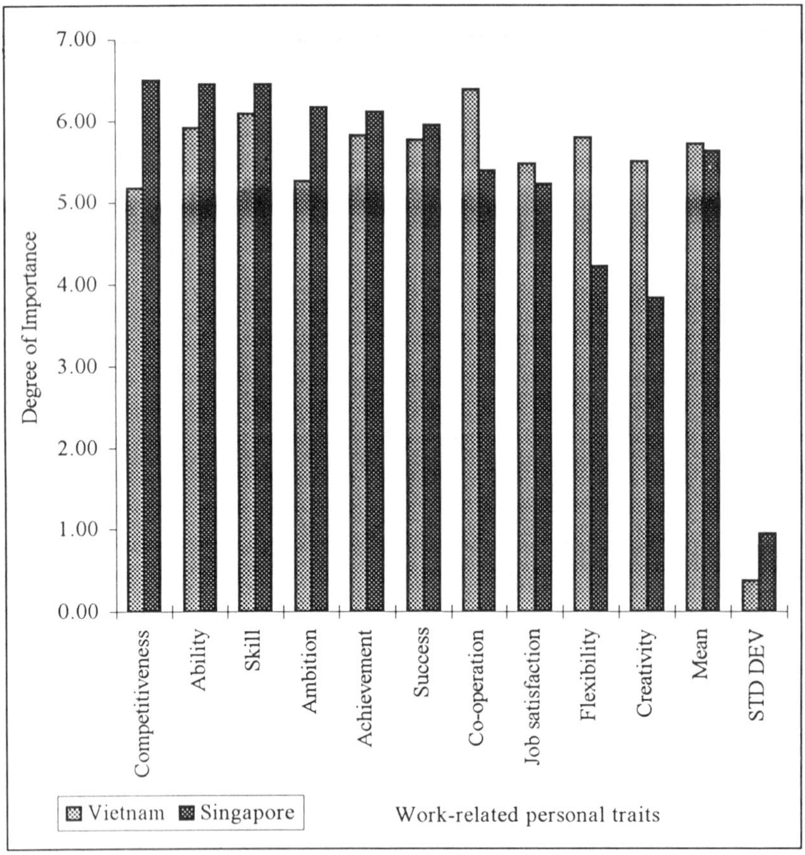

The 11 remaining characteristics in Table 25–3 all indicate significant differences in the mean scores between Singaporean and Vietnamese managers. With the exception of item (**k**), the former group is higher than the latter group. For item (**k**), dealing with perceptions of teamwork, Vietnamese managers' scores are much higher than the scores of Singaporean managers. This difference may not so much reflect a cultural difference as it might simply point to the temporary positioning of expatriate Singaporean managers who need to get the job done efficiently and effectively and then return home to the parent company.

TABLE 25–2
Work-related Values Expected by Managers of Their Subordinates, Colleagues and Superiors

	Subordinates		Colleagues		Superiors	
Values	**S'pore**	**Viet**	**S'pore**	**Viet**	**S'pore**	**Viet**
Competence	32%	12%	33%	21%	37%	29%
Co-operativeness	16%	31%	7%	24%	-	16%
Dependability	28%	24%	24%	23%	-	12%
Determination	8%	5%	6%	-	5%	10%
Fairness	16%	5%	19%	9%	26%	32%
Helpfulness	-	23%	-	-	4%	1%
Intelligence	-	-	11%	23%	9%	-
Integrity	-	-	-	-	19%	-
Total	100%	100%	100%	100%	100%	100%

Note: The numbers in the table refer to the percentage of respondents in each sub-sample who ranked the work-related value in the top three.

TABLE 25–3
Job and Organisation

Item	Job and Organisation Description	Mean S'pore	Mean Vietnam	p-value
a	Your job uses your skills and ability	5.16	4.74	*0.026
b	Doing job well brings recognition and respect	4.95	4.06	*0.001
c	Having influence to do the job well	4.32	3.53	*0.002
d	Get adequate feedback on the results of efforts	3.42	3.41	0.972
e	Department has clear-cut and reasonable goals/objectives	4.37	3.94	*0.016
f	Decisions made at levels where most adequate and accurate information is available	4.53	3.88	*0.001
g	Work activities sensibly organised in your agency/department	5.11	4.68	*0.046
h	The climate (policies, people and working conditions) encourages you to work hard	3.89	3.32	*0.048

TABLE 25–3 (cont'd)

Item	Job and Organisation Description	Mean S'pore	Mean Vietnam	p-value
i	Clear about what is expected of you in your job	4.32	4.00	0.184
j	The senior executives articulate their vision of the company's future	5.21	4.34	*0.000
k	Feel a sense of teamwork in your organisation	4.58	4.97	*0.011
l	Satisfied with your job	4.28	3.53	*0.018
m	Talk favourably about your organisation with people outside of work	4.00	3.91	0.631
n	While at work, think about issues or topics unrelated to your work	4.05	4.15	0.587
o	Effectiveness of organisation	4.80	4.14	*0.000

* p-values < 0.05 indicate that the two means are significantly different statistically at the 0.05 confidence level.

However, the organisational designs of Vietnamese private enterprises are generally structured along simpler lines. Their principal operating units are functional divisions under the control of chief executive officers who often are also the owners. Singaporean subsidiaries are structured along similar lines but they tend to have more hierarchical levels and are similarly authority-centred at the top management level.

Controls

Five control features were evaluated as indicated in Table 25–4. For each control feature, the responses were tabulated in percentage terms for each sub-sample of firms.

Both the Vietnamese firms and Singaporean subsidiaries in Vietnam indicated that top management exercises very strict control in managing their firms. The responses for each group were 90% and 70%, respectively.

The level of formalisation in a firm can be measured by official policies and procedures, and the number and frequency of reports required by management. The Singaporean subsidiaries exhibited a higher level of formalisation (80%) versus the Vietnamese firms (60%). The high percentages suggest that formalisation is fairly prevalent in the two groups of firms and it is consistent with the fact that rules and regulations are greatly emphasised in both countries.

TABLE 25–4
Level of Control in Vietnamese Firms and Singaporean Subsidiaries in Vietnam

Control Features	Vietnamese Firms	Singaporean Subsidiaries
Very strict control by top management	90%	70%
High level of formalisation	60%	80%
Centralised decision-making	95%	92%
High degree of delegation of authority	15%	40%
Greater extent of delegation of routine tasks	80%	40%

Decision-making was found to be highly centralised at the top management level in both groups of firms (95% and 92%, respectively). This result is relevant given that Vietnam is in the early stages of moving from a centrally planned economy to a capitalist economy. Therefore, in this transition phase, decision-making at the firm level is still highly centralised and this is especially so in state-owned enterprises (not shown in Table 25–4).

With respect to the delegation of authority to make major policy decision, managers in Singaporean subsidiaries are more likely to delegate than are Vietnamese managers. Only 15% of the managers in Vietnamese firms delegated authority to their subordinates as compared to 40% of the managers in the Singaporean firms. Finally, there is a high tendency for Vietnamese firms to delegate authority for decisions only on routine tasks (i.e., 80%) which implies that only 20% of all decision-making deals with non-routine tasks. For Singaporean managers, these proportions are 60% and 40%, respectively.

Planning

Considering both samples together, a majority of firms conduct medium range planning extending from five to nine years. However, a proportionately larger number of Singaporean subsidiaries are involved in longer range planning, extending beyond ten years, than are Vietnamese firms (20% versus 5%). One reason why the Vietnamese firms do not plan for the longer term may be due to the fragmentation of the economy into a large number of small local markets. This happens because enterprises fail to sell beyond their immediate local markets. A lack of distribution and marketing channels, a lack of information about consumer preferences and market potential elsewhere (even when such information is available), and an incapability of penetrating more distant markets are the main reasons for the fragmented and cellular markets (Ronnas, 1990).

In a transitional economy such as Vietnam, where the level of uncertainty is high, planning for the long-term is very difficult. Some companies use uncertainty-reducing methods to help strengthen their planning process and develop strategies. Examples of some uncertainty-reducing methods are the use of consultants, such as Price Waterhouse, and computer simulation models. Interestingly, there is a wide gap in the use of uncertainty-reducing methods between the Vietnamese firms and Singaporean subsidiaries. For example, 80% of the Vietnamese firms do not use any of these techniques while only 20% use them occasionally. On the other hand, 70% of the Singaporean subsidiaries use consultants and computer simulation models in their efforts to manage risk or uncertainty.

Communication

Both groups of firms reported that the communication structures in their companies are basically top down. In fact, 85% of the Vietnamese firms and 70% of the Singaporean subsidiaries reflect this type of communication structure. This is consistent with the findings on the bureaucratic structure of the two groups discussed earlier.

The effectiveness of a communication system is also determined by behaviour related to providing effective feedback. According to Robbins (1996), feedback is effective and positive when it is: (a) focused on specific behaviour; (b) given on an impersonal basis; (c) well-timed; and (d) understood by the recipient. Both groups indicated that feedback occurs very infrequently in their companies. Only 2% of the Vietnamese firms and 5% of the Singaporean firms reported that feedback is frequent. Even in limited cases where feedback is received, it is often done on an informal or *ad hoc* basis. This supports the findings of previous studies (Chong, 1987; Low, 1984) where Singaporean firms, particularly the Chinese local firms, did not have any formal feedback system.

Leadership

A large majority of Vietnamese (90%) and Singaporean (75%) managers reported a leadership style which may be characterised as authoritarian. These findings for the Singaporean subsidiaries confirm other research results which suggest that the Singaporean management style is largely paternalistic (Chong, 1987), which yields a leadership style that is authoritative or autocratic (Low, 1984).

Staffing

With respect to human resource management practices, Singaporean subsidiaries adopt a more formal and systematic approach to human resource planning and recruitment. Their approach appears to be in contrast to Vietnamese firms, where recruitment and resource planning are carried out either informally or on an *ad hoc* basis. Typically, Vietnamese labour management operates through a contract labour system (Gates, 1995) that hires workers for a fixed period of time on a fixed salary under fixed conditions. Consequently, it is probably difficult for Vietnamese companies to confidently plan their human resources.

In terms of the selection process, 75% of top management in the Singaporean subsidiaries and 80% in the Vietnamese firms make selection decisions in their organisations. Almost without exception, they decide on senior appointments but they also exert a strong influence in appointing middle and lower management positions. This is one aspect of management decision-making that is not readily delegated down the hierarchy. Furthermore, educational credentials are considered to be critical in deciding important career progress in the Vietnamese firms. Apparently, high fliers in these firms are earmarked for early responsibility and rapid promotion (Barsoux and Lawrence, 1991). The French influence in Vietnam may be a factor contributing to this situation where people are measured by their intellectual achievement rather than their last posting or present salary.

For the Singaporean firms, the criteria used in selecting and promoting senior and lower management personnel are usually determined by training, experience and education whereas non-management staff are usually promoted on the basis of training and experience.

The appraisal system used by the two sets of firms also shows similarities. Staff is mainly appraised by senior management on an annual basis. Singaporean subsidiaries in Vietnam do not have a formal performance appraisal system and they only have semi-formal programmes for their personnel. Table 25–5 indicates that for both groups of firms, more than one-half of the staff do not receive any form of feedback after the appraisal is done. Only 15% of the employees in Vietnamese firms receive feedback as compared to 39% for Singaporean subsidiaries.

TABLE 25–5
Comparison of Appraisal System

Appraisal System	Singapore	Vietnam
With feedback	39%	15%
Without feedback	61%	85%

CONCLUSION

Vietnamese firms tend to be highly centralised with tight control over the organisation by top management. A typical organisation has approximately five hierarchical levels and has a relatively high level of formalisation. The leadership style of the Vietnamese managers is authoritative, with a top-down communication approach. Little or no formal feedback is provided to their subordinates. These aspects of the management function are relatively similar in practice and form to the subsidiaries of Singaporean companies in Vietnam.

In contrast, there seems to be less delegation of decisions in the Vietnamese firms, especially for major decisions that are non-routine. The Singaporean subsidiaries, on the other hand, delegate more major decisions that are non-routine to their subordinates. Another difference is that although both groups of firms are operating in the same transitory economy of Vietnam, where planning is made difficult by the unpredictability and uncertainty of the future, the Vietnamese managers make little use of any uncertainty-reducing techniques compared to the Singaporean subsidiaries.

Differences appear to exist in the way Vietnamese and Singaporean managers attach importance to organisation values. For example, Vietnamese managers rated organisational stability as the most important for the organisation. With respect to personal values, they consider co-operation and helpfulness as important attributes that contribute to effective organisation performance. Singaporean managers, however, view organisational growth, efficiency and leadership as the most important organisational goals. And, unlike their Vietnamese counterparts, they consider skill, ambition and competitiveness as key personal values towards achieving organisational goals.

Finally, the findings from this study confirm earlier research results about how managerial and organisational behaviour differ between local firms and foreign subsidiaries operating in a host country (Negandhi, 1987). An important implication of this study is that as more firms increasingly globalise their business activities, they demand more sophisticated managers who need to be sensitive about how firms are cross-culturally managed in a foreign environment. This caveat may well apply to potential partnership arrangements, including joint ventures, with local businesses in Vietnam.

APPENDIX 25–1
Demographics of Survey Respondents (Percentages)

	Singapore	Vietnam
Type of Company		
Manufacturing (consumer)	79	62
Manufacturing (Industrial)	5	18
Finance/real estate/insurance	0	16
Construction	16	6
Number of Employees		
< 100	26	41
100 – 499	58	53
500 – 2,499	16	6
Age		
< 35	47	9
35 to 40	53	41
41 to 50	0	50
Educational Background		
Did not complete high school	0	18
Completed high school	26	44
Completed some college	26	26
Completed a bachelor's degree	26	3
Completed some postgraduate work	21	9
Position		
Supervisory manager	47	44
Middle manager	26	44
Executive manager	21	12

APPENDIX 25–1 (cont'd)

	Singapore	Vietnam
Others	5	0
Years of Managerial Experience		
< 10	63	82
10 to 19	37	18
Functional Area of Work		
General management	5	0
Marketing	11	9
Manufacturing	63	64
Finance	0	12
Research and Development	5	6
Others	16	9
Gender		
Male	84	91
Female	16	9
Marital Status		
Single	37	9
Married	58	85
Others	5	6

APPENDIX 25–2
Questionnaire for Organisational and Personal Values

1. Listed below are some organisational goals, groups of people, and personal traits. Please indicate their importance to you by assigning them a number according to the following scale:

Section A

	Of little or no importance to me						Very important to me
Organisational Goals							
(a) High productivity	1	2	3	4	5	6	7
(b) High morale	1	2	3	4	5	6	7
(c) Efficiency	1	2	3	4	5	6	7
(d) Effectiveness	1	2	3	4	5	6	7
(e) Strong organisational leadership	1	2	3	4	5	6	7
(f) Organisational growth	1	2	3	4	5	6	7
(g) Budget stability	1	2	3	4	5	6	7
(h) Organisational stability	1	2	3	4	5	6	7
(i) Organisation's reputation	1	2	3	4	5	6	7
(j) Organisation's value to the community	1	2	3	4	5	6	7

(k) Service to the public	1	2	3	4	5	6	7

Section B

Groups of People

(a) Clients/Consumers	1	2	3	4	5	6	7
(b) Owners	1	2	3	4	5	6	7
(c) Managers	1	2	3	4	5	6	7
(d) Employees	1	2	3	4	5	6	7
(e) Co-workers	1	2	3	4	5	6	7
(f) Technical employees	1	2	3	4	5	6	7
(g) White collar employees	1	2	3	4	5	6	7
(h) Craftsmen	1	2	3	4	5	6	7
(i) My boss(es)	1	2	3	4	5	6	7
(j) My colleagues	1	2	3	4	5	6	7
(k) Myself	1	2	3	4	5	6	7
(l) Elected public officials	1	2	3	4	5	6	7
(m) Government bureaucrats	1	2	3	4	5	6	7
(n) The general public	1	2	3	4	5	6	7
(o) Staff of elected officials	1	2	3	4	5	6	7
(p) My subordinates	1	2	3	4	5	6	7

Section C

Personal Traits

(a) Ability	1	2	3	4	5	6	7
(b) Ambition	1	2	3	4	5	6	7
(c) Skill	1	2	3	4	5	6	7
(d) Co-operation	1	2	3	4	5	6	7
(e) Achievement	1	2	3	4	5	6	7
(f) Job satisfaction	1	2	3	4	5	6	7
(g) Creativity	1	2	3	4	5	6	7
(h) Success	1	2	3	4	5	6	7
(i) Flexibility	1	2	3	4	5	6	7
(j) Competitiveness	1	2	3	4	5	6	7

2. Circle three (3) values (personal qualities or characteristics you look for or admire most in your subordinates, colleagues, and superiors).

Section D

Work-related Expectations of Managers

	Subordinates	Colleagues	Superiors
(a) Broadmindedness	1	2	3
(b) Competence	1	2	3
(c) Co-operativeness	1	2	3

(d)	Dependability	1	2	3
(e)	Fairness	1	2	3
(f)	Helpfulness	1	2	3
(g)	Imagination	1	2	3
(h)	Integrity	1	2	3
(i)	Intelligence	1	2	3

3. Below are a series of questions about your job and organisation. Please circle the number to indicate the extent to which each of these questions best describes your job and organisation.

Section E

Job and Organisation	**Very Little** 1	2	3	4	5	6	**Very Much** 7
To what extent does your job use your skills and abilities – let you do the things you can do best?	1	2	3	4	5	6	7
To what extent does doing your job well bring you things like recognition and respect?	1	2	3	4	5	6	7
To what extent do you have the influence necessary to do your job well?	1	2	3	4	5	6	7
To what extent do you get adequate feedback on the results of your efforts?	1	2	3	4	5	6	7
To what extent does your agency/department have goals and objectives that are both clear-cut and reasonable?	1	2	3	4	5	6	7
In your agency/department, to what extent are decisions made at those levels where the most adequate and accurate information is available?	1	2	3	4	5	6	7
To what extent are work activities sensibly organised in your agency/department?	1	2	3	4	5	6	7
To what extent does "the climate" (policies, people, working conditions) in your agency/department encourage you to work hard?	1	2	3	4	5	6	7
To what extent are you clear about what is expected of you in your job?	1	2	3	4	5	6	7
To what extent do the senior executives in your organisation articulate what their vision of the company's future is all about?	1	2	3	4	5	6	7
To what extent do you feel a sense of teamwork in your organisation?	1	2	3	4	5	6	7

To what extent are you satisfied with your job?	1	2	3	4	5	6	7
To what extent do you talk favourably about your organisation with people outside of work?	1	2	3	4	5	6	7
To what extent, while at work, do you think about issues or topics unrelated to your work?	1	2	3	4	5	6	7
To what extent is your organisation effective?	1	2	3	4	5	6	7

APPENDIX 25–3
Questionnaire for Management Practices

This questionnaire on the firm's management practices is to be completed in conjunction with an interview with the company CEO and at least 4 staff members in top management including the HRM director.

(Please tick/delete where appropriate)

Section A
Organisational structure

1. In general, how many levels are there in your organisational structure?
   (a) 3 levels (b) 3–5 levels (c) 5–7 levels (d) 7–10 levels?

Section B
Controlling

Level of Formalisation

1. To what extent are the management operations/activities dependent on manuals, policies and procedures?
   (a) very little (b) little (c) some (d) large (e) very large

2. To what extent are policies and procedures used for strategic and policy-level decision making?
   (a) very little (b) little (c) some (d) large (e) very large

3. Are formal/technical reports constantly required? Yes/No

Top Management Control

4. To what extent are management down the line directly involved in the allocation of resources?
   (a) very little (b) little (c) some (d) large (e) very large

5. Is relevant feedback given to staff periodically? Yes/No/Sometimes
   What areas of feedback are provided? Routine/non-routine

6. Who makes decisions on manpower and career development? On R&D? On marketing strategies?

7. Does management have an open-door policy/system? Yes/No

Nature of Decision-Making

8. Do you decide on policy issues alone? With top management staff? Or involve representative staff at all levels?

9. Are policy decisions made first by top management before implementation or discussed first with inputs from all levels?

10. To what extent are subsidiary managers allowed policy decisions? Routine decisions?

11. How many committees are there generally in your organisation? How are they used?

Locus of Decision-making and the use of Technology

12. How pervasive is technology usage (at some levels? every level? etc.)

13. How would you describe the nature and purpose of technology used in your organisation?

Delegation

14. Who makes unit (departmental/divisional) decisions on:
    (i) budgets
    (ii) marketing – customer needs
    (iii) marketing – advertising
    (iv) staffing; career development; training and manpower needs
    (v) technology

Section C
Planning

1. How long do you normally plan for strategic direction?
    (i) Long range planning (10 years and above)
    (ii) Medium range planning (5–9 years)
    (iii) Short-term planning (1–4 years)

2. Who participates in policy/strategic planning?

3. How frequently do you plan?
    (i) annually
    (ii) half-yearly
    (iii) quarterly
    (iv) ad-hoc (as and when needed)

4. Is planning done:
   (i) formally and systematic
   (ii) formally, not systematic
   (iii) informal and systematic
   (iv) ad hoc

Use of Uncertainty-reducing methods in planning

5. Do you conduct any environmental risk planning?
   (i) formal and systematic using computer models or other quantitative models
   (ii) informal planning
   (iii) ad hoc planning
   (iv) little or no planning at all

Section D

Communication

1. How often is feedback given to staff (on performance, career development, etc.)?
   (i) regularly (say, quarterly or half-yearly)
   (ii) annually
   (iii) sometimes
   (iv) little or no feedback

2. How is feedback given?
   (i) using formal and systematic approach (consultative and developmental)
   (ii) formal approach (merely reporting)
   (iii) informal feedback (confusion and causing uncertainty)
   (iv) ad hoc or no feedback (chaos and causing staff alienation)

3. In general, how would you describe the communication structure in your organisation in terms of the following (describe using/activities to substantiate)
   (i) network (all-round participation and information flow)
   (ii) upward information flow only
   (iii) downward information only
   (iv) little or no communication at all

Section E

Leadership styles

1. In general, how would you describe the leadership style of management in this company in terms of the following (describe using events/activities to substantiate):
   (i) autocratic
   (ii) democratic
   (iii) laissez fairre

Section F
Staffing

1. How do you conduct recruitment, selection, performance appraisals, training and manpower planning in terms of the following:

   A. (i) using formal and systematic approach
   (ii) using only formal approach
   (iii) using informal approach
   (iv) using ad hoc approach

   B. (i) involve CEO, relevant supervisor and HRM director
   (ii) CEO and relevant supervisor
   (iii) CEO and HRM director
   (iv) relevant supervisor and HRM director
   (v) only CEO
   (vi) only relevant supervisor
   (vii) only HRM director

REFERENCES

Barsoux Jean-Louis and Peter Lawrence, "In Search of Intelligence", *Journal of General Management*, Vol. 17, No. 2, Winter 1991, pp. 20–7.

Chong Li Choy, "History and Managerial Culture in Singapore: Pragmatism, Openness and Paternalism", *Asia Pacific Journal of Management*, Vol. 4, No. 3, May 1987, pp. 28–37.

Dean T. E. and A. A. Kennedy, *Corporate Culture: The Rights and Rituals of Corporate Life*, Addison-Wesley, Reading MA, 1982.

England G. W., "Managers and Their Value Systems: A Five-Country Comparative Study", *Columbia Journal of World Business*, Vol. 13, 1987, pp. 35–44.

England G. W., *The Manager and His Values*, Bullinger Publishing Company, Cambridge, 1975.

Gates Carolyn L., "Enterprise Reform and Vietnam's Transformation to a Market-Oriented Economy", *Asean Economic Bulletin,* Vol. 12, No. 1, July 1995, pp. 9–14.

Low Peter S., "Singapore-Based Subsidiaries of U.S. Multinationals and Singaporean Firms: A Comparative Management Study", *Asia Pacific Journal of Management*, September 1984, pp. 29–39.

Negandhi A., *International Management*, Allyn and Bacon, Boston,

1987.

Negandhi A. and B. D. Estafan, "A Research Model to Determine the Applicability of American Management Know-how in Differing Cultures and/or Environments", *Academy of Management Journal*, Vol. 8, No. 4, December 1965, pp. 309–18.

Peters T. J. and R. H. Waterman, *In Search of Excellence*, Harper and Row, New York, 1982.

Posner Barry Z. and Peter I. Low, "Australian and American Managerial Values: Subtle Differences", *International Journal of Management*, Vol. 7, No. 1, March 1990, pp. 89–97.

Posner Barry Z. and Peter I. Low, *Managerial Values in Perspective*, American Management Association Membership, Publication Division, New York, 1983.

Posner B. Z. and J. M. Munson, "The Importance of Values in Understanding Organisational Behaviour", *Human Resource Management*, Vol. 18, 1979, pp. 9–14.

Robbins S. P., *Organisational Behaviour*, Sixth Edition, Prentice Hall International, London, 1996.

Ronnas P., *Employment Generation Through Private Entrepreneurship in Vietnam*, International Labour Organisation/Swedish International Development Authority, Sweden, 1990.

Seibert D. V. and W. Proctor, *The Ethical Executive: A Top CEO's Program for Success With Integrity in the Corporate World*, Cornerstone, New York, 1984.

Sekaran U., "Are U.S. Organisational Concepts and Measures Transferable to Another Culture: An Empirical Investigation", *Academy of Management Journal*, Vol. 22, June 1984, pp. 409–17.

Yeh R. S., "Management Practices of Taiwanese Firms as Compared to Those of American and Japanese Subsidiaries in Taiwan", *Asia Pacific Journal of Management*, Vol. 8, No. 1, 1985, pp. 1–14.

Chapter 26

A Synopsis of Singapore's Investment Initiatives

BY
LUU Trankiem

INTRODUCTION

VIETNAM'S RECENT ECONOMIC success is attributable to an ambitious adjustment and reform programme which it has undertaken without significant support from the outside. After years of isolation, Vietnam can look forward to receiving an expanding volume of foreign aid and foreign direct investment (FDI). With its admission in 1995 as a full member of the Association of Southeast Asian Nations (ASEAN), Vietnam received over US$3 billion of FDI from ASEAN member nations. Singapore-based firms are active in Vietnam and currently represent a major overseas source of investment capital and management capacity.

The three preceding chapters provide detailed examinations of specific projects and industries in which Singapore has played a major role: the Vietnam-Singapore Industrial Park, Vietnam's construction and building development industries, and a cross-cultural comparison of management practices across Singapore and Vietnamese enterprises.

THE VIETNAM–SINGAPORE INDUSTRIAL PARK (VSIP)

The vision that led to the VSIP development grew not only out of a spirit of ASEAN co-operation and the strengthening relationship between Vietnam and Singapore, but it also grew out of Vietnam's intense desire to improve the country's economy. The idea of setting up the VSIP resulted from the emerging synergy between business and government leaders in the two countries. The VSIP will offer its manufacturing tenants the best of both worlds: the management expertise and reliable infrastructure of a Singapore-style industrial park combined with the highly productive work force and competitive cost structure in Vietnam.

VSIP, a joint venture between a consortium of Singaporean companies and Becamex, the Vietnamese partner, offers many advantages. These are discussed in detail in Chapter 23 and include the following highlights.

The Vietnam Advantage

Vietnam has a large and literate population of over 75 million potential consumers. It is also well-linked to the world and to the region, in particular. Trade with, and investment from, the dynamic economies of Southeast Asia, will accelerate with its ASEAN membership. The formal recognition of Vietnam by the U.S., with the likelihood of access to trade privileges such as generalised scheme of preference (GSP) treatment and most favoured nation (MFN) status, will further integrate the Vietnamese economy with the world and allow investors in Vietnam to reach out to the international market.

A Strategic Location

The VSIP is located near Ho Chi Minh City, the industrial and commercial hub of Vietnam. This location gives companies easy access to the international airport at Tan Son Nhat and the bustling seaports around Ho Chi Minh City which are connected by highway to the deep seaport in Vung Tau on the south coast. Within a 15 kilometre radius of VSIP is a working population of over 200,000 people providing a ready pool of labour.

The Singapore Advantage

Singapore's reliable infrastructure, comprehensive services and professional management will ensure its tenants a quick start and smooth operation. A powerful Management Board governing the industrial park will approve and issue investment licenses. This one-stop service is open to all applications of investment licenses for projects worth up to US$40 million.

Various types of investment structures, including 100% foreign-owned enterprises, joint ventures and local enterprises are allowed in the VSIP. Companies may export their production output or sell it in the domestic market. Tenants enjoy an exemption on profit tax for a period of two years from the first year of profit and a preferential profit tax rate of 12 to 18%, including import duties on equipment and raw materials.

The chapter highlights many investment problems such as inadequate infrastructure, limited term on land use rights, bureaucracy and red tape, unethical business practices and other economic risks. Similar to the Singapore–Suzhou Industrial Park in China, VSIP is a flagship project underscoring the co-operation between the Vietnamese and Singaporean governments. Both parties are interested in the success of the venture. This commitment could overcome many obstacles that currently beset FDI in Vietnam.

VIETNAM'S CONSTRUCTION AND BUILDING INDUSTRIES

After years of neglect as a consequence of war, Vietnam is now building infrastructure and developing quality hotels, office and residential properties. Chapter 24 examines fundamental issues of interest to consortium and related building development industries.

Establishing and protecting property rights is one of the important roles of the state in any market economy. In the case of Vietnam, the strengthening of laws on property rights in land and labour markets in recent years has been instrumental in sparking the large-scale recovery of the economy. Of particular importance is the right to use land: Vietnam is a country where land is the most important asset, followed by human resources. The lack of financing and an undeveloped banking system force foreign investors to arrange all their financing overseas. This results in slower implementation and higher transaction costs. The lack of acceptance for check banking services and the system's newness impose further constraints on construction project implementation since all transactions must be carried out in cash.

Problems in rights to use private property are pervasive in many areas, with notable impacts in the building industry. Foreign investors feel uncomfortable with the current weak, and sometimes poorly enforceable, legal framework. In the finance sector, borrowing is also constrained by a legal system which prohibits the use of real property as collateral for lending purposes. This is a key issue that the government needs to address as part of its reforms of the legal framework and the financial sector. These changes would facilitate growth in the construction and building industries. The findings in Chapter 24 show that 72% of the respondents believed that the laws in Vietnam do not adequately protect foreign companies in the event of a dispute.

Approximately US$20 billion will be spent on construction in Vietnam between 1996 and the year 2000. A large portion of this amount will be allocated to building the country's infrastructure. However, the task of achieving these development goals is thwarted by a shortage of skilled workers, lack of logistics to support construction and development projects, inadequate transportation system, lack of essential construction materials and high import duties levied on raw materials.

One of the most important findings in Chapter 24 is that, despite enormous difficulties encountered in the construction industry in Vietnam, foreign companies need to maintain their motivation, take challenges and continue to explore opportunities. This requires a long-term view of this fast-moving market economy, finding a good and reliable partner, and cultivating and maintaining friendships.

MANAGEMENT PRACTICES AND WORK-RELATED VALUES: VIETNAMESE FIRMS VERSUS SINGAPOREAN FIRMS

Since the *doi moi* reform, Vietnam has attracted an increasing amount of investment, particularly from countries in the Asia-Pacific such as Korea, Singapore, Malaysia and Hong Kong. These foreign investors bring their own managerial styles and practices to Vietnam. Vietnamese wages are low, although productivity is limited by traditions which make a large work force rather difficult to control. Further, expatriate managers report that urban workers are relatively well-educated but they tend to hop from job to job, so that turnover rates are very high and the value of their skills is diluted (*The Economist*, 21 September 1996). Since these issues can be contained only through competent human resource management practices, Chapter 25 is extremely relevant to joint ventures in Vietnam because they must make critical decisions about how to manage their local work force and whom to select as managers.

This chapter explores the managerial and organisational aspects of enterprises operating in Vietnam. It compares Vietnamese and Singaporean perceptions of work-related values and managerial expectations in the management of their organisations. The impact of personal values on managerial behaviour has generated much attention from practitioners. Values can give a sense of direction and provide guidelines on how employees can expect to be treated and, in turn, are expected to behave. The study presented in Chapter 25 deals with normalisation of the organisational structure, specialisation, planning, authority and feedback systems, the use of staff and committees in major policy decision-making, human resource management, performance appraisal systems, training and development.

Vietnamese firms tend to be highly centralised with tight control over the organisation by top management. The leadership style of the Vietnamese managers is authoritative with strong top-down communication. Little or no feedback is sought, nor is delegation of authority given to subordinates. Singaporean subsidiaries tend to delegate authority for non-routine decisions. Although both groups of firms operate in the same transitory economy, Vietnamese managers make little use of uncertainty-reducing techniques compared to managers in the Singaporean subsidiaries in Vietnam.

Vietnamese managers rated organisational stability as the most important factor for the organisation. With respect to personal values, they consider co-operation and helpfulness as important attributes that contribute to effective organisation performance. Singaporean managers, however, view organisational growth, efficiency and leadership as the most important organisational goals. And, contrary to their Vietnamese counterparts, they consider skill, ambition and competitiveness as key personal values necessary for achieving organisational goals.

The most important implication from the findings of this study is that as more firms globalise their business activities, they demand more sophisticated managers who need to understand and be sensitive to the way firms are cross-culturally managed in a foreign environment.

CONCLUSION

Regional interaction creates conditions that will push Vietnamese enterprises outward, and increase access to foreign investment capital, new technologies and regional markets; at the same time, potential investors gain access to Vietnam's growing markets and source of skilled and inexpensive labour. However, this interaction requires Vietnam to harmonise key laws and administrative procedures with those throughout the region.

The three chapters in this section address the perspective of regional interaction as a source of mutual benefit to Vietnam and her neighbours. VSIP will offer its manufacturing tenants the best of both worlds; management expertise and the reliable infrastructure of a Singaporean-style industrial park, combined with a highly productive work force and competitive cost structure in Vietnam.

There are many opportunities in the construction industry, as Vietnam is now building infrastructure and developing hotels, office and residential properties. The government needs to continue advancing the legal and regulatory framework for market activity. Property rights over land is an important legal and economic issue. The current regime for land use is not well-suited to a market economy; land use rights have a brief tenure, are not tradable and cannot be mortgaged. It is critical to have a revised land law lengthening the tenure of use rights over land, allowing land use rights to be traded in a free market and permitting land use rights to be mortgaged. Changes in the framework governing foreign investors are needed that abandon the veto power of minority partners in joint ventures and reduce the number of agencies approving foreign licenses.

As Vietnam accommodates these important tasks, the flow of capital and technology will increasingly enter Vietnam and production will rise rapidly. Once dynamic growth via regional interaction is set in motion, Vietnam will be well on its way to joining the other successful tigers in East Asia.

REFERENCE

"Asia's Costly Labour Problems", *The Economist*, 21 September 1996, p. 72.

CONCLUSION

Chapter 27

Vietnam: Some Current Challenges

BY
Ashish LALL

STATE OF THE ECONOMY

VIETNAM'S ECONOMIC PERFORMANCE thus far has been encouraging. Although economic reform, or *doi moi,* was introduced in 1986, serious implementation only began after the withdrawal of Vietnamese troops from Cambodia in 1989. This led to the normalisation of relations with western European and Asian countries. However, initial reform success suffered a setback due to the collapse of the Soviet Union that resulted in Vietnam's loss of Soviet aid and preferential trading arrangements among members of the Soviet bloc. Nonetheless, during the period 1991 to 1995, annual average real GDP growth exceeded 8%, resulting in a doubling of nominal per capita GDP which reached US$220 in 1995. Real per capita GDP increased by about 30% over the five year period (Country Report, 1996). The current macro economic climate remains delicate, with inflation in the double digit territory and growing twin deficits.

Unlike the newly industrialising economies, Vietnam is starting its journey toward industrialisation in an increasingly liberal trading environment. Thus, its economic growth cannot have protectionist and anti-competitive underpinnings as was the case in countries such as South Korea. In July 1995, Vietnam became the seventh member of ASEAN and in January

1996 it joined the ASEAN Free Trade Association (AFTA). This organisation is seeking free trade within ASEAN by 2003, reducing tariffs to 5% or less. Vietnam has until 2006 to meet this goal. The advantage to Vietnam is that the liberal trading regime will allow it much needed market access once commercial relations with the U.S. are normalised and it is granted most favoured nation (MFN) status by the U.S. under the Generalised Scheme of Preferences, but more so when it joins the World Trade Organisation (WTO). The disadvantage is that its economy is simply not competitive in many sectors.

A moderate slow-down is expected in the economic performance of Vietnam in 1997. In the first six months of 1996, 148 FDI projects worth US$2.6 billion were approved. Compared to the same period in 1995, these figures are lower by 58 projects and US$1.12 billion, respectively. For the first eight months of 1996, the trade deficit was US$3.25 billion as compared to US$2.3 billion for the whole of 1995 (*Vietnam Economic Times*, October 1996). Forecasts for 1997 by the Union Bank of Switzerland (*New Horizon Economics*, 1996) indicate real GDP growth of 8.6%, consumer price inflation at 9.5%, and an increase in the budget deficit and foreign debt.

While the various sections of the book have covered important sectors of the Vietnamese economy in terms of business and investment opportunities, two areas need to be highlighted. One is the agricultural sector. Not only is this sector the largest employer, but nearly three-quarters of Vietnam's population relies on agriculture for its livelihood. As a percentage of national output, agriculture declined to 29% in 1994 from 45% in 1988 (Country Report, 1996). However, there are rich opportunities in this sector. The second area is more critical and is related to the first. In order to sustain the momentum of reform, Vietnam needs to upgrade its infrastructure. This calls for both a supply response and demand management through appropriate pricing. The following discussion deals with these two areas.

PRODUCE AND POULTRY

Vietnam cultivates 600,000 hectares of fruit and vegetables at present and plans to increase this to 1.6 million hectares by the year 2000. However, the glorious days of the fresh produce industry were the 1980s when the Soviet bloc was Vietnam's biggest customer. In 1988, Vietnam's fresh produce exports to the Soviet Union were valued at

US$40 million. In addition, eastern European countries spent about US$8 million per year on Vietnamese fruit and vegetables. In 1995, however, exports of these products only brought in US$21.2 million (*Vietnam Economic Times*, October 1996).

The Vietnam Vegetable Export Company (Vegetexco) is the key player in this sector and it operates 17 processing factories which have antiquated equipment. As a result, packaging cost is a very high proportion (about 50%) of the total cost of processed produce. In addition, produce packaged by Vegetexco does not meet international hygiene standards. The master plan of the Ministry of Agricultural and Rural Development calls for $380 million to develop the industry; however, the state budget is only able to cover 0.2% of this amount. This sector is actively seeking foreign capital but, in the meantime, Vegetexco continues to look eastward and plans to open a subsidiary in Russia.

Marine products are the second ranked export after crude oil but Vietnam has no port specialising in marine products. In August 1996, the government approved a US$71 million project (of which US$57 is from the Asian Development Bank) to re-orient ten ports towards the fishing industry but, as with many other infrastructure projects, progress is slow and the completion date uncertain. Vietnam currently has 164 processing factories, about two-thirds of which are operating in the red because of outdated equipment. Moreover, most processing plants are located in cities, with few facilities such as refrigeration available in the farming areas. As a result, most of the exports are unprocessed. The government has set a target of producing 1.6 million tonnes of marine products with an export turnover of $1.3 billion by the year 2000. This will require an investment of US$600 million which is double the amount invested over the last 14 years. As of June 1996, there were 22 foreign projects worth only US$60 million in this sector.

Chickens and chicken feed are lucrative businesses in Vietnam. Vietnam's current consumption of chicken is between two and 2.4 kilograms per person per year and is expected to increase with growth in income. Consumption in neighbouring Thailand, for example, is three times larger. This industry provides quick and lucrative returns so the government has decided to allow local firms to share in the profits by restricting foreign involvement to joint ventures rather than allowing 100% foreign ownership.

While the major players are Thai, a French firm (Proconco) invested US$6.5 million in a farm in Dong Nai province and realised a turnover of US$38 million in 1995 and turnover is expected to increase to US$60 million in 1996 (*Vietnam Economic Times,* September 1996). The company is also entering the feed market and plans on setting up four factories in the next few years with each one expected to produce about 200,000 tonnes of feed per year. The major local company (Vietnam Poultry Farming Company) is unable to compete. Its production in 1995 was one-half that of the previous year. It is estimated that development of this industry will require a minimum investment of US$100 million over the next few years.

Coffee accounts for about one-quarter of the value of Vietnam's agricultural exports. Recently, there has been a resurgence in coffee production which had declined due to dwindling demand from the Soviet bloc. Because of *doi moi*, 75% of the coffee industry is now in private hands. In 1995, coffee exports generated US$200 million. Singapore is the major export market, accounting for 60 to 65% of total exports. Unfortunately this resurgence in demand is exacting a large social cost. In 1995, coffee cultivation grew by 30,000 hectares in the main growing region of Daklak, bringing the total area under cultivation to over 157,000 hectares (*Vietnam Economic Times,* July 1996). The immediate concern in the region is environmental as farmers have cut down 10,000 hectares of forest in the process. In addition, more than 300,000 people have migrated to Daklak over the last three years thus putting substantial strain on the existing infrastructure, health and education systems.

One common theme emerging from the above discussion is that there is little added value to Vietnam's agricultural and fishery exports. Processing these products prior to export would increase export earnings, generate employment in the rural sector and probably lead to more equitable growth. In the mid-1980s, about 70% of the population had incomes below the poverty line. Even with a decline to 50% in 1995 (*Vietnam Economic Times,* October 1996), regional disparities remain high. Nearly 71% of the population in the north and 33% of that in the south live below the poverty line, with 90% of the poor people living in the rural areas.

The second common theme that emerges is that equipment in the local processing industry is antiquated and the government can only provide a fraction of the required financing. One solution to this problem is leasing. World bank statistics show that, from 1988 to 1994, leasing in developing countries increased from US$13 to US$44 billion (*Vietnam Economic Times,* October 1996). Vietcom Bank provided Vietnam's first leasing service through a subsidiary established in 1995. In the first ten months, 23 contracts worth US$1.8 million were processed. However, the existing legal framework needs to be strengthened before an active leasing market can develop in Vietnam.

Similar to other countries in the region such as Thailand and Malaysia, Vietnam needs to actively seek FDI in its agriculture, forestry and fisheries sectors. As of 14 September 1996, the total stock of FDI committed to (but not there yet)Vietnam was US$22 billion (*Vietnam Economic Times,* October 1996). Agriculture and forestry accounted for US$385 million and fisheries a mere US$61 million. However, future development of the fisheries industry, and indeed that of the entire economy, critically depends upon infrastructure.

PHYSICAL INFRASTRUCTURE

Infrastructure, or lack thereof, plays a decisive role in the location of FDI. In 1995, the French company TOTAL spent millions of dollars on a feasibility study for setting up an oil refinery in south Vietnam. However, the preferred government site was Dung Quat (south of Da Nang in central Vietnam). This site is 1,200 kilometres from the offshore source of crude oil and its distance (by road) from the major demand centre, Saigon, is 800 kilometres. TOTAL withdrew from the project citing high transportation and infrastructure costs. The project is now slated for development by Petro Vietnam with Malaysian, South Korean and Taiwanese partners, but they also refuse to develop the infrastructure. Nonetheless, the project is expected to be operational by the year 2000.

There are some 8,000 bridges in Vietnam covering about 110 kilometres (*Vietnam Economic Times*, June 1996). Approximately 80% are in need of repair and many of them cannot support modern 20 tonne container-bearing trucks. In 1990, the World Bank agreed to provide a US$158 million loan to rehabilitate Highway 1, the country's main transportation artery. The project has been held up for two reasons. The first relates to compensation for those people who will be relocated, and the second is disagreement regarding the width of the right of way section on both sides of the highway. At present, the only source of funding for upgrading roads and bridges is overseas development assistance, primarily from the World Bank, Asian Development Bank (ADB) and Japan. The state limit on expenditures for roads over the period 1997 to 2003 is US$575 million while the expenditure needed is about US$4 billion.

Vietnam plans to raise power generating capacity by 2,600 MW before the year 2000 and by another 11,000 MW before the year 2010. Thus, planned production is expected to double from present levels to around 27 billion kilowatt hours by the year 2000 and increase further to 75 billion kilowatt hours by 2010. In addition, the country plans to renovate the transmission and distribution system.

Only 199 of Vietnam's 521 urban centres have a piped treated water supply. These water systems serve about 47% of the country's urban population, or about 7.5 million people. In Hanoi, for example, water capacity has doubled to 340,000 cubic meters per day since 1985 but this only meets the needs of 40% of the city's population. However, 71.4% of this is non-revenue water. A little less than one-half (43%) of non-revenue water represents leakage due to the age of the pipes and the remainder is accounted for by consumers who do not have water meters. Hanoi Water Business Company collects a flat tariff or a standard household fee of VND 4,000 per month. Over the period 1995 to 2000, Vietnam expects to receive US$1 billion for water sanitation and supply (*Vietnam Economic Times,* September 1996).

Vietnam's infrastructure development plans are reminiscent of the ambitious Soviet style plans. These ambitions are not matched by the planned budgetary outlay on infrastructure. Thus, the billion dollar question remains unanswered: where is the money going to come from? The pockets of parastatal bodies, such as the World Bank and ADB, are not deep enough. Build-operate-transfer (BOT) and its many variants are feasible alternatives, particularly for telecommunications, air and sea ports, and for electric power; however, the government has been unwilling to allow companies sufficiently long terms of operation. In addition, it has to allow for substantial price increases which may be politically unacceptable. The water pricing policy in Hanoi bears no relation to use and, therefore, it encourages water use. Presently, there are only three BOT projects under way in Vietnam: the gas-fired Phu May II, Phase II power plant; the Ben Dinh-Sao Mai port; and a thermal power plant in the northern province of Qunag Ninh (*Vietnam Economic Times,* August 1996).

THE ROAD AHEAD

An important issue that will determine the future of Vietnam is how well it is able to balance economic reform and its political ideology. The government would like the benefits of FDI while keeping out "foreign cultural influence and social ills". In order to further this objective, it recently proposed establishing party cells and party controlled unions in foreign enterprises (*Vietnam Economic Times*, August 1996). Foreign investors do not care about the political party in power; instead, they seek a transparent and stable business environment. Central to the contradiction between Vietnam's economic and political paradigms, is the issue of property rights. In order to function effectively, markets require well-defined and enforceable property rights. While it is unlikely that Vietnam is going to turn back on its chosen economic path, continuing on that path may necessitate a change in the political paradigm at some point in the future. Nonetheless, there are some very lucrative business opportunities in Vietnam ranging from sophisticated telecommunications systems to agricultural products.

In summary, Vietnam has achieved remarkable progress in a short period of time. More importantly for investors, Prime Minister Vo Van Kiet and members of Vietnam's National Assembly are acutely aware of the need to enhance competitiveness in export markets and to pursue vital infrastructure construction (*The Straits Times*, 16 October 1996). Concomitantly, the government wishes to preserve Vietnam's cultural identity while improving the per capita standard of living. Naturally, the government wants the population to share in the economic returns which motivate global investors to consider Vietnam's business opportunities. This is a delicate balance and there are no pre-ordained frameworks for success. Understanding this balance combined with transparent economic intentions is perhaps the golden key for successful foreign investment in Vietnam.

REFERENCES

Country Report, *Vietnam: Sustaining the Reform Momentum,* Union Bank of Switzerland Economic Research, 1996.

New Horizon Economies, 4th Quarter, Union Bank of Switzerland, 1996.

Vietnam Economic Times, June through October, 1996.

"Viet PM Highlights Social Problems", *The Straits Times*, Singapore, 16 October 1996.

AFTERWORD

This book paints a picture of Vietnam which, in one generation, has transformed itself from a Communist-led nation engaged in a post-colonial civil war to a peaceful member of the Southeast Asian family of nations, in steady transition from a centrally planned to a market-led economy. Beneath this level, we see many fundamental changes that combine to create a massive renovation, not only in the economy, but in the underlying structure of its society as shown in Table A.

As each one of these radical trends emerges in the remainder of the current decade, we can expect the resulting forces to interact both within and across domains. The outcomes are simply impossible to forecast with any degree of certainty. However, because the resulting economic, social, and political turbulence will necessarily create internal and external conflicts, we can explore both the opportunities and threats flowing from these conflicts, and trace them to the implications for government and business leaders.

The most visible sign of internal change is an emerging middle class, composed of upper-level public officials, managers of larger state-owned companies, and a new breed of young business leaders, many of whom are Viet Kieu. While Vietnam is banking on the rise of its young tourist industry as a key source of foreign exchange, this will bring not only much-needed hard currencies but, also, the flow of unwelcome new ideas and social norms across its borders.

TABLE A
Transitional Change

Domain	From	To	Reference
Economic Structure:			
Lead sectors	Agriculture, state enterprises	Manufacturing, services	17
Source of foreign inputs	Aid	Investment	
Control mechanisms	Central planning	Market-led	
Economic performance	Hyper-inflation, dual currency	Stable currency, 9% growth	
Infrastructure	War-torn and neglected	Modern, rapidly renewed	11
Policy focus	Domestic	Exports	
Local industries	Weak, protected	Competitive in region	5,7
Social Structure:			
Education	Indoctrination	Information	16
Access	Closed to foreigners	Open to investors, tourists	
Expectations	Subsistence	Consumerism	
Political Structure:			
Dominant ideology	Revolutionary struggle	Economic progress	1
Power base	Provinces, military and police	Urban, economic power	
Leadership	Worker and soldier	Middle class Professional	
International relations	Geopolitical isolation	Regionally connected	23

Prior to *doi moi*, non-competitive state-owned industries were the centrepiece of the economy; yet now, more than one-half of them have closed their doors. Any economic organisation that functions reasonably well is a soft form of capital because the whole is more than the sum of its parts, and to develop a replacement takes time. But it is difficult, and perhaps even impossible, to alter the core values of organisations where authority is conferred by external sources and rewards are not linked to performance. In its process of renovation, Vietnam must strike a balance between preserving order and the Schumpeterian forces of creative destruction.

Because the surviving state-owned industries are linked to the power structure and will expect protection, they are a potential source of external conflict with Vietnam's new partners in the Association of Southeast Asian Nations (ASEAN), and her ASEAN Free Trade Area (AFTA) neighbours, who will demand a level playing field. Another potential source of conflict stems from the natural desire of state-owned enterprises to capture and distribute any benefits from a joint venture investment to local stakeholders, at the expense of the foreign partner's expectations of a surplus that is sufficient to recover the original investment plus a reasonable profit.

These conflicts in values, coupled with a constant struggle to alter the mindset of mid-level bureaucrats who must somehow mediate between their socialist tradition and the expectations accompanying the current influx of foreign capital, creates reputation effects that may be very difficult to reverse. However, these are minor issues compared to the expected rise of neighbouring China as a global superpower. Given the Vietnamese position with their northern neighbour, the relationship between China and Vietnam is of great interest and one in which ASEAN membership is an important element.

CHANGE MANAGEMENT CHALLENGES FOR THE GOVERNMENT

Despite having achieved a lasting peace, and then obtaining support from aid donors, foreign investors, and friendly nations in the region and throughout the world, Vietnamese policymakers face a difficult policy agenda. Although much of the nation's war-torn and neglected physical infrastructure is in the process of renovation, even more remains to be accomplished, and the current challenge is to mobilise sufficient capital and organisational capacity to achieve their goals.

Assuming this renewal is possible, the new physical infrastructure is unlikely to add much value to the economy unless it is accompanied by a thorough transformation of the soft infrastructure, especially in education, law, and social services. It will be particularly difficult to manage change in these areas because they intersect both the functional values which support economic success and the political values which sustain deeper power.

CRITICAL SUCCESS FACTORS FOR OVERSEAS INVESTORS

Singaporean firms, prompted by their government, were among the first ASEAN-based investors to enter Vietnam and many of their joint venture projects are well-positioned for the long run. While not all of them are likely to be hugely profitable, the initial projects are raising local skill levels and generating a great amount of organisational learning for the Singaporean enterprises. Some of the early lessons are already apparent in the following trends:

Trend 1: Particularly in the early stages, investors must be able to tolerate high levels of uncertainty and ambiguity in demand, access to supplies and bureaucratic barriers. For example, when Singapore Telecoms International decided to enter the mobile phone service market a few years ago, the simplest way to get an operation underway was as a trial project in a joint venture with Ho Chi Minh City Posts & Telecoms. Within a few years, this mode has fallen into official disfavour, and few of the early trials are now expected to obtain full licenses, while well-financed latecomers offering European technology are welcomed with open arms.

Trend 2: Investors who demonstrate an interest in the long-term are more likely to be offered attractive opportunities. For example, because firms based in Southeast Asia have a weaker bargaining position than OECD-based (Organisation for Economic Co-operation and Development) investors who can promise access to the latest technology, they must structure investment proposals to emphasise their long-term contribution to developing a strong regional economy, in which Vietnam is an increasingly important actor. The key challenges are building capacity in infrastructure (such as port operations, airlines, and telecommunications) and skills, roles in which government-linked Singaporean investors have long been active. Nanyang Technological University has pledged its assistance to the Ministry of Education and Training and is providing postgraduate scholarships for studies in engineering and business. This assistance serves to support the Singaporean-based firms operating in Vietnam, not only because of its symbolic value, but in the practical sense that the returning Vietnamese will be familiar, and thus willing and able to work, with Singaporean ventures.

Trend 3: Although it is necessary to have good relationships with those who are currently in power, it is never too early to begin forming linkages with the rising young professional elite who will (perhaps sooner rather than later) take over power. For example, although deliberations during the 1996 Party Congress resulted in perhaps as many steps backward as forward for many overseas investors, a new generation of young technocrats is emerging who are more open to foreign investment and influences. Nanyang Business School, through its Vietnam Co-operation Project, is designing and implementing programmes to develop the management capacity of this younger generation in strategic domains ranging from tourism to technology transfer.

Trend 4: International joint ventures are conduits through which, not only capital and technology flows, but organisational knowledge, values and ethics as well. For example, the Vietnam-Singapore Industrial Park in Song Be, near Ho Chi Minh City will be organised so that its tenants, most likely foreign investors, can operate in an environment which resembles Singapore more closely. This facility will serve to reduce the business risk for many overseas investors who can deploy a two-stage entry strategy.

Trend 5: Rapid economic growth means that, in most cases, investors should expect to reinvest their returns rather than repatriate profits. For example, even though Asia Pacific Brewery's market entry strategy for Tiger Beer demanded heavy investments in distribution and promotion, the joint venture was able to earn profits early in its life cycle. However, market demand soon outstripped the capacity of the new Ho Chi Minh City brewery which subsequently led to even more investment in new brewing facilities in the north.

Trend 6: The rapid evolution in consumer and industrial markets means that today's successful business model may have a fairly short half-life and, therefore, businesses must be prepared to make radical changes in their operations within a relatively brief period. For example, only a few years ago most young people in Ho Chi Minh City or Hanoi rode bicycles while their parents rode tiny motor scooters. Today, because many bicycles have turned into a *Dream Hai* and scooters seem to have become automobiles, urban streets are crowded. Similarly, a paging device was unknown until recently, but a new generation views pagers as only a temporary substitute for the handphones that they see their superiors carry. In services, the transformation has been even more radical, with yesterday's crowded five-star restaurant becoming today's budget tourist package.

A. Lee GILBERT
John J. WILLIAMS
Luu TRANKIEM